JORDAN
ON
INVESTMENTS

JORDAN
ON
INVESTMENTS

BY

DAVID F. JORDAN
PROFESSOR OF FINANCE
NEW YORK UNIVERSITY

FOURTH REVISED EDITION

NEW YORK: 1942
PRENTICE-HALL, INC.

First Printing............September, 1919
Second Printing...........December, 1920
Third Printing.............February, 1922
Fourth Printing..............March, 1923
Fifth Printing..............January, 1924

FIRST REVISED EDITION

Sixth Printing............September, 1924
Seventh Printing................July, 1925
Eighth Printing.................June, 1926
Ninth Printing..............January, 1927
Tenth Printing.............December, 1927
Eleventh Printing...........January, 1929
Twelfth Printing.............March, 1930
Thirteenth Printing ....May, 1931

SECOND REVISED EDITION

Fourteenth Printing.........August, 1933

THIRD REVISED EDITION

Fifteenth Printing............August, 1934
Sixteenth Printing..........August, 1935
Seventeenth Printing.......February, 1936
Eighteenth Printing.........August, 1936
Nineteenth Printing...........June, 1937
Twentieth Printing..........August, 1939
Twenty-first Printing...........June, 1940

FOURTH REVISED EDITION

Twenty-second Printing.........June, 1941
Twenty-third Printing......February, 1942

TO

C. W. G.

PREFACE

The writing of a book in any field of specialized knowledge presupposes the fact that the subject matter is adequate and dependable—that certain procedures have gained general recognition as sound practice and that these procedures can be inculcated upon receptive minds.

It is not difficult to recognize the validity of a book on engineering. The problems of an engineer are primarily those of the measurement of physical forces. Consequently the errors of an engineer arise from faulty calculation of measurable forces such as weights and stresses.

It is less easy to accept a book in the field of medicine. The human body is a complex machine, the operation of which is imperfectly known even to the greatest of the medical practitioners. Science has made definite progress in the conquest of disease but is helpless in an embarrassing number of cases. Nonetheless, a great deal is known which is accepted as truth and which can be taught.

It is most difficult to justify a book in a specialized field of applied economics such as investments. The area of definitive knowledge on which the structure must be erected is so small as to endanger the stability of any work except one of moderate pretensions. All that economic research has thus far contributed to what is sometimes called *the science of investment* is painfully meager. Candor compels the admission that success in investment practice is as much dependent upon chance as upon intellect.

It therefore follows that there are distinct limitations to the extent to which investment knowledge may be taught.

There are principles that should be known and rules that should be learned as measures for the mitigation rather than the elimination of risk. The most elaborate formula that economic science has yet evolved is powerless to foretell the future in the lap of which is the fate of all securities now extant.

Investment wisdom must therefore begin with the appreciation that there are no securities which, in the words of a modern economist, afford "havens of safety in a changing world." The field of investment research provides an excellent illustration of the law of diminishing returns. The most intensive application to investment study results chiefly in a profound respect for the unpredictable hazards of economic change.

The purpose of this volume is to set forth those rules of procedure which have gained practical recognition in the area known as Wall Street, where the author has endeavored to teach investments, for the past quarter of a century, to university classes wherein the students are frequently the instructor and the instructor is the student.

*   *   *   *

The present volume is a rearrangement as well as a revision of the matter contained in previous editions. The previous arrangement was based upon an outline suggested, some twenty years ago, by the Education Committee of the Investment Bankers Association of America under the chairmanship of Lawrence Chamberlain. The new arrangement is based upon the sequence of instruction followed in the investment classes at New York University.

The book now comprises two parts—namely, investment principles and securities analysis. The section on investment principles is subdivided into investment instruments and investment management. Investment instruments are further divided into classes of securities, types of markets, types of dealers, and the tools of investment; investment management, into discussions related to supervision, safeguards, and applied procedure. The section on securities analysis is subdivided into public and corporate issues. The public group is further divided into Federal, state, and municipal bonds; the corporate group, into railroad, utility, industrial, financial, real estate, and foreign securities.

Recognition is given in this revised edition to outstanding changes which have developed in the investment world during the past decade. The securities of the United States Government and its agencies have become the outstanding investment medium for individual as well as institutional investors. Utility and industrial securities have grown in importance as railroad and financial securities have declined. Real estate securities are regaining investment popularity as interest in foreign securities has all but vanished. Federal regulation of securities markets has changed substantially the mechanism of distribution and brokerage operations. The traditional opposition to unlisted securities has largely disappeared in the growing importance of over-the-counter markets. Drastic changes in the Federal bankruptcy laws have affected the position of investors in corporate reorganizations. Most significant of all, possibly, has been the increased interest in common stocks as investment media. An attempt has been made to evaluate these changes in the light of demonstrated experience.

* * * *

The author is grateful to innumerable persons who have contributed directly and indirectly to this volume. Especially is he grateful to his former associates in the investment banking firm of Halsey, Stuart and Co. and in the securities brokerage firm of Sutro Bros. and Co. His former associates in the General Electric Co. and the National Cash Register Co. have been most helpful. His indebtedness to John H. Patterson and Gerard Swope for a practical training in industrial methods, to Harold Stuart and Richard Sutro for an invaluable experience in investment procedure, to John T. Madden and Charles W. Gerstenberg for a sound knowledge of business procedure, and to George B. Hotchkiss for an inspired training in the art of expression is beyond repayment.

It would be unfair to omit reference to the contributions of the members of the investment seminars at the Graduate School of Business Administration, representing practically every important institution in the Wall Street area in the past twenty years. More than anyone else, they have written the present volume.

Finally, the author is appreciative of the many suggestions made by his colleagues, Professors Thatcher C. Jones, Guy D. Plunkett, John H. Prime, Louis P. Starkweather, and C. Elliot Smith, and to Arnold LaForce.

D. F. J.

May 1, 1941.

CONTENTS

∗◆▯▮▮▮▮▮▮▯▯▮▮▮▮▮▯▮▮▮▮▯▮▮▮▮▮▯▮▮▮▮▮▯▮▮▮▮▯▮▮▮▮▮▯▮▮▮▮▯▮▮▮▮▮▯▮▮▮▮▯▮▮▮▮▮▯▮▮▮▮◆∗

PART I

PRINCIPLES OF INVESTMENT

xi

PART II

ANALYSIS OF SECURITIES

1

INTRODUCTION

Scope. The purpose of this chapter is to discuss the economic background of investments and to familiarize the reader with the meaning of technical terms used in investment practice. The order of discussion is: (1) the nature of investment, (2) the function of investment, (3) the forms of investment, and (4) the language of investment. The objective of the borrower of funds is to secure terms which are most favorable to the borrower and which, therefore, are least favorable to the lender. To use a military expression, the investor must employ "defensive" tactics to safeguard his funds against the "offensive" designs of the borrowers.

The nature of investment. Investment may be defined as the productive employment of capital. Productive, in this sense, does not necessarily apply to the use to which the capital is put but rather to the return received by the investor. It has been truly said that the service which the money renders is one of the best tests of investment safety because the borrower is thereby enabled to discharge the obligation. Deficit borrowing by governmental bodies is rarely for productive purposes, yet government bonds rank high as investments because investors usually receive interest payments promptly when due. To the true investor who is primarily concerned with the conservation of capital, the relative productivity of an investment is subordinate to the degree of

3

safety afforded. It is essential, however, that every investment worthy of the title should produce at least some income
to the owner and that the procurement of such income should
represent the main purpose in the making of the commitment.

Speculation may be defined as a financial commitment
made for the purpose of profit through appreciation in value
rather than through income from the use of capital. Because both investments and speculations are made for productive purposes, the difference between the two is more in
degree than in kind. Both commitments require the assumption of risk because, in both cases, productivity depends
upon future conditions which cannot be accurately foreseen.
The fact that every investment partakes of the nature of a
speculation, however, does not warrant the belief that there
is little difference between the terms. It is the extent of the
risk factor, not merely its presence, that determines the dividing line. The speculator ordinarily seeks a large profit in a
short time and assumes a large risk of loss in so acting. The
investor desires only as much regular income as is consonant
with the safety of capital. In one case, the hazard is
openly accepted; in the other case, the risk is reduced to a
minimum.

The theory is often advanced that speculators are not gamblers in that they endeavor to act intelligently and avoid un-
necessary risks. The contention has merit. Some speculators do study economic conditions carefully and act cau-
tiously. But after a quarter of a century of experience in Wall
Street, the writer is forced to the reluctant observation that
most speculators are gamblers, in many cases almost totally
ignorant of the risks assumed. Because few, if any, speculators profit from their commitments, the natural question
arises as to why speculation in securities should retain its
popularity. To the least informed, speculation offers "something for nothing," a profit obtainable without working for
it, an opportunity to "get rich quickly." To the more realistic, speculation offers a mental diversion, an absorbing pastime, to men of affairs who can afford to lose (as they usu-

ally do) but who enjoy matching their wits against what is generally acknowledged to be "an unbeatable game." [1]

It is significant to observe that speculation is rarely profitable and that investment is rarely unprofitable. Most of the money which has been lost by investors has been lost in speculations rather than in investments. Even the best investments can fail, but every intelligent investor distributes his "risks" in such fashion as to escape serious embarrassment when misfortune arises. It is also significant to observe that, although many authoritative volumes have been written on investment procedure, relatively few books on speculative practice have gained more than passing notice.

The demand for new capital. The demand for new capital comes from the productive enterprises of the nation which desire funds for expansion or replacement purposes. If consumptive capacity is increasing because of population growth or higher living standards, the productive agencies of the country must expand their facilities to keep pace. New products and new industries require the construction of new equipment and new factories. Moreover, old equipment which has become worn out or obsolete must be replaced constantly if output is to be maintained. Few enterprises are able to finance such requirements from their own funds; most of them must seek outside capital.

The opinion is frequently expressed that the United States has reached a stage of economic maturity wherein the demand

---

[1] "If you are ready and able to give up everything else—to study the whole history and background of the market and all the principal companies whose stocks are on the board, as carefully as a medical student studies anatomy—to glue your nose at the tape at the opening of every day of the year and never take it off till night—if you can do all that, and in addition you have the cool nerve of a great gambler, the sixth sense of a kind of clairvoyant, and the courage of a lion, you have a Chinaman's chance.

"But if you try dodging in and out it's like a man trying to sail a ship in a typhoon—he doesn't know what causes it, which way it is going or how fast, or where it will wind up. He's just a sucker. The percentage in favor of a crapshooter is ten times better.

"Buying and paying outright for a stock because it pays an income and because careful expert study shows that it is highly likely to continue is like buying a drygoods store. All business is a hazard, and this no greater hazard than any other."—Statement by B. M. Baruch, quoted by Gen. H. S. Johnson, in syndicated article in *New York World-Telegram* on Oct. 15, 1937.

for new capital has practically ceased. Evidence in support of this viewpoint is offered in the declining rate of population growth, in the growing spread of nationalism throughout the world closing export markets to American goods, and especially in the prolonged depression which characterized almost the entire decade of the 'thirties. Concurrently with these developments, the larger companies have been able to build up cash reserves sufficient to meet their needs indefinitely. So widespread has such thinking become that it has been accepted as almost self-evident. Although it is admittedly impossible to prove that such opinions are fallacious, it is highly regrettable that this philosophy has gained such wide acceptance, even to the point of influencing governmental policies in major economic problems.

In a nation as young and as dynamic as the United States, it is difficult to conceive of a "finished economy." So long as population increases, even though at a slower rate, so long as higher standards of living add to consumptive capacity despite restricted buying power in wide areas, and so long as inventive genius makes productive equipment obsolete faster than does deterioration from use, it seems premature to talk of the attainment of economic frontiers. It is possible for economic progress to stop at times, as recurring periods of depression prove, but the cumulative effect of the underlying forces must sooner or later assert itself. If the contention is true that this nation is still growing, only sufficient time is necessary to correct what may appear to be a chronic maladjustment of industrial activity. Even during depressions, population grows, goods are consumed, and productive equipment wears out or becomes obsolete.

In more specific reply to the proponents of a "finished economy" in the United States, there may be cited many important industries where existing equipment is either inadequate or obsolete. An outstanding example is afforded in the steam railroad industry, wherein two out of every three locomotives in use are beyond twenty years old, an age which usually terminates their service-life. A second example, less conspicuous but equally important as a factor in National Defense, is to be found in the electrical power field, wherein existing loads already approximate generating capacities which include equipment installed decades ago. Other examples are to be found in the older basic industries, such as iron and steel and allied products, wherein, for the most part, the equipment in use has already outlived normal service lifetime.

The productive employment of capital. Capital flowing from investors and investment institutions to corporate and public borrowers is used to accomplish many different purposes. The more important of these functions are here illustrated:

(1) *To finance a new enterprise.* Promoters of new enterprises usually need capital in excess of their personal funds.

(2) *To finance the expansion of an established enterprise.* Many established enterprises need outside capital for the purchase of additional buildings and equipment.

(3) *To finance the betterment of existing facilities.* It is frequently advisable for industries to seek new capital in order to replace obsolete equipment and thereby reduce costs and lower sales prices.

(4) *To finance public improvements.* Governmental bodies customarily borrow money in order to spread the cost of permanent improvements over long periods.

(5) *To finance public expenditures.* During periods of low tax revenues or of high expenditures, governmental bodies borrow money in order to cover deficits in fiscal budgets.

(6) *To finance foreign trade.* Exports to nations which are not offset by equivalent imports are customarily settled by promises to make future payment, which promises in turn are offered to investors.

(7) *To finance private consumption.* Companies which make personal loans and which discount installment purchase contracts require new capital to meet larger demands for their services.

The supply of new capital. New capital is created in any community which produces more than it consumes. The individuals who possess this surplus in the form of savings naturally desire to put it to productive use. Their decision to postpone immediate consumption arises out of a time preference or a savings incentive. In the former case, they believe that their surplus will be more valuable to them at a future time, as evidenced in purchasing a deferred annuity or in making a pension contribution. In the latter case, they are motivated by a more immediate incentive such as the regular receipt of an attractive interest payment for the use of their capital. In either event, their savings become available to borrowers either directly through the transfer of securities or indirectly through the financial institutions where the savings may be held. It should be observed in this regard that deposits made in savings institutions and life insurance companies enter the capital market even more rapidly than if retained by the saver for direct investment.

While it is probably true that some new capital would be always available to borrowers even at negligible interest rates, it necessarily follows that the promise of a favorable rate of return acts as a powerful stimulant to saving. The abnormally low interest rates available to savers in recent years have undoubtedly deterred saving, as illustrated in the case of the savings banks in New York State where total deposits remained at about the same level from 1930 to 1940.

Despite a lower volume in savings in the United States during the past decade, a concurrent decline in the demand for new capital has resulted in little, if any, adverse effect upon business conditions. Ultimately, however, as the demand for capital revives, the problem of a shortage of new capital may appear more serious than it has been during the past decade. The economic progress of a nation is directly related to and eventually dependent upon the saving habits of its people.

The position of the investor. The person who has savings to invest and who desires to act intelligently and prudently faces many problems requiring careful consideration. His needs are relatively simple: (a) a place where his funds will be adequately safe and where he can recover them at short notice if necessary, (b) a reasonable rate of return for the use of his capital, and (c) assurance that he is dealing with reliable parties. In the achievement of these objectives, however, economic road maps afford only limited assistance. It is as important to know the detours as to know the main highways which sometimes are dangerous. Unfortunately, there is no one best way to invest safely and there are many investment problems which cannot be answered with assurance of accuracy, even by financial experts.

The investor must first determine the relative advisability of placing his funds in some form of property other than securities. If he has a family, the purchase of a home might readily prove a preferable investment, if social as well as economic advantages are to be considered. Apart from home-ownership, some of the largest American fortunes have been founded upon real estate investments. The purchase of basic commodities of commerce, such as grains, metals, and textiles, is becoming increasingly popular with investors who have knowledge of values in those fields.

As a further alternative to the purchase of securities, the investor may entrust his savings to a financial institution for reinvestment. Included in this group are the life insurance companies, the savings banks, the savings and loan associations, and the investment trust companies. Under the provisions of the Federal Social Security law, most of the workers in the United States are now compelled to buy deferred annuities with part of their income. In all these cases, however, the investor is merely delegating to another the choice of securities into which his funds will be invested.

Under the assumption that a decision has been reached to buy securities, the next question is whether to purchase the issues of governmental bodies or of private corporations. In either case, the choice is a wide one, ranging from Treasury bonds of the Federal Government to school district bonds of a rural community and from first mortgage bonds of a leading utility company to the common stock of a local iron foundry. In corporate securities, the investor faces a risk hazard which compels him to choose between the position of a creditor who will be satisfied with a moderate rate of interest return on his loan and the position of an owner who seeks to make a larger profit through the enhancement in value of his property. As a bondholder, his risk will be limited, but as a stockholder, his hazard is unlimited. He faces technical questions as to whether he should confine his purchases to issues "listed" on National Securities Exchanges, or to issues which are "legal" for trustee purchase, or to issues which are "exempt" from certain taxes, or to issues which have been outstanding long enough to become "seasoned." He must choose between issues which are called "short-term" because they will be repayable within a few years and issues known as "long-term" because of distant maturity dates.

He then finds that there are opportune and inopportune times in which to buy or sell securities, depending upon the current position of the business cycle. He likewise learns that separate industries have their own cycles and that the choice of the industry may be more important than the choice of a particular company. He finds that prudent investors do not concentrate their commitments even in the most promising areas but prefer to spread their risks over groups of securities.

He next finds that the market place for securities may be on regularly established exchanges or may be "over the counters" of investment firms that act as dealers. He finds that he may deal directly with one of these firms but learns that most investors buy and sell through brokerage houses or banks that charge a small commission for their services. He learns that prices of securities frequently must be negotiated in accordance with the size of the order and the condition of the market.

He eventually learns that not all of his purchases will prove satisfactory and that he must be willing at times to accept minor losses in order to avoid major ones and that at other times he must have the patience and courage to stay through a prolonged reorganization in order to protect his investment.

At all times he has the choice of delegating the supervision of his investments to another party by establishing a trust fund. Or he may prefer to employ investment counsel to assist him in his problems. Or he may elect to handle the entire matter personally, relying on his own skill and prudence in the management of his funds. It is to the credit of such individuals that they frankly realize that they will make mistakes of judgment and that they also appreciate that the employment of the most skilled investment advisors is no assurance against loss. It is primarily for the benefit of this latter group that the present volume has been written.

Definition of terms. In order to avoid misapprehension as to the meaning of certain terms which have already been used and which will recur frequently in subsequent discussions, the following definitions may be be found helpful:

An *investment* is a financial commitment, usually evidenced by a negotiable instrument, made for a productive purpose. For the purpose of this book, a true investment is one in which the risk of loss is limited to a reasonable extent and in which the purpose of the investor is to derive dependable income rather than potential profit.

Income is the compensation received by the investor for the use of his capital, usually in the form of interest or dividend payments.

Yield is the rate of return, expressed as a percentage of the capital investment, which the annual income bears to the principal sum. A bond costing $1,000, paying an income of $40 yearly, is said to yield 4 per cent to the owner.

Basic yield is the annual rate of return obtainable at any given time from the safest securities available in the market. It is often called "the riskless rental value of money." The basic yield, at least to investors in the United States, is indicated by the prevailing rate of return at which the longest-term Federal Treasury bonds may be purchased. At the time of writing, this yield was 2.20 per cent, which indicated the highest rate of return available to investors who desired the maximum degree of safety.

Premium for risk is the additional compensation obtainable from the purchase of securities which are not of the highest quality. Although New York City bonds are generally regarded as good investments, they were available at the time of writing on a yield basis of around 2.90 per cent. The difference of 0.70 per cent between the yields on the Federal

Treasury bonds and the New York City bonds was the "premium for risk" obtainable to the buyers of the latter issue for their willingness to purchase the lower-quality issue.

A true investment is one in which the premium for risk does not exceed the basic yield. Consequently, securities which yield returns of over 4.40 per cent at a time when the basic rate is 2.20 per cent are regarded as being too risky for conservative purchase.

Securities are negotiable instruments which evidence either indebtedness, in the case of bonds and mortgages, or ownership, in the case of stock. In view of the fact that many "securities" have proved to be poor investments, it has been suggested that a more realistic approach would be to term these instruments "risks." As will be shown, the test of a good investment is not its title but in its character.

Investment dealers are financial firms which act as wholesale buyers of securities and as retail distributors. They provide the mechanism through which new capital is transferred from investors to the public and private enterprises in need of funds. These dealers are technically known as "underwriters."

Investment brokers are financial firms which act as agents for the buyers and sellers of securities. They are usually members of securities exchanges on which their orders are completed. Unlike dealers who derive a trading profit on their sales, brokers charge commissions for their services as agents.

Securities exchanges are established market places for securities where orders are executed for the purchase or sale of issues "listed" thereon.

Unlisted dealers are financial firms which make a practice of buying and selling securities which are not listed on the various exchanges.

Securities are bought either for *cash,* which means that full payment must be made on delivery, or *on margin,* which is a combination cash and credit transaction under which the security purchased is held as collateral for a loan represented by the unpaid balance.

2

CHARACTERISTICS OF BONDS

Scope. The purpose of this chapter is to discuss the characteristics of bonds from the viewpoint of the investor. The order of discussion is: (1) titles based upon the underlying security, such as *first mortgage;* (2) titles based upon the purpose of issue, such as *refunding;* (3) titles based upon the form of issue, such as *registered;* (4) titles based upon the manner of redemption, such as *serial;* and (5) titles based upon the manner of participation in earnings, such as *income.* The outstanding importance of bonds in the investment field is clearly indicated in a summary which shows that bonds represented more than ninety per cent of all new securities issued in the decade from 1930 to 1940.

The bond instrument. Bonds are certificates of indebtedness usually secured by the pledge of specified property. The title of a bond may be as simple as Ohio Edison First Mortgage 4's of 1965 or as involved as United New Jersey Railroad and Canal General Mortgage 4½'s of 1979. The face amount of each bond is customarily $1,000 and represents part of a large issue that has been divided into small units for convenience in distribution. A fixed annual interest rate, seldom less than 3 or more than 6 per cent, is stated on each bond, interest payments usually being made semiannually. Interest is collected by the owner through the deposit of coupons detached from the bond or of a check received from the issuer. Practically all bonds bear definite maturity dates; a small group, however, are permanent loans. Usually, bonds are *secured* obligations, but many important issues are not. Peculiarly enough, the highest-grade issues are, technically speaking, *unsecured* bonds.

Bondholders are creditors, since their commitment is essentially a loan. They are preferred creditors only when the nature of the preference is definitely stated in the instrument, as illustrated in the case of a first mortgage pledge. They are entitled only to the amount of income fixed by the specified interest rate. They exercise no voice in the management of the enterprise, save in the event of default in payment of interest or of principal. Failure on the part of the debtor to meet the promises made in the bond indenture gives the bondholder, through the trustee appointed to hold the mortgage indenture, the right to foreclose on the pledged property or to sue for breach of contract. These various provisions clearly indicate the investment position of the bondholder. He has made a loan to, rather than participated in, an enterprise. His return is strictly limited to a fixed rate of interest, which, theoretically, is certain to be paid. He anticipates a full return of his capital at a definite future date. He does not willingly assume any risk of business loss.

Although all bonds are essentially similar as representations of indebtedness, many variations are found in practice. The chief difference between bonds is in the nature of the claim that the bondholder has against the issuer. That bond which has a prior claim naturally represents the safer security, taking precedence over any other bonds issued by the same debtor. The title of the bond, which seldom indicates the degree of priority, is usually taken from the nature of the instrument, such as *first mortgage, collateral,* or *debenture;* or from the purpose of issue, such as *adjustment, refunding,* or *consolidated;* or from some special feature, such as *sinking fund, convertible,* or *external.* In numerous cases, a combination title is used, such as *first consolidated, adjustment income,* or *first and refunding.* The title, however, serves to distinguish the issue more than to reflect the investment position.   Not all first mortgages are so in fact, and, even when correctly named, may prove inferior to many unsecured issues.

Further to confuse the investor, one company may have several issues outstanding, with the question of priority of claim most complicated.   Moreover, one company with numerous bonds of its own may be directly or indirectly responsible for the payment of bonds issued by affiliated companies. The Pennsylvania Railroad has, in all, nearly seventy-five bond issues, many of which are subdivided into different series. Each one of these bonds fits into a definite sequence of claim upon earnings.   The bonds of the Philadelphia, Baltimore, and Washington division are protected by a mortgage on that property and by the earnings of the entire Pennsylvania system.   Such a multiplicity of bond issues is not confined to the railroad field.   The Public Service Corporation of New Jersey had forty different bond issues of subsidiary companies outstanding in 1940.   Industrial companies, however, usually have relatively few bond issues, and these are of a correspondingly simpler nature.

Titles based upon security.   The most popular designation of a bond title is that which is based upon the nature of the security behind the obligation.   The inference is plausible that, in many cases in which the title is based upon another consideration, the cogent reason is to avoid a term that would indicate a weak underlying situation.   Numerous issues that represent little better than unsecured claims adopt harmless titles such as *gold 5's* or *sinking fund 4's*.   The *Plain Bonds* of the Boston and Maine Railroad constituted a rare example of corporate frankness in this interesting matter of terminology.   Under ordinary conditions where definite security is available, a title is selected that patently carries this assurance to the investor, such as *first mortgage 3's, refunding mortgage 4's,* or *prior lien 3½'s.*

As the customary form of security is a mortgage, investors should be cognizant of certain features in corporate mortgages that may operate helpfully or harmfully, according to the nature of the specified provisions.   The *open* feature of many corporate mortgages is a good illustration. Investors naturally prefer *closed* mortgages because the inability of the company to increase the obligation under the indenture tends to protect holders against diminution in the value of their claims. Corporations, however, have found that such issues tend to make future financing difficult, especially when the closed mortgage contains an *after acquired* clause carrying priority of claim upon future acquisitions. The *open* form was devised to meet this situation, at first on a limited basis up to a stated maximum, and later on an unlimited basis. The authorization on the Commonwealth Edison (Chicago) First Mortgage is unlimited in amount. Investors buying open mortgage bonds should require either or both of the following covenants in the indenture: (1) additional bonds to be issued only in proportion (not exceeding 75 per cent) to new property acquired, and (2) additional bonds to be issued only when aggregate fixed interest charges are adequately earned (not less than one and one-half times). A further covenant that all investors should seek is the penalty clause for failure to meet the various covenants in the indenture, under the terms of which default in any specified promise renders the entire principal immediately due and payable.

Mortgage bonds may be divided into senior and junior liens, the adjectives referring to priority of claim rather than to date of issue. The senior liens, which hold the first claim upon both earnings and assets, comprise first mortgages and prior liens. As the title indicates, *first mortgage* bonds have precedence of claim upon earnings and properties. The Duquesne Light (Pittsburgh) First Mortgage bonds illustrate such an issue. At times, usually those resulting from corporate financial reorganizations, the senior issues are called *prior liens,* illustrated in the Erie Railroad Consolidated Prior Lien bonds which are the senior issue of the company but which are junior to three issues of bonds of a predecessor company which were not disturbed in the reorganization. As a consequence the Prior Lien bonds constitute only a fourth lien on the main line of the system. Mortgages given in payment for property purchased are styled *purchase money mortgages* and take precedence over claims against the property acquired, despite *after acquired* clauses in mortgages previously issued by the purchasing company. The senior group also includes a goodly number of apparently junior issues, which are, in many cases, a combination of a large senior claim and a small junior position, or which have a small amount of prior bonds, or which have gradually advanced in rank with the retirement of earlier claims. The Pennsylvania Railroad Consolidated Mortgage bonds are junior to only $3,000,000 in prior liens. The Louisville Gas and Electric First and Refunding 3½'s of 1966 are likewise junior to only $1,000,000 in prior lien issues.

The junior bonds are those that have a secondary claim upon the corporate property. From the viewpoint of the investor, it would be most helpful if every bond bore a numerical adjective indicating the position of the security, as shown in the case of the New York and Erie Railroad First Mortgage 4's, Second Mortgage 5's, and Third Mortgage 4½'s. Corporations, however, are reluctant to disclose thus openly the position of junior issues; they prefer less significant and, in some cases, misleading titles, such as *general*, or *unified*, or *consolidated*, or *first refunding*, or *first leasehold*. All refunding mortgages, as the title indicates, are originally, at least, junior claims, even when a definite part is reserved to retire the existing first mortgage. Eventually, as before stated, the refunding mortgage may become a first claim, but, practically speaking, few such instances are to be found outside of the public utility field. The Long Island Railroad Refunding Mortgage 4's of 1949, of which over $37,000,000 were outstanding in 1940, were subordinate in claim to only about $3,500,000 in the few prior liens that then remained unpaid. On the other hand, the Kansas City Southern Refunding and Improvement 5's of 1950, of which nearly $21,000,000 were outstanding in 1940, were then subject to nearly $30,000,000 in prior liens.

Bonds which are secured by the deposit of other bonds and stocks are generally termed *collateral trust notes,* although the term *notes* in investment finance usually implies short-term, unsecured obligations. Collateral trust notes are ordinarily issued by holding companies and investment trusts, neither of which is in a position to offer mortgage bonds. Holding companies usually pledge a few securities in large blocks, as illustrated in the case of the Alleghany Corporation, which, in 1940, had collateral bonds outstanding which were secured by deposited stocks of only five companies including that of the Chesapeake Corporation, another holding company. The Chesapeake Corporation itself had an issue of notes secured exclusively by Chesapeake and Ohio Railway stock. Investment trusts, seldom interested in control policies, usually pledge a wide variety of securities in small blocks. Collateral trust notes, as a class, are in relative disfavor with current investors. In too many cases, notably in the public utility and railroad fields, the interests of the investors have been subordinated to what might be termed the ulterior purposes of the management. The experience of investors during the past decade with Kreuger & Toll collateral bonds and with Insull Utility Investment collateral notes proved most unfortunate because, in both cases, securities originally pledged as collateral were not available to the collateral bondholders when default occurred. In the first instance, poor securities were substituted for good issues, and, in the second case, securities reserved for the protection of noteholders were pledged for bank loans which went into default. Subsequent litigation indicated that adequate protection is rarely provided to buyers of collateral issues.

A third group of bonds consists of those secured by the guarantee of companies other than the issuers. These bonds, mostly found in the railroad field, are the obligations of small companies which, through leases or consolidations, are now parts of large systems. Such bonds bear not only the original name but also an added title, such as *guaranteed,* or *assumed,* or *endorsed.* The guarantee may be as to principal and interest, as in the case of the Albany and Susquehanna Railroad First Consolidated Mortgage, or as to interest only, as in the case of the Rensselaer and Saratoga Railroad First

Mortgage, both guaranteed by the Delaware and Hudson Railroad. The Southeastern Power and Light Debenture bonds were assumed by the Commonwealth and Southern Corporation after the latter company acquired the assets of the former in 1929. Most guaranteed bonds are assumed without actual endorsement by the guaranteeing company, although some carry the stamped endorsement, as in the case of the United New Jersey Railroad and Canal General Mortgage 4½'s of 1979, guaranteed by the Pennsylvania Railroad. An interesting section of this guaranteed group is found in cases such as the Kansas City Terminal First Mortgage bonds, where several companies give joint and separate guarantees. When these companies include such strong systems as the Atchison, the Burlington, and the Union Pacific, the bonds occupy a most favorable position. The investment position of guaranteed bonds depends primarily upon the value of the underlying property and secondarily upon the credit standing of the guaranteeing company. The unconditional guarantee of principal and interest by the Mexican Government has not prevented a long series of defaults on the Vera Cruz and Pacific Railroad First Mortgage bonds. The strategic position of the leased New York and Harlem property, on which Grand Central Terminal has been erected, causes the guaranteed First Mortgage bonds of that company to rank on a basis of equality with the senior mortgage bonds of the guaranteeing New York Central Railroad Company.[1]

A fourth group of bonds comprises the *debenture* issues, which ordinarily are unsecured promises. Some of these bonds, however, because of the absence of prior obligations, have a senior claim, as shown in the case of the Socony-Vacuum 3's of 1964. Others, by the operation of the *equal coverage* clause, have become secured obligations concurrent with the later issuance of mortgage bonds, as shown in the case of the New York, New Haven, and Hartford Debenture

---

[1] A notable recent addition to the guaranteed bond group are those bonds which have been issued by Federal agencies such as the Home Owners Loan Corporation and which are directly guaranteed by the Federal Government. Nearly $5,000,000,000 in such bonds were outstanding in 1940.

4's of 1956. Debenture bonds are not necessarily poor by reason of lack of pledged security. All bonds, including debentures, are primarily secured by the intangible asset of earning power. Despite interesting exceptions to the rule, however, debenture bonds of holding companies are generally inferior to those of operating companies. The Debenture bonds of the American Gas and Electric Corporation apparently have a first claim upon earnings, but an examination of the consolidated balance sheet of the company and the subsidiaries for 1939 would disclose the fact that over $195,000,000 in subsidiary bonds had a prior claim upon operating profits, even thought not guaranteed by the parent company. To show extreme liberality in the use of bond titles, one might cite the misnamed Debenture "B" bonds of the Green Bay and Western Railroad (Wisconsin), which are a species of deferred stock entitled to interest only after a specified dividend rate has been declared on the common stock of the company. On the other hand, the Consolidated Debenture stock of the Canadian Pacific Railway would be termed a bond if issued by a company in the United States, since income thereon is paid as a fixed interest charge.

Titles based upon purpose of issue. The purpose for which the bonds have been issued forms a second basis for the selection of a title. The underlying reason may be to take advantage of a favorable investment attitude toward certain classes of securities, as illustrated in the case of equipment trust notes; or to avoid the admission of a junior lien through the use of a title such as adjustment mortgage. This method of styling bonds is, however, not without advantages, irrespective of the motive. Investors should be very much interested in the use to which their funds are put, since that alone is an important test of safety.

Adjustment bonds are issued in the reorganization of companies in financial difficulties. In practically all cases, they are received by investors in exchange for old securities retired in the new plan, under conditions whereby interest is payable only if earnings permit. Although these bonds are usually issued on a speculative basis, the eventual success of the reorganization, as shown in the case of the Atchison, Topeka, and Santa Fe Railway Adjustment Mortgage 4's of 1995 (issued in 1895), places the bonds in the investment category. The Adjustment Mortgage bonds of the Chicago, Milwaukee, St. Paul, and Pacific Railroad (issued in 1925) have fared less auspiciously. Although adjustment bonds are usually protected by a junior mortgage, the general provision is that foreclosure is permitted for default in the payment of principal only.

Bridge bonds are issued to finance the construction of bridges. Bonds issued by public authorities for the construction of bridges (such as the George Washington Memorial Bridge between New York and New Jersey, which cost more than $50,000,000) are secured primarily by the revenues of the bridge, and, in some instances, by the taxation power of the public authorities. Bonds issued to finance the construction of railroad bridges (such as the Hell Gate Bridge in New York) are chiefly the mortgage obligations of a subsidiary operating company (the New York Connecting Railroad Company) guaranteed by the roads using the bridge (the Pennsylvania and the New Haven). Such bonds are likewise highly regarded. Bonds issued by private corporations for the construction of automobile toll bridges, however, are generally regarded as speculative, largely because of their poor record over recent years. Noteworthy examples of unfavorable experience with bridge bonds of private companies are afforded in the cases of the Detroit International Bridge and the San Mateo-Hayward Bridge across San Francisco Bay.

Equipment trust obligations in the form of notes or certificates are issued to finance the purchase of railway rolling stock on the partial payment plan. Since modern railroad equipment is expensive, as evidenced by costs now running as high as $185,000 for a steam locomotive and $250,000 for an electric locomotive, and as much as $1,450,000 for Diesel-powered streamline passenger trains, the purchase of such equipment on a quantity basis requires substantial expenditures. Funds for the payment of such purchases are obtained through the sale of serial obligations payable over a period

Specimen Offering of Equipment Trust Obligations at Extremely Low Interest Rates in 1940.

of years. In 1937, the Atchison, Topeka and Santa Fe Railway purchased 7 Diesel-electric locomotives and 43 stainless-steel passenger-train cars at a total cost of $4,880,000. The purchase was financed through a cash payment of $980,000 (20%) and the sale of $3,900,000 in equipment trust certificates, payable at the rate of $390,000 annually for 10 years. In 1935 the Pennsylvania Railroad purchased 10,000 freight cars at an average cost of $2,456, and a total cost of $24,560,000; the purchase was financed through a cash payment of $6,140,000 (25%) and the sale of $18,420,000 in trust certificates, payable at the rate of $1,228,000 annually for 15 years.

Under one method, known as the Philadelphia plan, the equipment is leased to the road for the period by a trustee, the installment payments are regarded as rent, and the investors receive "dividends" on their equipment trust *certificates*. Under another method, known as the New York plan, the equipment is purchased from the trustee under a conditional bill of sale whereby title immediately reverts to the trustee in the event of default, and the investors receive "interest" on their equipment trust *notes*. Although some investors prefer the Philadelphia, or lease, plan, the conditional sale plan has worked out as well in practice. Equipment trust obligations are usually regarded as excellent investments, owing to: (1) the essential nature of the underlying property; (2) the quality of mobility that would facilitate repossession; (3) the gradual increase in the value of the equity due to the liquidation of the debt on a scale faster than the depreciation of the equipment, which normally lasts well beyond fifteen years; and (4) the excellent investment record of these securities, as illustrated in the fact that in only one recent instance, that of the Florida East Coast Railway, were holders of equipment obligations required to assume any loss during recent years. There are probably less than five similar cases in the past fifty years. Receivers and trustees in charge of companies in insolvency usually continue to pay interest charges on equipment bonds despite the fact that they allow the mortgage bonds of the company to remain in default.

EQUIPMENT TRUST TABLE

(Fifteen-Year Basis)

Year	Depreciated Value at 5%*	Unpaid Notes	Equity of Notes
New	100.00%	75%	33%
1	95.00	70	36
2	90.25	65	39
3	85.73	60	43
4	81.45	55	48
5	77.37	50	55
6	73.50	45	63
7	69.83	40	74
8	66.34	35	89
9	63.02	30	110
10	59.87	25	139
11	56.88	20	184
12	54.04	15	260
13	51.34	10	413
14	48.77	5	875
15	46.33	0	—

* Master Car Builders Association standard rate on steel equipment.

Municipal bonds are those issued by public authorities and, in investment parlance, include the broad group of state and county as well as city obligations. The purpose for which the funds are being borrowed is usually stated in the title of the bond, as, for example, *Bridge, Fire Equipment, Grade Crossing, Highway, Park, Public Works, Sewer, School, Street Improvement, Water Supply.* Municipal bonds are essentially different from corporate bonds. Municipal bonds are almost always debenture issues, whereas corporate bonds seldom are; municipal bonds depend upon taxation power rather than earning power; and legality of issue, a minor consideration in corporate bonds, becomes a major factor in municipal issues. [2]

Refunding bonds are those issued for the more obvious purpose of paying an existing loan and the less obvious purpose of getting new capital on a favorable basis. Just as the

[2] A large part of the debt of New York City is called "Corporate Stock," which is really a long-term bond redeemable from a sinking fund, as distinguished from serial maturities.

conversion of a short-term debt into a long-term debt is known as a funding operation, the payment of a maturing debt with the proceeds of a new loan is called refunding. As the refunding purpose of the loan is generally a minor consideration, and is seldom immediately effective, the title is used primarily to avoid the more fitting designation of second mortgage. In some instances, however, especially in the public utility field, the refunding bonds eventually become the senior security of a company, as illustrated in the case of the Pacific Telephone and Telegraph Refunding Mortgage 3¼'s of 1966.

Revenue bonds are those issued by public authorities, usually municipalities, repayable out of revenues specifically received from the projects which the bonds finance. Unlike other forms of municipal obligations, revenue bonds are not payable from tax collections. Because these bonds have been used to provide funds for the construction of many spectacular enterprises such as the Golden Gate Bridge in San Francisco, the Triborough Bridge in New York, and the Pennsylvania Turnpike from Harrisburg to Pittsburgh, they have become well known to present-day investors.

Terminal bonds are those issued by railroad associations which are formed by a group of railroad companies for the purpose of financing the construction of terminal facilities in large cities to be used by all of the participating companies. These companies, either separately (severally) or collectively (jointly), usually assume proportionate responsibility for all operating and financial expenses of the association. The companies which proportionately guarantee the bonds of the Terminal Railroad Association of St. Louis include several of the most important systems in the country. An interesting observation in connection with terminal bonds is that companies in default on their mortgage bonds usually continue to make their proportionate payments on terminal contracts in order to retain the use of an essential facility.

Titles based upon form of issue. The form in which the bond is issued occasionally affords the basis for its title. An example is offered in the international field. In the United

States, *domestic* bonds are the obligations of American issuers, and *foreign* bonds are those issued by debtors outside of the United States; *internal* bonds are those issued in the country of the debtor and in the currency of that country, whereas *external* bonds are issued outside the country of the debtor and within the country of the creditor and in the currency of the latter. An external bond always remains so, even if owned in the country of the issuing debtor. When England suspended gold payments in 1931, the British internal bonds were harmed to a greater extent than were the British external bonds owned in the United States.

Bonds are issued in either *coupon* or *registered* form. Some, but not all, are interchangeable for a small service fee. Coupon bonds are payable to bearer and carry detachable interest coupons. Registered bonds are payable only to the registered owner to whom interest checks are mailed, except in the case of bonds registered as to principal only. The coupon bond may be more conveniently transferred and hence often commands a price slightly higher than that of the registered bond.

Interim bonds are temporary certificates issued pending the preparation of the *definitive* bonds. Approximately six months are required for the preparation, engraving, and printing of the regular bonds. In the meanwhile, the interim certificate evidences ownership and may be as readily disposed of as the permanent bond. Temporary receipts from investment dealers are not interim bonds, however, and should be accepted for brief periods only.

Titles based upon redemption. In certain instances, the title of a bond is taken from some feature with respect to redemption. In such cases, the bond may be a secured or an unsecured obligation; if secured, the claim is usually a junior lien, since the company would naturally select a more indicative title for a senior obligation.

Annuity bonds are those that represent permanent obligations and might more properly be termed *perpetual interest-bearing certificates,* as is done in the case of such an issue sponsored by the Public Service Corporation of New Jersey.

Certain Lehigh Valley Railroad Consolidated Mortgage bonds, which bore an original maturity date of 1923, were converted, by mutual agreement, into perpetual obligations and bear the title of *Irredeemable*. The well-known British Government "Consols" (an abbreviation of Consolidated) are perpetual bonds. Some long-term domestic issues, such as the West Shore Railroad 4's of 2361 and the Elmira and Williamsport 5's of 2862, might readily be classed as annuity bonds for all practical purposes.

Extended bonds are those on which the maturity date has been extended under a mutual agreement with the bondholder. The Illinois Central Railroad First Mortgage 3½'s of 1950 were originally issued as 5's in 1876, but, at maturity in 1905, they were extended to 1950 at a lower interest rate; incidentally, whereas the original obligation was payable in pounds sterling, the extended bonds are payable in dollars.

Gold bonds are those which are expressly payable in gold coin of specified weight and fineness. Gold payment clauses in domestic obligations, both public and private, were abrogated through Federal legislation on June 5, 1933, with respect to past and future contracts. Such action made the gold clause inoperative and therefore ineffectual for the designed purpose of protecting investors against currency depreciation.

Redeemable bonds, also known as *callable,* are those which may be paid at the option of the issuer during a specified period prior to maturity date. The price at which the bonds may be repaid is usually on a sliding scale providing for a relatively high premium of as much as $50 or $100 in the event of early redemption and for a small premium of as little as $5 or $10 for late redemption. It is an unfortunate feature of callable bonds from the investor's viewpoint that these bonds are most likely to be called at a time when reinvestment opportunities are unfavorable. Few investors seem to realize the handicap a call price puts on a bond. At a time when callable bonds of comparable quality were selling close to par value, noncallable 5 per cent bonds of the Bell Telephone Company of Pennsylvania were selling around 135 and noncallable 8 per cent bonds of the Public Service Electric and Gas Company of New Jersey were selling around 220. The buyer of a redeemable bond faces the prospect of being forced to accept less income if interest rates fall but of not being able to obtain more income if interest rates rise. A more general appreciation of this disadvantage would result in the issuance of fewer redeemable bonds. It is significant that the noncallable feature is emphasized when such bonds are offered to investors.

Serial bonds are those on which the maturities are spread over a succession of years rather than in a single year. The Pennsylvania Railroad Equipment 2¾'s (series "J") were issued in 1939 in the total amount of $8,865,000 repayable at the rate of $591,000 annually from 1940 to 1954. In interesting contrast to the general practice of having all bonds in a serial issue carry the same interest rate, the United States Steel Corporation brought out a serial issue in 1940 on a semi-annual basis from 1940 to 1955 with interest rates gradually increasing from ⅜ of 1 per cent on the earliest maturity to 2.65 per cent on the bonds payable in 1955. [3]

Series bonds are those that are issued in sequential series under the same indenture. Although all bonds thus issued have the same security, each series has distinctive features such as interest rate, maturity date, and call price. This type of financing gives the corporation a maximum degree of flexibility and allows each new issue to meet the prevailing conditions in the market. The Commonwealth Edison (Chicago) First Mortgage Series "I" bonds brought out in 1938 with an interest rate of 3½ per cent represented the ninth issue of bonds under this mortgage, the first issue having been sold in 1923.

Sinking fund bonds are those that require the establishment of a fund to be built up during the life of the issue to sink, or liquidate, the debt. Such bonds are more prevalent in foreign

---

[3] This issue was the first serial maturity bond to be listed on the New York Stock Exchange. Previous serial issues were not admitted because of probable confusion in price quotations arising out of varying maturity dates on the same issue.

and industrial issues than in railroads or public utilities. The amounts annually appropriated for the sinking fund may be: (1) a definite sum fixed in advance; or (2) an amount varying with earnings; or (3), in the case of extractive industries, an amount proportionate to physical output. The sinking fund may be used: (1) to redeem, either by purchase in the open market or by call, outstanding bonds of the same issue; or (2) for investments in other securities; or (3) for plant improvements. From the investor's viewpoint, the first method stated in each case is preferable. The expression "subject to call for sinking fund only" applies to bonds which are otherwise nonredeemable. Bonds which are called are drawn by lot, usually in the presence of witnesses representing the trustee and the underwriters, and must be surrendered to avoid loss of interest. A frequent source of embarrassment and irritation to investors is the return to them of unpaid interest coupons which are deposited for collection six months after that particular bond has been called for redemption for the sinking fund. As corporations keep no record of the names of owners of coupon bonds, there is no way of notification of redemption other than by newspaper advertising. Such notices are often missed by bondholders.

Titles based upon participation. Some bonds that carry income payments directly or indirectly contingent upon the earnings of the issuer bear a title reflecting that condition. As a general rule, these bonds are unsecured debts and in many cases bear a distinct resemblance to stocks.

Income bonds are those on which the payment of interest is contingent upon the amount of current earnings and is not a mandatory charge. They are generally issued as part of a reorganization plan under which bond interest charges are "scaled down" to an amount within the reasonable capacity of the enterprise. Income bonds are being used to a large extent at the present time in connection with railroad reorganizations. The practice of completely replacing fixed interest bonds with income bonds has been employed extensively in real estate foreclosure proceedings. The payment of interest on income bonds is contingent upon and proportionate to earnings available. Payments may be made at rates even below 1 per cent per annum. The income bond has the merit of being a realistic instrument even though it can never be popular with investors. It is unfortunately true that, in the older income bonds at least, companies have taken unfair advantage of their right to omit all interest payments on income bonds at times when partial payments might safely be made. It might also be noted that many income bonds provide for annual rather than semiannual interest payments as is customary in other bonds. Although some income bonds carry a "cumulative" feature entitling holders to eventual payment of deferred interest, the present tendency is to make payment "noncumulative." [4]

Participating bonds are those that are entitled to share in the net earnings of the company, in addition to receiving interest in full on a fixed charge basis. A participating bond is an anomaly, since it seems to combine stock income with bond safety. Very few such bonds—in fact, none of any important companies—are now outstanding. The modern method of bond participation is through the indirect procedure of conversion or stock purchase options.

Convertible bonds are those that may be transferred into stock at the option of the holder. These bonds make a strong appeal to investors who like a privileged opportunity to share in the future earnings of those companies to which they loan money. The conversion feature may extend over the entire life of the bond, as it does in the case of the Alleghany Corporation Collateral 5's of 1944; or over a limited period during the early life of the bond, as in the case of the American International Convertible 5½'s of 1949, which lost their conversion privilege in 1934; or over a limited period during the later life of the bond, as in the case of the New Haven Railroad Convertible 6's of 1948, which were issued in 1907 but which did

---

[4] The Colorado Fuel and Iron Income Mortgage 5's of 1970, which were issued in connection with the reorganization of the company in 1936, are entitled to full interest if earned in the preceding year and to cumulative arrearages if not paid in any year. The cumulative feature was largely accountable for the payment of full interest charges on these bonds in 1939 despite operating losses in 1938.

not become convertible until 1923. The conversion ratio may be par for par, one $1,000 bond for ten shares of $100 par stock, or in any fixed ratio, usually expressed in terms of a conversion price for the stock. The Phelps-Dodge 3½'s of 1952 are convertible at $50 per share, which means that one $1,000 bond may be exchanged for as many shares of stock as $50 is contained into $1,000, or 20 shares.

The peculiar advantage of convertible bonds over stock is that, in a declining market, the bonds will not fall below their investment value as straight bonds, whereas the stock, not having that intrinsic strength, may fall to an extremely low level. In an advancing market, the bonds will advance fully proportionate to the stock after the conversion parity has been passed. The Commonwealth Edison Debenture 3½'s of 1958 were convertible at $25 a share in 1940 at a time when the stock was selling at $30 a share. The market value of the bonds was therefore $1,200 (120) despite the fact that the First Mortgage 3½'s of 1968 were currently around $1,100 (110).

Bonds *with warrants* are those that bear stock purchase option warrants giving the holder the privilege of buying a certain number of shares of stock at a fixed price. The warrants may or may not be detachable, and may be valid for a limited or an unlimited period. The warrants attached to the National Dairy Products Debenture 3¾'s of 1951 were not detachable until exercised, and gave the bearer the right to purchase up to May 1, 1940, 10 shares of common stock at $28 per share. The warrants attached to the Remington-Rand Debenture 4¼'s of 1956 were detachable and gave the bearer the right to purchase up to March 1, 1944, 15 shares of common stock at prices gradually increasing up to a maximum of $38.69 per share. Although many of these warrants became highly valuable during the active stock market period from 1925 to 1929, investors should realize that in warrant bonds, as well as in convertible bonds, the participating feature has been added mainly to enhance the marketability of issues that lack fundamental investment quality. Investors who seek participating benefits should realize that a large measure

NEW SECURITY ISSUES IN THE UNITED STATES [5]
(Amounts in Millions)

Public Bonds

Year	Domestic	Foreign	Total
1931....................	$1,385	$ 50	$1,435
1932....................	1,010	65	1,075
1933....................	610	60	670
1934....................	1,660	60	1,720
1935....................	2,365	115	2,480
1936....................	1,495	130	1,625
1937....................	1,345	220	1,565
1938....................	2,245	65	2,310
1939....................	3,590	70	3,660
1940....................	2,045	0	2,045
Total..................	$17,750	$835	$18,585
Average...............	$1,775	$85	$1,860

Private Corporation Issues

Year	Bonds	Stocks	Total
1931....................	$2,245	$345	$2,590
1932....................	620	25	645
1933....................	230	155	385
1934....................	455	35	490
1935....................	2,115	150	2,265
1936....................	4,065	570	4,635
1937....................	1,675	760	2,435
1938....................	2,040	100	2,140
1939....................	1,960	235	2,195
1940....................	2,390	330	2,720
Total..................	$17,795	$2,705	$20,500
Average...............	$1,780	$270	$2,050

Purpose of Issue

Year	New Capital	Refunding	Total
1931....................	$3,115	$ 910	$4,025
1932....................	1,190	530	1,720
1933....................	715	335	1,050
1934....................	1,385	825	2,210
1935....................	1,475	3,270	4,745
1936....................	1,975	4,280	6,255
1937....................	2,100	1,900	4,000
1938....................	2,355	2,105	4,460
1939....................	2,300	3,555	5,855
1940....................	1,945	2,820	4,765
Total..................	$18,555	$20,530	$39,085
Average...............	$1,855	$2,055	$3,910

[5] Data from *The Commercial and Financial Chronicle.*

of safety must necessarily be sacrificed. Appearances to the contrary, convertible or warrant bonds rarely combine potential appreciation with adequate safety.

Stock purchase option warrants are being used to an increasing degree in connection with bonds issued in corporate reorganizations. The purpose of the warrants is to give bondholders who have accepted a drastic reduction in interest payments an opportunity to share in any subsequent improvement in the earning power of the enterprise.

The investment position of bonds. Bonds have traditionally been regarded as the most conservative form of investment in the country. To the investor who has complete freedom in the choice of his commitments, they provide a combination of safety and convenience surpassing that available in any alternative form of investment. To the investing institution which, for reasons of fiduciary safety, is restricted in the choice of securities, bonds provide the most satisfactory medium of investment as evidenced in the billions of dollars carried by these institutions in bondholdings. For obvious reasons, transactions in bonds and changes in their market prices do not attract public attention in the sense that activity in the stock market does. Moreover, the argument that stocks make better long-term investments than do bonds is advanced from time to time, impressing many persons who lack investing experience. Relatively few investors have lost money buying good bonds or have made money buying good stocks.

The investment business is primarily that of investing in bonds and only incidently that of investing in stocks. Every true investment may not necessarily be a loan, but the position of a creditor must necessarily be safer than that of a debtor, which every stockholder is, either actually or potentially.

During the ten-year period from 1930 to 1940, as shown in the accompanying table, 39 billion dollars in new securities were issued to American investors, of which bonds represented 36 billion dollars, or over 90 per cent, and stocks about 3 billion dollars, or less than 10 per cent.

3

CHARACTERISTICS OF STOCKS

Scope. The purpose of this chapter is to discuss the characteristics of stocks from the viewpoint of the investor. The order of discussion is: (1) preferred stocks, (2) guaranteed stocks, and (3) common stocks. With respect to common stocks, the advantages and disadvantages are summarized in the light of practical experience, and the conclusion is reached that, in most instances, common stocks do not make good investments.

Corporate stock. Corporate stock represents the ownership of a corporation as divided into uniform units, called shares. On December 31, 1939, the corporate stock of the Eastman Kodak Company comprised 2,500,000 shares, each of which represented a $\frac{1}{2,500,000}$ share of the net assets of the company. A stock certificate evidences the ownership of a certain number of shares, usually one hundred.[1] The certificate may be for any number of shares, and even for a fractional part, such as $\frac{35}{100}$, which is called "scrip."[2] The stock certificate is always a registered, never a bearer, instrument. The name of the owner, personal or corporate, appears on the

---

[1] For market convenience, large investors generally hold stock in one-hundred-share certificates.

[2] Dividends are not paid on scrip. Investors holding fractional shares should buy or sell the proper fractional interest to carry full-share lots only. Certain firms deal in fractional shares at prices close to the prevailing market for full shares.

face of the certificate and on the books of the company. The certificate states the number of shares, the date of issue, the signatures of the company officials, the registrar, and the transfer agent.

Corporate stock may have nominal *par* value, usually $100 per share, or *no par* value. Since 1912, when New York legalized no par stock, the trend away from a definite par value has been quite noticeable. Only in the regulated industries, such as the steam railroads, the commercial banks, and the public utility operating companies, where nominal value bears an important relationship to intrinsic value, do par stocks predominate. From the viewpoint of the investor, the distinction is not important. The chief objection to the use of par value is that uninformed purchasers might be misled into believing that the stated par value represents the true value of the stock.

The market value of a share of stock is determined by factors other than par value, as illustrated in the cases of Pennsylvania Railroad and General Motors during recent years. The former stock has been selling for less than half and the latter stock for more than double the respective par values.

Legal position of stockholder. Stockholders, as part proprietors of corporations, have certain well-defined rights and obligations, depending upon the corporation laws of the state in which the company is chartered. Although state laws vary widely with respect to powers of corporations, the position of the stockholder is fairly uniform in most states.

The stockholder has a right to receive dividends when earned by the company and when declared by the directors. In other words, the income claim of a stockholder is a contingent one, differing fundamentally from that of the bondholder, who has a fixed definite claim. The stockholder shares in the fortunes of the business, and his share may be large or small. Even when earnings are large, stockholders cannot ordinarily compel dividend payments if the management desires to reinvest the profits in the business.

The stockholder has a right to subscribe to new issues of stock proportionate to old holdings, before such new stock may be offered to outsiders. This preëmptive right may be denied only when so stated in the charter. As these privileged subscriptions are generally made below the prevailing market price, this right is often valuable.

The stockholder has a right to inspect the corporate books. This right applies to the general books, such as the minutes of the stockholders' meetings and the list of stockholders, rather than to the ledgers and the books of financial record.

The stockholder has a right to vote in the selection of the board of directors and on all matters affecting the corporate property as a whole, such as sale or merger or liquidation of the business. The voting privilege may be restricted to one class of stock or to one group of stockholders.

The stockholder is liable for the debts of the corporation only to the amount of unpaid subscriptions to the capital stock, and to the difference between subscription price and par value, in the event the former is lower. This limited liability feature of corporate stock, in contrast to the unlimited obligation that exists in partnerships, is one of the great advantages afforded by the corporate form of organization.

The stockholder is generally liable for wages of employees for limited periods. This provision applies to employees in subordinate positions, for periods not exceeding three months, under somewhat technical conditions. Although the stockholder is liable for the payment of assessments in the event that the capital of the company is impaired by losses, he is seldom called upon to meet this obligation.

The position of stockholders in the reorganization of defaulting companies has been greatly strengthened by recent amendments to the Federal Bankruptcy Act (better known as Section 77 and Chaper X). Although the priority rights of bondholders are duly recognized, the stockholders are given a longer period in which to submit an acceptable reorganization plan, and may not be "frozen out" in the event that any equity remains after all creditor claims have been met.

Preferred stock. The capital stock of a company may be divided into two classes, one of which, usually called preferred stock, has priorities over the other, uniformly called common stock in the United States but more accurately termed ordinary stock in England.

The chief priority of preferred stock is that with respect to dividend payments, since no dividends may be paid on the common stock of a company in any year in which the full preferred dividend has not been paid.   The amount of the annual dividend to which the preferred stock is entitled and to which it is limited is stated in the charter of the company and on the stock certificate either in dollars per share or as a percentage of par value.   The payment of the preferred dividend is not a fixed charge in the sense that the company is required to make the payment.   Preferred dividends, like common dividends, are contingent upon the financial condition of the company and the discretion of the management as represented by the board of directors.   Even though the available profits may be adequate for the payment and the cash position may be strong, the directors may decide to conserve the funds in the business rather than to pay out dividends.

Cumulative preferred stock is that type under which dividend payments omitted at any time accumulate in the form of arrearages.   These arrearages must be paid in full before any dividend payments may be made on the common stock of the company.   *Noncumulative* preferred stock is the other type which has no future claims on dividends omitted in any particular year.   The advantage of cumulative over noncumulative preferred stock is not so great as it might seem.   A prolonged period of poor earnings may result in an accumulation of dividend arrearages beyond the capacity of the company to pay.   A situation is thereby created wherein a solvent company is almost permanently enjoined from paying any dividends to the common stockholders who are the actual managers of the enterprise.   Such a situation scarcely contributes to efficient management.   Even when the amount of arrearage is not discouragingly large, the holder of cumulative preferred stock is usually persuaded to accept other securities in lieu of cash.   The existence of an enormous accumulation of unpaid preferred dividends has proved to be a formidable deterrent to the reorganization of public utility holding companies as required under the Federal law enacted in 1935. [3]

Some companies have adopted a practice of issuing different classes of preferred stock which may share the same rank of priority or which may have varying priorities. A large public utility company in New Jersey has four classes of preferred stock, all ranking equally in priority, but having dividend rates of $8, $7, $6, and $5, respectively. Another well-known company has three classes of which two carrying rates of $7 and $6, respectively, are known as Preferred and have dividend priority over the third, known as Second Preferred, which carries a rate of $7. The term *prior preferred* is sometimes used to designate the particular preferred stock which has priority of claim, although the term *first preferred* is more generally used for this purpose. In such cases, the senior issue is entitled to its full dividend rate before any payment may be made on the junior issue.

Preferred stocks, especially in the industrial field, usually have priorities in the distribution of assets (in the event of dissolution) as well as in the distribution of profits. The amount of such preference is usually stated in dollars per share and generally approximates the original value of the stock. This preference "as to assets" is rarely of practical value. Most companies dissolve as the result of failure, a condition which usually finds the creditors in possession of the assets, with little if anything available to the stockholders.

Redeemable preferred stock is stock which may be retired by the issuing company upon the payment of a definite price stated in the instrument. Although the call price provides for the payment of a premium which may be as much as $25 above the face value of the stock, such issues are not popular with investors. Recent experience has shown that holders

---

[3] The market price of a cumulative preferred stock includes the right to receive all dividends in arrears. It is therefore significant to observe that many such issues are priced below the accumulated dividend arrearages, indicating a negative value for the stock iteslf. Despite this fact, the common stock of the company will frequently enjoy a popularity attributable only to ignorance or speculation.

of redeemable issues have been forced either to accept the return of their funds at an unfavorable time or to witness an arbitrary market value limited by the price at which their stock may be called. Several instances might be cited at the time of writing where nonredeemable preferred issues are selling at prices far above the prices of comparable redeemable preferred issues. Although a call price of $120 could readily hold down the market price of a $7 Preferred stock, the thought that a similar call price could limit the market price of a $5 Preferred stock probably never occurred to the management of General Motors when that issue was originated. Redeemable preferred stocks appear to be even more objectionable than redeemable bonds from the investor's viewpoint.

Convertible preferred stock is that type which may be exchanged into common stock at the option of the holder. Preferred stocks which carry this privilege are likely to be deficient in quality because it is rarely necessary that this feature be included in order to attract investment buyers. The exchange ratio is stated in the instrument and, under modern practice, is on a sliding scale whereby the conversion price increases during the conversion period. A large industrial company has issued convertible preferred stock on which the conversion price which is now $50 a share will increase to $66⅔ in 1942 and $75 in 1944, which prices indicate that, respectively, 2 shares, 1½ shares, and 1⅓ shares of common stock will be exchanged for 1 share of preferred stock.

Participating preferred stock is that type which is sometimes entitled to a further share in the earnings of the company after the payment of the regular preferred dividend. A well-known electrical company has preferred stock which is entitled to a 7 per cent priority dividend, and, in the event that the common stock receives more than 7 per cent, is entitled to the same dividend rate as that paid on the common stock. Under a similar provision, the preferred stock of a western utility company has been on an 8 per cent dividend basis for many years, although it is entitled to a priority dividend of only 5 per cent. Very few important preferred stocks are participating, however.

Preferred stocks as investments. Preferred stock occupies an intermediate investment position, offering more income but less safety than bonds, and less income but more safety than common stocks. Admittedly a compromise security, it was designed to attract investors who desired what might be called a favorable rate of return and who were willing to assume the attendant risk. It might be said that some preferred stocks resemble bonds in their investment position but that the majority of preferred issues might more properly be regarded as common stocks.

Some preferred stocks belong in the bond category because of their technical position. Certain companies, such as International Harvester, Eastman Kodak, General Motors, and American Smelting and Refining, have no bonds outstanding. Consequently, the preferred stocks of these companies have claims on earnings which are not subordinate to or lessened by bond interest payments. So long as this condition continues, these preferred stocks are the senior securities of the enterprise.

Other preferred stocks belong in the bond category because of the prosperity of the issuing companies. Certain railroad companies, such as Union Pacific and Norfolk and Western, public utility companies, such as Cleveland Electric and Pacific Telephone, and industrial companies, such as National Biscuit and Corn Products, have established impressive records of earnings over long periods of years, thus placing their preferred stocks in a strong investment position. Included in this group are many rather small public utility operating companies which have unbroken dividend records on preferred stocks running back many years.

The great majority of preferred stocks of utility holding companies and of industrial companies, however, are in the common stock category because of inadequate earnings protection. In too many instances, investors have bought preferred stocks upon the apparent assumption that the payment of dividends was no less certain than the payment of interest on bonds. Unfortunately, there appears to be no medium-grade of preferred stocks and, even more unfortunately, the poor issues greatly outnumber the good ones.

Guaranteed stocks. Guaranteed stocks are those upon which dividend payments are guaranteed by some company other than the issuer. Obviously, no company can guarantee dividends on its own stock. The guarantee usually arises out of a consolidation of properties under a lease. Such stocks, confined almost entirely to the railroad field, may be preferred or common. Guaranteed stocks partake more of the nature of bonds, since dividend payments are fixed, rather than contingent, charges. The amount of the guaranteed dividend is either the regular rate stated on the preferred certificate or a contractual rate agreed upon in the case of common stock.

The investment position of guaranteed stock depends upon the nature of the guarantee, the value of the underlying property to the guaranteeing company, and the financial responsibility of the guaranteeing company. The ideal guaranteed stock would be one protected by an unqualified guarantee of a definite dividend rate under a long-term lease contract, covering property of strategic value to a prosperous guaranteeing company. Such a security is to be found in the case of the common stock of the United New Jersey Railroad and Canal Company, which forms part of the main line between New York and Philadelphia of the guaranteeing Pennsylvania Railroad. The common stock of the New York and Harlem Railroad is highly rated, more because of its underlying value in providing terminal facilities to the New York Central Railroad than because of the credit position of the guaranteeing company. It is significant to observe that not even the receivership of the guaranteeing company necessarily means a breach of the guarantee. During the receivership of the old Chicago and Alton Railroad, dividends on the guaranteed Joliet and Chicago common stock were paid regularly although no interest was being paid on the Chicago and Alton bonds. A further favorable factor in connection with guaranteed preferred stocks is that they are seldom redeemable.

A notable example of a strong guaranteed stock is shown in the case of Pittsburgh, Fort Wayne and Chicago Preferred, which not only is secured by valuable underlying property (being on the main line from Pittsburgh to Chicago) and by a prosperous guaranteeing company (the Pennsylvania) under a long lease, but also has first claim on the property because of the absence of prior indebtedness.

The general decline in railroad prosperity during recent years has resulted in a weaker position for guaranteed stocks as a group. Although the popularity of the stocks guaranteed by the companies of weaker credit has measurably diminished, the issues guaranteed by the more prosperous companies are regarded on a parity with the bonds of those systems.[4]

Common stock. Common stock represents the basic ownership of the company. The claim of the common stockholders to income and assets is subordinate to all other claims, except in the relatively few instances where preferred stock is not preferred as to assets. Common stocks are often called *equities,* since they usually represent only part of the total capitalization as contributed by the owners, in contrast to the remainder supplied by the creditors. In some instances, the common stock comprises the sole security issued by the company, as notably illustrated in the cases of General Foods, General Electric, and Standard Oil of California in their recent balance sheets. The common stocks of such companies enjoy a fundamentally sound position that is rarely met in equity investments.

Income payments to stockholders are made in the form of dividends which, as the title implies, represent a division of profits. Dividend payments are usually made quarterly

---

[4] Reference might be made at this point to the remarkable trust fund created by Cornelius Vanderbilt (grandson of Commodore Vanderbilt) in 1899 under his will for the benefit of his widow. This fund, comprised almost entirely of guaranteed railroad stocks, had a value of about $7,000,000 in 1899 and was appraised at more than $6,000,000 at the time of the death of the beneficiary in 1934, after having produced a total income of $12,250,000 during the period.

and are payable in cash. The payments may be made semi-annually or annually, and are occasionally in some form other than cash. In some instances, dividends are declared in the form of short-term promissory notes, called scrip. In rare cases, certain of the corporate assets are distributed as property dividends.

Investors are often confused by dividends in the form of stock, since the distribution appears to be simply a matter of dividing the ownership into a larger number of units, and, therefore, not a true distribution of earnings. While this assumption is correct, the result would not be different if the disbursement were made in cash and the money reinvested in new stock offered by the company. Stock dividends are the external evidence of internal reinvestment of profits in the business. Stockholders who do not desire to increase their investment in the company should sell their stock dividends. [5]

Dividend policies. Investors in common stocks should become acquainted with the dividend policy of any company in which they are interested. Corporations usually adopt a certain policy which characterizes their dividend distributions for long periods of time. These policies may be divided somewhat arbitrarily in the following fashion:

Regular dividend irrespective of current earnings. This policy, as followed by the American Telephone and Telegraph Company for many years, is regarded as the investment ideal. The only disadvantage is that the dividend rate may be maintained too long after earning power has declined, as illustrated in the classical example of the New Haven Railroad in the early years of the present century. [6]

---

[5] During recent years, the American Telephone and Telegraph Company has paid a cash dividend on the fifteenth of January, April, July, and October to all stockholders who were listed on the corporate books on the twentieth of the preceding month. The interval between the "record date" and the "dividend date" is provided in order to allow the checks to be prepared for mailing. The magnitude of this task is indicated by the fact that more than 600,000 separate stockholders receive checks quarterly from this one company. A mailing schedule is prepared under which all stockholders throughout the country receive their checks at the same time, irrespective of place of residence.

[6] The establishment of an impressive dividend record is not necessarily indicative of an equally impressive record of earnings. During the twelve-

Regular dividend proportionate to current earnings. This policy has become increasingly popular during recent years in recognition of rapidly changing business conditions. One effect of the Federal tax on undistributed profits when it was in effect during the years of 1937 and 1938 was to encourage many companies to adopt this policy. General Motors and General Electric are now following this method of dividend distribution.

Regular dividend at minimum rate. This policy permits companies to pay a small but dependable dividend at all times and to reinvest most of current earnings for expansion purposes. This policy is characteristic of many companies in the petroleum industry, and forms the basis for occasional extra distributions, usually in the form of stock.

Regular dividend payable in stock. This policy enables companies to make a distribution to stockholders which they may convert into cash if they desire, but which allows the retention of all profits in the business.

Regular dividend payable partly in cash and partly in stock. This policy, which represents a combination of two methods, is used by a few companies. In such cases, the cash payments are made quarterly, but the stock payments are made either semiannually or annually to avoid the effect of rapid compounding.

Experience has taught corporate stockholders two important considerations respecting dividends. The first is that common stockholders should not expect to receive all available earnings as dividends. The management is certain to retain part of the profits in the business, a conservative policy that unfortunately has been carried too far. The market values of numerous common stocks during recent years have been substantially below the aggregate reinvested surpluses of the five years from 1925 through 1929, a condition especially true in the steam railroad industry. The indicated aggregate market value of the common stock of the New York Central

---

year period from 1927 through 1938, the Pullman Company paid dividends aggregating $128,500,000 in contrast to aggregate net profits of only $80,400,000 during the same period.

Railroad throughout the decade from 1930 to 1940 was frequently less than the aggregate surpluses reinvested in property in the preceding decade from 1920 to 1930. At no time during recent years has the indicated market value of the common stock of Western Union Telegraph even approached the amount of surplus earnings reinvested in property between 1920 and 1930. In other words, the reinvestment of surplus earnings is not always to the advantage of the stockholder, and is especially dangerous in those industries that are in the saturation zone of development.

The second important consideration is that stockholders should not rely upon accumulated surplus reserves to carry dividends through poor years. Despite the almost universal belief that one of the chief reasons for partial distribution of earnings is the creation of a reserve for dividends in lean years, recent experience has clearly demonstrated the fallacy of reliance upon such consideration. Numerous examples might be cited to evidence this statement. Not even the existence of a special reserve for this purpose (American Car and Foundry) nor a definite statement of management policy (American Smelting and Refining) has protected stockholders against dividend reductions in poor years. Corporate management has clearly indicated a reluctance to pay dividends in excess of current earnings over any extended period in order that the cash position may not become impaired.

Advantages of common stocks. The position of common stocks as investments has been a matter of controversy for many years. The traditional viewpoint that bonds should be bought for investment and common stock for speculation has been seriously challenged during recent years. Many bank officials have advocated that common stocks might advantageously be placed in trust funds and have not hesitated to do so when they had proper authority. A new school of financial economists has developed which holds that common stocks make better long-term investments than do bonds and presents confirmatory evidence to show that stocks consistently offer greater stability of value and afford larger net income than do bonds over extended periods of time. Conservative institutions which have not accepted this theory of stock investment are criticized as being nonprogressive and unwilling to recognize a radical change in the field of finance.

The increased popularity of common stocks is due in part to contributory developments in the bond market. In the first place, the rate of return which bonds afford has declined to such a low level as to discourage investors who prefer, under such conditions, to assume the higher risks in order to receive the larger income that stocks return. In the second place, many large companies have substantially reduced their bonded debts during recent years and have thereby created a distinct scarcity of high-grade bonds. In the third place, an important group of companies, such as General Electric and Standard Oil of California, have only common stock outstanding, thereby compelling prospective investors in those enterprises to buy common stocks if they desire to participate. In the fourth place, the almost complete collapse of the foreign government bond market in the United States has diverted capital which normally would buy such issues. In the fifth place, recent experience with real estate mortgages has lessened their popularity and further diverted capital from that field. In short, an impressive combination of circumstances has tended to reduce the popularity of bonds and thereby stimulate the demand for stocks.

The increased popularity of common stocks, however, is not due entirely to the changed status of bonds. There have been positive as well as negative advantages. The redemption in whole or in part of corporate indebtedness has reduced the burden of fixed interest charges and thereby enhanced the position of the stock. The rate of dividend return is not only more favorable than interest yields but also is backed by ample margins of safety over sustained periods. [7] The prospect of higher living costs arising out of higher prices

[7] The dividend record of American Telephone and Telegraph is most impressive on three counts: (1) unbroken record for more than 50 years; (2) no reduction in dividend rate for the same period; and (3) present rate of $9 annually in effect for nearly 20 years.

due to inflationary influences makes stock-ownership a protective "hedge" against the decline in the purchasing power of money, a condition under which the bondholder would be distinctly vulnerable. Most potent, however, in the appeal of common stocks to the average investor is the potential profit which may come from appreciation in market value.

The statistical evidence available further evidences the popularity of stocks as investments. The aggregate number of stockholders of record (excluding buyers on margin) of American Telephone, General Motors, and General Electric increased from 200,000 in 1920, to 450,000 in 1925, to 950,000 in 1930, and to 1,250,000 in 1940. The total dividends paid by American corporations in the decade from 1928 through 1937 aggregated over $60,000,000,000, or an annual average of more than $6,000,000,000. Dividend income reported by taxpayers for a typical year (1936) amounted to 14½ per cent of total income received, the percentages varying from 5 per cent in the case of individuals with total incomes of less than $5,000, to 40 per cent of those in income brackets around $100,000, and to 60 per cent of those in income brackets around $1,000,000. It is obvious that any opinion to the effect that stocks are bought primarily as speculations applies chiefly to short-term buyers. There are many important stocks in which the total transactions in a full year amount to less than one tenth of the number of shares outstanding.[8] It is one of the anomalies of finance that such trading, which literally takes place on the "fringe" of the issue, should establish the prevailing value of the entire issue. Such a price appraisal ignores the large holdings which are not offered for sale either because the price is not satisfactory or because the holders are not interested in selling.

Disadvantages of common stocks. The prospective buyer of common stocks cannot afford to overlook distinct disadvantages which are involved in such commitments. Regarded

---

[8] Total sales of General Motors common stock on the New York Stock Exchange in 1940 amounted to 2,659,000 shares, including duplications arising out of resales during the year, in comparison with 43,500,000 shares outstanding.

collectively, they present a problem which requires the application of all the skill, intelligence, and good fortune with which the investor may be endowed.

From a *technical* viewpoint, common stocks suffer the double handicap of being junior securities and having only contingent claims upon earnings. Any argument which might be used to demonstrate the safety of common stocks must necessarily be an even stronger argument in favor of bonds, since bonds invariably have a prior claim on earnings. Furthermore, the stockholder faces the probability of a reduction in income and the possibility of a complete loss thereof in periods of economic stress in contrast to the contractual right of the bondholder to be paid irrespective of prevailing earnings.

From an *economic* viewpoint, common stocks suffer the double handicap of being subject to the vicissitudes of the business cycle and to the adverse influences of industrial trends. In periods of prosperity, earnings are good, dividends are regular, and the situation is favorable; but in periods of depression, earnings are poor, dividends are irregular, and the situation of the stockholder is unenviable. Over longer periods, certain industries grow as others decline, an almost inevitable condition which often means that increased earnings in one field are at the expense of decreased profits elsewhere. A policy of alertness and adaptability is essential to protect capital investments under these changing circumstances.

From a *political* viewpoint, common stocks suffer the double handicap of being subject to public regulation in varying degrees and to public competition in extreme cases. Even though the enterprise may not be under the restricting influence of a regulatory commission as the railroad and utility companies are, the company may face increased costs in the form of heavy taxes and higher wage scales which cannot be passed on to buyers of their products, and which reduce income available to stockholders without, incidentally, decreasing interest payment due to bondholders. Moreover, in an increasing degree, public ownership has become a distinct threat to many industries under the unpleasant alternative of public competition on a basis of subsidized costs. [9]

From a *market* viewpoint, common stocks suffer the double disadvantage of affording one of the most popular forms of speculation in a country in which wagering is a major pastime and of being vulnerable to a method of taxation which places a heavy burden on profits from appreciation without providing equivalent exemption on loss from depreciation. As a result of speculative activity, the market value of common stocks is unreasonably high in periods of prosperity when investors have funds to invest, and is unreasonably low in periods of depression when many investors are compelled to sell their holdings in order to meet living expenses. [10]   It

[9] Despite industrial activity, current and prospective, at record-breaking levels in the latter part of 1940, the outlook for higher dividends was regarded as unfavorable by the Chairman of the General Motors Corporation, who made the following comments on October 27, 1940, with reference to the effect of increased taxation upon corporate earnings available for dividends:

"In view of the fact that over recent years industry has been subjected to a constantly increasing burden of taxation, even excluding the excess profits tax to which special considerations apply, and in view of the impossibility of any management being able progressively to increase the efficiency of operations to the degree that this increasing burden may be offset, stockholders must expect to receive a diminishing return as this trend of increasing taxes proceeds."

[10] "We have recently referred to the difference in yield obtainable on British and American equities and it should be realised that this is due to a fundamental difference affecting the two markets.   British securities are held by people all over the world for investment purposes; holders are genuinely interested in British industry and are more or less quick to respond to the normal changes in general conditions, being prepared to sell their investment holdings in one industry for reinvestment in others as the various industries are favourably or otherwise affected. The principle behind investment in the British market is the desire for an income return on capital invested.   Public interest in the American market is on quite a different basis.   Although here again, interest is world-wide, very few holders of the shares really follow American industry or the news regarding individual companies.   Their interest is confined to the prices of their shares, with the result that changes in Wall Street are cabled throughout the day all over the world, thus fostering the gambling spirit and the search for capital appreciation.   In the capitals of many countries American Brokers have their own offices with a price board on which fluctuations are recorded, and, when the market is active large numbers of speculators are attracted to these rooms to watch the changing prices. In almost every important city in the world it is possible to be kept informed of the prices of leading American shares all day and every day, whereas very few British security prices are quoted in European capitals and even then are somewhat difficult for the public to obtain."—Quoted from weekly letter, issued by prominent London investment firm in 1938.

is the usual experience for buyers of common stocks in this fashion to lose through buying dear and selling cheap. In the event that an investor in common stocks is fortunate enough to obtain a substantial profit from the sale of his securities in any year, his profit is subject to a relatively high income tax; if his losses exceed his profits, however, in any year, he is not permitted to reduce his taxable income to the same extent.

From a *practical* viewpoint, therefore, it is scarcely surprising that relatively few people of limited means find the purchase of common stocks profitable. Surely the evidence available as to the practical results of a policy of investing in common stocks is discouraging, to say the least. It would be invidious to cite specific cases to show how difficult is the problem of stock investing. One is reminded of the experience of a large life insurance company in Canada which had such severe losses on its common stock investments during the past decade as to result in parliamentary action restricting such companies against placing more than one quarter of their assets in this field. Another noteworthy illustration is afforded in the investment record of the largest chemical enterprise in Great Britain which, despite the supervision of perhaps the most skilled industrial management in the world operating in an industry which has made astonishing progress in the past twenty years, reported a net loss of £100,000 from the purchase of securities, principally stocks, aggregating £13,000,000 in value over the twelve-year period from 1926 through 1937. A third example is presented in the case of an investment trust company sponsored by one of the best-known investment firms in America and having the advantage of long experience in finance, which suffered a depreciation of 90 per cent in portfolio values between 1929 and 1932, representing a dollar loss of nearly $290,000,000. A fourth example might be cited in the case of one of the best-known American endowment foundations, which reported for the year ended June 30, 1939, a loss of 18 per cent on common stocks and a loss of only 1 per cent on bonds sold during the year, and a further 29 per cent depreciation on common stocks still held, despite the fact that the foundation bought only common stocks of distinct investment character. If institutions skilled in investment methods suffer such misfortune on common stock purchases, it is apparent that individual investors face a most difficult task. [11]

The investor who buys common stocks for long-term holding endeavors to select those industries and those companies which appear to have the most favorable prospects. Accurate foresight in this respect has yet to be demonstrated in actual practice. Of the ten most popular common stocks chosen in a prize contest conducted by a prominent financial periodical in 1925, only two showed any appreciation in value in 1939, and the other eight showed depreciations ranging from 22 to 89 per cent; in a similar contest held in 1939, only one of the original ten appeared among the most popular issues. The investment inquiry department of the leading financial newspaper in the United States prepared, in 1927, a list of twenty-five common stocks which offered the best prospect for the ensuing twenty years; ten years later, in 1937, only five of the issues showed any appreciation in value, whereas the twenty others showed depreciation from 1927 values; over one half of the issues showed losses of more than 50 per cent. A study made in the early part of 1933 showed that a certain public utility stock was the most popular stock held by the investment trusts of the country at that time; within two years that stock had declined to the lowest point in its history. Although 1937 was generally regarded as a good business year, more than one half of the 500,000 corporations which filed income tax returns for that year reported a net loss for the year.

----

[11] The vulnerability of common stocks to drastic depreciation in market value was vividly illustrated in the sale of 17,325 shares of New Haven Railroad common stock on the New York Stock Exchange on December 10, 1940, at a price of $\frac{1}{16}$, or $6\frac{1}{4}$ cents per share. Although this block of stock had a value in excess of $4,000,000 in 1910, the net proceeds to the seller in 1940 resulted in an expenditure of $389.82 because total expense of $1,386 for transfer taxes plus $86.63 for brokerage commission exceeded the revenue of $1,082.81 from the sale of stock. The owner was willing to pay nearly $400 to get rid of stock (apparently for tax purposes) which had a former value of more than $4,000,000.

The final comment may be made that practically all informed men in Wall Street regard the stock market as an unbeatable game. Such an opinion does not indicate that they believe that the purchase of stocks for long-term holding is never wise. Rather do they infer that the person who hopes to derive a satisfactory income from market fluctuations is almost certain to be disappointed. [12]

---

[12] However, as merchants of investment securities of established character, we do not consider that it is sound practice for us to offer common stock over our own name to the general public through banks and dealers. Consequently, in the few equity operations which we undertook, we invited to join us, not primarily institutions and dealers who distribute investment securities to the general public, but individuals capable of sharing and understanding the risk; and with one minor exception we asked them to join us in the stock purchase at the same price that we paid. It would not have been prudent banking to keep all these common stocks in our own portfolio. We wished, therefore, to sell part of them as a businessman's investment to those having knowledge of business and general conditions, who would understand exactly what they were buying and who, as joint venturers, would share with ourselves the profit and the risk of the stock purchase.—From a statement prepared by J. P. Morgan and Co., in connection with the Federal Securities Investigation in 1933.

4

❖❘❙❙❙❙❙❙❘❙❙❙❙❙❙❘❙❙❙❙❙❙❘❖

SECURITIES MARKETS

❖❙❙❙❙❙❙❙❙❙❙❙❙❘❙❙❙❙❙❙❙❙❙❙❙❙❘❙❙❙❙❙❙❙❙❙❙❙❙❘❙❙❙❙❙❙❙❙❙❙❙❙❘❙❙❙❙❙❙❙❙❙❙❙❙❘❙❙❙❙❙❙❙❙❙❙❙❙❘❙❙❙❙❙❙❙❙❙❙❙❙❘❖

Scope. The purpose of this chapter is to discuss securities markets from the viewpoints of (1) securities exchanges and (2) unlisted markets. With respect to the exchanges, the order of discussion is: (1) function, (2) regulation, (3) registration requirements, (4) report requirements, (5) credit, or margin, requirements, and (6) price manipulation. With respect to the unlisted market, the order of discussion is: (1) unlisted securities, (2) types of dealers, and (3) method of operation. The interesting conclusion is reached that listed securities have lost a large part of their traditional advantage over unlisted issues, many of which have active markets in over-the-counter trading.

Listed and unlisted markets. The principal function of the securities exchanges is to provide a convenient central point for the execution of buying and selling orders. The securities which have been regularly admitted to trading privileges on these exchanges have traditionally been called *listed* issues in contrast to all other securities, which are known as *unlisted* issues. As a practical matter, however, only those securities admitted to the New York Stock Exchange are regarded as listed issues because of the predominant position of that exchange in the investment markets of the country; this distinction is especially true with respect to bonds, since the other exchanges largely confine their operations to stocks.

The distinction between listed and unlisted securities still exists, but material changes in the nature of the securities markets have made the distinction less unfavorable to the unlisted group. In the first place, the number of unlisted issues has grown tremendously during recent years with respect to quality as well as quantity. In the second place, many unlisted issues have been admitted to trading facilities on the securities exchanges with the official approval of the Federal authorities. In the third place, the investment firms which deal principally in unlisted issues provide trading facilities comparable to the organized markets for listed issues. In the fourth place, the volume of trading on the exchanges has declined to such a point that assurance no longer exists that more than a relatively small amount of securities may be bought or sold at the prevailing price. In the fifth place, certain issues of undoubted quality, because of either small capitalization or limited distribution, cannot meet the listing requirements of the exchanges. And, lastly, relatively reliable quotations on prices of many unlisted securities are now obtainable in the daily newspapers.

The preference which investors have long shown for listed issues has become somewhat outmoded in the light of these developments. So extensive has become the unlisted market embracing issues of the highest quality, such as Treasury notes, municipal bonds, and railroad equipment obligations, that even the most conservative investors buy as freely from the unlisted group as from the issues listed on the securities exchanges.

Function of the exchanges. Securities exchanges in the United States are of the auction type in the sense that brokers for sellers deal directly with brokers for buyers in competitive bidding and offering. In contrast, the London Stock Exchange affords a noncompetitive market in which brokers must buy and sell through jobbers who are dealers acting as middlemen. Under the American system, the broker for the buyer tries to obtain the lowest possible price, while the broker for the seller tries to obtain the highest possible price; consequently, prices tend to change from sale to sale according to the urgencies of the customers, thus creating a situation which encourages speculation. Under the British system, the jobber makes the prevailing market by maintaining prices with a small spread between that at which he is willing to buy and that at which he is willing to sell; consequently, prices tend to change slowly, being determined more by the volume of buying or selling orders than by the anxieties of customers. The London method in providing relatively stable prices tends to protect both buyer and seller to a greater extent than does the New York method. Unlike the American auction plan which encourages speculation, the British jobber plan is designed to discourage speculative operations. [1]

Members of the securities exchanges generally act as brokers who execute orders sent to them by their respective clients. They may, and often do, act as principals in purchasing and selling for their own account. In the latter capacity, they are not permitted to take advantage of their position in the filling of their own orders but must give precedence to orders held for others at the same price. Their principal advantage over nonmembers is the saving in time through actual presence on the floor of the exchange and in commission charges. [2]

The primary purpose of a securities exchange is to provide a market for seasoned issues. The secondary purpose in creating a market for new issues has questionable economic justification, save in the cases of new issues by companies that already have previous issues listed. It is scarcely the

---

[1] Another significant difference between the New York and London stock exchanges is the absence of "margin" accounts in London and the fortnightly settlement dates. Only persons with financial responsibility may carry accounts with London brokers.

[2] The New York Stock Exchange is not a corporation but a voluntary association of 1,375 individuals, of whom about one half are commission brokers, about one quarter are specialists, about one tenth are representatives of odd-lot dealers, and the remainder consists of either individual traders or inactive members. Firms which advertise as members of the Exchange have one or more partners who hold the so-called "seats."

function of the securities exchanges to help in the distribution of new issues by investment houses, except in indirect fashion through encouraging original purchases by investors who prefer to hold listed securities. Some exchanges emphasize the point by refusing to list new issues until the securities have been satisfactorily distributed.

Securities exchanges are allowed to have two groups of securities, those that are regularly listed and those that are unlisted but admitted to trading privileges. Unlisted issues which may be bought and sold on those exchanges which permit this practice are in three groups: (1) those which had already been admitted prior to March 1, 1934; (2) those which are regularly listed on another securities exchange; and (3) the securities of companies on which there is available information substantially equivalent to that required for duly listed securities. Although all of the 2,530 securities admitted to trading on the New York Stock Exchange on June 30, 1939, were regularly listed, over 60 per cent of the 1,475 securities admitted on the New York Curb Exchange on the same date were unlisted issues.

Securities Exchange Act. The securities exchanges of the United States were brought under Federal control for the first time under the provisions of the Securities Exchange Act of 1934. This law created a Federal Securities and Exchange Commission appointed by the President. It provides for the registration with the Commission of any exchange as a National Securities Exchange. It forbids the operation of any unregistered exchange except those which may be exempted by reason of a limited volume of transactions. It places the control of the credit used in the purchasing or carrying of securities with the Board of Governors of the Federal Reserve System. It prohibits the manipulation of security prices and the use of deceptive devices for such purpose. It requires all companies which have securities listed on the registered exchanges to file comprehensive information of their affairs and to keep the information reasonably current. It empowers the Commission to control the over-the-counter market. It imposes severe penalties for violations. In short, it aims to eradicate the more serious abuses in securities trading.

The Securities Exchange Act of 1934 may be regarded as a logical supplement to the Securities Act of 1933. The purpose of the Securities Act is to provide adequate protection to investors in the purchase of new issues. The objective of the Securities Exchange Act is to safeguard investors in brokerage transactions involving the purchase or sale of seasoned securities. Through such legislation, the Federal Government has assumed drastic regulatory control of the investment markets of the United States.

The Securities and Exchange Commission. A Federal commission, called the Securities and Exchange Commission, has been created for the purpose of administering the Securities Act of 1933 and the Securities Exchange Act of 1934. This Commission comprises five members appointed by the President and has wide discretionary powers in the administration of the laws. Registration statements, listing applications, and periodic reports must be prepared according to the detailed requirements of this Commission. Important exemption powers are granted to the Commission with respect to exchanges, securities, and reports. It has already assumed an importance in the investment business exceeding that attained by the Interstate Commerce Commission in the field of transportation.

National Securities Exchanges. The Federal law now requires, in effect, that all securities exchanges in the United States become National Securities Exchanges through registration with the Securities and Exchange Commission. Such registration obligates the exchange to comply with all rules and regulations of the Commission with respect to listing requirements and operations. The Commission, however, may exempt certain small exchanges from registration when, "by reason of the limited volume of transactions effected on such exchange, it is not practicable and not necessary or appropriate in the public interest or for the protection of investors to require such registration." Transactions on unregistered exchanges which have not been specifically exempted are unlawful.

Registration requirements. Transactions on National Securities Exchanges are restricted to those securities which have been officially registered with the Exchange and with the Commission, or which are legally exempted under the provisions of the law. The exempted group comprises, in general, public issues of domestic origin, including Federal obligations and instrumentalities, and state and municipal bonds. Companies which desire to have their securities listed on a National Securities Exchange must arrange registration by submitting detailed information of their affairs at the time of application, and must agree to keep such information reasonably current thereafter. The nature of the required information is shown in the following summary:

1. The organization, financial structure, and nature of the business.

2. The terms, position, rights, and privileges of the different classes of securities outstanding.

3. The terms on which securities are to be and during the preceding three years have been offered to the public or otherwise.

4. The directors, officers, and underwriters, and each security holder of record holding more than 10 per cent of any class of any equity security of the issuer, their remuneration and their interests in the securities of and their material contracts with the issuer and any person directly or indirectly controlling or controlled by or under direct or indirect common control with the issuer.

5. Remuneration to others than directors and officers exceeding $20,000 a year.

6. Bonus and profit-sharing arrangements.

7. Management and service contracts.

8. Options existing or to be created in respect of their securities.

9. Balance sheets for not less than the three preceding fiscal years, certified by independent public accountants.

10. Profit and loss statements for not less than the three preceding fiscal years, certified by independent public accountants.

11. Any further financial statements which the Commission may deem necessary or appropriate for the protection of investors.

In addition to the registration requirements as set forth in the Federal law, each of the securities exchanges has adopted certain requirements for admission to its particular facilities. The New York Stock Exchange requires: (1) that the company be a substantial going concern of national reputation with demonstrated earning power; (2) that the management agrees to be bound by established standards of responsibility to security holders in the publication of reports, in the appointment of trustees, and in the repurchase of its securities; (3) that investors be assured of the purchase of valid securities; (4) that a sufficient volume of securities be outstanding to provide a national market; (5) that independent registrars be selected; and (6) that adequate transfer facilities be provided in the vicinity of the exchange.[3]

Report requirements. Issuers of securities registered on a National Securities Exchange are required to keep the information filed with the Commission and the Exchange "reasonably current" and to submit such annual and quarterly reports as may be prescribed. These reports must be prepared in such detail and according to such accounting procedure as is required by the Commission. The Commission is empowered to prescribe the methods to be followed in the preparation of the reports, the appraisal or valuation of assets and liabilities, the determination of depreciation and depletion, the differentiation of investment and operating income and of recurring and nonrecurring income, and in the matter of separate and consolidated income statements and balance sheets.

---

[3] The New York Stock Exchange reported total sales of $12,360,000,000 in the year ended June 30, 1939, or nearly 90 per cent of the aggregate sales of $14,210,000,000 on all registered exchanges. The New York Curb Exchange reported total sales of $1,150,000,000, or 8 per cent of the aggregate. The other 18 registered exchanges in the nation handled only 2 per cent of the aggregate volume.

Credit control.   The amount of credit which may legally be extended by investment houses and commercial banks for the purchasing and carrying of securities is subject to the rules and regulations of the Board of Governors of the Federal Reserve System.   The present margin requirement is a cash payment of at least 40 per cent of the cost price.   Should the price later decline, however, the buyer is not compelled to maintain the full 40 per cent margin and would not be called upon for more cash unless his equity were greatly reduced.   Under the present rules of the New York Stock Exchange, the minimum equity requirement is 30 per cent of the unpaid balance.   If stock is purchased at $50 per share under a 40 per cent margin payment, the buyer's equity of $20 is 67 per cent of the unpaid balance of $30.   If the stock should decline to $45, the buyer's equity of $15 would be 50 per cent of the debit balance of $30. If the stock should decline to $40, the equity of $10 would be 33 per cent of the debit balance of $30.   Additional margin would therefore be required only if the price should fall below $40 a share.

Manipulation of prices.   One of the most interesting provisions of the Exchange Act is the restriction prohibiting the manipulation of market prices.   The law forbids the execution of matched orders or "wash sales" made for the purpose of creating a false impression of market activity.   It prohibits the dissemination of false or misleading information with respect to market prices or values.   Short sales, stop-loss orders, price-pegging, and stabilizing operations are forbidden except as the Securities Commission may prescribe.   Such restrictions are aimed directly at pool operations and have measurably reduced speculative activity in securities.

Over-the-counter market.   The Securities Exchange law prohibits public dealings in any registered security on other than a registered exchange.   It further empowers the Securities Commission to set up rules and regulations for transactions on over-the-counter markets, and for the registration of dealers and securities in such markets.   Such restrictions, however, do not apply to transactions in those securities which, as previously stated, are specially exempted from registration, or to unregistered securities which have principally a localized market.

Advantages of listing. The object of listing securities is to gain marketability. Other advantages exist, but the chief aim is to make the security more desirable by increasing its market. A listed security can be bought or sold on the exchange on which it is listed—where buyers and sellers are accustomed to meet, where the value of the security is best known, and where the most favorable price is obtainable. Moreover, if one is not immediately interested in buying or selling, he can keep in touch with the market by observing the prices at which the security is being sold, as reported in the transactions of the exchange. If he is an owner, a downward trend in the price may warn him that an exchange is desirable and an upward trend may enable him to realize a profit if he believes the movement is temporary. If he is not an owner, repeated publication of current prices acts as a constant invitation to buy, particularly if the price is attractive.

Listing adds to the collateral value of a security. In making loans, banks prefer as collateral those securities that are readily marketable. The bank is interested in the security not as an investment, but rather as a pledge that the loan will be paid. The chief consideration of the bank is the relative convenience with which the collateral may be converted into cash if the loan is not paid. Bankers usually have neither the time nor the facilities for investigating the intrinsic value of each security offered as collateral, and therefore accept the market quotation as their chief criterion. Listed securities enjoy a distinct advantage in this regard.

Listing has much greater significance in the case of stocks than in the case of bonds. It is customary to buy and to sell stocks through the exchanges, whereas bonds are usually bought and sold privately. Although the larger part of the shares of stock bought and sold in New York is handled through the exchanges, less than ten per cent of the bonds bought and sold are covered in exchange transactions. Even at this, some of the stocks listed on the New York Stock Exchange are not represented in a full year's transactions, and even the busiest days have only about two thirds of the listed stocks included. Over 1,200 stocks are listed, and transactions in 800 different issues are construed to represent an active day. Some listed issues sell as infrequently as once or twice a year. The great bulk of the transactions is confined to relatively few securities. A spread of five full points (forty times the minimum of one eighth of one point) between the bid and asked prices is not regarded as unusual for a listed stock. Such spreads have been known to exceed twenty-five points. Reference to the prices of inactive listed securities as reported in the periodicals will bear out this point. And it should be remembered that such compilations include only those securities which are usually dealt in, but which were inactive that day. If a similar compilation of the really inactive listed stocks were possible, the evidence would be still more striking.

Bond listing is less advantageous than stock listing. Although nearly 1,400 bonds are listed on the New York Stock Exchange, less than 500 provide over 95 per cent of the transactions. In other words, 1,000 listed bonds are dealt in so seldom that their aggregate volume is less than 5 per cent of the total. Moreover, as already stated, the stock exchange transactions in bonds represent a very small part of the total for the city.[4]

Unlisted securities. A very substantial volume of securities is not listed on any of the securities exchanges. Though less important in the aggregate value than the listed issues, the unlisted group is much larger, because of the inability or the unwillingness of corporations to gain listing privileges for their securities. In interesting comparison with the approximately 6,000 securities listed on the various national exchanges, there are about 60,000 additional issues in which an active market is maintained throughout the country. The importance of the

---

[4] Recent statistics show that monthly sales of stocks on the New York Stock Exchange, including numerous duplications, average only about 2 per cent of the total number of shares listed; and that monthly sales of bonds average only about one half of 1 per cent of the total par value of listed bonds.

MARKETS FOR SECURITIES

Classes of Securities	Securities Exchanges	Over-the-counter
United States:		
Treasury Notes...............	0	xxx
Treasury Bonds...............	x	xx
Agency Bonds................	x	xx
Territorial...................	0	xxx
State..........................	0	xxx
Municipal......................	0	xxx
Railroad:		
Bonds and Stocks.....	xxx	0
Equipments..................	0	xxx
Public Utility....................	x	xx
Industrial......................	xx	x
Bank and Insurance.............	0	xxx
Investment Trust...............	x	xx
Real Estate....................	0	xxx
Foreign.......................	xx	0

0   = Rarely, if ever.
x   = Minor degree.
xx = Major degree.
xxx = Almost exclusively.

unlisted group is shown in the following list of issues which are usually in this classification:

1. United States Treasury notes and bills.
2. United States Territorial bonds.
3. Federal Land Bank and Federal Home Loan Bank bonds.
4. State bonds.
5. Municipal bonds.
6. Railroad equipment trust notes.
7. Many public utility bonds and stocks.
8. Most industrial bonds and stocks.
9. Most serial maturity bonds.
10. Bank and trust company stocks.
11. Insurance company stocks.
12. Investment trust issues.
13. Foreign internal bonds.
14. Most real estate bonds and mortgages.

So extensive has the group of unlisted securities become that few intelligent investors now confine their commitments to the listed group. The point has already been established that listing, even on an important exchange, does not assure ready marketability. It may further be noted that the activity of many unlisted dealers has resulted in the creation of an open market in which many unlisted securities have gained a degree of marketability as active as that of the average listed issue. Furthermore, the achievement of a satisfactory diversification grouping almost necessitates the holding of some unlisted securities. Firms that provide markets in unlisted securities make no attempt to cover the entire field. One group will specialize in municipals, another in bank and insurance company stocks, and still another in investment trust issues. Not only must the investor ascertain the particular firms that handle issues in which he is interested, but he must further appreciate that transactions in unlisted securities are handled differently from dealings in listed issues.

The market in unlisted securities is made by dealers at prices reached through *negotiation,* which means through bargaining bid and offered prices. Although popularly called the *over-the-counter* market, it might more fittingly be called *over-the-telephone,* as the bulk of the business is handled in the latter fashion. Unlike the exchanges that are open only during established hours, such as "ten to three," the unlisted dealers make their own hours and are generally willing to trade from "nine to five," and even earlier and later. Each dealer makes a market dependent upon the general course of prices on the exchanges and upon the demand and supply in the particular issue. Competition among unlisted dealers keeps prices around a uniform level in each issue and the quotation spread within reasonable limits.

The market quoted by an unlisted dealer is generally *subject to confirmation* and represents the range in which he is willing to bargain. A quotation of "92-94" means that he is willing to pay at least 92 and does not expect to sell for more than 94. He is usually willing to *close the spread* to secure an order, and in the preceding case might bid 92½ for 100 shares or offer 100 shares for 93½ on a *firm* basis, generally subject to immediate acceptance.

The quotations on unlisted securities which appear in the newspapers are given in the form of bid and asked prices rather than those of actual transactions. The quotations represent an approximate average of prices as reported by representative dealers and are supplied in most instances by the National Association of Securities Dealers. This association includes about 3,000 of the dealers in unlisted securities and is a self-regulatory group registered with the Securities Commission and designed to maintain sound practices in the field without the continuous direct supervision of the government. Obviously, the newspapers have space for the publication of only a limited number of quotations and usually give preference to local issues. Comprehensive lists of quotations on unlisted securities are available to all investment dealers, however, who are usually able to provide an immediate quotation on any important unlisted security.

5

BROKERAGE ORDERS

Scope. The purpose of this chapter is to discuss the manner in which orders are placed with investment brokers for the purchase and sale of listed securities through the facilities of the exchanges. The order of discussion is: (1) price-limit orders, (2) function of the specialist, (3) time-limit orders, (4) stop-loss orders, (5) short-selling, (6) odd-lot orders, (7) put-and-call option contracts, (8) delivery time, (9) commission charges, and (10) transfer requirements. The rules and regulations in vogue in these respects are established by the respective exchanges under the general supervision of the Securities and Exchange Commission.

Buying and selling orders. The method employed in the purchase or sale of a security is determined largely by the type of issue. Certain securities which have been admitted to the list of those traded on the securities exchanges of the country are known as "listed" issues; orders for the purchase or sale of these issues are normally placed with brokerage firms which are members of the particular exchange involved. "Unlisted" issues are bought and sold directly by investment firms which act as dealers in such issues. Investors who do not have their own brokers usually have their banks place their orders for them.

New issues of securities are ordinarily bought from investment dealers at a fixed price without a commission charge.

Subsequent purchases and sales are usually handled by brokerage firms which charge a commission for their service. In the case of unlisted issues, investors who buy and sell directly with dealers are not charged any commission.

Market and limit orders. Orders for the purchase or sale of securities may be placed on a *market* (no price limit) or a *limit* basis. An order "at the market" means "at the best price available"; on a quotation of 92 (per cent) bid, 93 (per cent) asked, an order to buy at the market would be executed at 93 ($930 for a $1,000 bond) and an order to sell at the market would be executed at 92 ($920 for a $1,000 bond). Although the broker will try to get better prices on such orders, he cannot afford to delay because other orders may intervene. On limit orders, the investor places a price limit which the broker may not violate; on a selling order, the broker must not sell for less than the price limit but may accept more, whereas, on a buying order, the broker must not pay more but may pay less than the price limit set by the investor.

Whether "market" or "limit" orders are the more advisable is a debatable question. The great advantage of the market order is in immediate execution; the chief disadvantage is at times an unsatisfactory price. The great advantage of the limit order is the avoidance of an unsatisfactory price; the chief disadvantage is delay in execution and possible loss of the prevailing market quotation. Market orders are probably more satisfactory in securities of good marketability as shown in a narrow spread between bid and asked prices; limit orders are more advisable in securities which do not have good marketability.

Price quotations on securities represent bids and offers for limited quantities. Orders exceeding the established unit of trading (which is usually one $1,000 bond or 100 shares of stock) frequently cannot be filled at the prevailing quotation. An order to buy at the market 1,000 shares of a certain stock which is quoted 52½-53 may be filled on a basis of 100 shares at 53, 200 at 53⅛, 100 at 53¼, 200 at 53½, and 400 at 53¾. An order to sell 1,000 shares under the same conditions might be filled on the basis of 200 at 52½, 100 at 52¼, 300 at 52, and

To Every Investor and Speculator We Offer this Statement of our Basic Policy

1. Our customer's interest must come first. Upon our ability to satisfy him rests our chance to succeed.

2. Our business deals with people and their money. This creates financial and ethical responsibilities which we accept completely.

3. Eliminating all expensive frills which do not make a direct contribution to the fundamental requirements of our customers, we offer simple offices, competent manpower and efficient, impartial service.

4. When our relationship with a customer is other than that of a commission broker, the fact will be made known before the transaction. When supplying printed reports concerning a security in which the firm is not acting as principal, we intend to indicate the extent of the aggregate direct and indirect ownership, as of the date of the report, by the firm and its general partners. The purpose of such disclosure is to help the customer estimate the possibility and extent of bias on the part of the firm in its presentation of facts relating to a particular security.

5. Salaries of our Registered Representatives (Customers' Men) are related primarily to their success in satisfying the service requirements of customers—thus eliminating conditions which indirectly create pressures to increase the trading of customers.

6. We think it is impossible for us to operate successfully as investment counsel. Therefore all reports issued by our Research Department will be limited to facts—absolutely ungarnished with advice. Advice is out—unless it is specifically asked for, and then only with the approval of one of our partners or managers who are available for consultation with all customers, large or small.

7. During periods of extraordinary activity, no new accounts will be opened on any day when the volume of trading at any time indicates that the facilities of the firm may be overtaxed.

8. Our working capital position will at all times exceed the requirements of the law, the New York Stock Exchange and other exchanges, and our financial statements will be issued in a form designed for maximum clarity and understanding.

9. We heartily support the laws and other controls designed to protect the investor by preventing manipulation and fraud.

(Statement issued by a prominent securities brokerage firm in 1940.)

400 at 51¾.   An order to sell $10,000 of a certain bond issue quoted at 88-90 might be executed on a basis of $2,000 at 88, $2,000 at 87, $1,000 at 86, and $5,000 at 85.   So "thin" are the markets on some bonds that an offer of $10,000 in such bonds may cause the price to drop as much as five points.

Function of the specialist.   Orders which are placed for execution at prices which are "away" from the prevailing market customarily are turned over by brokers to other brokers who act as "specialists" in the particular stocks.   These "specialists" maintain records, known as "books," in which these orders are entered in the sequence received.   The accompanying illustration shows the volume of such orders in a certain stock at prices between 28 and 42; other orders not shown are held below 28 and above 42.   As here shown, the highest bid is for 100 shares at 33, and the lowest offer is for 100 shares at 33⅞, thus making the quotation 33-33⅞.   An order to buy 500 shares at the market would be thus executed: 100 at 33⅞, and 400 at 34.   An order to sell 500 shares at the market would be thus executed: 100 at 33, 200 at 32, 100 at 31½, and 100 at 31.   In either event, the specialist himself or other brokers may intervene if they care to make prices more advantageous than those which are on the unfilled list.   In other words, the specialist might supply stock from his own account to fill 100 shares on the buying order at 33⅞, which price would be less than 34, the lowest price then available on the buying side of the book.   In similar fashion, the specialist might buy stock for his own account to take the last 100 shares on the selling order at 31⅛, which price would be higher than 31, the highest price then available on the selling side of the book.

The principal advantage which the specialist offers is that of providing a convenient concentration point for orders which otherwise could not be expediently handled by the regular brokers.   His willingness to buy and sell stock for his own account does tend to narrow the spread between bid and asked prices, but his intimate knowledge of potential buying and selling orders gives him what many persons believe is an unfair advantage over other buyers and sellers in the issue.   The specialist obviously takes little risk in buying stock at prices only slightly above that on actual buying orders on his books, or in selling stock at prices only slightly less than that on actual selling orders on his books.

Day and open orders. Orders for the purchase or sale of securities may be placed on an *open* or a *day* basis. The investor may state that the order is to be held until it is executed, which, in the case of price limit orders, may require several months or longer. Such orders are known as G.T.C. orders, or "good until canceled." Unless there are specific instructions that the order is to remain "open," however, it is understood to be a "day" order, in which event it is regarded as automatically canceled if not executed on the day it is placed.

UNFILLED ORDERS ON "BOOK" OF SPECIALIST[1]

Buying Orders	Last Sale	Selling Orders
200 at 28	—	—
200 at 30	—	—
200 at 31	—	—
100 at 31½	—	—
200 at 32	—	—
100 at 33	—	—
—	33⅞	100 at 33⅞
—	—	700 at 34
—	—	100 at 40½
—	—	400 at 41
—	—	200 at 42
1,000 shares	—	1,500 shares

Although the placing of orders on an "open" basis would seem preferable to the investor who is in no hurry to act and who is not satisfied with prevailing prices, such practice will not always work to his advantage. Frequently, open orders to buy at prices below the prevailing market are executed to the extreme discomfiture of an investor when adverse developments, which make the security much less attractive, come too quickly to allow him to cancel the order. It is not uncommon for open orders to be executed to the subsequent surprise—and

[1] As reported in *The New York Times* on April 9, 1939.

sometimes chagrin—of investors who had completely forgotten the commitment while engrossed in other affairs.

Stop-loss orders. Investors who desire to limit the loss which they may incur in the holding of securities sometimes place orders to be executed at prices below the prevailing market. Although this practice is more common with speculators in stocks, it is at times employed by investors in both bonds and stocks. An investor who has bought 100 shares of a certain stock at $50 a share, and who desires to limit his maximum loss to about $5 a share, places an order to sell at "45 stop." This order is not an instruction to sell at $45, but rather an order to sell at the market "if and when" the price should decline to $45. This type of order is also used to protect profits gained from price advances as well as to limit losses on short sales. In the preceding case, the investor holding stock quoted at $60 which cost $50 places an order to sell at "55 stop," thereby insuring the retention of a profit of at least $5 a share. A speculator who has sold "short" 100 shares at $50 per share may place an order to buy at "60 stop" in order to limit his loss to around $10 a share.

The advisability of placing stop-loss orders is questioned in many informed circles. A market which has many stop-loss orders just below prevailing prices is technically weak since a limited volume of selling would bring prices down to the stop limits. The automatic execution of these orders would further depress the price, thereby "setting off" stop orders at lower limits. After the cumulative effect had run its course, the price would tend to rise, to the embarrassment of those who were sold out at lower levels. It would seem wiser for such investors not to place selling orders until they were ready to sell. Experience has shown that it is usually wiser to place an immediate order to sell at the prevailing price than a deferred order to sell at a lower price.

Short selling. Orders for the sale and immediate delivery of securities may be placed by persons who do not own the securities at the time but who expect to purchase them later at a lower price. The securities needed for delivery to the buyer—who is not aware that he has purchased from a "short seller"—are secured through a securities loan which will be liquidated when the subsequent purchase is arranged. The securities loans involved in short sales are arranged by the brokers through the use of securities held by them for their own account or for other customers who have allowed their securities to be used for this purpose.

Under present regulations, orders for short selling must be so designated when placed, and cannot be executed at prices below that established in the last preceding regular (as distinguished from short) sale. The purpose of this rule is to prevent the use of short sales to depress the market price of the issue.

As short selling is purely a speculative device, many persons believe that the practice should be outlawed as detrimental to investment values. Others claim that it serves a necessary function in providing a corrective check to abnormally high prices as well as a protective cushion to declining prices. It is noteworthy in the latter regard that short selling seems much more prevalent in periods of depression than in periods of prosperity and that the effect of buying orders to cover short positions rarely changes the trend of the market. Instead of acting as a brake on an advancing market, short selling frequently results in higher prices as frightened short sellers rush to place buying orders to cover their positions when favorable developments cause prices to advance.

Odd-lot orders. Orders for the purchase or sale of less than the established unit of trading on the various exchanges are handled through so-called odd-lot dealers. For the great majority of stocks on the New York Stock Exchange, 100 shares is the established minimum, although 10-share markets have been established for a group of stocks in which activity is limited for various reasons. Brokers who receive orders to buy or sell less than 100 shares place these orders with odd-lot dealers who fill them at prices slightly different from prevailing prices on 100-share lots. On odd-lot orders "at the market," the price is set at 12½ cents a share away from the prevailing price on full lots, higher on buying orders and lower on selling orders. On odd-lot "limit" orders, execution does not take place until the prevailing price reaches the 12½-cent differential. An order to buy 25 shares at 37 is not filled until the regular price reaches 36⅞; an order to sell 25 shares at 27 is not filled until the regular price reaches 27⅛. The odd-lot price differential is not in lieu of commissions which must be paid in addition. The importance of odd-lot orders is indicated by an average volume of about 30 per cent of the full-lot transactions.

Although the ordinary differential for odd-lot orders on the New York Stock Exchange is 12½ cents a share, somewhat higher differences are in vogue. On orders for less than the unit of trading in 10-share stocks, the differentials range from 25 cents to $2 a share. On other exchanges, odd-lot differentials are more commonly set at 25 and 50 cents a share.

Puts and calls. The term *options* is applied to contracts which involve the right to buy or sell securities at specified prices within stated times. A *put* is a contract which gives an investor the right to sell a certain number of shares (usually 100) at a designated price (usually slightly below the prevailing market) within a limited time (usually 30 days). An investor holding 100 shares of a certain stock selling at $50 a share who fears that the price may decline substantially because of an impending development but who otherwise desires to keep his stock may purchase a "put" giving him the right to sell his stock at, say, $45 a share to the seller of the option at any time within, say, 30 days.

A *call* is a contract which gives an investor the right to buy a certain number of shares (usually 100) at a designated price (usually slightly above the prevailing market) within a limited time (usually 30 days). An investor considering the purchase of 100 shares of a certain stock selling at $50 a share who feels that the time is not opportune but fears that the price might rise suddenly while he is waiting may purchase a "call" giving him the right to buy the stock at, say, $55 a share from the seller of the option at any time within, say, 30 days.

The differentials between the market prices and the option prices are set by the option dealers and are determined by the condition of the market. The spreads are naturally smaller on low-price stocks and in inactive markets. The cost of these option contracts is currently $137.50 per 100 shares on a 30-day basis. Although the contracts are used chiefly by speculators, they are occasionally used by investors, as here illustrated, as a sort of insurance against contingencies which may not occur.[2]

Time of delivery. Securities which are bought and sold on the securities exchanges must be delivered within the time specified under the rules of the exchange. Under the rules of the New York Stock Exchange, delivery is required on the second full business day (thereby excluding Saturdays, Sundays, and holidays) following the day of sale. Sales not made in the regular way may be made for *cash,* which means for delivery and payment on the same day as that of sale. Sales may also be made for *delayed delivery,* thus giving sellers a specified time, such as a week or a month, in which to arrange delivery. Short sellers, however, are not allowed to use the delayed delivery option, which is restricted to actual owners of securities. The prices at which securities may be sold on a cash or delayed delivery basis are usually slightly lower than those prevailing on regular deliveries because either of these options operates to the benefit of the seller more than to the benefit of the buyer. As the buyer must be prepared to accept delivery at any time within the delayed period, he is entitled to accrued interest on bonds on the basis of the date of sale rather than on the basis of the date of delivery.

In the event that the seller fails to make delivery within the designated time, the buyer has the right to a *buy-in,* whereby his broker repurchases the securities from another seller on a cash basis and holds the original seller liable for any higher cost. In practice, however, buy-ins are resorted to only after repeated failures to deliver.

When unlisted issues are bought or sold through dealers, the time of delivery is set more by informal agreement than by formal rules. In general, however, the practice closely conforms to that of the listed group.

---

[2] At the end of 1940, 30-day puts and calls were obtainable on American Telephone stock, quoted around $160, at $10 down and $8 up; on Chrysler stock, quoted around $80, at $8 down and $6 up; and on United States Steel Stock, quoted around $60, at $4 down and $3.50 up.

Commission charges. When securities are purchased or sold by investors directly from or to investment dealers, no commission charge is made since both parties are acting as principals in the transaction. When securities are bought or sold through brokerage houses, a commission charge is made which is paid by both the buyer and the seller. Minimum commission rates are usually established under the rules of the exchanges where the securities are sold. Competition between brokerage houses tends to keep rates on a uniform basis at the established minima. Although at one time a uniform commission of ⅛ of 1 per cent of par value was charged on all security transactions, under more recent procedure, graduated scales are in vogue varying, in the case of bonds, with issuer, price, and maturity and, in the case of stocks, with market price.

The accompanying table shows the minimum commission rates in effect on the New York Stock Exchange in 1940. These rates were placed in effect in 1937, subject to change at any time. Although the practice of dividing commission charges with outside persons is elsewhere regarded as acceptable procedure, such practice is forbidden under the present rules at New York.

The total purchase price for buying $5,000 in par value of Atchison General 4's of 1995 (interest payable April 1 and October 1) on September 18, 1940, at 105 would be computed as follows:

Principal: $5,000 at 105%......................	$5,250.00
Interest: $5,000 at 4% for 5 mo. and 19 days.....	93.89
Commission: 5 bonds at $2.50..................	12.50
Total cost..............................	$5,356.39

In the foregoing illustration the accrued interest is computed up to, but not including, the day of delivery, which would be September 20. The entire payment of $93.89 for accrued interest would be recovered on October 1, when interest amounting to $100.00 would be collected for the six months thus ending. The net cost to the buyer would therefore be $5,262.50.

MINIMUM COMMISSION RATES ON BONDS

Corporate and Foreign (long-term).................... $2.50 per $1,000 bond
Corporate and Foreign (short-term)................... 1.25 per $1,000 bond
Government, State, and Municipal.................... 1.25 per $1,000 bond

MINIMUM COMMISSION RATES ON STOCKS

Selling Price	Commission Per Share	Selling Price	Commission Per Share
$1 to $2..............	5¢	$10 to $20.............	14¢
$2 to $3..............	6¢	$20 to $30.............	15¢
$3 to $4..............	7¢	$30 to $40.............	16¢
$4 to $5..............	8¢	$40 to $50.............	17¢
$5 to $6..............	9¢	$50 to $60.............	18¢
$6 to $7..............	10¢	$60 to $70.............	19¢
$7 to $8..............	11¢	$70 to $80.............	20¢
$8 to $9..............	12¢	$80 to $90.............	21¢
$9 to $10.............	13¢	$90 to $100............	22¢

Each additional $10 .... 1¢ additional

Minimum commission:
Under $50.............. $1.00
$50 or more............ $3.00

The total purchase price for buying 100 shares of Union Pacific common stock on September 19, 1940, at 85 would be computed as follows:

Principal: 100 shares at $85.................... $8,500.00
Dividend: (included in price)................... 0
Commission: 100 shares at 21¢................. 21.00

Total cost............................. $8,521.00

In both of the preceding illustrations, the respective proceeds to the seller would be less than the amounts shown as the commission charges would be deducted rather than added. Furthermore, transfer taxes would be paid by the seller.

Transfer of securities. Bonds and stocks are negotiable instruments, the title to which may be transferred by simple delivery, in the case of coupon bonds which are payable to bearer, or by endorsement or assignment and delivery, in the case of registered bonds and all classes of corporate stock.   As in the case of a bank check, endorsement in blank converts an instrument payable to a specified party into an instrument payable to the holder thereof.   As the law generally upholds the title of an innocent purchaser to a negotiable instrument, it follows that buyers and sellers of securities should be most careful in arranging transfers.   As dividend payments are made only to stockholders of record, new owners should arrange for immediate transfer to ensure the receipt of future payments.   In the event of loss through delay, such owners may recover only from the former owners.

Every seller of a negotiable instrument gives three implied promises in the transfer to a buyer.   These guarantees are: (1) that the instrument is genuine; (2) that the seller is not aware of any defect in its validity; and (3) that the seller is the legal owner with full power to sell.

The transfer of stock.   Stock certificates are always registered in the names of the owners.   Sometimes, owners prefer to have their stocks registered in the names of nominees, in which case the nominees have the right of transfer.[3]   The certificates may be transferred by endorsement or through an attached written assignment.

Each certificate is numbered; states the total number of authorized shares and the number of shares represented by the certificate; and bears the name of the registered owner, the signature of two properly designated officers of the company, and the respective authentications of the registrar and transfer agent.   On the reverse side of each certificate usually appears a transfer order which represents a combination of a bill of sale and a power of attorney with authority to transfer.

The signature on the assignment must correspond in every way, without alteration, enlargement, or any change whatever, with the name written on the face of the certificate. The endorsement must be guaranteed by a responsible finan-

---

[3] Eighteen of the thirty largest stockholders of the Pennsylvania Railroad in 1937 were nominees who held nearly 500,000 shares for the benefit of more than 2,000 different owners whose names were not on the records of the Company.

cial institution. Buyers prefer 100-share certificates and may refuse to accept larger denominations. The actual transfer on the books of the company is usually arranged by the new owner, but the seller may sometimes make the transfer to be assured that his name no longer appears as a stockholder.

The transfer of stock held by a corporation, or in the name of a decedent or an estate, or in the name of a trustee or guardian, or by an alien or nonresident requires additional documents of a nature too technical for discussion in this volume.

INVESTMENT BANKING

❖⬛⬛⬛⬛⬛⬛⬛⬛⬛⬛⬛⬛⬛⬛⬛⬛⬛⬛⬛⬛⬛⬛⬛⬛❖

Scope. The purpose of this chapter is to discuss the work of the investment banking houses which originate and distribute the new securities which are offered to the public. The order of discussion is: (1) economic function, (2) type of organization, (3) private placements, (4) competitive bidding, (5) purchase negotiations, (6) underwriting contracts, (7) syndicate operations, (8) retail distribution, (9) advisory function, (10) protective function, and (11) operating departments. The preparation of registration statements and prospectuses on issues is discussed in a subsequent chapter (Chapter 10—"Protection in Purchasing").

Function of investment banking. The chief function of investment banking is the distribution of new issues of securities. The position of the investment banker in the commercial world is similar to that of the merchant who buys goods on a wholesale basis and resells them at retail. Just as some of the larger mercantile houses conduct a wholesale business with smaller firms, so the larger investment banking firms act as wholesalers in supplying securities to smaller dealers. The investment banker who deals in securities performs the economic function of the merchant who deals in commodities. In both instances, middlemen are needed in order to make the articles readily available to buyers. Both have an equal economic justification. Criticism is warranted in either case only if the service is inefficient or if the compensation is unreasonable.

In acting as merchants who are engaged in the business of distributing securities, investment bankers differ from commercial bankers who act primarily as the custodians of funds which have been deposited with them. The commercial banks, in loaning these funds, are, in effect, using capital which belongs to other people and which they must be prepared to return at short notice. Commercial bankers, therefore, are not in a position to supply long-term funds. Investment bankers, who are not allowed to engage in deposit banking, must supply their own funds for use in purchasing securities. Like merchants, they have placed their capital in inventories which must be resold before additional securities may be purchased.[1] They buy for resale, not for investment, the obligations of governments and corporations which are customarily sold to investors and institutions other than commercial banks.[2]

Investment dealers should not be confused with brokers, even though some houses act in both capacities. Dealers buy and sell for their own account and profit through price differences; brokers merely execute orders for which they are paid commissions. Investment dealers, as a matter of convenience for customers, will accept orders for the purchase and sale of securities in which they have no interest, and usually charge a commission for the service. Brokerage houses often maintain investment departments which deal in securities without any commission charge to customers. Investment dealers are principally engaged in distributing new issues, whereas brokerage houses are mostly concerned with transactions in older

---

[1] "The essential interest of the private banking business, the issuing business, is that the banker buys securities of such nature that he feels reasonably confident that he can sell them to the public, and having sold them, he is then free to go on with other business. If he locks himself up by retaining his own goods, he will very soon be so locked up that his usefulness as a banker will have ceased."—From testimony of the late Otto H. Kahn, at Congressional Investigation of Foreign Loans, December 21, 1931.

[2] During recent years, commercial banks have been making "term loans" for periods as long as five years in contrast to the traditional limit of one year for bank loans. This innovation has enlarged the scope of commercial banking and reduced the field of investment banking.

issues that have passed through the distribution stage. The general statement that investment houses deal in bonds and brokerage houses deal in stocks remains true, but to a more limited extent than a decade ago.

Organization of investment firms. Investment banking houses may be classified as national or local, depending upon their field of activity; as partnerships or corporations, depending upon the form of organization; as underwriters or distributors, depending upon the volume of business handled. Although many of the larger investment houses (such as Halsey Stuart and First Boston) do a nation-wide business with offices in the principal cities, some of the very largest are local, with no out-of-town offices (such as Morgan Stanley and Kuhn Loeb). Investment firms which have memberships on the New York Stock Exchange are required to operate as partnerships, but firms which do not have such affiliation are usually corporations, except in the smaller cases. Firms which are able to distribute relatively large portions of new issues usually join in the original underwriting in order to secure the larger profit margin thus obtainable; other firms are known as distributors, although the underwriting firms act also as distributors. Commercial banks participate in the distribution of corporate securities only to the extent of placing orders received from customers with investment firms as they are not allowed to act as principals in underwriting, or as distributing groups, or as dealers in corporate securities. They may, however, act as dealers in government issues.

The internal organization of an investment banking house depends chiefly upon the size of the firm. The larger houses, which handle a wide variety of issues, have departmental organizations comparable to a mercantile firm. The smaller houses necessarily combine many activities into a few operating departments. From a functional viewpoint, the work of an investment banking house, as distinguished from a securities brokerage firm, may be divided into five fields. The buying function is that of purchasing, through underwriting or otherwise, securities to be offered for resale. The selling function is that of distributing, either at wholesale through other dealers or at retail to the public, the securities previously purchased. The advisory function is that of giving professional advice to issuers and buyers of securities. The protective function is that of protecting the interests of holders of securities through the provision of secondary markets and in the reorganization of companies in trouble. The operating function is that of providing the necessary facilities for the conduct of the business.

Distribution methods. New securities are placed in the hands of investors either through direct sales or through investment banking houses. Direct selling may take the form of "private placements," whereby a corporation sells bonds in large blocks directly to large investing institutions such as life insurance companies. Direct selling is also employed by the Federal Government in the issue of new obligations to the general public. Securities are distributed through investment banking houses either through competitive bidding on the part of the bankers or through privately negotiated sales. The securities of public borrowers such as state and municipal governments are usually acquired through competitive bidding. Corporate issues, however, are customarily bought as the result of private negotiations.

The practice of many large companies in securing distribution of new issues through private placement with investing institutions has become a matter of serious concern to investment bankers. Nearly 45 per cent of the new corporate securities issued in the United States in 1939 were placed in this way in comparison with less than 10 per cent in 1936. The popularity of private placements is due partly to the requirements of the Securities Act of 1933 with respect to issues publicly offered. The time, labor, and expense involved in the registration of new issues for public sale are saved in private placements. A further economy is gained in the elimination of the underwriting profit of the investment bankers. A technical disadvantage is found in the ineligibility of such securities for resale to the public at a later date unless the proper registration procedure is then completed. The major disadvantage, however, is the fact that the investing public is not only prevented from participating in the better quality of new issues which are thus preëmpted by relatively few large institutions but also is deprived, through refunding operations, of bonds called for redemption with the proceeds of new issues. Another disadvantage, in the future more than in the present time, is the ultimate harmful effect upon investment banking if the rising trend of private placements is not checked.

The traditional custom of investment bankers in buying new corporate securities through private negotiations rather than through competitive bidding has been the subject of regulatory criticism during recent years. The claim is made that such purchases tend to create monopolistic groups in the field, who obtain unreasonable profits through dealing from a favored position (rather than at "arm's length") and prevent the corporations from realizing the most favorable prices for their issues. Investment bankers, while admitting that competitive awards have operated satisfactorily in the field of municipal finance, claim that competitive bidding in the corporate field would deprive corporations of the benefit of a "continuing relationship" whereby the corporation receives the benefit of expert financial advice at all times from bankers familiar with the problems of the industry. The offering prices of new issues are more likely to be reasonable to investors in contrast to the maximum prices which would be necessitated by high competing bids. The future prices of all securities of the company are likely to be more favorable because of the friendly interest of the established underwriters. Perhaps the best argument in favor of the traditional method of private negotiations is the fact that it seems to give general satisfaction to all parties directly interested—the corporations, the investing public, and the majority of investment bankers. It is noteworthy that all public sales of new securities by subsidiaries of registered holding companies must now be sold through competitive bidding.

The effect of compulsory competitive bidding for new corporate issues may eventually prove generally beneficial, but it will necessitate many changes in investment banking.

The more important effects as foreseen by an outstanding investment banker are here listed:

(1)   The investment banker's sense of responsibility will be minimized, and his professional relations with his client will be destroyed.

(2)   There will be a strong tendency toward overpricing of securities and high-pressure salesmanship.

(3)   The practice will encourage the issuance of securities of poorer quality.

(4)   Coöperation with corporations in connection with registration data will be largely eliminated.

(5)   The practice will tend to eliminate the small dealers from participation in the distribution of securities.[3]

The buying function.   The buying department of a large investment banking firm is ordinarily divided into three groups—corporate, municipal, and foreign.   The smaller underwriting firms have either corporate or municipal buyers. The firms which act as distributors rather than underwriters do not have buying departments, inasmuch as the new securities offered for sale by these firms are obtained from underwriting firms through sales agreements.

Although numerous foreign securities were underwritten by American houses in the decade from 1920 to 1930, the flotation of such issues has virtually stopped, with the sole exception of Canadian offerings.   The cessation of foreign issues during recent years was due in part to political and economic troubles abroad, in part to international hostilities, and in part to the effect of the Johnson Act of 1934, which prohibited loans to nations in default on World War debts to the American Government.   The practice of American investment houses in the purchase of foreign securities has been to send buying representatives to conduct negotiations in the countries of issue rather than to deal with an authorized negotiator in this country.   Competition between rival investment firms for the privilege of making the loans was not conducive

---

[3] Adapted from memorandum submitted by Harold Stanley of Morgan, Stanley and Company, to Temporary National Economic Committee, dated November 29, 1939.

to the most conservative lending practices or to the best interests of American investors who purchased the bonds.

Municipal securities are purchased through competitive bidding. When the proposed issue is larger than single firms can handle, bids are placed for a designated part of the issue. Because the aggregate price obtainable from the best combination of partial bids is frequently less than the price offered by bidders for the entire issue on an "all-or-none" basis, buying firms usually offer group bids for the entire issue. The work of the buying department in making a bid for a new issue of municipal bonds is chiefly mathematical. After estimating carefully the price which could be received from the sale of the bonds to the public with due consideration to interest rate and maturity date, a profit differential is subtracted, and a bid price is determined. If it is assumed that the bonds could be sold on a 2.80 per cent yield basis which would indicate a sales price of 104 ($1,040 per bond) for 3 per cent bonds at a 30-year maturity, a profit margin of one point ($10 per bond) might be subtracted, thus leaving an indicated bid price of 103 ($1,030 per bond). In the strong municipal bond market, the profit margin might be cut to ¾ of 1 per cent ($7.50 per bond), indicating a bid price of 103.25 ($1,032.50 per bond). As other bidders have probably calculated along the same lines, the actual bids placed are seldom in simple fractions but in involved decimals such as 101.5134, which is slightly higher than 101.50 or 101.51 or even 101.513.

Corporate securities are purchased, customarily, through private negotiations between the investment house and the corporation. The usual procedure of an investment banking firm in making an original purchase of a security issue may be divided into three major steps. The first is the preliminary, or office, analysis. The second is the plant, or physical, examination. The third is the negotiation conference, at which the final decision is reached.

The office analysis is conducted at the office of the investment banker and covers the financial statements and the general history of the company. Most proposals do not get beyond this stage. The prime requirement is that the company show a satisfactory earning record over a period of at least several years. It may be assumed, however, that the preliminary analysis is favorable and that the negotiations reach the second stage.

The plant examination is conducted at the place of 'the corporation. Representatives in the service of the investment house conduct a searching inquiry into the internal affairs of the company. Appraisers value the buildings, equipment, and inventories. Auditors verify the financial records and inspect the accounting methods, with particular regard to such important practices as depreciation policy. Industrial engineers observe production methods. Marketing specialists analyze the distribution of the product and determine the position of the company in its field. Legal counsels pass upon franchises, leases, and contracts. Reports on all of these phases are received by the house, and, if favorable, the negotiation conference is arranged.

At the negotiation conference, a final decision is reached. Agreement upon the nature of the security (whether stock or bond), the exact kind, the interest rate, the maturity date, and the purchase price completes negotiations. At all stages, the house must be most vigilant. The purchase is made for resale, not for investment. The security must be good in every respect, and the purchase price must be based upon the expected sale price. The margin is close, seldom exceeding three points, which is equivalent to three dollars on each hundred dollars of face value. The risk of loss is large, as the entire issue must be marketed and selling expenses must be paid. If the purchasing function is properly performed, however, the house now owns an issue that should be readily marketed. [4]

The underwriting of securities. When negotiations between the originating banking firm and the corporation have been completed, an underwriting contract is drawn up for signature by the corporation officials as one party and by

---

[4] The profit margin is usually about one point (1 per cent) on municipal bonds, two to three points on railroad and utility issues, and three to five points on industrial and foreign issues.

representatives of investment houses as the other party. While the negotiations between the originating house and the corporation were approaching completion, a group of investment houses were invited to share in the purchase as joint underwriters. The determination of the number of firms to be invited to participate, the choice of the particular firms, and the size of the individual participations are made by the originating bankers who become known as the "syndicate managers," the term *syndicate* being traditionally applied to underwriting and distributing groups. The underwriting contract states precisely the respective participations, the underwriting price, and the time for payment and delivery of the securities.

As a consequence of the provisions of the Securities Act of 1933, underwriting contracts now are materially different from those in vogue previous to that time. Under the former practice, only the originating firm signed the purchase contract under a binding agreement which became irrevocable except under extreme contingencies. Under the present practice, the underwriting contract is signed by all participating firms, each responsible only for its designated share, each having the option of withdrawing under numerous "escape" clauses, and each being guaranteed indemnity by the corporation for loss claims arising out of violations of the Securities Act in omissions or misrepresentations on the part of the corporation. The present practice eliminates the buying groups which were formerly created by the originating bankers.

An illustration of the organization of an underwriting operation was afforded in the bond issue of the Ohio Power Company in 1938, which took the form of $55,000,000 in $3\frac{1}{4}\%$ mortgage bonds, due in 1968. The underwriting group comprised 83 investment houses who purchased the bonds at two points ($20) less than the price at which they were resold to the public. A much larger number of houses were members of a selling group which obtained their bonds from members of the underwriting group at $\frac{7}{8}$ of a point ($8.75) less than the price set for public resale. Banks and smaller dealers who executed orders to purchase the bonds through members of the underwriting or selling groups obtained bonds at ⅛ of one point ($1.25) less than the price set for public resale.

Before new corporate securities may be offered to the public, registration statements must be filed with the Securities and Exchange Commission at Washington, and prospectuses must be printed for the use of prospective buyers. As considerable time is required to prepare the detailed information essential for registration, much of this work has already been completed when the underwriting contract is signed. In view of the fact that market conditions may change during the "waiting period" between the date when the registration material is filed and the date when it becomes effective, it is customary to leave the exact price of the issue and the complete list of underwriters open until the time when the statement becomes effective and when the bonds may be offered for sale to the public.

On the date set for the completion of the terms of the underwriting contract, the so-called "delivery date," each underwriter delivers to the managing house a certified bank check made out to the order of the corporation. These checks are delivered to the corporation at a designated bank in exchange for the bonds which are usually in the form of temporary certificates, called *interim receipts,* exchangeable later for definitive bonds. Underwriting firms "take down" only that part of their subscription which they plan to sell directly and leave the remainder for distribution to members of the selling group, from whom they will receive reimbursement through the underwriting managers.

The selling function. Under sales agreements either expressed in contracts or implied in understandings, all firms participating in the distribution of new securities agree not to offer new securities either before a specified time or under a minimum price.[5] The securities may then be purchased

---

[5] The time is set exactly, as, for example, November 15, 1940, at 9 A.M. Eastern Standard Time. The expression *beating the gun* applies to solicitation before the stated time.

directly through any members of the underwriting or selling groups or indirectly through hundreds of small dealers and banks throughout the country. In either event, all orders are subject to confirmation unless accepted on a "firm" basis. In many cases, the demand for popular issues is so great as to exceed the available supply, thereby necessitating a plan of allotment under which many orders have to be refused. In such cases, the entire issue may be sold within a few hours, thereby necessitating the use of telephones and telegrams instead of personal calls by salesmen.

Not all offerings are quickly absorbed, however. Due to unforeseen market conditions, new issues of even high-grade securities become difficult to sell or "sticky" in financial parlance. A large issue of New York City bonds, which was bought by an investment group early in 1937 at a price of around 102, found very few buyers at 103 and eventually had to be sold under 100 to close out the purchase. Shortly thereafter, a large issue of bonds of a well-known steel company was underwritten at 98 and had to be sold as low as 80 before the holdings were entirely sold. A similar loss of even greater magnitude was incurred in the underwriting of an issue of more than $40,000,000 in the preferred stock of a large petroleum company during the same year. In the latter case, the underwriting agreement had been kept in effect nearly a year in a vain attempt to realize the original price.

It is the invariable practice of underwriting groups to "support the market" while offering new securities. In order to avoid the harmful effect of reported transactions at prices lower than that set in the public offering, the underwriting manager places buying orders in the market for the purchase of limited quantities of the bonds at the public offering price. Similar buying orders are sometimes placed for the purchase of other securities of the same company if these issues seem more attractively priced than the new issue. As a consequence, the market price of a new issue is not allowed to fall below the established price during the period of distribution. It is not uncommon, when new issues are selling slowly, for price concessions to be made to investors who agree not to offer the securities for resale until the termination of the selling group contract. Even though such market stabilization is a form of price manipulation in the official opinion of the Federal regulatory commission, it has been approved as an essential part of security distribution.

The sales department of an investment firm keeps in contact with investors and investing institutions through telephone conversations and personal interviews. The solicitation of buying orders over the telephone is justifiable only when time is of the essence (as when new issues are sold out quickly) and when the salesman is personally acquainted with the buyer. The practice of telephone canvassing by strangers is generally regarded as inimical to the best interests of the investor. The use of "high-pressure" selling methods is also regarded as unethical, although there is frank difference of opinion as to the point at which this stage is reached in solicitation. Unsolicited calls at the homes of prospective buyers are also regarded as objectionable under the assumption that such calls are properly made only in places of business. Very little selling of securities is done by correspondence, chiefly because of the importance of time as affecting values and prices, as well as to the handling of negotiable instruments which might come into the hands of third parties. With dealers in securities located in every city of moderate size in the country able to make prices as favorable as those in metropolitan centers, there is little occasion or incentive to buy through correspondence.

Salesmen employed by investment dealers are almost invariably compensated on a commission basis. Even when regular salaries are paid, the rate is based upon their earning power in terms of profit to the firm. The natural consequence is that salesmen seek a maximum volume of business, frequently to the injury of their customers. Unlike salesmen who sell consumable goods for which there is a constant resale market, security salesmen sell durable goods which last for decades. The buying power of customers is therefore limited to relatively few annual purchases unless they can be persuaded to make frequent exchanges from old to new issues. Some salesmen attempt, in this fashion, to sell a customer $30,000 to $40,000 in new securities each year for each $10,000 the investor possesses. The ultimate effect is more likely to harm than to help the average quality of the securities owned.

The American custom of security *selling* by direct solicitation is in interesting and unfavorable contrast with the English custom of investment *buying*. The American practice places the initiative upon the salesman, who seeks out the investor; the English practice puts the initiative upon the investor, who seeks out the investment dealer. American investors are accustomed to dealing directly with soliciting salesmen; British investors, bearing proper letters of introduction, must call at the offices of the investment firm for personal consultation. While the English method would probably work as poorly in America as the American plan would in England, it is certainly true that some reform must be accomplished in security distribution methods in the United States if manifest evils are to be eradicated. Blind confidence on the part of investors, high-pressure efforts on the part of salesmen, and imprudent recommendations on the part of investment houses have caused serious financial losses which might readily have been avoided under a system of distribution based upon buying rather than upon selling.

In fairness to the investment house, investors should realize that all securities offered by that house are not of uniform quality and are therefore not equally suitable for all buyers. As explained throughout this book, securities range in quality from very good to very poor. While reputable investment houses naturally avoid poor securities, yet they do not confine themselves to those of the highest grade. The more conservative houses instruct their salesmen not to offer securities indiscriminately but to recommend issues suitable to the position of the investor. Investors, in turn, should not assume that all securities offered by a house in which they have confidence are desirable commitments for them. The proper selection of investment securities is among the most important problems of the investor. It is more than a duty; it is a responsibility that can be evaded only with grave danger to the safety of the funds involved. Investors should seek advice but should make their own decisions.

The advisory function. Investment houses act in an advisory capacity with relationship to issuers of securities as well as to buyers of securities. A corporation that desires to raise capital through the sale of securities will consult with the investment house which usually handles its issues before determining the nature of the offering. The investment house is constantly in touch with market conditions and is in a position to recommend the type of security that will prove most popular under existing conditions. Moreover, provision must be made for future needs and market conditions, as well as for those of the present. The manner in which this advisory function operates has been explained by a prominent investment banker: [6]

When a company desirous of raising capital funds first goes to an investment banking firm, the company frequently has not even decided what type of security it wishes to offer—whether, for example, it should be a mortgage bond, a convertible debenture, a collateral trust note, or a preferred or common stock. The issuer is seeking advice on that primary question and also on the related questions of the terms (such as probable price, maturity, and interest rate), the amount of money to be raised, and the time best suited for the offering. Such problems must be considered not only with the existing financial structure of the issuer in mind, but with an eye to the future. They are often studied jointly by the banker and the issuer for months. Some are frequently decided promptly; others (such as the public offering price, interest rate, conversion provisions, and redemption terms) cannot be finally fixed until a day or two before the issue is placed on the market. If the securities are to be issued under a trust indenture, weeks may be spent in considering the covenants and other provisions that it should contain for the proper protection of both the issuer and the investor.

Investment houses endeavor to act in an advisory capacity to investors in various ways. They are always willing to discuss the suitability of a particular security to the needs of the inquiring investor, either in personal consultation or by

---

[6] From memorandum submitted by Harold Stanley, of Morgan, Stanley and Company, to Temporary National Economic Committee, dated Nov. 29, 1939.

correspondence. Many houses invite their customers to submit investment lists for periodical examination, on the basis of which recommendations are made for changes believed to be beneficial. Most houses will cheerfully prepare an analysis of any security in which a customer may be interested, even though the firm may have no interest in the issue. Charges are seldom made for these services beyond the profit obtained on securities bought through the house.

The protective function. As explained more fully in another chapter, investment houses usually act to protect the interests of customers in securities issued by the house which later meet default. They form protective committees which endeavor to arrange the most equitable settlement on behalf of the security holders. In the words of an outstanding investment banker:[7]

> The issuing house considers it its responsibility to do everything in its power to reconstitute and re-establish the solvency and good credit of the property; to protect the bondholders against any undue exactions that might be demanded of them; to work out the best possible plan of reorganization, and to give advice in all fairness to the bondholders concerned; to give its efforts, its experience, its ability fairly and properly to deal with the situation after the default has been created.

As a further method of protecting the interests of its customers, investment houses usually maintain trading departments. These departments provide what is called a "secondary market" for securities originally sold by the firm which customers desire to dispose of. In all cases where securities are received on an exchange basis, the credit allowed to the customer depends upon the price the house can obtain through its trading department, which keeps in touch with the various security markets. The trading department usually "makes a market" in securities previously issued by the house, by maintaining bid and asked prices in the issues. Orders for the purchase and sale of securities not issued by the house are handled through this department. Requests for price quotations from customers are likewise answered

---

[7] From testimony of the late Otto H. Kahn, of Kuhn, Loeb & Co., in the Congressional Investigation of Foreign Loans, December 21, 1931.

by this division. The work of the trading department is especially valuable in connection with unlisted securities, because of the lack of reliable quotations in this important group. Unlike the trading department of a brokerage house, which is operated for the prime purpose of direct profit, the trading department of an investment house is maintained principally to assist the sales department in the distribution of new issues.

The service function. Investment houses perform many minor services of considerable benefit to customers who take advantage of them. They protect securities in their vaults in special safekeeping envelopes. They collect interest and dividend payments when so requested. They notify investors of called bonds and of opportunities to profit from sinking fund offers or conversion options. They keep files of customer security holdings which are constantly revised. They maintain statistical departments that contain official sources of information available to customers of the house. They advise the customers on income and estate tax problems in connection with security holdings. It is not customary to make any charges for these services, which are performed as part of the operating facilities of the house.

The operating function. The operating departments of an investment banking firm embrace many activities peculiar to the business. Besides the usual bookkeeping, stenographic, filing, and cashier divisions, there are securities divisions which take care of the receipt of securities bought and the delivery of securities sold. The larger firms have private wire systems which interconnect their various offices. Some firms maintain special libraries devoted chiefly to references on economic and financial topics. Correspondence departments handle inquiries from customers regarding the many details involved in the ownership of securities. Most of this work is of a routine nature and seldom brings the workers in contact with the customers of the firm. The overhead expense is considerable, however, and must be paid out of the narrow margin of gross profit on which investment firms operate.

7

SOURCES OF INFORMATION

Scope. The purpose of this chapter is to discuss the various sources of information which are available to investors who desire to keep informed currently on their commitments. The order of discussion is: (1) financial periodicals, (2) business periodicals, (3) banking periodicals, (4) industrial periodicals, (5) general periodicals, (6) information on specific classes of securities, (7) the statistical services, (8) the advisory services, and (9) investment counselors. The suggestion is made that every investor should subscribe to, or have regular access to, at least one periodical devoted to financial discussions.

The tools of investment. Intelligent investment is largely a matter of adequate knowledge. Although all securities are wagers upon future developments which can be foreseen only imperfectly, the greater knowledge the investor has of the degree of risk involved in the purchase of certain securities, the more satisfactory his subsequent experience should be. For many years, the purchase of securities in this country was based primarily on good faith because adequate information was not available to individual investors. Owing in part to the publicity requirements of the new Federal Securities laws and in part to a growing appreciation of the value of public goodwill, the corporate issuers of securities are now making available an almost complete disclosure of their financial condition. The investor who purchases securities without a careful study of the pertinent advantages and disadvantages has only his own carelessness to blame for subsequent misfortune.

It has been said that "no lawyer knows the law but a good lawyer knows where it can be found." In similar fashion it might be stated that no investment expert can possibly keep informed on all new developments affecting the values of securities, but that a good analyst knows where to obtain information which will enable him to make an intelligent appraisal of any security on relatively short notice. This information is available from many different sources, depending upon the particular type of investment under consideration.

It is one of the truisms of the investment business that news quickly becomes obsolete. It is but natural that the minds of investors should be always trying to read the future in the light of the present. Accordingly, the records of the past are given an importance far below that of the developments of the present. The insatiable demand of the investing public for news has created a situation wherein information, to be useful, must not be more than a few months old.

This information, which is constantly being supplied by the corporations of America for the benefit of investors, is available on an instantaneous basis during business hours in the electric news services, on a morning and evening basis in the daily newspapers, and on a weekly and monthly basis in various financial periodicals. The information appears in more permanent form in the publications of the statistical services, which, however, are not generally available to the public.

In addition to the information supplied by individual companies with respect to their particular activities, certain publications available to investors are devoted to topics of more general financial nature such as conditions in industry, banking, and commerce.

Financial periodicals. Practically all financial periodicals cover the fields of banking and commodities as well as securities. Those which are chiefly devoted to investments are:

(1) *The Wall Street Journal,* a daily newspaper published in connection with the Dow-Jones news service, is devoted almost entirely to information concerning securities.

(2) *The Journal of Commerce* (Chicago), a daily newspaper, is devoted largely to securities with particular regard for local issues.

(3) *Barron's,* a weekly periodical published by the Dow-Jones Co., is devoted entirely to the securities market.

(4) *The Bond Buyer,* a weekly periodical, is devoted entirely to municipal securities.

(5) *The Commercial and Financial Chronicle,* a weekly periodical devoted to an almost exhaustive presentation of the weekly development in the financial, banking, industrial, and commodities fields, is the outstanding source of current reference throughout the investment world. In addition to its regular edition which is almost encyclopedic in scope, supplements are issued which cover current price quotations (monthly), corporate earnings (monthly), state and municipal statements (semiannually), railway and industrial reports (semiannually), and public utility reports (semiannually).

(6) *The Exchange,* a monthly magazine published by the New York Stock Exchange, gives information of general interest regarding securities listed therein.

Business periodicals. Certain periodicals which are published for general business reference frequently give valuable investment information. Those which deserve special commendation are as follows:

(1) *The Journal of Commerce* (New York), a daily newspaper, has an excellent financial section in addition to a broad coverage of the mercantile markets.

(2) *Business Week,* a weekly magazine, covers the general business field and has an interesting financial section.

(3) *United States News,* a weekly magazine, covers political developments at Washington as interpreted from the financial viewpoint.

(4) *The Economist,* a weekly periodical published in England, gives an excellent survey of international economic developments.

(5) *Nation's Business,* a monthly magazine, contains articles by authoritative writers on general business subjects.

(6) *Fortune,* a monthly magazine, presents a picture of American business enterprise in greater detail than is elsewhere available.

Banking periodicals. Periodicals that are published primarily for readers interested in banking since they contain informative investment information would include the following:

(1) *Banking,* a monthly magazine published under the sponsorship of the American Bankers Association, usually contains several articles on investments.

(2) *Trusts and Estates,* a monthly magazine, covers primarily the administration of trust funds.

(3) *The Federal Reserve Bulletin,* a monthly periodical, is the official publication of the Federal Reserve System and contains statistical data of great value to investors.

(4) The monthly bulletins issued by individual banks, such as the Federal Reserve Bank and the National City Bank in New York and the Cleveland Trust Company, provide informative comment on current conditions in the financial and investment markets.

Industrial periodicals. Magazines devoted to special industries, better known as "trade journals," are excellent sources of information in their particular fields. Among many might be mentioned the following: *Coal Age, Electrical World, Factory, Food Industries, The Iron Age, Petroleum Age, Public Utilities Fortnightly, Railway Age,* and *Textile World.*

The *Industrial Bulletin* published by Arthur D. Little, Inc.

(Cambridge, Mass.), is especially recommended to investors who are interested in the newer developments in the field of industrial research.

General periodicals. The development of the new type of weekly news magazine with excellent financial departments, as illustrated in *Time* and *Newsweek,* is of especial interest to investors. The comment which appears in these publications affords a much better perspective than that obtainable in the daily papers.

Information on government securities. The primary sources of information on United States Government securities are the official reports of the Treasury Department issued on the following basis:

(1) Circular giving specific information on each issue prepared at the time of issue.

(2) Daily report of Treasury operations showing revenue and disbursements for year to date and the amount of the Federal debt.

(3) Monthly statement showing composition of Federal debt and the amount of each class of debt outstanding.

(4) Annual report of the Secretary of the Treasury giving a comprehensive picture of Federal fiscal operations during the year.

(5) Annual report of the Farm Credit Administration giving information on the bonds of the Federal Land Banks and Joint Stock Land Banks.

(6) Annual report of the Federal Home Loan Bank Boards giving information on Federal Home Loan Banks and Federal Savings and Loan Associations.

(7) Annual report of the Federal Housing Administration giving information on insured mortgages.

The secondary sources of information on United States Government securities (in addition to the statistical services later mentioned) include:

(1) *Securities of the United States Government and Its Instrumentalities,* published annually by The First Boston Corporation.

(2) *United States Government Securities,* published annually by C. J. Devine and Co. (New York).

Information on state securities. The primary sources of information on securities issued by state governments are the annual reports prepared by the financial officers of the respective states. These reports vary in size from a brief financial statement to a comprehensive booklet such as that which has been issued during recent years by the Comptroller of New York State.

The secondary sources of information on state securities (except the statistical services) include:

(1) *Financial Statistics of States,* prepared at irregular intervals by the Federal Department of Commerce. The most recent edition covers the year 1937.

(2) *Resources and Debts of the Forty-eight States,* prepared at irregular intervals by Dun and Bradstreet.

(3) *State and Municipal Compendium,* issued semiannually (in June and December) by *The Commercial and Financial Chronicle.*

Information on municipal securities. The primary sources of information on securities issued by municipal governments are the annual reports of the respective financial officers.

The secondary sources of information on municipal securities (except the statistical services) include:

(1) *Financial Statistics of Cities,* prepared at irregular intervals by the Federal Department of Commerce.

(2) *State and Municipal Compendium,* issued semiannually (in June and December) by *The Commercial and Financial Chronicle.*

(3) Special reports on selected cities prepared by the Municipal Service Department of Dun and Bradstreet.

(4) Annual reports of state tax commissions, especially those of New York State, which give a detailed picture of the financial condition of each town, city, and county in the state.

Information on railroad securities. The primary sources of information on railroad securities are:

(1)   Annual reports to stockholders, which reports give complete summaries of the operating and financial results of each year.

(2)   Monthly reports of earnings to the Interstate Commerce Commission, which reports usually appear in the newspapers in summary form.

(3)   Annual reports of the Interstate Commerce Commission which has regulatory power over interstate traffic.

The secondary sources of information on railroad securities (except the statistical services) include:

(1)   *Earning Power of Railroads,* a statistical study of railroad earnings prepared annually by J. H. Oliphant and Co.

(2)   *A Review of Railway Operations,* a general survey of railway operations prepared annually by the Association of American Railroads.

(3)   *A Yearbook of Railroad Information,* a statistical and graphic study of railroad operations prepared annually by the Western Railways' Committee on Public Relations.

(4)   *Equipment Trust Securities,* a statistical study prepared annually by Freeman and Company.

(5)   *The Railway and Industrial Compendium,* a statistical analysis of corporate earnings, published by *The Commercial and Financial Chronicle,* the railway sections being issued semiannually in May and November.

Information on public utility securities. The primary sources of information on public utility securities are:

(1)   Annual reports to stockholders which summarize the results of each year.

(2)   Quarterly reports to stockholders which show the earnings for each quarter of the year.

(3)   Monthly reports of earnings which are prepared by some of the larger companies but which do not appear in the general newspapers.

(4)   Registration statements which are filed with the S. E. C. when new securities are sold to the public.

(5)   Prospectuses which are compiled from the registration statements and are available to prospective as well as actual buyers of new issues.

(6)   Financial statements filed with the S. E. C. annually under the provisions of the Securities Exchange Act, which frequently give more information than do the annual reports to stockholders.

(7)   Annual reports to the Securities and Exchange Commission with particular regard to the enforcement of the provisions of the Public Utility Act of 1935.

(8)   Annual reports of the Federal Power Commission with particular regard to the supervision of water-power companies.

(9)   Annual reports filed with the public service commissions of the respective states by all operating companies.

(10)   Annual reports of the respective state public service commissions.

The secondary sources of information on public utility securities (except the statistical services) would include:

(1)   *The Public Utility Compendium*, a corporate manual issued semiannually (in April and October) by *The Commercial and Financial Chronicle*.

(2)   Monthly report on electrical power production, compiled by the Federal Power Commission.

(3)   Annual report on the outputs and capacities of the principal electric power companies, prepared by the *Electrical World*.

(4)   Monthly report on the sale of manufactured and natural gas, prepared by the American Gas Association.

(5)   *Bell Telephone Securities*, an annual publication prepared by the American Telephone and Telegraph Co. covering all securities issued by the companies in the Bell group.

(6)   Weekly and monthly reports on the outputs of the larger electrical power systems compiled by the Edison Electric Institute.

Information on industrial securities. The primary sources of information on industrial securities are:

(1) Annual reports to stockholders.

(2) Quarterly reports to stockholders (nearly three quarters of all companies whose securities are listed on the New York Stock Exchange now publish earnings quarterly).

(3) Registration statements filed with the S. E. C. when new issues are sold.

(4) Prospectuses issued when new securities are sold.

(5) Financial statements filed with the S. E. C. annually under the provisions of the Securities Exchange Act.

The secondary sources of information on industrial securities (except the statistical services) would include:

(1) *The Railway and Industrial Compendium*, published by *The Commercial and Financial Chronicle*, the industrial sections being issued semiannually in June and December.

(2) *Survey of American Listed Corporations*, a statistical analysis of the financial reports filed with the S. E. C. under the provisions of the Securities Exchange Act.

(3) Articles in *Fortune* magazine on specific companies and industries.

Information on securities of financial institutions. The primary sources of information on securities of financial institutions are:

(1) Annual reports to stockholders.

(2) Quarterly reports of banks, which are called "statements of condition."

(3) Quarterly reports of investment trust companies showing detailed holdings and indicating purchases and sales during the period.

(4) Registration statements filed with the S. E. C. at the time of new issues of securities.

(5) Prospectuses prepared from registration statements, available to the general public.

The secondary sources of information on securities of financial institutions (except the statistical services) would include:

(1)   Comparative analyses of the bank statements prepared by local investment dealers on the banks in their areas, which analyses are reprinted in the local papers in many instances.

(2)   Comparative analyses of the annual statements of leading insurance companies prepared by investment dealers for private distribution but occasionally reprinted in financial periodicals.

(3)   Comparative analyses of the quarterly statements of investment trust companies, which analyses appear in *Barron's* weekly magazine.

(4)   Annual reports of the Federal Deposit Insurance Corporation showing in great detail the condition of the commercial banks of the United States, with respect to loans, investments, deposits, and capital position.

Information on real estate securities.   Information on real estate securities is rarely available to investors from primary sources.   Only in the cases of exceptionally large properties are annual reports prepared for general distribution.   Investors generally obtain the necessary information from the various manuals prepared by the statistical services, as later described.

Information on foreign securities.   As in the case of real estate securities, information on foreign securities is seldom available to investors from original sources.   Investors obtain whatever information is available from the statistical manuals or from the Institute of International Finance or the Foreign Bondholders Protective Council, both of which are private organizations designed to help investors in foreign securities.

The statistical services.   Three large statistical organizations are engaged primarily in the publication of statistical data for the guidance of investors.   It is the practice of these organizations to compile financial data on all companies in which there is definite investment interest. The information is supplied in yearly manuals (with loose-leaf weekly supplements) or on cards which are filed in convenient cabinets and frequently revised. The information is largely statistical and usually covers periods of from five to ten years previous, being compiled either from the annual reports to stockholders or from reports to the S. E. C.

In addition to the general information provided by the services, an attempt is made to rank securities according to quality through the so-called "ratings" which are given to the more important issues. These ratings, which vary from legends such as "AAA" or "A1+" for the highest group and "AA" and "A1" for the second highest, enjoy wide popularity with investors who have found them to be useful guides in the selection of suitable issues. Few investors, however, and certainly no one professing an ability to judge quality in securities, would be guided solely by such ratings in the purchase of securities. The mere fact that previous ratings are constantly being changed by the services indicates that the value of any rating is limited to the time when it is determined and is subject to change without notice.

The services which are included in this group are:

Standard & Poor's Services.
Moody's Investors Service.
Fitch Services.

The advisory services. Certain organizations make a business of selling advisory service to investors as distinguished from supplying statistical information. It is the function of these firms (the best known of which is the Babson Statistical Organization) to analyze general business conditions as well as specific industries and individual companies in order to recommend those securities which appear to be most promising and, incidentally, to recommend the sale of those securities which appear to be least promising. These firms, as a general rule, do not manage or supervise the accounts of clients but make recommendations which subscribers are at liberty to accept or reject. In this important respect, they differ from investment counsel firms which are in the business of supervising the accounts of their clients.

A constructive step in the development of the advisory services has been the recent requirement that all such organizations must register with the S. E. C. and thereby become subject to Federal regulation.

Investment counselors. The growth of investment counsel firms has been a noteworthy development of recent years. These firms believe that the average investor is not qualified to select securities or to manage his investments without professional help. They claim that the fees which they charge for their advice are more than offset in savings gained by their clients, either through larger income or through fewer losses. The growth in this field was realistically described in a recent article in a prominent financial periodical in this fashion: [1]

Investment counsel as an independent profession is only of recent origin. The first firm was established in 1921. There were only 10 or 20 in 1923, and not a great many more by 1928. Estimates of the number today vary from 3,000 to 8,000. There are no legal requirements. Anyone can call himself an investment counselor and dispense advice on investments. As a consequence, the ranks have been swollen by ex-bankers and brokers, former customers men, unemployed statisticians, ex-bond salesman, young college graduates with little or no experience—in fact by many whose chief qualifications are a few good contacts, the money to hire an office and a bent for telling other people what to do with their money. There has been no supervision: Like Topsy—the profession just "growed."

The service which these firms render covers the entire field of security operations from the most conservative investments to the most radical speculations. Some firms base their advice upon a very careful analysis of the position of the client, whereas others merely try to foretell the fluctuations of the stock market. Some firms base their annual fees upon the number of securities owned by their clients,

[1] From article by L. C. Duncan in *Barron's, The National Financial Weekly,* issue of February 28, 1938.

whereas others charge a uniform percentage, usually one half of 1 per cent of the value of the entire fund under supervision. Very few of these firms handle the securities of their customers, giving their instructions either directly to the customers or to the brokers of the customers. Some of these firms are affiliated with investment dealers and brokers, whereas others operate independently. Some firms advertise their ability to foretell market trends to the intense discomfiture of other firms that believe such publicity does more harm than good to a business which has yet to demonstrate its right to be regarded as a profession.

In a field where training and experience receive no official recognition, a wide variety of practitioners is likely to be found. There are many conscientious investment counselors in the country who are doing a capable job in the field where exact measurements are unknown. They are the firms which place safety and income as the prime essentials of investment policy and which give no speculative advice. They advertise conservatively, if at all, and charge a uniform fee for their services. They are rarely associated in any way with an investment house and therefore are neither directly nor indirectly interested in the securities handled or in the brokerage commissions involved. They maintain offices properly equipped and capably staffed.

Unfortunately, the majority of the people in the business of investment counsel are not included in such a recommended group. Too many of the so-called investment counselors are selling speculative advice on how to play the stock market. Their clients quickly become "stock-minded" and lose the investment viewpoint. The unfavorable record which even skilled and experienced investors have had in stock purchasing, as referred to elsewhere in this volume, should be the strongest possible argument against the claims of such firms.

It is the general custom of the reputable investment counsel firms to charge a minimum fee of $500 to $1,000 annually for each account under supervision, if the account is valued at less than $100,000. Such a charge is prohibitive to the person who seeks advice for the investment of smaller funds.

A capable investment counsel service within the means of people of moderate wealth, who need it the most, has yet to be developed in this country.

Until such time as the business of investment counsel is restricted to individuals who have demonstrated their knowledge of security values through competent examination and who are not directly or indirectly engaged in the business of buying and selling securities, investment counselors can scarcely hope to gain professional recognition.[2]

---

[2] Under the provisions of Federal legislation enacted in 1940 (Investment Advisers Act), individuals or firms which are engaged in the business of investment counsel must register with the Securities and Exchange Commission. Investment advisers may not be compensated on a basis of a share of the profit gained by clients, nor may they, acting as principals, sell any securities to, or buy any securities from, their clients.

8

INTERPRETING FINANCIAL NEWS

Scope. The purpose of this chapter is to discuss in interpretative fashion the financial news which appears in the daily newspapers. The order of discussion is: (1) bond price quotations, (2) stock price quotations, (3) price-averages, (4) the Dow theory, (5) interest rates, (6) commodity prices, (7) business indexes, (8) corporation earnings reports, and (9) a glossary of financial terms with particular reference to investment usage. As economic interpretation is imperfect at best, complete reliance upon outside advice does not represent investment wisdom. It is the duty of every investor to form some opinion of his own as to how his funds should be invested.

Financial reporting. Every important American newspaper now includes a financial news section. In striking contrast to the practice of confining financial news to a single page, which was customary during the early decades of the present century, the newspapers now devote several pages of their daily issues to business news. Investors are thus afforded a chance to keep constantly informed on all developments which are of major significance to the position of their securities.

The information contained in the financial section of the papers is either statistical or general. The statistical news comprises price quotations on securities and commodities as reported on the various exchanges and markets as well as

financial statements as released by public and private institutions. The general news consists of comments on developments throughout the business world, with particular regard to the trend of prices in securities and commodities.

The news items which appear on the financial pages have
not been compiled by the paper as a rule but have been supplied in the form of formal statements and "news releases,"
prepared, in many instances, by the publicity departments of
the institutions concerned. As time is of the essence in news
reporting and as such information is usually received from reliable sources, these items are usually published without edi-
torial revision beyond that required by limitations of space.

Price quotations on securities are secured by the papers,
in the case of listed issues, from reporting services such as
the mechanical price "tickers" which are operated from the
securities exchanges and, in the case of unlisted issues, from
investment firms which maintain markets in such issues.

Supplementing the work of the great news-gathering organizations such as the *Associated Press* and the *United Press,*
which endeavor to cover all news items of general interest, the
Dow-Jones service is devoted entirely to the field of finance.
Items obtained by Dow-Jones reporters and correspondents
who are located in the principal cities of the world are dis-
seminated by means of mechanical news printers and bulletin
sheets, as rapidly as received, to subscribing financial institutions and newspapers. *The Wall Street Journal,* which is
the best known of the strictly financial newspapers, is published by the Dow-Jones Company.

Bond price quotations. Price quotations on bonds are
given in the form of actual prices on completed transactions
in the case of listed bonds and in the form of bid and asked
prices at the close of the day in the case of unlisted bonds.
In either case, the price quoted is in terms of percentage of
par value.

The following information on a specified United States
Government bond appeared in the financial section of *The
New York Times* on September 21, 1940, reporting transac-
tions as of September 20 in the New York Stock Exchange:

Issue: Treas. 3s, 1955-51 (signifying Treasury bonds bearing a 3 per cent interest rate, payable in 1955 but redeemable by the Government at any time between 1951 and 1955).

Range since date of issue: High 112.26—June 5, 1939, Low 82.3 —Jan. 12, 1932 (the highest price reached was $112^{26}\!/_{32}$ or $1,128.12½ for a $1,000 bond, and the lowest price was $82^{3}\!/_{32}$ or $820.94, on the respective dates).

1940 Range: High 111.30, Low 107.20 (the highest price reached in 1940 up to September 21 was $111^{30}\!/_{32}$ or $1,119.37½ per bond, and the lowest price was $107^{20}\!/_{32}$ or $1,076.25).

Sales in 1,000's: 1 (only one $1,000 bond was sold on this date).

High: 111.7 (the highest price of the day was $111^{7}\!/_{32}$ or $1,112.19).

Low: 111.7 (the lowest price of the day was $111^{7}\!/_{32}$ or $1,112.19).

Last: 111.7 (the final price of the day was $111^{7}\!/_{32}$ or $1,112.19).

Net change: + .4 (the last price on this day was $\frac{4}{32}$ or $1.25 per $1,000 bond higher than the last price on the preceding day).

Closing: Bid 111.5, asked 111.7 (the best bid at the close of the exchange was $111^{5}\!/_{32}$ or $1,111.56, and the best offer was $111^{7}\!/_{32}$ or $1,112.19).

In contrast to extensive current information supplied in the case of the Treasury 3's of 1955, which are listed on the New York Stock Exchange, is the decidedly meagre information on the Panama Canal 3's of 1961 (an unlisted issue), which merely stated that the bonds were quoted at 122¾ bid ($1,227.50) and 123¾ asked ($1,237.50).

Bonds such as railroad equipment notes, which are due in serial installments, are quoted on the basis of the rate of income return instead of the percentage of face value. The Illinois Central Equipment Trust 3's, due annually until 1952, were quoted 2.50 bid and 2.00 asked at the time of writing. Buyers were offering to pay a price which would afford a rate of income return of 2½ per cent annually; sellers were offering to sell at a price which would afford a rate of income return of 2 per cent annually.

Stock price quotations. Price quotations on corporate stocks follow the same practice as in the case of bonds. Actual prices on completed transactions are shown on listed issues, whereas bid and asked prices are shown on unlisted stocks.

The following information on a leading industrial common stock which is listed on the New York Stock Exchange is also taken from *The New York Times* on September 21, 1940, covering transactions as of September 20:

Stock: Eastman Kodak.

Dividend (6): (dividends were being made at the rate of $6.00 a share annually).

Range 1940: High 166¾, Low 117 (the highest price reached during the year up to September 21 was $166.75 per share, and the lowest price was $117 per share).

First: 133 (the first sale took place at $133 per share).

High: 135⅛ (the highest price reached was $135.12½ per share).

Low: 133 (the lowest price reached was $133 per share).

Last: 135⅛ (the last sale took place at $135.12½ per share).

Net change: + *2⅛* (the final price of $135.12½ was $2.12½ higher than the final price on the preceding day).

Closing: Bid 134½ asked 136 (the best bid at the close of the exchange was $134.50 per share, and the best offer was $136 per share).

Sales: 500 (the total number of shares sold during the day amounted to 500).

On the same date, the common stock of the Bankers Trust Company (of New York), which is an "over-the-counter" security, was quoted at 49 bid ($49 per share) and 51 asked ($51 per share), with no further information beyond the statement that the dividend rate was $2 annually and that the bid price on the previous day was 48¾ ($48.75 per share).

Price averages.   It is customary for newspapers to publish average prices of selected groups of securities for the previous day.   The averages may be compiled directly by the paper but are more commonly supplied by one of the reporting services such as the Dow-Jones Company or the Standard & Poor's Corporation.   The purpose of these averages is to enable the reader quickly to observe the trend of prices more reliably than from the movement of a few leading issues.   The Dow-Jones average of closing prices on a representative group of industrial stocks showed a broad upswing from 88.33 in 1924 to 381.17 in 1929 and an even greater decline to 41.22 in 1932.   Subsequently, prices recovered to 194.40 in 1937, fell to 98.95 in 1938, and were around 130 in 1940. The Dow-Jones average of a selected group of railroad stocks moved from 79.98 in 1924 to 189.11 in 1929, but fell to 13.23 in 1932, advanced to 64.46 in 1937, declined to 19.00 in 1938, and were around 30 in 1940.

A second function of price averages is to indicate the trend of the market by classes of securities. Some newspapers show separate averages for utility, oil, steel, food, motor, and other groups of stocks and thus enable their readers to compare

DOW-JONES AVERAGES
CLOSING PRICES ON REPRESENTATIVE COMMON STOCKS (AS COMPUTED DAILY)

Year	Industrials		Railroads	
	High	Low	High	Low
1924	120.51	88.33	99.50	79.98
1925	159.39	115.00	112.93	92.98
1926	166.54	135.20	123.33	102.41
1927	202.40	152.73	144.82	119.29
1928	300.00	191.33	152.70	132.60
1929	381.17	198.69	189.11	128.07
1930	294.07	157.51	157.94	91.65
1931	194.36	73.79	111.58	31.42
1932	88.78	41.22	41.30	13.23
1933	108.67	50.16	56.53	23.43
1934	110.74	85.51	52.97	33.19
1935	148.44	96.71	41.84	27.31
1936	184.90	143.11	59.89	40.66
1937	194.40	113.64	64.46	28.91
1938	158.41	98.95	33.98	19.00
1939	155.92	121.44	35.90	24.14
1940	152.80	111.84	32.67	22.14

the prices of any particular group with the general trend of the market. Such group averages are especially helpful as a guide to the trend of bond prices. A widening of the normal spread between the prices of first-grade and second-grade bonds is generally regarded as an unfavorable development indicating less confidence in the business situation, just as a shortening of the spread indicates greater optimism.

Any attempt to indicate what might be regarded as a "normal zone" for any set of averages such as Dow-Jones would be hazardous. In a volume written in 1926, at a time when the industrial average was around 160, the writer ventured the opinion that that level was abnormally high on the basis of historical data. Subsequently, as is shown in the accompanying table, the averages went above 380 in 1929 before dropping to 40 in 1932. Although the averages again went above 160 in 1937, the advance was not sustained. Until such times as a more trustworthy guide is available, therefore, buyers of stocks might well regard 160 as a danger signal in these averages.[1]

The Dow theory. It has been long observed that the market prices of common stocks tend to move upward or downward over extended periods of time, a movement which is obscured by short-term fluctuations. An early observer of these price movements (Charles H. Dow, one of the founders of the Dow-Jones services) formulated a method of interpretation known as "the Dow theory of price movements," which has gained wide recognition among students of market conditions.

Stated in its simplest form, the Dow theory is a mechanism which indicates the major trend of the market without forecasting the extent of the movement in time or degree. A comparison of the successive high and low points reached in the normal fluctuations of the stock market enables an observer who notices that the successive high and low points are advancing or declining thus to determine the trend of the market. If the price average should rise from a low point of 120 to a high point of 130, then fall to 125 and advance to 135, an upward trend was indicated when the decline stopped at 125 and was confirmed when the new advance went above 130. If the upward trend continues until the price average reaches 150, a subsequent change in the direction of the market trend would not be indicated until a recession from that level was followed by a recovery to less than 150 and a subsequent recession to a lower point than on the preceding decline. In an advancing market, a change in the direction of the trend is indicated when an advance fails to carry higher than the pre-

---

[1] D. F. Jordan, *Practical Business Forecasting*, p. 101 (1927).

ceding advance and when a decline goes lower than the preceding decline.   In a declining market, a change in the direction of the trend is indicated when an advance goes higher than the preceding advance and when a decline does not go so low as did the preceding decline.

Even more serious than the inability of the Dow theory to forecast the duration and degree of price movements is the failure in many instances to indicate a change in the direction of the trend until long after the change has taken place.   In 1937, industrial stock prices reached a high point of 194 in March and had declined to 165 before the downward trend was confirmed under the Dow theory five months later. Subsequently a low point of 99 was reached in March of 1939, but the Dow theory did not confirm an upward reversal until the average was above 140 some six months later.

As explained elsewhere in this volume, the Dow theory is based upon the use of both industrial and railroad stock prices and is valid only when the movements of both averages are confirmatory.

Interest rates.   The prevailing rates of interest on short-term, medium-term, and long-term loans indicate the condition of the money market reflecting the factors of demand for and supply of capital funds.   The rates usually published in the financial pages of particular significance to investors are as follows (as of September 20, 1940):

Call loans—1%.   This rate applies to loans arranged by brokers and dealers secured by bonds and stocks, payable on demand.   For many years previous to 1930, the call loan rate was normally around 3 per cent but during more recent years has remained consistently below this figure.   The failure of low interest rates to encourage greater activity on the securities exchanges has been a matter of widespread comment.   High call rates usually indicate the culmination of bull markets in stock prices.

Rediscount rate—1%.   This rate applies to loans made by member banks through the Federal Reserve Banks on loans secured by eligible collateral.   The prevailing rate of 1 per cent is the lowest in the history of the System.   Changes in the rediscount rate are highly significant as representative of major changes in the business situation.

Treasury notes—0.50%. This was the effective rate of return obtainable from the purchase of United States Treasury notes due in four years. The extremely low rate prevailing on these notes was due to short maturity and tax-exemption.

Treasury bonds—2.25%. This was the effective rate of return obtainable from the purchase of United States Treasury bonds of the longest maturity outstanding. *This rate is the most important interest rate in the money market from the investment viewpoint.* It is the common denominator of all investment values and provides a continuous standard by which to judge the riskless rental value of money. Conservative investors never buy bonds which yield more than 2 times the Treasury bond yield and usually regard one and one half times the Treasury bond yield as a safer limit.

Prices of commodities. The trend of prices in the basic raw materials of commerce is closely watched by investors as indicative of prevailing conditions in general business and in specific fields of industry. Advancing prices usually indicate that demand is increasing relative to the available supply just as declining prices are usually due to available supplies exceeding current demands. The leading metropolitan newspapers publish daily the current prices on the principal commodities as shown in the accompanying table. In addition to such individual prices, the Bureau of Labor Statistics at Washington publishes a weekly index of wholesale prices, using 1926 prices to represent a base of 100. The opening of hostilities in Europe in September of 1939 caused a sharp rise in this index from 75 to 79 in a single month. The fact that this initial advance was not followed by further advances during the subsequent months was regarded as highly significant by investors who inferred that prices of stocks probably would not advance despite wartime conditions unless prices of commodities also advanced.

Business indexes. The degree of business activity prevailing throughout the country is measured by means of index numbers which are now compiled by both public and private analysts and are available in monthly and weekly series in the leading newspapers. Probably the most popular of these indexes is the monthly index of production published by the Board of Governors of the Federal Reserve System. The Federal Reserve index uses as a 100 per cent base the average degree of activity which prevailed over the five-year period from 1935 to 1939 inclusive. From an estimated position

WHOLESALE PRICES OF COMMODITIES [2]
(Cash Prices in Primary Markets)

Items	Unit	High—1940	Low—1940	December 10, 1940
Foods				
Wheat.............	bushel	$ 1.32	$ 0.86⅜	$ 1.10⅝
Corn.............	bushel	0.85¼	0.71⅜	0.78½
Coffee............	pound	0.07⅝	0.06⅝	0.07¼
Sugar.............	pound	0.047	0.042	0.0435
Metals				
Iron.............	ton	24.84	24.84	24.84
Copper...........	pound	0.12½	0.10½	0.12
Lead.............	pound	0.0580	0.0475	0.055
Textiles				
Cotton.............	pound	0.1174	0.0966	0.1037
Silk..............	pound	4.35½	2.52½	2.52½
Miscellaneous				
Rubber...........	pound	0.24	0.1817	0.2106
Hides.............	pound	0.15	0.09½	0.13
Crude oil..........	barrel	0.96	0.96	0.96

of 114 in June of 1929, productive activity declined to a low point of 53 in July of 1932, subsequently advanced to 121 in May of 1937, but declined to 80 in May of 1938. In the latter part of 1940, the index had again advanced beyond 120.

Experience has shown that the usual range of productive activity is between 90 and 110 per cent of what might be considered normal. An index position under 90 would indicate a period of industrial depression when prices of cor-

[2] From *The New York Times*, Dec. 11, 1940.

porate stocks are relatively cheap. An index position above
110 would indicate a period of industrial prosperity when
prices of corporate stocks are relatively dear.

Corporate earnings reports. In addition to the annual
report of earnings which corporations customarily issue, interim reports on a semiannual or quarterly basis are now published by the great majority of the more important companies.
A recent compilation showed that 73 per cent of the companies
whose securities are listed on the New York Stock Exchange
now publish quarterly income statements, and 15 per cent
additional publish semiannual reports, leaving only 12 per
cent which report earnings solely on an annual basis. It is
the practice of all steam railroad companies and of certain
public utility companies to publish monthly statements.

This information which is available to all investors in the
newspapers allows them to keep in close touch with the earnings records of companies in which they have invested and
enables them to act quickly if necessary for the protection
of their interests.

Investors should make proper allowance for seasonal influences upon interim reports. Earnings for the first quarter
of the year are rarely a dependable guide for the entire year.
Because of increased volume of crop movements during the
harvest months, earnings of railroad companies during the
second half of the year are generally much better than during
the first half.

Financial terms. Certain terms which are frequently used
in the financial world have meanings somewhat different from
those understood in common parlance.

Accumulation is a term applied to the gradual purchase of
a large volume of a particular security in order to gain a more
favorable price than would ordinarily be possible in an immediate transaction, just as the term *distribution* is applied
to selling in the same manner. In restricted markets, such
as have existed in recent years, with limited buying and selling
orders in the hands of brokers, any attempt to execute a
large order immediately would have an unfavorable effect
upon the prevailing price.

Arbitrage represents concurrent dealings in the same security in different markets or in equivalent securities in the same market. If United States Steel common stock is selling at a slightly lower price on the London Stock Exchange than on the New York Stock Exchange as disclosed by an interchange of cablegrams (with due regard to currency exchange rates), the concurrent purchase of 100 shares in the cheap market (London) and sale of 100 shares in the dear market (New York) should result in a profit to the operator. Similarly, if rights to purchase a certain stock are selling below their equivalent value, concurrent orders to buy the rights and sell the stock should result in a profit. The natural effect of arbitrage transactions is to maintain prices on an equivalent basis.

Bulls and *bears* represent, respectively, persons who are buying stocks in anticipation of higher prices and persons who are selling stocks in anticipation of lower prices. An optimistic forecast is termed "bullish," while a pessimistic forecast is called "bearish."

Closing the books is the term applied to the action of a company in setting a final day for the transfer of stock prior to the payment of a forthcoming dividend. Checks will be sent to holders of record on the closing date. The term *ex dividend* is applied to stock which is purchased after the closing date and which is therefore not entitled to the dividend. The market price of the stock customarily declines the amount of the dividend on the day the stock first sells on an ex dividend basis.

Declaring a dividend refers to the action taken by the directors of a company in announcing the payment of a dividend to be made to stockholders registered on the books of the company as of a specified date, known as the *record date*.

Discounting the news is the term applied to the action of the market prior to the publication of important developments. Stock prices often advance before favorable news is published and decline before unfavorable news is published because of transactions by persons who have what is known as "inside information." The requirement that corporate officers must hold securities for at least six months in order to retain any profit derived therefrom has eliminated a large part of "informed" trading. Consequently, prices no longer are so prophetic as formerly.

Long and *short* are terms applied respectively to the positions of persons who hold securities previously purchased and of persons who have previously sold securities which they expect to be able to buy later at a lower price. *Short covering* refers to the purchasing of securities for the purpose of closing short positions.

Passing the dividend is the term applied to the failure on the part of a company to declare a dividend at the customary time.

Regular, flat, and *premium* are terms applied to stock loans arranged to allow short sellers to make deliveries on their sales. As the full cash value must be deposited as security for the loan, the lender of the stock pays interest on the cash held (regular), or pays no interest (flat), or is paid interest by the borrower (premium). A premium is paid only when the loanable supply of the security is very scarce.

Abbreviations. A short explanatory list of the abbreviations frequently used in the financial world is here shown:

Bonds

J-J	—Interest payable in January and July.
F-A	—Interest payable in February and August.
M-S	—Interest payable in March and September.
A-O	—Interest payable in April and October.
M-N	—Interest payable in May and November.
J-D	—Interest payable in June and December.
adj.	—adjustment.
col.	—collateral.
con., cons.	—consolidated.
cou., coup.	—coupon.
ct., conv.	—convertible.
deb.	—debenture.
div.	—division.
eq.	—equipment.
ext.	—extension.
f.	—flat (no interest charge).
gen.	—general.

gtd.	—guaranteed.
imp.	—improvement.
inc.	—income.
mtg.	—mortgage.
pr. ln.	—prior lien.
r.e.	—real estate.
ref.	—refunding.
reg.	—registered.
ser.	—series.
s.f.	—sinking fund.
w.w.	—with warrants.
x.w.	—without warrants.
1st 4's	—first mortgage 4 per cent bonds.
'65	—due in 1965.

Stocks

com.	—common.
ctfs.	—certificates.
ex. div.	—without next dividend.
gtd.	—guaranteed.
pf.	—preferred.
rts.	—rights.
vtc.	—voting trust certificates.
w.i.	—when, as, and if issued.

9

MATHEMATICS OF INVESTMENT

Scope. The purpose of this chapter is to discuss the mathematical problems which arise in investment practice. The order of discussion is: (1) definition of terms, (2) accrued interest on bonds, (3) rate of return on stocks, (4) rate of return on bonds, (5) present values on bonds, (6) the use of bond yield tables, (7) values of convertible securities, (8) values of stock subscription rights, and (9) values of stock purchase option warrants. The discussion of present values involving the use of algebraic and logarithmic formulae may be omitted by other than advanced readers. The investor who can appreciate that the price of a security is determined by the rate of income return, and not conversely, has gained a true realization of investment value.

Investment mathematics. The determination of a fair price for an investment security usually involves mathematical calculations which may be simple, as in the case of bond interest, or complex, as in the case of bond yield. In the latter case, however, reference tables are available which greatly simplify what would otherwise require the knowledge of advanced algebraic principles.

The mathematical problems which occur most frequently in investment practice may be placed in the following groups:

(1) The calculation of accrued interest on bonds.

(2) The calculation of yield on stocks.

(3) The calculation of yield on bonds.

(4) The calculation of equivalent values on convertible bonds.

(5) The calculation of the value of stock subscription rights.

Mathematical terms. Many of the mathematical terms used in the field of investments have meanings which are not always applicable in other fields. The first group of terms are those used in connection with the prices of securities:

Market price is the value as shown in the last previous transaction or as indicated by the prevailing quotations expressed in terms of the best price that any prospective buyer is willing to pay.

Bond prices are expressed as percentages of face value (a price of 103½ means 103½ per cent of $1,000, or $1,035), whereas stock prices are expressed in dollars per share (a price of 46¾ means $46.75 per share).

The difference between market price and face value of bonds is known as *discount* when the market price is lower and as *premium* when the market price is higher.

Conversion price is the fixed price at which stock will be issued to holders of convertible bonds in exchange for their bonds.

Subscription price is the fixed price at which additional stock will be sold to existing stockholders.

The second group of terms are those used in connection with interest calculations:

Accrued interest is the amount of interest that has accumulated on a bond since the last preceding semiannual payment date.

Accumulation is the appreciation in the value of a bond bought at a discount, between the purchase date and the maturity date when it is payable at face value.

Amortization is the depreciation in the value of a bond

bought at a premium, between the purchase date and the maturity date when it is payable at face value.

Nominal yield is the annual income rate specified on bonds and preferred stocks.   The actual yield to the investor will be higher or lower than the nominal yield if the cost price is less or more than the face value.

Current yield is the annual income rate as determined by the cost price without regard to accumulation or amortization. (A 4 per cent bond bought at 105, due in 20 years, provides a current yield of about 3.80 per cent per annum.)

Net yield (or *yield to maturity*) is the annual income rate as adjusted to the cost price and the amount of annual accumulation or amortization.   (A 4 per cent bond bought at 105, due in 20 years, provides a net yield of about 3.65 per cent per annum.)

Accrued interest on bonds.   Bond prices are quoted on an "and interest" basis.   In addition to the agreed price, the buyer will be expected to advance to the seller the amount of interest accrued since the preceding interest date because interest for the full six months will be paid to the buyer on the next interest date.

Accrued interest on bonds is calculated on the 360-day-year basis, except in the case of certain United States Government bonds on which the 365-day-year basis is used.   Under the 360-day basis, each month is considered to have 30 days irrespective of the calendar.   The seller is entitled to interest up to, but not including, the day of delivery.

If a 4 per cent bond with interest payment dates on January 1 and July 1 (J-J) is sold on Monday, October 14, for regular two-day delivery on Wednesday, October 16, the seller is entitled to interest for three months (July, August, and September) and 15 days (up to, but not including, October 16) at 4 per cent, or $11.67.   If a 3 per cent bond with interest payment dates on March 1 and September 1 (M-S) is sold on Friday, October 18, for delivery on Tuesday, October 22, the seller is entitled to interest for one month (September) and 21 days (up to but not including October 22) at 3 per cent, or $4.25.

BOND INTEREST TABLE

INTEREST ON $1,000 FROM ONE DAY TO SIX MONTHS

Days	2 Per Cent	3 Per Cent	4 Per Cent	5 Per Cent	6 Per Cent
1.........	$ 0.0555	$ 0.0833	$ 0.1111	$ 0.1389	$ 0.1667
2.........	0.1111	0.1667	0.2222	0.2778	0.3333
3.........	0.1667	0.2500	0.3333	0.4167	0.5000
4.........	0.2222	0.3333	0.4444	0.5556	0.6667
5.........	0.2778	0.4167	0.5555	0.6944	0.8333
6.........	0.3333	0.5000	0.6667	0.8333	1.0000
7.........	0.3889	0.5833	0.7778	0.9722	1.1667
8.........	0.4444	0.6667	0.8889	1.1111	1.3333
9.........	0.5000	0.7500	1.0000	1.2500	1.5000
10.........	0.5555	0.8333	1.1111	1.3889	1.6667
11.........	0.6111	0.9167	1.2222	1.5278	1.8333
12.........	0.6667	1.0000	1.3333	1.6667	2.0000
13.........	0.7222	1.0833	1.4444	1.8055	2.1667
14.........	0.7778	1.1667	1.5555	1.9444	2.3333
15.........	0.8333	1.2500	1.6667	2.0833	2.5000
16.........	0.8889	1.3333	1.7778	2.2222	2.6667
17.........	0.9444	1.4167	1.8889	2.3611	2.8333
18.........	1.0000	1.5000	2.0000	2.5000	3.0000
19.........	1.0555	1.5833	2.1111	2.6389	3.1667
20.........	1.1111	1.6667	2.2222	2.7778	3.3333
21.........	1.1667	1.7500	2.3333	2.9167	3.5000
22.........	1.2222	1.8333	2.4444	3.0555	3.6667
23.........	1.2778	1.9167	2.5555	3.1944	3.8333
24.........	1.3333	2.0000	2.6667	3.3333	4.0000
25.........	1.3889	2.0833	2.7778	3.4722	4.1667
26.........	1.4444	2.1667	2.8889	3.6111	4.3333
27.........	1.5000	2.2500	3.0000	3.7500	4.5000
28.........	1.5555	2.3333	3.1111	3.8889	4.6667
29.........	1.6111	2.4167	3.2222	4.0278	4.8333
30.........	1.6667	2.5000	3.3333	4.1667	5.0000
Months					
1.........	1.6667	2.5000	3.3333	4.1667	5.0000
2.........	3.3333	5.0000	6.6667	8.3333	10.0000
3.........	5.0000	7.5000	10.0000	12.5000	15.0000
4.........	6.6667	10.0000	13.3333	16.6667	20.0000
5.........	8.3333	12.5000	16.6667	20.8333	25.0000
6.........	10.0000	15.0000	20.0000	25.0000	30.0000

In the event that interest is not paid at the subsequent payment date, the buyer may not recover the amount advanced to the seller but must endeavor to collect from the issuer.

Accrued dividend on stocks. The amount of dividend which accumulates on corporate stock from each payment date to the next is automatically included in the quoted price of the stock which includes all accrued dividends, if any. No calculation of dividend accrual is therefore involved, as is necessary in the case of bond interest.   If no other influences were affecting the market price of a stock on which a quarterly dividend of $2.25 is being paid, the market price would gradually advance $2¼ per share from one dividend record date (say March 20) to the next record date (June 20), after which time it would normally decline the entire amount of the dividend.   Dividend payments involve declaration dates (say March 1), record dates (say March 20), and payment dates (say April 15).   Persons buying the stock on or before the record date are entitled to receive the forthcoming dividend. Because buyers after the record date (March 20) are not entitled to the next dividend (on April 15), the market price is said to be "ex dividend" and usually declines the amount of the quarterly payment around the record date.

Yields on stocks. The rate of return, or yield on investments in corporate stocks, is determined by dividing the annual dividend payment (in dollars) by the cost price.   A stock which cost $150 per share and which is paying an annual dividend of $9 per share is affording a yield of 6 per cent. Subsequent changes in the market price do not affect the rate of return to existing holders but do change the rate of return available to new buyers.   The prevailing yield therefore affects relatively few holders, most of whom have cost prices either higher or lower than prevailing quotations.   Subsequent changes in the dividend rate do affect the rates of return of all holders.

The calculation of the yield on preferred stocks has greater warrant than in the case of common stocks.   Dividend rates on preferred stocks are fixed in time and amount and therefore provide a more dependable basis for the calculation of an estimated rate of income return.   Dividend payments on the common stocks of even the largest corporations have become increasingly irregular in amount during the economic disturbances of recent years. An examination of the dividend record of two representative American companies during the decade from 1930 to 1940 discloses the complete absence of any uniform dividend rate on which an estimated rate of return might be based in these instances.

Unlike the case of bonds where the yield directly indicates the quality of the security, the rate of return on stocks is not directly significant of quality except in the case of high-grade preferred stocks with dependable dividends. For the most part, common stock prices reflect appreciation possibilities as foreseen by speculators more than dividend income as anticipated by investors.

TEN-YEAR DIVIDEND RECORD (1931-1940)

Year	Pennsylvania Railroad	General Motors
1931	$3.25	$3.00
1932	0.50	1.25
1933	0.50	1.25
1934	1.00	1.50
1935	0.50	2.25
1936	2.00	4.50
1937	1.25	3.75
1938	0.50	1.50
1939	1.00	3.50
1940	1.50	3.75

Yield on bonds. It is the general custom of the investment business to calculate the annual rate of income on bonds on the basis of net yield to maturity. Although this method of calculation is obviously misleading if the bonds are not held to final maturity, or if full payment is not made at maturity date, it is the only method of measurement which has general acceptance in the securities business. The experience of recent years, however, has possibly outmoded this method of calculation. A survey made in 1940 showed that no less than 2.5 billion dollars in corporate bonds listed on the New York Stock Exchange were already in default on interest payments, or 15 per cent of the total corporate bonds listed. A substantial additional volume of bonds were selling at such large discounts as to indicate considerable uncertainty concerning final payment. Despite almost universal practice to the contrary, the suggestion is made that a more practical method of calculating the yield on bonds bought at a discount is to ignore the maturity basis and to use the current method.

The current yield on bonds is determined by dividing the cost price into the annual interest payment. A 3½ per cent bond purchased at 90 would afford a current yield of 3.89 per cent as thus calculated:

annual interest......... $ 35 (3½ per cent of $1,000)
    divided by
cost price.............. $900
        equals
current yield...........   .0389.

The net yield (to maturity) on bonds is determined by dividing the average cost price (as adjusted by accumulation credits or amortization charges) into the annual income (interest plus annual accumulation or minus annual depreciation). A 3 per cent bond due in 25 years which was purchased at 90 would afford an approximate net yield (to maturity) of 3.58 per cent as thus calculated:

annual interest......... $ 30 (3 per cent of $1,000)
        plus
annual accumulation.... $ 4 ($1,000 − $900 = $100 ÷ 25 yrs.)
        equals
total income........... $ 34
        divided by
average cost........... $950 ($900 + $1,000 = $1,900 ÷ 2)
        equals
net yield (to maturity)..   .0358.

A 4 per cent bond due in 20 years purchased at 110 would afford an approximate net yield (to maturity) of 3.33 per cent as calculated on the following page.

annual interest......... $ 40 (4 per cent of $1,000)
        minus
annual amortization.... $ 5 ($1,100 − $1,000 = $100 ÷ 20
                                   yrs.)
        equals
annual income......... $ 35
        divided by
average cost.......... $1,050 ($1,100 + $1,000 = $2,100 ÷ 2)
        equals
net yield (to maturity)..   .0333.

The net yield (to maturity) as calculated in the two preceding examples is an approximate, rather than an exact, method. From a mathematical viewpoint, the annual amortization or accumulation would not be a uniform amount, and the average cost would be somewhat higher or lower than the figures here shown. For practical purposes, therefore, a more accurate method is necessary which requires the use of advanced mathematics in order to determine the value of future payments of principal and interest compound discounted to the present time. To expedite such calculations, tables have been prepared and published which permit the ready determination of accurate yields when prices are known or of exact prices when yields are given.

Compound interest formula. The formula for determining the future value of money invested at compound interest is:

$$(1 + N)^n,$$

in which N is the interest rate per year and n is the number of years.

Assume that $1.00 is invested at compound interest credited annually, for 20 years at 3 per cent:

$$(1 + N)^n = (1 + .03)^{20} = (1.03)^{20}$$
$$\text{Log } (1.03) = 0.012837$$
$$\text{Log } (1.03)^{20} = 0.25674$$
$$0.25674 = \log 1.806 = \$1.806.$$

The indicated value of $1.00 would therefore be $1.806 and of $1,000 would be $1,806.

Present worth formulae. The formula for determining the value of a principal sum of money payable at a future time, compound discounted to the present time, is the reciprocal of the compound interest formula:

$$\frac{1}{(1 + N)^n},$$

in which N is the discount rate per year and n is the number of years.

Assume that $1.00 payable in 20 years is to be compound discounted at 3 per cent:

$$\frac{1}{(1 + N)^n} = \frac{1}{(1 + .03)^{20}} = \frac{1}{1.806} = \$0.553.$$

The indicated value of $1.00 would therefore be 55.3 cents. The present worth of a $1,000 bond payable in 20 years, compound discounted at 3 per cent per annum, would be $553.

The formula for determining the value of the total annual interest payments on a bond payable over a period of years, compound discounted to the present time, is here shown:

$$\frac{C}{N}\left(1 - \frac{1}{(1 + N)^n}\right),$$

in which C is the coupon interest rate, N is the net interest rate or yield, and n is the number of years.

Assume that a $1,000 bond payable in 20 years carries a 4 per cent coupon interest rate and the interest payments are to be compound discounted at 3 per cent:

$$\frac{.04}{.03} (\$1,000 - \$553) = \frac{4}{3} (\$447) = \$596.$$

The total present worth of both principal and coupons on a $1,000 bond bearing a 4 per cent interest rate payable in 20 years would therefore be the sum of $553 (the present worth of the principal) plus $596 (the present worth of the coupons), or $1,149.

The formula for determining the present worth of a bond payable at a future date is obtained by combining the respective formulae for present worth of principal and present worth of coupons as follows:

$$\frac{1}{(1+N)^n} + \frac{C}{N}\left(1 - \frac{1}{(1+N)^n}\right).$$

This formula may be reduced and expressed more simply as:

$$\frac{N + C(1+N)^n - C}{N(1+N)^n}.$$

The preceding case of the 4 per cent $1,000 bond payable in 20 years may now be applied to the simplified combined formula in order to determine the present value of the bond on a 3 per cent yield basis:

$$\frac{.03 + .04(1+.03)^{20} - .04}{.03(1+.03)^{20}} = \frac{.03 + .04(1.806) - .04}{.03(1.806)}$$

$$= \frac{.03 + .07224 - .04}{.05418} = \frac{.06224}{.05418} = 1.149 = \$1,149.$$

The total value of the bond in question would therefore be $1,149, which confirms the separate values of $553 as determined by the principal formula and of $596 as determined by the interest formula.

In the preceding cases, the problem was to determine the price of a bond when the yield is given. In other cases, the problem may be to determine the yield when the price is given.

Assume that a 3 per cent bond due in 60 years is purchased at 105. The net yield would be thus determined through substitution in the combined formula:

$$1.05 = \frac{N + .03(1+N)^{60} - .03}{N(1+N)^{60}}$$

$$1.05N(1+N)^{60} = .03(1+N)^{60} + N - .03.$$

The bonds having been purchased at a premium, it is evident that the net yield is less than .03 per annum. Solving by approximation, .029 may be tried.

$$1.05 \times .029(1+.029)^{60} = .03(1+.029)^{60} + .029 - .03$$
$$1.05 \times .029(1.029)^{60} = .03(1.029)^{60} - .001.$$

The solution from this point will be facilitated through the use of logarithms.

Left Side of Equation		Right Side of Equation	
log 1.05	= 0.02119	log .03	= 8.47712 − 10
log .029	= 8.46240 − 10	log (1.029)^{60}	= 0.74520
log (1.029)^{60}	= 0.74520		
log	9.22879 − 10	log	9.22232 − 10

$$\left. \begin{array}{l} \log 1.05 = 0.02119 \\ \log .029 = 8.46240 - 10 \\ \log (1.029)^{60} = 0.74520 \\ \hline \log \qquad 9.22879 - 10 \end{array} \right\} = \left\{ \begin{array}{l} \log .03 = 8.47712 - 10 \\ \log (1.029)^{60} = 0.74520 \\ \\ \hline \log \qquad 9.22232 - 10 \end{array} \right\} - .001$$

.1693   .1678
                               .001
―――   ――――
.1693   >   .1668

.028 may next be tried: (.028 — .03 = — .002).

$$\left. \begin{array}{l} \log 1.05 = 0.02119 \\ \log .028 = 8.44716 - 10 \\ \log (1.028)^{60} = 0.71940 \\ \hline \log \qquad 9.18775 - 10 \end{array} \right\} = \left\{ \begin{array}{l} \log .03 = 8.47712 - 10 \\ \log (1.028)^{60} = 0.71940 \\ \\ \hline \log \qquad 9.19652 - 10 \end{array} \right\} - .002$$

.1541   .1572
                               .002
―――   ――――
.1541   <   .1552

The net yield is apparently between .029 and .028 as, in the first case, the left side was the greater, and, in the second, the right was larger.   The comparative equality being greater at .028, .0281 may next be tried: (.0281 — .03 = — .0019).

$$\left. \begin{array}{l} \log 1.05 = 0.02119 \\ \log .0281 = 8.44871 - 10 \\ \log (1.0281)^{60} = 0.72180 \\ \hline \log \qquad 9.19170 - 10 \end{array} \right\} = \left\{ \begin{array}{l} \log .03 = 8.47712 - 10 \\ \log (1.0281)^{60} = 0.72180 \\ \\ \hline \log \qquad 9.19892 - 10 \end{array} \right\} - .0019$$

.1554   .1581
                               .0019
―――   ――――
.1554   <   .1562

.0282 may be tried: (.0282 — .03 = — .0018).

$$\left. \begin{array}{l} \log 1.05 = 0.02119 \\ \log .0282 = 8.45025 - 10 \\ \log (1.0282)^{60} = 0.72420 \\ \hline \log \qquad 9.19564 - 10 \end{array} \right\} = \left\{ \begin{array}{l} \log .03 = 8.47712 - 10 \\ \log (1.0282)^{60} = 0.72420 \\ \\ \hline \log \qquad 9.20132 - 10 \end{array} \right\} - .0018$$

.1569   .1589
                               .0018
―――   ――――
.1569   <   .1571

As the assumed net yield of .0282 brought the two sides of the equation in almost exact balance, it is evident that the bond in question has been bought at a price which affords a yield of 2.82 per cent per annum.

Relative values of principal and interest. The present value of the principal of a bond is determined, not by the interest rate that the bond bears, but by the prevailing rate of income return on similar securities. The present worth of the right to receive $1,000 in 20 years is determined by compound discount and is equivalent to the amount which accumulates to $1,000 in 20 years at compound interest at the prevailing rate of income return. (The present value of $1,000 payable in 20 years, compound discounted at 3 per cent per annum, is $553; or, stated otherwise, an investment of $553 will accumulate to $1,000 in 20 years at 3 per cent compound interest.) The present worth of the right to receive the interest payments on a bond, as established by the fixed interest rate, is determined by compound discounting of the aggregate payments from their respective due dates to the present time. (The present value of the aggregate coupons on a 4 per cent-20 year $1,000 bond, amounting to $800 in face value, would be $596 if the respective interest payments are compound discounted at 3 per cent annually.) It is thus apparent that the investor who pays $1,150 for a 4 per cent bond due in 20 years is paying more for the right to receive the interest payments ($596) than for the right to receive the principal at maturity ($553).

Yields on callable bonds. Many bonds contain provisions whereby they may be redeemed by the issuer after a certain date and prior to maturity date. The conservative investor will remember that the option is with the issuer and redemption will be made only when it is to the issuer's advantage, and, conversely, probably to the holder's disadvantage. The holder of a redeemable bond purchased at a discount should therefore base his maturity at the final date of payment, whereas the holder of a bond purchased at a premium should base his maturity at the earliest possible date of redemption. The yield on bonds on the basis of a premium redemption cannot be determined by the use of ordinary bond tables. Special premium tables based upon a complicated formula are necessary in such cases.

Bond tables. The mathematical problems most frequently arising in connection with bond investment are, first, the problem of determining the net yield of a bond when price, redemption value, and maturity are known; and, second, the problem of ascertaining the price at which a bond of known redemption value and maturity must be purchased to yield a certain desired return. In either case, the solution is simplified through the use of bond table books.

At the outset it may be stated that bond tables are not complete. Complete bond tables in the true sense of the word would show the net yield on every amount invested at every possible rate of interest for every possible maturity. Such a compilation is, of course, out of the question. Bond tables may be constructed within any desired limitations. Those illustrated are the Rollins, the Sprague, and the Johnson tables. [1] The Rollins tables show the value, to the nearest cent, of a bond for $100, bearing interest at the rates of 2, 2½, 3, 3½, 4, 4½, 5, 6, and 7 per cent and yielding from 2 to 7 per cent. The Sprague tables show the value, to the nearest cent, of a bond for $1,000,000, bearing interest from 3 to 7 per cent and yielding from 1¼ to 10 per cent. The Johnson tables show the yields obtainable from bonds of standard denomination, maturities, and interest rates.

Use of the Rollins tables. A specimen page from the Rollins tables is shown on page 140. The maturity, 20 years, appears at the top of the page. Assume that a bond, maturing in 20 years and bearing 4 per cent interest, is purchased at 111¾ ($1,117.50); required, the net yield. Since the first horizontal row shows the nominal yields, reference is made to the column headed 4 per cent. In this column, 111.75 appears opposite 3.20 per cent in the first vertical column, which shows the net yield. The required net yield is therefore 3.20 per cent.

---

[1] *Bond Values*, Montgomery Rollins; *Complete Bond Tables*, Charles E. Sprague; *Bond Yields*, D. C. Johnson and others.

20 YEARS. INTEREST PAYABLE SEMI-ANNUALLY

Per cent per an.	3%	3½%	4%	4½%	5%	6%	7%
2.90	101.51	109.06	116.60	124.15	131.70	146.80	161.89
3.	100.00	107.48	114.96	122.44	129.92	144.87	159.83
3.10	98.52	105.93	113.34	120.75	128.16	142.98	157.81
3⅛	98.15	105.55	112.94	120.33	127.73	142.52	157.31
3.20	97.06	104.41	111.75	119.09	126.44	141.13	155.82
3¼	96.34	103.66	110.97	118.28	125.59	140.21	154.83
3.30	95.63	102.91	110.19	117.47	124.75	139.30	153.86
3.35	94.93	102.17	109.42	116.66	123.91	138.40	152.89
3⅜	94.58	101.81	109.04	116.27	123.49	137.95	152.41
3.40	94.23	101.44	108.66	115.87	123.08	137.51	151.93
3.45	93.54	100.72	107.90	115.08	122.26	136.62	150.98
3½	92.85	100.00	107.15	114.30	121.45	135.74	150.04
3.55	92.17	99.29	106.41	113.52	120.64	134.87	149.11
3.60	91.50	98.58	105.67	112.75	119.84	134.01	148.18
3⅝	91.16	98.23	105.30	112.37	119.44	133.58	147.72
3.65	90.83	97.88	104.94	111.99	119.04	133.15	147.26
3.70	90.17	97.19	104.21	111.24	118.26	132.30	146.35
3¾	89.51	96.50	103.50	110.49	117.48	131.46	145.44
3.80	88.86	95.82	102.78	109.74	116.70	130.63	144.55
3⅞	87.90	94.81	101.73	108.64	115.56	129.39	143.22
3.90	87.58	94.48	101.38	108.28	115.18	128.98	142.78
4.	86.32	93.16	100.00	106.84	113.68	127.36	141.03
4.10	85.09	91.86	98.64	105.42	112.20	125.76	139.32
4⅛	84.78	91.54	98.31	105.07	111.84	125.37	138.90
4.20	83.87	90.59	97.31	104.03	110.75	124.19	137.63
4¼	83.27	89.96	96.65	103.35	110.04	123.42	136.80
4.30	82.68	89.34	96.00	102.66	109.33	122.65	135.98
4⅜	81.80	88.42	95.04	101.65	108.27	121.51	134.75
4.40	81.51	88.11	94.72	101.32	107.93	121.14	134.35
4½	80.35	86.90	93.45	100.00	106.55	119.65	132.74
4.60	79.22	85.72	92.21	98.70	105.19	118.18	131.16
4⅝	78.94	85.42	91.90	98.38	104.86	117.82	130.77
4.70	78.11	84.55	90.99	97.43	103.86	116.74	129.61
4¾	77.57	83.98	90.39	96.80	103.20	116.02	128.84
4.80	77.02	83.40	89.79	96.17	102.55	115.32	128.08
4⅞	76.22	82.56	88.90	95.24	101.59	114.27	126.95
4.90	75.95	82.28	88.61	94.94	101.27	113.92	126.58
5.	74.90	81.17	87.45	93.72	100.00	112.55	125.10
5.10	73.86	80.09	86.31	92.53	98.76	111.20	123.65
5⅛	73.61	79.82	86.03	92.24	98.45	110.87	123.29
5.20	72.85	79.02	85.19	91.36	97.53	109.87	122.22
5¼	72.34	78.49	84.64	90.78	96.93	109.22	121.51
5.30	71.85	77.97	84.09	90.21	96.33	108.57	120.81
5⅜	71.11	77.19	83.27	89.36	95.44	107.60	119.77
5.40	70.87	76.94	83.01	89.07	95.14	107.28	119.42
5½	69.90	75.92	81.94	87.96	93.98	106.02	118.06
5⅝	68.72	74.68	80.64	86.59	92.55	104.47	116.38
5¾	67.57	73.46	79.36	85.26	91.15	102.95	114.74
5⅞	66.43	72.27	78.11	83.95	89.78	101.46	113.13
6.	65.33	71.11	76.89	82.66	88.44	100.00	111.56

If the exact cost price does not appear in the column, a process known as interpolation, which is later described, is necessary. The second assumption is that the bond has the same maturity, 20 years, and bears 4 per cent interest; required, the purchase price to yield 3.75 per cent. Reference is made to the column headed 4 per cent, and directly opposite 3.75 per cent, the desired net yield, appears 103.50, which shows the required purchase price to be $1035.00 (103½) for a $1,000 bond. Interpolation is again necessary if the required net yield is not given in the yield column.

It should be observed that maturity means, in the calculation of bond yields, the number of years which a bond has still to run. A 30-year bond issued in 1935 had a maturity of only 25 years as of 1940.

Use of the Sprague tables. A sample page from the Sprague tables is shown on page 142. A difference from the Rollins tables is immediately apparent. The entire page is devoted to the 5 per cent rate for five maturities: 18, 18½, 19, 19½, and 20 years. Similar pages are provided for semiannual maturities from 1 to 50 years; also for maturities at 5-year intervals from 50 to 100 years. As previously stated, the values are shown to nine places instead of to five. Assume that, a 5 per cent bond due in 20 years is purchased at $1,100 (110); required, the net yield. Reference is made to the 5 per cent page, which contains the column headed 20 years, and in that column opposite 1,100,369.73 is found 4.25 per cent, the approximate net yield. If the exact purchase price does not appear, interpolation, explained in the following paragraph, is again necessary. The second assumption is that a 5 per cent bond matures in 18 years; required, the purchase price to yield 4.75 per cent. Upon reference to the 5 per cent page containing the 18 years column, in that column opposite 4.75 per cent is found 1,030,023.41. The required cost of a $1,000 bond is therefore $1,030 (103). If the desired net yield does not appear in the first column, interpolation is necessary.

Interpolation. Rarely do the bond tables give the desired information directly, because either the exact cost of the

SPRAGUE TABLES
VALUES, TO THE NEAREST CENT, OF A BOND FOR
$1,000,000 AT 5% INTEREST, PAYABLE SEMI-ANNUALLY

Net Income	18 Years	18½ Years	19 Years	19½ Years	20 Years
2.50	1,360,590.84	1,368,484.78	1,376,281.27	1,383,981.50	1,391,586.66
2.55	1,351,885.91	1,359,551.62	1,367,120.83	1,374,594.75	1,381,974.57
2.60	1,343,250.69	1,350,691.70	1,358,037.21	1,365,288.46	1,372,446.66
2.65	1,334,684.58	1,341,904.35	1,349,029.70	1,356,061.88	1,363,002.10
2.70	1,326,186.97	1,333,188.92	1,340,097.60	1,346,914.26	1,353,640.12
2.75	1,317,757.27	1,324,544.78	1,331,240.23	1,337,844.86	1,344,359.91
2.80	1,309,394.89	1,315,971.29	1,322,456.89	1,328,852.95	1,335,160.70
2.85	1,301,099.23	1,307,467.81	1,313,746.92	1,319,937.81	1,326,041.71
2.90	1,292,869.72	1,299,033.73	1,305,109.64	1,311,098.71	1,317,002.18
2.95	1,284,705.78	1,290,668.42	1,296,544.39	1,302,334.95	1,308,041.34
3.00	1,276,606.84	1,282,371.27	1,288,050.52	1,293,645.83	1,299,158.45
3.05	1,268,572.34	1,274,141.68	1,279,627.36	1,285,030.65	1,290,352.77
3.10	1,260,601.71	1,265,979.04	1,271,274.29	1,276,488.71	1,281,623.55
3.15	1,252,694.41	1,257,882.75	1,262,990.65	1,268,019.34	1,272,970.07
3.20	1,244,849.87	1,249,852.23	1,254,775.82	1,259,621.87	1,264,391.60
3.25	1,237,067.56	1,241,886.89	1,246,629.17	1,251,295.62	1,255,887.44
3.30	1,229,346.93	1,233,986.16	1,238,550.08	1,243,039.92	1,247,456.88
3.35	1,221,687.45	1,226,149.45	1,230,537.94	1,234,854.13	1,239,099.22
3.40	1,214,088.60	1,218,376.20	1,222,592.13	1,226,737.59	1,230,813.76
3.45	1,206,549.83	1,210,665.85	1,214,712.06	1,218,689.67	1,222,599.82
3.50	1,199,070.65	1,203,017.83	1,206,897.13	1,210,709.71	1,214,456.72
3.55	1,191,650.52	1,195,431.61	1,199,146.75	1,202,797.10	1,206,383.79
3.60	1,184,288.94	1,187,906.62	1,191,460.33	1,194,951.21	1,198,380.36
3.65	1,176,985.40	1,180,442.33	1,183,837.29	1,187,171.42	1,190,445.78
3.70	1,169,739.40	1,173,038.19	1,176,277.07	1,179,457.11	1,182,579.39
3.75	1,162,550.44	1,165,693.69	1,168,779.08	1,171,807.68	1,174,780.55
3.80	1,155,418.04	1,158,408.28	1,161,342.77	1,164,222.54	1,167,048.61
3.85	1,148,341.69	1,151,181.45	1,153,967.57	1,156,701.08	1,159,382.95
3.90	1,141,320.92	1,144,012.68	1,146,652.94	1,149,242.71	1,151,782.94
3.95	1,134,355.26	1,136,901.45	1,139,398.34	1,141,846.86	1,144,247.96
4.00	1,127,444.21	1,129,847.27	1,132,203.20	1,134,512.94	1,136,777.40
4.05	1,120,587.32	1,122,849.62	1,125,067.01	1,127,240.39	1,129,370.64
4.10	1,113,784.12	1,115,908.01	1,117,989.23	1,120,028.64	1,122,027.08
4.15	1,107,034.14	1,109,021.94	1,110,969.32	1,112,877.12	1,114,746.14
4.20	1,100,336.93	1,102,190.92	1,104,006.78	1,105,785.29	1,107,527.22
4.25	1,093,692.04	1,095,414.48	1,097,101.08	1,098,752.59	1,100,369.73
4.30	1,087,099.00	1,088,692.12	1,090,251.71	1,091,778.47	1,093,273.10
4.35	1,080,557.39	1,082,023.38	1,083,458.17	1,084,862.41	1,086,236.76
4.40	1,074,066.75	1,075,407.78	1,076,719.94	1,078,003.86	1,079,260.13
4.45	1,067,626.66	1,068,844.86	1,070,036.54	1,071,202.29	1,072,342.67
4.50	1,061,236.66	1,062,334.15	1,063,407.48	1,064,457.19	1,065,483.81
4.55	1,054,896.35	1,055,875.19	1,056,832.26	1,057,768.03	1,058,683.00
4.60	1,048,605.29	1,049,467.53	1,050,310.40	1,051,134.31	1,051,939.69
4.65	1,042,363.05	1,043,110.73	1,043,841.42	1,044,555.50	1,045,253.36
4.70	1,036,169.23	1,036,804.33	1,037,424.85	1,038,031.11	1,038,623.46
4.75	1,030,023.41	1,030,547.89	1,031,060.21	1,031,560.65	1,032,049.47
4.80	1,023,925.17	1,024,340.98	1,024,747.05	1,025,143.61	1,025,530.87
4.85	1,017,874.11	1,018,183.17	1,018,484.91	1,018,779.50	1,019,067.13
4.90	1,011,869.83	1,012,074.01	1,012,273.32	1,012,467.85	1,012,657.74
4.95	1,005,911.92	1,006,013.10	1,006,111.83	1,006,208.18	1,006,302.20
5.00	1,000,000.00	1,000,000.00	1,000,000.00	1,000,000.00	1,000,000.00

bond or the desired net yield, as the case may be, does not appear therein. This situation must necessarily exist, because the tables are incomplete. On the specimen page of the Sprague tables, which are the most complete published, it will be noted that there are 51 out of the 39,158,666 different possible prices between $1,000,000 and $1,391,586.66. It would be remarkable if the exact amount should be found among the amounts stated, when the fact is considered that there is only one chance in 767,817 that the amount will be found directly.

Interpolation is a matter of proportion, as it is based upon the assumption that the changes in the bond table values are proportionate. This assumption is not absolutely correct, but the degree of variance is too small to be serious.

Assume that a 5 per cent bond is to run 20 years and is purchased at 103½; required, the net yield. Using the Rollins table, the nearest amounts that appear are 103.20 and 103.86, which give net yields of 4.75 per cent and 4.70 per cent, respectively. The required net yield is therefore between 4.75 per cent and 4.70 per cent. The difference in amount is .66; in per cent, .05 per cent. The given price, 103.50, being .30 greater than 103.20, will therefore yield $\frac{30}{66}$ of .05 per cent less than 4.75 per cent, or $\frac{30}{66}$ of .05 per cent greater than 4.70 per cent, making the net yield 4.727 per cent.

The second assumption is that a 5 per cent bond is to run 20 years; at what price should it be purchased to yield 4.95 per cent? The nearest net yields that appear in the Rollins table are 4.90 per cent and 5.00 per cent, which require a cost of 101.27 and 100, respectively. The difference of .10 in rate represents a difference of 1.27 in price. The difference of .05 per cent between 4.90 per cent and 4.95 per cent must therefore cover a difference of .635 in price (.10:1.27 as .05:.635), making the required price 101.27 — .635, or 100.635 (100⅝).

A third assumption may be that, with maturity, purchase price, and net yield given, it is desired to determine the interest, or coupon, rate. Although unusual, such a question might conceivably arise. A 20-year bond is purchased at

3%

BOND

Yields in per cent per annum,
correct to the nearest five ten-thousandths of one per cent,
interest payable semi-annually.

Price	18 Years	18½ Years	19 Years	19½ Years	20 Years	20½ Years	21 Years	Current Income
45	9.389	9.273-	9.163-	9.059	8.961	8.868	8.780	6.667-
46	9.192-	9.079-	8.972-	8.871-	8.775	8.685-	8.599	6.522-
47	9.000	8.890	8.786	8.688-	8.595-	8.507-	8.423	6.383-
48	8.814	8.707	8.606-	8.510	8.420-	8.334-	8.253-	6.250
49	8.633	8.529	8.431-	8.337	8.249	8.166	8.087-	6.122
50	8.457	8.356-	8.260	8.170-	8.084-	8.003-	7.926-	6.000
51	8.286	8.187	8.094	8.006	7.923-	7.844	7.769	5.882
52	8.119	8.023	7.933-	7.847	7.766	7.689	7.617-	5.769
53	7.956	7.863	7.775	7.692	7.614-	7.539-	7.468	5.660
54	7.798-	7.707	7.622-	7.541	7.465-	7.392	7.323	5.556-
55	7.643-	7.555-	7.472	7.394-	7.319	7.249	7.182	5.455-
56	7.492-	7.406	7.326-	7.250-	7.178-	7.110-	7.045-	5.357
57	7.344-	7.261	7.183	7.109	7.039	6.973	6.910	5.263
58	7.199	7.119	7.044-	6.972	6.904	6.840	6.779	5.172
59	7.058	6.981-	6.907	6.838-	6.772	6.710	6.651-	5.085-
60	6.920	6.845-	6.774-	6.707-	6.643	6.583-	6.526-	5.000
61	6.785-	6.712	6.643	6.578	6.517-	6.458	6.403	4.918
62	6.653-	6.582	6.516-	6.453-	6.393	6.337-	6.283	4.839-
63	6.523	6.455-	6.391-	6.330-	6.272	6.218-	6.166-	4.762-
64	6.396	6.330	6.268	6.209	6.154-	6.101-	6.051-	4.688-
65	6.272-	6.208	6.148	6.091	6.038-	5.987-	5.938	4.615
65½	6.210	6.148-	6.089-	6.033	5.980	5.930	5.883-	4.580
66	6.149	6.088	6.030	5.976-	5.924-	5.875-	5.828-	4.545
66½	6.089	6.029	5.972	5.919-	5.868-	5.819	5.773	4.511
67	6.030-	5.971-	5.915-	5.862	5.812	5.765-	5.720-	4.478-
67½	5.971-	5.913-	5.858	5.806	5.757	5.711-	5.666	4.444
68	5.912	5.855	5.802-	5.751-	5.703-	5.657-	5.613	4.412-
68½	5.854	5.799-	5.746-	5.696-	5.649-	5.604-	5.561	4.380-
69	5.797-	5.742	5.691-	5.642-	5.595	5.551	5.509	4.348-
69½	5.740	5.686	5.636-	5.588-	5.542	5.499	5.458	4.317-
70	5.684-	5.631	5.581	5.534	5.490-	5.447	5.407	4.286-
70½	5.628-	5.576	5.528-	5.482-	5.438-	5.396	5.357-	4.255
71	5.573-	5.522	5.474	5.429	5.386	5.346-	5.307	4.225
71½	5.518-	5.468	5.421	5.377	5.335	5.295	5.258-	4.196-
72	5.463	5.415-	5.369	5.326-	5.285-	5.246-	5.209-	4.167-
72½	5.409	5.362	5.317	5.275-	5.234	5.196	5.160	4.138-
73	5.356	5.310-	5.266-	5.224	5.185-	5.147	5.112-	4.110-
73½	5.303	5.258-	5.215-	5.174	5.135	5.099-	5.064	4.082-
74	5.251-	5.206	5.164	5.124	5.087-	5.051-	5.017-	4.054
74½	5.198	5.155-	5.114-	5.075	5.038	5.003	4.970	4.027-
75	5.147-	5.104	5.064	5.026	4.990	4.956-	4.923	4.000
75½	5.096-	5.054	5.015-	4.978-	4.943-	4.909	4.877	3.974-
76	5.045-	5.004	4.966-	4.930-	4.895	4.863-	4.832-	3.947
76½	4.994	4.955-	4.917	4.882	4.848	4.817-	4.786	3.922-
77	4.944	4.906-	4.869	4.835-	4.802	4.771-	4.741	3.896
77½	4.895-	4.857	4.822-	4.788-	4.756-	4.726-	4.697-	3.871-
78	4.846-	4.809-	4.774	4.741	4.710	4.681-	4.653-	3.846
78½	4.797-	4.761	4.727	4.695	4.665-	4.636	4.609-	3.822-
79	4.748	4.714-	4.681-	4.650-	4.620	4.592	4.565	3.797
79½	4.700	4.667-	4.635-	4.604	4.575	4.548	4.522	3.774-
80	4.653-	4.620-	4.589-	4.559	4.531	4.505-	4.479	3.750
80½	4.605	4.573	4.543	4.514	4.487	4.461	4.437-	3.727-
81	4.559-	4.527	4.498-	4.470	4.444-	4.419-	4.395-	3.704-
81½	4.512-	4.482-	4.453	4.426	4.401-	4.376	4.353	3.681-
82	4.466-	4.436	4.409-	4.382	4.358-	4.334	4.312-	3.659-
82½	4.420-	4.391	4.365-	4.339	4.315	4.292	4.270	3.636
83	4.374	4.347-	4.321-	4.296	4.273-	4.251-	4.230-	3.614
83½	4.329	4.303-	4.277	4.254-	4.231-	4.209	4.189	3.593-
84	4.284	4.259-	4.234	4.211	4.189	4.169-	4.149-	3.571
84½	4.240-	4.215-	4.191	4.169	4.148-	4.128-	4.109-	3.550
85	4.196-	4.172-	4.149-	4.127	4.107-	4.088-	4.069	3.529

Yields in per cent per annum,
correct to the nearest five ten-thousandths of one per cent,
interest payable semi-annually.

3%
B O N D

Price	18 Years	18½ Years	19 Years	19½ Years	20 Years	20½ Years	21 Years	Current Income
85	4.196-	4.172-	4.149-	4.127	4.107-	4.088-	4.069	3.529
85½	4.152-	4.129-	4.107-	4.086-	4.066	4.048-	4.030-	3.509-
86	4.108	4.086-	4.065-	4.045-	4.026-	4.008-	3.991-	3.488
86½	4.065-	4.043	4.023	4.004-	3.986-	3.969-	3.952	3.468
87	4.022-	4.001	3.982-	3.963	3.946-	3.929	3.914-	3.448
87½	3.979	3.959	3.941-	3.923	3.906	3.891-	3.875	3.429-
88	3.937-	3.918-	3.900	3.883	3.867	3.852-	3.837	3.409
88½	3.895-	3.877-	3.860-	3.843	3.828	3.814-	3.800-	3.390-
89	3.853-	3.836-	3.819	3.804	3.789	3.776-	3.762	3.371-
89½	3.811	3.795	3.780-	3.765-	3.751	3.738-	3.725	3.352-
90	3.770	3.755-	3.740-	3.726	3.713-	3.700	3.688	3.333
90½	3.729	3.715-	3.701-	3.687	3.675-	3.663	3.652-	3.315-
91	3.689-	3.675-	3.662-	3.649	3.637	3.626	3.615	3.297-
91½	3.648	3.635	3.623-	3.611-	3.600-	3.589	3.579	3.279-
92	3.608	3.596-	3.584	3.573	3.563-	3.553-	3.543	3.261-
92½	3.568	3.557-	3.546-	3.536-	3.526-	3.517-	3.508-	3.243
93	3.529-	3.518-	3.508-	3.498	3.489	3.480	3.472	3.226-
93½	3.489	3.479	3.470	3.461	3.453-	3.445-	3.437	3.209-
94	3.450	3.441	3.432	3.424	3.417-	3.409	3.402	3.191
94½	3.411	3.403	3.395	3.388-	3.381-	3.374-	3.367	3.175-
95	3.373-	3.365	3.358	3.351	3.345-	3.339-	3.333-	3.158-
95½	3.335-	3.328-	3.321	3.315	3.309	3.304-	3.299-	3.141
96	3.296-	3.290	3.285-	3.279	3.274	3.269	3.265-	3.125
96½	3.259-	3.253	3.248	3.244-	3.239	3.235-	3.231-	3.109-
97	3.221-	3.216	3.212	3.208	3.204	3.201-	3.197	3.093-
97½	3.184-	3.180-	3.176	3.173-	3.170-	3.167-	3.164-	3.077-
98	3.146	3.143	3.141-	3.138-	3.135	3.133-	3.131-	3.061
98½	3.109	3.107	3.105	3.103	3.101	3.099	3.098-	3.046-
99	3.073-	3.071	3.070-	3.069-	3.067	3.066	3.065-	3.030
99½	3.036	3.036-	3.035-	3.034	3.034-	3.033-	3.032	3.015
100	3.000	3.000	3.000	3.000	3.000	3.000	3.000	3.000
100½	2.964-	2.965-	2.965	2.966	2.967-	2.967	2.968-	2.985
101	2.928	2.930-	2.931-	2.932	2.934-	2.935-	2.936-	2.970
101½	2.893-	2.895-	2.897-	2.899-	2.901-	2.902	2.904	2.956-
102	2.857	2.860	2.863-	2.865	2.868-	2.870	2.873-	2.941
102½	2.822-	2.826-	2.829-	2.832	2.835	2.838	2.841	2.927-
103	2.787-	2.791	2.795	2.799	2.803	2.807-	2.810-	2.913-
103½	2.752	2.757	2.762	2.767-	2.771-	2.775-	2.779-	2.899-
104	2.718-	2.723	2.729-	2.734-	2.739-	2.744-	2.748	2.885-
104½	2.683	2.690-	2.696-	2.702-	2.707	2.712	2.717	2.871-
105	2.649-	2.656	2.663-	2.669	2.676-	2.681	2.687-	2.857
106	2.581	2.590-	2.598-	2.606-	2.613-	2.620-	2.626	2.830
107	2.514	2.524	2.534-	2.542	2.551-	2.559	2.567-	2.804-
108	2.448-	2.459	2.470-	2.480	2.490-	2.499-	2.508-	2.778-
109	2.382	2.395-	2.407-	2.418	2.429	2.439	2.449	2.752
110	2.317	2.331	2.345-	2.357	2.369	2.381-	2.391	2.727
111	2.253	2.269-	2.283	2.297-	2.310	2.323-	2.334	2.703-
112	2.190-	2.206	2.222	2.237	2.251	2.265	2.278-	2.679-
113	2.127-	2.145-	2.162	2.178	2.194-	2.208	2.222-	2.655-
114	2.065-	2.084	2.102	2.120-	2.136	2.152-	2.167-	2.632-
115	2.003	2.024-	2.043	2.062-	2.079	2.096	2.112-	2.609-
116	1.942	1.964	1.985	2.005-	2.023	2.041-	2.058-	2.586
117	1.882	1.905	1.927	1.948-	1.968-	1.986	2.004	2.564
118	1.823-	1.847-	1.870	1.892-	1.913-	1.932	1.951	2.542
119	1.763	1.789	1.813	1.836	1.858	1.879-	1.899-	2.521
120	1.705-	1.732-	1.757	1.781	1.804	1.826	1.847-	2.500
121	1.647	1.675	1.702-	1.727-	1.751-	1.774-	1.795	2.479
122	1.590	1.619	1.647-	1.673	1.698	1.722-	1.744	2.459
123	1.533-	1.563	1.592	1.620-	1.646-	1.670	1.694-	2.439
124	1.477-	1.508	1.538	1.567-	1.594-	1.620-	1.644-	2.419
125	1.421	1.454-	1.485	1.515-	1.543-	1.569	1.594	2.400

$1,035 (103½) to yield 3.75 per cent. The Rollins table shows 103.50 appearing in the 4 per cent column opposite the 3.75 per cent yield; 4 per cent is therefore the coupon rate.

The Johnson tables. The more recently published Johnson tables differ from the older Rollins and Sprague tables. The older tables give a greater number of varying prices and relatively few yields, thus requiring almost constant interpolation to determine the exact yield. Prorating is necessary in all cases where the yield is not in exact eighths or tenths. The Johnson tables give a greater number of varying yields and relatively few prices. But the prices that are shown in the Johnson tables are those at which bonds are usually quoted, such as 96½, whereas the prices in the older tables, such as 96.57, seldom conform exactly with bond quotations, which are always in eighths.

Specimen pages are shown on pages 144 and 145, which cover maturities from 18 to 21 years on a 3 per cent bond. If the yield is desired on such a bond, due in 20 years, with the market price at 102, reference to the table shows the yield to be 2.868 per cent. The negative sign indicates that the exact yield is less than 2.868 per cent but more than 2.8675 per cent.

Interpolation is simpler with the Johnson tables. If the exact price is not given, the nearest price is usually close and at a distance of a readily workable fraction, such as one-quarter. In the preceding illustration, had the market price been 91¼, inspection would show that 91¼ is halfway between the stated prices of 91 and 91½, with respective yields of 3.637 per cent and 3.600 per cent. One half of the difference in the yields (0.037 per cent) is 0.0185 per cent, which, added to 3.600 per cent, gives 3.6185 per cent as the required yield.

Conversion parities. The calculation of the equivalent values of convertible bonds in terms of the stocks into which they are exchangeable requires knowledge of the established conversion ratio and the prevailing market prices of both the bonds and the stocks in question. The conversion ratio is usually expressed in terms of an arbitrary value placed upon the stock. If the conversion price is set at $50 (as in the case of Phelps-Dodge 3½'s of 1952), a $1,000 bond may be converted into as many shares of stock as $50 is contained into $1,000, or 20 shares.

To compute the conversion parity of the bond, the market price of the bond (not the cost price or the face value) is divided by the number of shares obtainable in exchange. In the case of a bond with a conversion value of $50 per share and a current market price of 112, the conversion parity would be a value of $56 per share for the stock. ($1,120 ÷ 20 shares = $56). The conversion value of the bond would be determined by multiplying the number of shares obtainable by the prevailing market price per share. A bond convertible at $50 per share has a conversion value of $800 when the stock is selling at $40 per share ($1,000 ÷ $50 = 20 × $40 = $800).

Bonds rarely, if ever, sell below their conversion values, owing to the higher value thus obtainable. The conversion feature on a bond favorably affects the market price even though the conversion price may be considerably higher than the market price. At the end of 1940, certain bonds of the Great Northern Railway (Series G 4's of 1946) which were convertible into stock at $40 a share were quoted around 105, whereas almost identical bonds of the same company (Series H 4's of 1946) which were convertible at $75 a share were quoted around 98, although the stock was then selling around $28 a share, which was substantially below either of the conversion prices. Some years ago, the Pennsylvania Railroad 3¼'s of 1952, convertible at $50 a share, sold at 109 (despite a conversion value of 80 indicated by the prevailing price of $40 on the stock) at a time when other issues of the company bearing a higher interest rate sold several points lower.

Subscription rights. When new stock is issued by a corporation, it is customary to offer the shares to old stockholders at a price below the prevailing market price for the old shares. The value of this privilege is calculated in terms of each old share outstanding expressed as one "right." The issuance of these rights is usually announced in advance of a certain "record date." All stockholders of record on that date are entitled to participate in the new issue.　The market price of the "old" stock includes the right to participate in the new offering until the record date and is therefore said to be "cum rights."　Because the market price of the old stock after the record date does not include the right to participate in the new offering, it has proportionately less value and is said to be "ex rights."　As the market price of the old stock is the chief determining factor in the value of the rights, a slightly different method of calculation is required before the record date than thereafter.

The value of a right as determined *before* the record date is calculated by dividing the difference between the prevailing market price for the old stock and the subscription price for the new stock by *one more* than the number of old shares required for a subscription to one new share.　To illustrate: If new stock is being offered to old stockholders in the ratio of one new share for four old shares at $30 a share, the value of one right, as calculated before the record date with the old stock selling at $40 a share, would be $2 ($40 — $30 = $10 ÷ 5 = $2).

The value of a right as determined *after* the record date is calculated by dividing the difference between the prevailing market price for the old stock and the subscription price for the new stock by the *exact* number of old shares required for a subscription to one new share.　To illustrate:　If new stock is being offered to old stockholders in the ratio of one new share for six old shares at $20 a share, the value of one right, as calculated after the record date with the old stock selling at $29 a share, would be $1.50 ($29 — $20 = $9 ÷ 6 = $1.50).

In the event that any dividends are payable prior to the expiration date of the rights, the market price of the old stock must be reduced by the amount of the dividend payment before calculating the value of the rights, inasmuch as the new stock will not be entitled to the dividend payment.

Rights are received by stockholders in the form of negotiable stock purchase option warrants which must be exercised on or before a specified expiration date.　As each warrant is an option to buy one new share, a stockholder owning 100 shares of old stock would receive 100 *rights* in the form of 20 *warrants* if the rate of increase is 20 per cent. Market quotations are made in terms of rights and not in terms of warrants. In the case just mentioned, five rights would be required for the purchase of one share of new stock at the subscription price.

Stock purchase option warrants. Certain companies have followed the practice of issuing long-term option warrants for the purchase of their common stocks at prices specified in the instrument, usually considerably above the market value at the time of issue. These warrants have no mathematical value so long as the market price remains below the option price; they do, however, have a practical value in that they provide a "call" on the stock over a long period. Warrants issued by the Colorado Fuel and Iron Corporation in 1936 give the holder the privilege of buying common stock at the price of $35 per share until February 1, 1950. In 1940, these warrants had a market value of $5 each despite the fact that the market value of the stock was only $21 per share. In 1937, the market value of the warrants was nearly $25, or nearly $8 higher than the indicated mathematical value of $17 suggested by the prevailing price of $52 on the stock. The value of these warrants is determined, not by any mathematical formula, but by the opinion of speculators as to the future value of the stock into which they may be converted.

10

PROTECTION IN PURCHASING

Scope. The purpose of this chapter is to discuss the protective measures which operate to assist the investor in the selection of securities. The order of discussion is: (1) Federal Securities Act, (2) work of the Securities and Exchange Commission, (3) state blue-sky laws, (4) private safeguards, (5) corporate promotions, (6) investment timing, (7) trend of interest rates, and (8) importance of quality. The intelligent investor realizes that his greatest protection against loss is his own capacity to judge the securities which should be bought and the time at which they should be sold.

Public and private protection. The selection of sound investments requires the exercise of care and prudence. Thousands of securities of varying quality are available to the investor, who necessarily must choose but a few out of a great many. Certain issues that may be suitable for one person are inadvisable for others. Many securities, honestly issued, represent the obligations of new companies that have not established definite earning power. The statement is probably true that, for every sound investment security, there are several unsound issues the purchase of which would almost certainly result in loss.

Legislation purposed to prevent losses arising from poor investments has proved of limited value because it is based upon the eradication of fraudulent practices and not upon investment merit. Consequently, each investor must erect his own safeguards, fashioned to meet his individual requirements, and thus supplement the limited degree of public protection which the law provides with the more rigid specifications of private protection, which the investor sets up for himself.

The scope of the present chapter is to differentiate between sound and unsound investments rather than to discuss intervening gradations. The measurement of the precise amount of quality in any separate security involves a thorough analysis of many influencing factors. The differentiation, however, between securities that are probably good and those that are probably poor seldom requires more than the employment of common-sense principles. It seems amazingly illogical that funds which are carefully accumulated as a result of wise personal policies are so often invested with almost complete disregard of the ordinary precautions which a simple consideration of safety plainly demands. The dividing line between good and poor securities is too easily ascertainable to warrant ignorance on the part of any investor.

Good securities are not always profitable, and bad securities are not invariably unprofitable to investors. Time brings many things and may occasionally show declines in good securities and advances in poor securities. In the great majority of cases, however, the purchase of sound issues is profitable and the purchase of unsound securities is fraught with grave danger.

Federal Securities Act. Legislation designed to protect the public in the purchase of investments made a decided advance in the passage of the Securities Act of 1933. So far-reaching are the provisions of this law that it is not an exaggeration to state that it represented the passing of an old order and the beginning of a new epoch in the business of security marketing. As aptly remarked by President Roosevelt in recommending such legislation, the old slogan of "Let the buyer beware" has been amended to "Let the seller also beware." No longer may "hedge clauses" be inserted in security circulars for the purpose of releasing the investment house from any responsibility for the accuracy of information given. The obligation of telling the whole truth in connection with new security offerings has been placed upon the issuing corporation and the distributing investment house.

The Federal Securities Act does not automatically eliminate state security commissions and blue-sky laws, or interfere in the security-approval functions of the Interstate Commerce Commission· or the state public service commissions explained elsewhere in this volume. The Federal law aims to supplement existing state laws which have not proved sufficiently rigorous in preventing severe losses to the investing public.

The purpose of this discussion is to indicate the nature of the protection afforded in the new law rather than to summarize the provisions of the entire Act. In general, the law requires that specific information on new security offerings be filed with the Securities and Exchange Commission prior to the sale of such issues to the public and that the issuers of the securities be held responsible for the completeness and accuracy of such information. Certain classes of securities and kinds of transactions are exempted.

Exempt securities. Certain classes of domestic securities are exempted from the provisions of the Securities Act. The list of such issues is here shown:

(1) United States Government obligations;

(2) Territorial bonds;

(3) Federal instrumentalities, such as Federal Land Bank bonds;

(4) State bonds;

(5) Municipal bonds;

(6) Railroad securities;

(7) Receiver's certificates;

(8) Certain issues aggregating less than $100,000, at the option of the Commission.

(9) Securities of Savings and Loan Associations.

Exempt transactions. Certain kinds of transactions are exempted from the Securities Act, as shown on the next page.

(1) Transactions in new issues, not through an underwriter and not involving a public offering;

(2) Brokerage transactions, executed upon unsolicited customers' orders;

(3) Exchanges of securities in recapitalizations and reorganization plans.

Registration statement. Before new securities may be offered to the public, a registration statement which becomes effective 20 days later, or earlier as the Commission may determine, must be filed with the Commission. This statement must be signed by designated officials of the company, and copies must be made available to the public. The Commission has the right to serve a stop notice in any case where it appears that the statement is incomplete or inaccurate in any material respect. The law requires that the registration statement give specific information on no less than 32 designated points, among which are the following:

(1) Purpose of issue;

(2) Price at which offered to the public;

(3) Price at which offered to any special group;

(4) Disclosure of any purchase option agreements;

(5) Promotion fees;

(6) Underwriting profit;

(7) Net proceeds to the company;

(8) Remuneration of any officers receiving over $25,000 annually;

(9) Disclosure of any unusual contracts such as managerial profit-sharing;

(10) Detailed capitalization statement;

(11) Detailed balance sheet;

(12) Detailed earnings statement for three preceding years;

(13) Names and addresses of officers, directors, and underwriters;

(14) Names and addresses of stockholders owning more than 10 per cent of any class of stock;

(15) Copy of underwriting agreement;

(16) Copy of legal opinions;

(17) Copy of articles of incorporation or association;

(18) Copies of indentures affecting new issues.

A separate group of 14 requirements is provided in connection with new issues of foreign governments and subdivisions. The requirements include the following:

(a) Purpose of issue;

(b) Complete debt statement;

(c) Default record for 20 preceding years;

(d) Revenues and expenditures for 3 preceding years;

(e) Net proceeds from securities sold in United States;

(f) Price to the public;

(g) Cost of distribution (underwriting fees);

(h) Copy of legal opinions;

(i) Copy of underwriting agreement.

The prospectus. The term *prospectus* is applied to any notice, circular, advertisement, or letter, written or broadcast, which offers a security for sale. The information contained in the prospectus must coincide with that in the registration statement, with the omission of certain technical features, as stated in the law and as determined by the Commission.

Civil liability. In the event that the registration statement contains any untrue statement of a material fact or omits any material fact, any purchaser unaware at the time of purchase of such situation may take legal action for recovery of loss against the persons mentioned in the statement as officers or directors of the company, as professional advisers, or as underwriters. Such persons, to escape liability, must prove that they had no reasonable ground for the belief that the information was incomplete or inaccurate. Since the standard of reasonableness in this respect is "that required of a prudent man in the management of his own property," it follows that investors are in a much stronger position than ever before to recover damages in a suit involving misrepresentation of new issues of securities.

Financial statements. In connection with the balance sheets and earnings statements required in the registration statement, the Federal Comission is empowered to prescribe the forms in which the information is to be submitted, the items to be shown, and the methods to be followed in the preparation of accounts in the appraisal of assets and liabilities, in the determination of depreciation and depletion, and in the differentiation between charges to capital account and to operating expense.

Speculative securities. The purpose of the Securities Act is not to prevent the sale of speculative issues, but rather to stop the sale of fraudulent securities. The main objective is to place before the investor all the facts necessary for intelligent judgment of the merits of the issue. Investors must rely upon their own opinions in arriving at a decision to purchase. The position of the Federal Commission in this important respect has been officially stated as follows:

The public should thoroughly understand that the commission is not authorized to pass in any sense upon the value or soundness of any security. Its sole function is to see that full and accurate information as to the security is made available to purchasers and the public, and that no fraud is practiced in connection with the sale of the security.

Speculative securities may still be offered and the public is as free to buy them as ever.

The commission's duty is to see that the security is truthfully presented to prospective purchasers. The fact that a description of the security and of the concern issuing the security is filed with the commission is in no sense and must not be regarded as an endorsement or approval of the security or the concern by the commission.

State blue-sky laws. With a few important exceptions (New York, New Jersey, Delaware, and Maryland) practically all states now have in effect legislation, popularly termed "blue-sky laws," to prevent the sale of fraudulent securities. In no state, however, are the requirements for the approval of new security issues so severe as those stated in the Federal Securities Act. In many instances, the requirements are met in a perfunctory manner through the filing of a questionnaire which is not subjected to a searching scrutiny. Consequently, numerous examples of the sale of securities of doubtful merit are to be found, despite the approval of state commissions.[1]   The primary cause of the enactment of the Federal Securities law in 1933 was the failure of the state securities laws to function effectively.

The regulatory powers of the Interstate Commerce Commission with respect to the issuance of railroad securities, and of the state public service commissions with regard to the issuance of certain public utility securities, as discussed in later chapters, are excellent illustrations of preventive legislation that has worked out admirably.   The fact that such approvals are not to be interpreted as investment recommendations does not contradict the fact that careful scrutiny generally precedes formal approval.[2]

Personal protection.   Public and private agencies can offer only a limited amount of protection to the individual investor. To a major extent, he must rely upon his personal judgment in the choice of his securities.   Unfortunately, investment clinics are not available to the man of limited means.   The cost of expert investment advice is prohibitive to all but wealthy investors.   Thus the problem of the man with limited means is not only to avoid securities that are outright speculations, but also to evade issues that contain a risk greater than he is in a position to assume.   To the latter problem, the book as a whole is directed; to the former, the ensuing discussion is devoted.

The purchase of poor securities may usually be attributed to either ignorance or avarice.   Ignorance, in this respect, connotes more than simply lack of knowledge, since it also implies unwarranted reliance upon the judgment of others. It is manifestly unfair and unreasonable to expect an impartial opinion on the quality of an investment from an interested

---

[1] A noteworthy illustration was the promotion of an automobile company in the Middle West some years ago. The sale of stock in this company was approved by the commissions of several states, yet resulted in the loss of about $10,000,000 to 75,000 purchasers of the stock over a period of twelve months, before the license was revoked.

[2] It is interesting to note that in New York State, which has no blue-sky law, new security offerings must be publicly advertised. The Attorney General's office, as a matter of policy, investigates all such offerings and often prevents losses, through court injunctions, before formal complaints are made.

source. To cite an extreme case, an American opinion that United States Government bonds are the safest investment in the world would scarcely prove the point. United Kingdom Government bonds are sold to British investors on precisely the same argument.

Avarice is a more understandable human weakness. The desire for wealth, which is apparently congenital with the great majority of persons, is seldom lessened by the realization that the acquisition is denied to all but a very few. The fact that, in rare instances, a small investment has returned a magnificent reward is enough to spur the gambling instinct in the average man, who appreciates that only a lucky chance can bring him fortune. Modern writers are inclined to make some concession to human frailty in this respect, provided it is not carried too far. This point has been admirably brought out by a British economist:

> But the gambling instinct is human, normal, unescapable. We all want something for nothing; still more, we want to import into our lives a little excitement, a little colour. What you want is something exciting and terrific, shares in diamond mines, in turtle fisheries, or even in collapsible flats—upon which you have put, not your shirt, but let us say a collar-band. Most likely, you will lose your money, but it will keep you quiet while you invest the rest sanely.[3]

The earmarks of a poor security are numerous and readily ascertainable. In many instances, several appear in connection with a single offering. While it is true that some of these methods are employed at times in the distribution of acceptable securities, the presence of any of them should put the prospective investor on his guard. Good investments will stand close inspection; poor investments will not. The more prevalent practices in this regard may be grouped as follows:

(A) With respect to safety:

1. *The promise of absolute safety.* Such a promise is obviously false, since even the best securities are only relatively safe.

---

[3] George, W. L., *How to Invest Your Money*, p. 14.

2. *The irresponsible guarantee.* The value of any guarantee depends primarily upon the responsibility of the guarantor.

(B) With respect to income:

3. *The promise of large yields.* As yield varies directly with risk, the possibility of securing a large yield requires the assumption of a high degree of risk endangering the entire commitment. Good investment securities rarely can be obtained at a yield exceeding 5 per cent per annum.

4. *Comparative figures.* Figures showing profits derived by investors in other companies do not ensure similar fortune in the new enterprise.

(C) With respect to profit:

5. *The promise of big profits.* The human but unreasonable desire to "get rich quick" leads many persons to assume large risk in an endeavor to gain sudden wealth.

6. *The artificial market.* The market price quoted on new securities is usually arbitrarily controlled by the distributors until the issue is sold. The purchaser may later find a very poor market if he cares to sell.

7. *The fictitious advance.* Statements on the part of distributors to the effect that the price will advance on a certain date clearly indicate the existence of an artificial market.

8. *The ground-floor analogy.* Statements to the effect that the investor is being offered securities on the same terms as the promoters should be open to suspicion.

9. *The inference of confidential information.* Statements to the effect that the distributor has "inside information" are difficult to verify and are seldom authentic.

(D) With respect to purpose:

10. *Oil promotions.* Spectacular profits from oil investments realized in past years by prominent men have encouraged many small investors to try to share in these earnings. With many large, established companies unable to show satisfactory earnings, the chances of a new oil company are not overbright.

11. *Mining fallacies.* The peculiar belief that mineral products are the free gift of nature combines with the atmos-

phere of mystery which surrounds mining operations to make mining securities appeal to the credulous investor.

12. *Patent delusions.* The natural, almost fanatic, confidence that inventors have in their inventions leads them to underestimate the development costs and to overestimate probable earning power. Financing patent ideas is scarcely investing.

13. *Popular industries.* New industries that gain wide publicity in the current periodicals are usually made the basis for security promotions. In recent years, television, natural gas, radio, and aviation have been conspicuous examples.

(E) With respect to method:

14. *The telephone canvass.* Although a large amount of legitimate security selling is transacted over the telephone, such practice is advisable only when both parties are personally acquainted. Telephone solicitation by strangers is especially objectionable in the investment field.

15. *The limited offer.* Statements to the effect that only a limited number of selected persons will be allowed to subscribe, or that a limited number of shares can be purchased, or that the offer is open for a limited time, should be liberally discounted.

16. *The appeal to prejudice.* Statements critical of Wall Street, of savings banks, of low yields on other securities, and of public exploitation tend to conceal the weakness of the proposed security by diverting attention on a prejudicial basis.

17. *High-pressure selling.* Attempts on the part of distributors to force a quick, favorable decision on the part of the investor should be effectively resented. Conservative investment is based on prudence and caution.

18. *The statement of opinion.* A willingness to state many opinions but few facts is an outstanding characteristic of the fraudulent appeal. Investors should not invest without an adequate knowledge of the facts in the case.

19. *The partial payment plan.* The suggestion that

installment payments will be acceptable if full payment is inconvenient is not customarily made by legitimate investment dealers.

20. *The use of prominent names.* Numerous examples might be cited where the names of prominent men have been used in security promotions, either without authorization or under false pretenses. From the investor's viewpoint, the security should stand on its own merits.

The development stage. It is axiomatic that the securities of companies in the development stage do not deserve investment consideration. Only those persons who are able and willing to assume large risk of loss should place their funds in such enterprises. Admittedly, the rewards obtainable from an early commitment in a successful undertaking greatly exceed those that come to investors who wait until earning power has been clearly demonstrated. The financing of new enterprises is a worthy and necessary function for people who are in a position to assume risk, but scarcely the duty of investors who should primarily seek safety.

A careful study was made in 1930 of 58 companies formed in Great Britain in 1928 for the purpose of establishing new businesses. The survey showed that only one of the 58 companies had paid a dividend, whereas 14 were in compulsory liquidation, 13 in voluntary liquidation, and at least 16 of the remaining companies were in serious difficulties. It was estimated that 95 per cent of the capital invested (about $75,000,000) in these 58 companies was lost. [4]

American investment experience with companies in the development stage has been no more favorable than the British record. The chance of success is so slight as to make the average commitment in such companies a pure gamble and certainly not an investment. The automobile industry has had a most spectacular and successful development in the United States; yet, less than 40 cars were still being produced in 1940 out of nearly 1,000 placed on the market since

---

[4] Address by Henry Morgan, President of the Society of Incorporated Accountants and Auditors, at the Conference of the Society in 1930.

1895. Over 96 per cent of the cars placed on the market proved commercial failures. [5]

The problem which the investor faces in the selection of particular industries involves the avoidance of "overage" as well as "underage" companies. The fact that industries have life cycles through sequential stages of experimentation, development, saturation, and decline is not fully appreciated by investors. The biological analogy has been admirably stated by an outstanding financial economist in the following quotation: [6]

Industries and corporations have their birth and youth. They suffer from the crudities and struggles incident to rapid growth and economic adjustment. Capital is difficult to obtain from the outside, but what is invested in a youthful industry or youthful corporation—through confidence in the future rather than results of the past—yields large returns. But such an investment to be more than a mere gamble must be made with a broad knowledge of the risks involved and a prophetic knowledge of economic values. Such investments are never recommended by the trustee-lawyer or the country banker. Following the period of youth, industries and corporations have their stage or epoch of maturity. They become acknowledged. They compete on a reasonable basis with other established industries and established corporations for banking credit and investment funds. Consequently the returns on capital invested in such industries or such corporations yield a fair rate of interest with a reasonable, though not excessive compensation for risk. Were it possible to forecast the length of time, which varies greatly, that an industry or corporation will remain in this maturity

---

[5] Estimates of the prospective earning power of new enterprises are notoriously optimistic to an extreme degree. Prior to the construction of the Detroit International Bridge, an engineering firm of national reputation prepared estimates of the prospective revenues, which compared with actual receipts as here shown:

Year	Estimated	Actual	Per Cent
1931	$2,295,000	$506,000	22.1%
1932	2,622,000	321,000	12.3
1933	2,944,000	246,000	8.5
1934	3,265,000	232,000	7.0
1935	3,597,000	247,000	6.8
1936	3,921,000	302,000	7.7
1937	4,248,000	366,000	8.6
1938	4,573,000	328,000	7.1

[6] From article by Arthur S. Dewing, in *Harvard Business Review*, July, 1923.

stage, investment of capital here would be sound and relatively permanent, neither increasing nor decreasing so long as the industry or corporation remained in this "balanced" condition. And then finally there is the old-age stage. The industry, and particularly the corporation, lives on, buoyed up for a considerable time by its past accomplishments. If we are considering a corporation in the old-age stage, it will show large capital assets, large bookkeeping surplus, but relatively low current earnings. Nevertheless, its stock will be eagerly bought by the lawyer-trustee because of its long dividend record. Those who by training and cast of mind are wont to forecast the future entirely by the weight of accumulated precedent will regard the old-age industry or corporation, even on the brink of final dissolution, as thoroughly sound, eminently "conservative." At the final break of the New Haven bubble, its stock was held by upwards of 7,000 trustees, a large proportion of them lawyers, extremely conservative in their investment ideas.

The time factor. Experience of recent years has served to emphasize the importance of the time factor in the purchase of securities. Changes in business conditions definitely affect investment values, operating favorably at one time and adversely at another time. Irrespective of the quality in any security, there are times when its purchase would be inadvisable and other times when it might be most advantageous. The purchase of common stocks at a time of great business prosperity is dangerous, even though the particular issues may have excellent records. On the other hand, the purchase of high-grade bonds during a period of extreme business depression is not altogether sagacious, despite the natural desire for safety at such a time. The fact that large investors, such as the life insurance companies, are continuous buyers of securities, regardless of current conditions, should not unduly influence the private investor. Life insurance companies must keep their funds invested at all times and would quickly have an embarrassing accumulation of capital if they were to stop purchasing over a prolonged period. Moreover, this policy enables them automatically to average their costs over good and bad times. The theory that "the time to invest is when you have the money" appears to have originated with investment dealers rather than with investors.

The trend of business. The trend of business conditions traces an irregular line, now advancing, now receding. At times, the advances become so pronounced that they are apparent to everyone in the form of greater activity and increased earnings. At other times, the recessions become equally pronounced and are apparent in the form of unemployment and decreased earnings. As there is a natural tendency for periods of prosperity to be followed by periods of depression and vice versa, the successive stages are popularly termed *cyclical movements.* The term *business cycle,* however, has been too freely applied to such fluctuations in business activity, which rarely follow a curve of regular ascent or descent. The absence of uniformity in the extent and the duration of business movements may make economic forecasting a most difficult problem, but it should not prevent the achievement of an investment policy consonant with existing conditions.

In a period when business is recovering from an inactive stage, prices of bonds and stocks both advance, the increased earning power of business enhancing the safety position of bonds and improving the dividend prospects for stocks. In a period of business activity, bond prices decline somewhat, owing in part to the effect of higher interest rates and in part to the increased popularity of stocks; during this same period, stock prices continue to advance practically to the peak of the boom, reflecting continued increases in corporate earnings. In a period when business is declining, prices of stocks fall more rapidly than prices of bonds, owning chiefly to the realization that earning power was too liberally estimated in prosperous times. In a period of business depression, prices of bonds strengthen, because of the safety factor, whereas prices of stocks reach low levels. It might be observed that bond prices tend to move ahead of stock prices rather than conversely. In periods of prosperity, stock prices are high and bond prices are low; in periods of depression, bond prices are strong and stock prices weak.

Investment timing. The policy of the investor in these successive stages is not open to serious question. In periods of prosperity, he should adopt a cautious attitude toward stocks and a courageous attitude toward bonds; in periods of depression, he should reverse this policy. Obvious as such procedure would appear to be in the light of economic experience, it is admittedly unnatural from a psychological aspect. Stocks are popular when earnings are good, and unpopular when the reverse is true. Bonds are popular when earnings are poor, and unpopular when business prospers. The careful investor eventually learns that to act naturally in matters of investment policy is usually to act unintelligently. Psychology should be subordinated to logic and experience in this most important phase of investing. [7]

The strict observance of an investment policy synchronized with changes in business conditions is a matter of extreme difficulty, relatively simple though it may seem. In the first place, the investor must have the courage to act somewhat contrary to his natural inclinations. In the second place, he must have the capacity of intelligently interpreting the trend of business activity. In the third place, he must have the patience to await the opportune time to buy, as well as to sell. The ideal combination of the essential qualities of courage, capacity, and patience is found, unfortunately, in relatively few investors. Although courage and patience may be congenital, capacity is not, especially in the question of economic interpretation. [8]

---

[7] In a recent report issued by the Securities and Exchange Commission, this statement appeared: "To buy securities cheap is folly if they continue to grow cheaper." Such a statement seems both gratuitous and fallacious unless it is assumed that the decline is never to be recovered. The art of investing is largely that of buying when prices are relatively low. To postpone buying until the very lowest prices are reached is as fallacious as to postpone selling until the very highest prices are reached. Either attempt is almost certain to result in lost opportunity.

[8] The problem of investment timing presents many practical difficulties. Investment companies in England have found the problem no easier than have their American counterparts. A trust company formed in London in 1931 to buy and sell in accordance with the swings of the market suffered a loss of one half of its invested capital within two years. The four securities (Courtaulds, Kreuger & Toll, General Motors, and Woolworth) suggested by the prize winner in an investment contest in London in 1928 suffered an average depreciation of 80 per cent within the next four years. See *Work of the Stock Exchange* by S. Killek.

Business indexes. Investors of a decade ago were largely compelled to formulate their own opinions as to the state of business activity. The idea of an economic thermometer to show the current condition of general business was chiefly a theoretical concept prior to the First World War. During recent years, numerous indexes have been devised that are readily available to the general public. While it may be admitted freely that none of these indexes approaches the accuracy of a thermometer, as a result of refinement based upon experience, they do provide an approximate yardstick, adequate for the purpose of the investor.

The customary method of constructing a business index is to establish an estimated normal position, based upon an extensive analysis and projection of historical data. For this purpose, physical units rather than monetary values are employed to avoid distortion through changes in price levels. Data used include items such as pig-iron output, electric-power production, and freight-car loadings. The normal position is adjusted to a long-term trend to allow for the growth of the country, and is corrected for seasonal variation in different months of the year. The normal position is regarded as 100 (per cent). An index number of 96 would indicate 4 per cent below normal, just as 103 would indicate 3 per cent above normal. (The most popular of the business indexes is the monthly Federal Reserve production index, which has been previously discussed on page 121.)

Experience has shown that business is in a period of prosperity when the index is above 110 and in a period of depression when the index is below 90. Although the index number has rarely exceeded 115 in periods of prosperity, it has on several occasions gone below 85 in periods of depression. A low point of 75, however, marks a severe depression. When the index is substantially above the normal position, the investor should purchase bonds, since stocks reach dangerously high levels at such times. When the index is substantially below normal, stocks may be purchased with less risk of loss through depreciation. Bonds purchased at such times are likely to suffer price depreciation later, when business conditions improve and interest rates advance. [9]

The foregoing discussion is offered as a guide for the investor rather than as a basis for speculative operations. In all cases, it is assumed that the securities concerned, whether bonds or stocks, have intrinsic investment merit and are being purchased primarily for income. True as it is that the investor does not buy for appreciation, it is even more valid that he should avoid depreciation. The purchase of even the best securities at the wrong economic hour is almost certain to result in depreciation. It is the plain duty of the investor to avoid this loss insofar as he is able.

The trend of interest rates. Interest rates on loans vary according to the condition of the money market, the position of the borrower, and the duration of the loan. Interest rates on commercial loans for less than one year tend to vary with the business cycle, whereas interest rates on investment loans for upwards of 20 years are affected more by longer-term influences. Although the short-term commercial and the long-term investment interest rates are dependent upon the supply of loanable funds available in the market, and thus tend to move together, the investment rate is relatively more stable than the commercial rate which fluctuates over a wider area with changes in the business cycle. A notable example of this tendency was illustrated in 1929 when the interest rate on call loans—the shortest of all commercial loans—was over 10 per cent and the comparable rate on investment loans was around 4 per cent. A decade later in 1939, the interest rate on call loans was 1 per cent and the rate on long-term investments was around 3 per cent.

Interest rates on long-term investments follow secular trends which are separate from cyclical influences. The first 40 years of the present century provide an illustration. The prevailing rate of return on high-grade long-term bonds

---

[9] Weekly and monthly business indexes are now prepared and published by many periodicals of general circulation, as well as by the statistical services. Those available in the New York area include *The New York Times* (Sunday edition), *The New York Herald-Tribune* (Thursdays), *The Business Week,* and *Monthly Bulletin* of the Federal Reserve Bank of New York.

in 1900 was around 3 per cent with no indication of higher rates for years ahead.[10]   A decade later, the comparable yield had risen to 3.75 per cent and, in 1920, had advanced to 5.25 per cent, which marked the culmination of the long advance.   By 1930, the average rate had fallen to 4.30 per cent and, in 1940, had declined further to 2.60 per cent, or below the rate which had prevailed in 1900.

Experience has demonstrated the futility of attempting to predict the time of turning points in long-term interest rates.   If economic history is to prove a reliable criterion, however, the statement appears reasonably sound that such interest rates will not long continue above 5 per cent or under 3 per cent.   Although the next decade may prove otherwise, the record shows that interest rates on high-grade long-term bonds are about normal when they are between 3½ and 4 per cent.

Investors who purchase bonds near the end of a long decline in interest rates face an added hazard in prospective depreciation in market value when interest rates rise.   At times when interest rates are abnormally low, the purchase of relatively short-term bonds is more advisable than long-term issues.   The closer the maturity date of a bond is, the greater is its price stability.   A 4 per cent bond due in *ten years* is worth 108½ in a 3 per cent market and is worth 100 in a 4 per cent market; a rise in interest rates from 3 to 4 per cent would cause a decline of *eight per cent* in market value.   A 4 per cent bond, however, due in *twenty years* is worth 115 in a 3 per cent market and is worth 100 in a 4 per cent market; a rise in interest rates from 3 to 4 per cent would cause a decline of *thirteen per cent* in market value.   A similar 4 per cent bond due in *forty years* is worth 123¼ in a 3 per cent market and is worth 100 in a 4 per cent market; a rise in interest rates from 3 to 4 per cent would cause a decline of *nineteen per cent* in market value.

---

[10] A large life insurance company in New York asked 50 of the leading financiers of the country in 1900 if higher interest rates were likely to develop over the next 20 years. Every reply was to the effect that rates would remain the same or go lower. Not one reply predicted higher rates!

The natural desire on the part of investors to buy short-term bonds in periods of low interest rates so increases the demand for these issues as to result in higher market prices. In 1930 when interest rates were fairly close to normal, the rates of return obtainable from short-, medium-, and long-term bonds were about the same. In 1940, however, with interest rates abnormally low, a wide variation existed, as illustrated in prevailing yields of $\frac{1}{2}$ of 1 per cent on two-year bonds, $1\frac{1}{4}$ per cent on five-year bonds, $1\frac{3}{4}$ per cent on ten-year bonds, $2\frac{3}{8}$ per cent on twenty-year bonds, and $2\frac{5}{8}$ per cent on thirty-year bonds. In 1920, when interest rates were abnormally high, the comparable rates were in striking contrast, as shown in prevailing yields of $9\frac{1}{2}$ per cent on two-year bonds, $7\frac{1}{2}$ per cent on five-year bonds, 6 per cent on ten-year bonds, $5\frac{1}{2}$ per cent on twenty-year bonds, and $5\frac{1}{4}$ per cent on thirty-year bonds.

The importance of quality. The desire on the part of investors to obtain a favorable rate of return from their investments frequently results in the assumption of risk beyond a reasonable limit. Although a dividing line may be drawn between good and poor securities at that rate of return which is equal to twice the rate obtainable from long-term Federal Treasury bonds, it does not follow that all bonds within that category make acceptable investments for all buyers. The highest-grade issues afford the lowest yields because they are exceptionally well secured and have the greatest price stability. The lower-grade issues afford higher yields because they are less secure and are more subject to fluctuations in market value. In the drastic decline of the bond market between 1930 and 1932, a representative group of bonds declined about 30 per cent in total market value. The first-grade bonds declined only 10 per cent; the second-grade bonds declined about 25 per cent; the third-grade bonds declined about 40 per cent; and the lowest-grade bonds declined about 50 per cent. In view of the fact that the purchase of the lower-grade bonds in 1930 would have afforded rates of return only about 1 per cent higher than the higher-grade issues, the additional compensation was not commensurate with the greater hazard involved.

Although there is ground for debate on the question as to whether second-grade bonds should ever be regarded as attractive investments, there is little question but what they should be bought only by persons who can afford to assume a high degree of risk. It is an axiom of the investment business that the higher grade the securities are, the smaller will be the market depreciation. While it is true that high-grade bonds sometimes prove to be poor investments, seldom indeed do low-grade bonds prove to be good investments. On the whole, securities tend to lose quality over periods of time, thus emphasizing the great desirability of buying the better-grade issues.

Investment precautions. The investor who is realistically inclined and who is seeking a practical approach to the problem of selecting suitable securities might well observe certain precautions which are widely recognized in the professional field. The author is indebted to a well-known investment banker for permission to reprint the following suggestions to prospective investors:[11]

First of all, remember that corporations, and businesses in general, die easily and frequently—much more frequently than human beings. This suggests that our average investor should try to pick sturdy companies of good quality and reasonable life expectancy. No matter what stage of the business cycle one is in, no investment is "good enough to buy with your eyes shut."

Second, remember to be extra careful when everything begins to look good. No level of prices continues unchanged for long.

Third, remember that you are buying risks and not securities. Risk in varying degrees is present in all investments. The safest bond you can buy is still only gilt-edged insecurity.

Fourth, remember that governments break promises just as businesses do, and frequently for the same reasons. There is no such thing as absolute safety in investments.

Fifth, remember that no investments worth having are permanent. They should be watched all the time, and some responsible and impartial investment man or banker ought to be consulted at frequent intervals for news of your companies.

---

[11] By Robert A. Lovett, of Brown Bros. Harriman Co., in *The Saturday Evening Post,* April 3, 1937.

11

PROTECTION IN HOLDING

Scope. The purpose of this chapter is to discuss the protective measures which operate to assist the investor in the management of an investment fund. The order of discussion is: (1) investment hazards, (2) diversification theories, (3) diversification practices, (4) exchanging of securities, and (5) safeguarding of securities. A sound plan of diversification affords the most practical method of avoiding serious investment losses.

Investment management. The management of an investment fund necessitates a degree of care and prudence equal to, if not exceeding, that required in the purchase of securities. Conditions are always changing, with material influence upon investment values. Securities that appear in an impregnable position at the time of purchase may become highly speculative in the short space of a few years. Extraordinary events, such as wars, earthquakes, and climatic disturbances, may adversely affect security values overnight. To a major extent, these factors are uncontrollable and therefore unpredictable. Investment policy must be sufficiently flexible to permit ready adjustment to the unexpected. The experience of recent years has taught the invaluable lesson that a rigid investment policy is unwise procedure. No investment policy should assume that occasional losses are avoidable or that the intrinsic value of any security is not subject to change.   Investors have learned only too well what investment houses are reluctant to admit: that the element of risk is present in all securities.   Intelligent investors formulate investment policies which recognize this element of reasonable risk by taking advantage of certain practices which have been found helpful.

Our own responsibility in the premises can be neither evaded nor avoided.   Our first loyalty is to the public—and our enduring welfare depends on intelligent conception of our fiduciary relationship with the public.   We must constantly remind our clients that we live in a loss as well as a profit economy; that inherent in every investment is the element of risk.   To stress security and to say nothing about the risk is to lack frankness.   To speak about the possibility of gain and to be silent on the possibility of loss leaves half the story untold.[1]

While investment management comprehends the problem of selection as well as of supervision, it is with the latter phase that this discussion is concerned.   The proper supervision of an investment fund has three distinct aspects.   A plan of diversification should be adopted to secure proper distribution of the risks assured.   A plan of continuous scrutiny should be worked out to take advantage of favorable exchange opportunities.   A plan of safeguarding should be devised to protect the actual security instruments from loss caused by theft or otherwise.   The conservation of an investment fund is as dependent upon care in supervision as it is upon caution in selection.

The problem of diversification.   The advantages arising from diversification of risk are too obvious to necessitate elaboration.   As conditions change, governments rise and fall, corporations grow more and less prosperous, social and economic developments help some enterprises and harm others, personal fortunes advance and decline, and the tide of business activity surges and ebbs.   Progression in one economic trend is often concurrent with retrogression in another.   The convenient notion that the quality in a security is inherent and

---

[1] From general letter by Charles R. Gay, President of New York Stock Exchange, to all members and associates, January 15, 1937.

unchangeable has lulled innumerable investors into a false sense of security, as recent harsh awakenings amply testify. If security values were established primarily by the tangibility of physical assets, some price equilibrium might exist indefinitely. But investment values are governed chiefly by the intangibility of earning power, which provides a most unstable base for the vital function it performs.

Experienced investors realize that even the greatest amount of caution in the selection of securities does not guarantee complete safety. Some bonds that seem ultrasafe at the time of purchase become unsatisfactory investments. To the protection afforded by the careful selection of commitments, the intelligent investor will add the safeguard of diversification. Through a distribution plan over a number of issues, he does not lessen the risk attendant upon any one security but he does limit the loss that would be encountered if a substantial part of his fund were concentrated in an issue which depreciated in value. The application of a principle in mathematics, loosely termed *the law of averages,* based upon the improbability of the concurrence of unrelated unfavorable factors, underlies this policy of diversification.[2]

Diversification is more than a theory. It is accepted as sound practice by all large investors and has been officially recognized by legislative bodies and courts. The New York State law definitely limits the proportion of funds that savings banks may invest in real estate mortgages (65 per cent), in railroad bonds as a group (25 per cent) and as single companies (10 per cent), in electric and gas bonds as a group (10 per cent) and as single companies (2 per cent), and in telephone bonds as a group (10 per cent) and as single companies (2 per cent). The courts have held that trustees should diversify trust funds and have, in at least one case, surcharged a trustee for a substantial loss sustained from an unduly large investment in a single issue.[3] Moreover, as will

---

[2] In interesting contrast to his well-known admonition to "put all your eggs in one basket and watch that basket," as suggested by Andrew Carnegie in *The Empire of Business,* his estate contained the securities of more than 50 different companies.

[3] 183 Massachusetts 499 (1903).

be shown, banks, insurance companies, and other large investors almost universally practice diversification methods.[4]

The methods by which investment funds may be diversified
are numerous, but may be classified into two groups. The
purpose of diversification is usually to increase the degree of
safety by decreasing the amount of risk. The more important
methods fall in this group. A secondary purpose is to improve
what might be termed the convenience of the fund. Convenience would concern such details as regularity of income,
tax status, and reinvestment problems. This second purpose
of diversification increases in importance with the size of the
fund.

The simplest manner in which diversification is accomplished is through limitation upon the proportion of the total
fund that may be invested in any distinct category. The
more popular applications of such restrictions, from the aspect
of safety, are limitations of the amounts which may be invested
in: (1) any one security or company, (2) any one kind of enterprise, (3) any one grade of securities with respect to (a)
yield and (b) marketability, and (4) any one geographical
district. From the viewpoint of convenience, restrictions
apply less rigidly to: (1) income payment dates, (2) maturity
dates, and (3) maximum and minimum commitment
amounts.

The proportion of the total fund that may be invested in
any single issue should be limited to a reasonable degree. The
quality of the issue has direct influence in this respect, since
the percentage may be higher in the case of exceptionally good
investments, such as United States Treasury bonds. Five
per cent of the total fund would appear to be a reasonable
maximum for any single issue, excluding United States Government bonds, in a fund of average size.[5]

---

[4] The New York Life Insurance Company held over 1,200 different securities
on December 31, 1939, exclusive of real estate mortgage loans.

[5] A noteworthy illustration of the danger of investment concentration in a
single company is afforded in the recent experience of Western Union. Prior
to 1930, Western Union securities were regarded as high-grade investments evidenced by a splendid record of sustained earning power dating back over 70
years. Two years later, the bonds were regarded as medium grade and the
stock as speculative.

The proportion to be invested in any one kind of enterprise should also be limited. As before, the investment position of each group should be considered so that higher ratios may be established for the more promising fields. The various groups into which investments may be classified for this purpose are as follows:

     I.   United States Government obligations, including guaranteed issues.

     II.   United States Government instrumentalities, including Federal Farm Loan and Federal Home Loan bonds.

     III.   Domestic state and municipal bonds, including both general lien and reserve issues.

     IV.   Domestic steam railroad securities.

     V.   Domestic public utility securities.

     VI.   Domestic industrial securities.

     VII.   Domestic bank and insurance stocks.

     VIII.   Investment trust securities.

     IX.   Real estate securities.

     X.   Foreign securities.

It is not suggested that some part of the fund should be invested in each of these ten groups. The principle of diversification does not require such extreme conformance. It is suggested, however, that an investment fund should not be concentrated in any one of these groups to the exclusion of the others. The acquisition of many separate issues in a single group is diversification of a nature much more limited than that considered in the present discussion. The investor, for example, who believes that he is practicing diversification through the simple expedient of confining his purchases to the securities of public utility companies located in different parts of the country is operating under a false interpretation of the term. Thirty-five per cent of the total fund would appear to be a reasonable maximum for any of the specified groups.[6]

---

[6] Numerous examples might be cited of the dangers of group concentration. The present critical condition of the steam railroad industry, the securities of which have long been regarded as the best in the corporate group, has brought considerable misfortune to many conservative investors who held principally railroad securities.

The proportion of the fund to be invested in relatively high-, medium-, and low-yielding securities will depend largely upon the position of the investor and his ability to assume risk. Under normal conditions, first-grade securities yield under 4 per cent; second-grade, under 5 per cent; and third-grade, under 6 per cent. The average yield, therefore, should be around 4 per cent on the aggregate fund.[7] A higher yield usually indicates the presence of too many relatively poor issues. Accordingly, a limit of 20 per cent might reasonably be placed upon high-yielding issues, and of 30 per cent on medium yields, to assure a minimum of 50 per cent in the low-yielding group.

The proportion of the fund to be invested in securities of limited marketability will also depend upon the position of the investor. A substantial part of the fund must necessarily be invested in marketable securities if the likelihood exists that the fund may have to be converted into cash at short notice. The improbability of such development, however, should not lead the investor to ignore the question of marketability.[8] A natural spirit of prudence would dictate a maximum limitation of 50 per cent in issues of limited marketability.

The diversification of an investment fund according to geographical boundaries affords more theoretical than actual advantages to the American investor. The British investor, because of limited opportunities at home, has been compelled to invest abroad and naturally has sought to limit his risks through geographic diversification; moreover, in the far-flung reaches of the British Empire, he could find international investment opportunities under the protection of his country. The American investor has always been able to find plenty of opportunities at home and therefore has not been put to

---

[7] It is not generally recognized that an average return of 4 per cent upon invested capital over an extended period of years requires investment skill of a high order. The better grade of securities does not consistently offer a rate of return as high as 4 per cent.

[8] The value of marketability in an investment fund has been clearly indicated in the recent experience of commercial banks with investment portfolios. Emergency calls on the part of depositors compelled all banks to keep as liquid as possible. Many banks were obliged to close because of *frozen assets,* a term applied to unmarketable investments.

the same necessity of seeking foreign investments. Large as some countries are, however, geographical distribution on a national basis is much less significant than on an international basis.[9] Differences in economic conditions are more likely to exist between nations than within the borders of a single country.

The American investor who endeavors to practice national distribution finds the task complicated because of limited opportunities in certain sections and because of the nation-wide activities of the more important companies. Only in the cases of investors with extremely large funds, such as life insurance companies, is geographic diversification of practical value.[10] To the average American investor, the principle of geographic diversification serves its purpose when it prevents the concentration of investment in any one section. Securities of the American Telephone and Telegraph Company represent national diversification in themselves, just as securities of the General Electric Company represent international diversification.

Diversification according to income payment dates is based upon the fact that bond interest is generally paid semiannually and stock dividends quarterly. It thus becomes possible to arrange a fund in such fashion that an approximately equal amount of income is receivable monthly or quarterly. It is questionable, however, if the slight advantage gained in this way offsets the additional work involved in the selection of such securities with varying payment dates.

Diversification according to maturity dates endeavors to minimize the losses which may be involved in reinvestment. Large maturities are inconvenient in years of low interest rates, since the new securities bought with the proceeds of

---

[9] The world-wide depression of recent years completely refutes the former belief that all nations cannot suffer from depression at the same time. It would seem that international diversification has proved less profitable than national concentration in recent years.

[10] Geographic diversification is a normal by-product in the average investment account. Exceptional is the case of a large fund that had 85 per cent invested in securities located in a single state. Prudent investment policy should precede state loyalty in such a case.

maturing obligations will give a less satisfactory rate of return. Large investors endeavor to distribute maturity dates to avoid concentration in any particular years and generally refer to their *maturity calendars* before buying new issues. The average investor will usually find it more convenient to distribute his holdings into the three chronological groups of short-term (up to five years), medium-term (five to twenty years), and long-term (over twenty years), limiting his commitment in any group to 40 per cent of his fund.

The size of the investment unit should be proportionate to the amount in the fund. A fund of $100,000 might reasonably comprise 20 different securities averaging $5,000 (5 per cent), with a maximum of $10,000 (10 per cent) and a minimum of $2,000 (2 per cent) in any single issue. A fund of $1,000,000 might comprise 50 securities averaging $20,000 (2 per cent), with a maximum of $50,000 (5 per cent) and a minimum of $10,000 (1 per cent). A fund of $10,000,000 might comprise 100 securities averaging $100,000 (1 per cent), with a maximum of $250,000 (2½ per cent) and a minimum of $50,000 (½ of 1 per cent).[11]

The achievement of a satisfactory degree of diversification in a fund of relatively small size is practically impossible. A maximum commitment of 5 per cent in a fund of $10,000 would require the purchase of bonds in inconvenient denominations of $500. It is unfortunate that the investment trust companies which have been formed to provide diversification advantages to investors of limited means have not operated more conservatively in the choice of their securities. Until such time as these companies prove more worthy of public confidence, investors with limited capital should confine their purchases to units of $1,000 in each commitment. So definite is the risk hazard in all securities that investors with a few hundred, or even a few thousand, dollars would do well to place their funds in a savings bank rather than directly in a few securities.

---

[11] An extreme case of diversification carried to an absurd extent was a fund of $130,000 comprising 120 different securities. The disadvantage involved in the management of such a fund offsets the benefit diversification might provide.

Diversification practices. A study of the portfolios of leading American investment institutions discloses the fact that diversification is widely practiced, but with considerable lack of uniformity. Each type of institutional investor endeavors to adapt its investment procedure to its particular needs. The greater need of liquidity on the part of the commercial banks is naturally reflected in the large volume of short-term Government bonds held by such investors. On the other hand, the limited need for liquidity on the part of the savings banks has permitted the holding of a large volume of long-term mortgages.

The leading life insurance companies of the United States had invested 28.2 billion dollars at the close of 1940. As shown in the accompanying table, about one quarter (25.6 per cent) of this total was invested in real estate securities, about one quarter (28.1 per cent) in government bonds, about one third (31.1 per cent) in corporation issues, and the remainder (15.2

DISTRIBUTION OF INVESTMENTS HELD BY LEADING
AMERICAN LIFE INSURANCE COMPANIES

Class	1930	1940
Farm mortgages..........................	10.9%	2.8%
City mortgages..........................	29.6	16.1
Real estate.............................	2.4	6.7
Total.............................	42.9	25.6
United States Government..............	1.8	19.8
State and municipal....................	3.4	6.3
Canadian Government...................	2.3	2.0
Total.............................	7.5	28.1
Steam railroad.........................	17.0	10.7
Public utility..........................	9.7	14.4
Industrial.............................	3.1	6.0
Total.............................	29.8	31.1
Other assets...........................	19.8	15.2
Grand total....................	100.0%	100.0%

per cent) was principally in loans to policyholders. A comparison of the 1940 distribution with that of a decade previous in 1930 shows substantial changes in policies, as reflected in a decline in real estate commitments from 42.9 to 25.6 per cent (with farm loans falling from 10.9 to 2.8 per cent), and an increase in public loans from 7.5 to 28.1 per cent (with United States Government loans gaining from 1.8 to 19.8 per cent). Corporation loans remained around 30 per cent, but railroad issues dropped from 17.0 to 10.7 per cent. Utility issues increased from 9.7 to 14.4 per cent, and industrial issues increased from 3.1 to 6.0 per cent. A further indication of the policy of the life insurance companies to adapt their purchases to changing conditions is shown in the fact that nearly one third (30.9 per cent) of new investments made in 1940 were United States Government bonds, and nearly one fifth (19.0 per cent) were public utility issues.

The insured commercial banks in the United States had invested 27.0 billion dollars at the close of 1939. As shown

THE DISTRIBUTION OF INVESTMENTS HELD BY INSURED
COMMERCIAL BANKS ON DEC. 31, 1939

Farm mortgages	$ 535,000,000	2.0%
City mortgages	3,605,000,000	13.3
Real estate	420,000,000	1.6
Total	$ 4,560,000,000	16.9
United States Government	$15,565,000,000	57.6
State and municipal	3,695,000,000	13.7
Foreign issues	220,000,000	0.8
Total	$19,480,000,000	72.1
Steam railroad	$ 910,000,000	3.4
Public utility	760,000,000	2.8
Industrial	770,000,000	2.8
Total	$ 2,440,000,000	9.0
Corporate stocks	$ 520,000,000	2.0
Grand total	$27,000,000,000	100.0%

in the accompanying table, about one sixth (16.9 per cent) of this total was invested in real estate loans, about two thirds (72.1 per cent) in government loans, and about one tenth (9.0 per cent) in corporation issues. The most significant feature of the investment policy of these banks has been the placing of more than one half (57.6 per cent) of total holdings in United States Government bonds.

DISTRIBUTION OF INVESTMENTS HELD BY NEW YORK STATE SAVINGS BANKS ON OCT. 31, 1940

Mortgages......................	$3,042,000,000	53.0%
Real estate.....................	310,000,000	5.4
Total....................	$3,352,000,000	58.4
United States Government........	$1,709,000,000	29.7
State and municipal..............	341,000,000	6.0
Total....................	$2,050,000,000	35.7
Steam railroad...................	$ 207,000,000	3.7
Public utility....................	101,000,000	1.7
Total....................	$ 308,000,000	5.4
Miscellaneous....................	$ 28,000,000	0.5
Grand total..............	$5,738,000,000	100.0%

The savings banks in New York State which are obliged to observe legal restrictions in the diversification of their investments, as previously explained, had invested in 1940 more than 5.7 billion dollars in securities in the proportions shown in the accompanying table. Real estate investments represented more than one half (58.4 per cent) of total holdings, government issues about one third (35.7 per cent), and corporation bonds less than one tenth (5.4 per cent). Like the life insurance companies, the savings banks have changed their investment policies to meet the new conditions which have developed. During the past decade, real estate investments were reduced from nearly 70 to less than 60 per cent, and railroad investments were reduced from 14 to 4 per cent, whereas Federal bonds were increased from 4 to 30 per cent.

Exchanging securities.   The importance of vigilance in the management of an investment fund was admirably stated in a recent report of the Carnegie Corporation as follows:

> The funds of a great endowment can be kept intact only by a systematic revision month by month of all the securities of the endowment and by a continuous process of sale and exchange, as circumstances may affect the financial soundness of this or that security which the trust holds.

Circumstances are continually arising to change investment values collectively and separately. Some industries enter the stage of expansion as others fall into decline.   One company prospers at a time when other firms in the same field are operating under deficits. Investment popularity swings from one type of security or enterprise to another.   As the old order gives way to the new, values in the less popular fields decline as prices in the more interesting groups advance. While diversification tends to minimize the losses often sustained in these changes, the sale of securities which face unpromising prospects is even more effective as a safeguard against depreciation.

Security exchanging is an important phase of investment management.   The once popular theory that some securities were adequately safe for investors to "buy and forget" has been invalidated in the experience of recent years. Neglect of a regular scrutiny of investment holdings does more than result in the loss of favorable exchange opportunities; it may lead to a most serious decline in the aggregate value of the fund.   As with diversification, however, exchanging may be overdone, as happens when it develops into promiscuous trading.   An exchange of securities is justifiable only when the position of the investor is improved as a result.   The conditions under which such betterment is possible are not many:

1.   Greater safety at the same yield.
2.   Higher yield with equal safety.
3.   Greater marketability at the same yield.

4. Improved tax position.
5. Improved diversification.
6. Better appreciation opportunity.

As no two securities have the same quality, it naturally follows that exchange opportunities are constantly afforded to the vigilant investor. His principal concern is to be assured that the advantage to be gained in one respect is not more than offset in the sacrifice necessitated elsewhere. If all security buyers were purely investors, exchange opportunities would be fewer; but since prices are influenced by speculators who have little interest in the income aspect, investors often find good exchange opportunities. As yield does not always vary with quality, because of the presence of such technical factors as seasoning, convertibility, marketability, taxability, legal status, and redemption option, investors who are cognizant of these features are frequently in a position to make advantageous exchanges resulting in an enhanced rate of return upon their securities.

Exchanges should never be made solely to realize a profit obtainable from an advance in the market value of a purchased security. Unless a good additional reason exists, such as a gradual increase in the degree of seasoning, or a temporary advance arising out of a conversion option, or the attainment of the call price,[12] or an unusual opportunity to purchase an alternative security, the appreciation should be ignored by investors other than those who are frankly trading in securities. Even more emphatically, exchanges should not be made upon the importunity of a bond salesman who usually has a new issue to sell, unless it is clearly evident that advantage is to be derived from the exchange.

The average investor has limited opportunity to follow the trend of the investment market and thus to keep closely in touch with the position of his securities. He should endeavor, however, to keep posted to the following extent.

---

[12] Investors often find the sale of redeemable bonds advisable when the market price reaches the call price, in the belief that further appreciation is unlikely. A bond rarely sells above its redemption price.

1. Current quotations on all securities should be secured at least monthly. Unusual changes should be investigated as possible portents of serious developments.

2. Corporate earnings reports should be scrutinized on a comparative basis. These reports are generally published quarterly and afford a continuous check upon the prosperity of the enterprise.

3. Changes in management should be carefully observed. The more important the changes are, the more significant the results may be.

4. External factors, such as the enactment of important legislation, the development of new industries, and the trend of business activity, directly influence investment values. The problem of the investor is to relate these developments to the particular securities which he is holding.

The reluctance on the part of the average investor to accept a small loss on a security is a natural reaction which frequently results in substantial depreciation. While it is true that all security prices fluctuate and that many declines are subsequently recovered, a more realistic attitude would recognize a weakening situation before a serious condition is reached. The suggestion is here made that any investment which shows a depreciation of 10 per cent from its cost price should be disposed of unless there is ample reason for believing that the decline is temporary. Such a reason would be a general decline in all similar securities due to the influence of changing interest rates. Although the price might rise subsequent to such "forced" sale, the probabilities are that an even larger decline is ahead. The old adage that investors should "cut their losses short" is entitled to considerable respect. Too often investors unwilling to take a ten-point decline hold on until the major part of the investment has been lost. What appears to be economic courage at such a time might more properly be regarded as the reverse. Selling in order to prevent losses requires a keener intelligence than selling in order to take profits.

The problem of investment management is as much concerned with selling as buying. It may not be appropriate to regard securities as inventories, but the analogy has some justification. In the ultimate sense, at least, securities are bought to be resold just as inventories are. In both cases, vigilance is necessary in order to offset the loss in value resulting from changes in the economic world. Advantage should be taken of favorable opportunities to sell as well as to buy.

Safekeeping of securities. Security instruments should be carefully guarded through deposit in a protected place. Bonds and stock certificates should preferably be kept in a locked metallic box, either in a bank vault or in a safe. Most banks offer safe-deposit box service at a low annual rental. A duplicate list of the securities should be prepared (one to remain in the box) showing the number of each security, the amount, the name, the maturity date, and the rate and dates of income payments. Stock certificates should be transferred into the name of the new owner upon delivery. Bonds bought for long-term holding should be registered in full, or at least as to principal. No writing or marks of any kind, other than endorsements, should be made on security instruments. If a security is lost, notice with full description should be sent immediately to the issuing corporation and also to the firm through which it was purchased. Bond coupons should not be detached prior to due dates.

Investors who desire to be relieved of the detail involved in the handling and care of securities may establish *custodian accounts* with banking institutions. In this event, the bank, for an appropriate fee, handles all of the details under instructions from the investor. The securities of each investor are kept in a segregated group, apart from the general assets of the bank. The services provided by the bank include the following:

1. Collection of interest, dividends, and principal.
2. Purchase and sale of securities.
3. Rendition of periodical statements of the account.
4. Provision of income tax information.
5. Special reports on securities held.

6. Information on called bonds, stock rights, protective committees, and sinking fund offers.

The advantage of a custodian account is that of convenience as well as of safety. In the event of sickness or absence from home, the securities are available for use of the owner, through letter, telegram, or cable instructions to deliver, sell, or pledge as collateral for a loan. Obviously, however, since the bank has full access to the securities, the institution with which the account is placed should be of unquestioned financial responsibility.

12

PROTECTION IN REORGANIZATIONS

Scope. The purpose of this chapter is to discuss the problems which arise in the reorganization of companies which are in default to their creditors. The order of discussion is: (1) market depreciation, (2) equity proceedings, (3) reorganization plan, (4) statutory reorganizations, (5) railroad reorganizations, (6) Section 77 proceedings, (7) industrial reorganizations, and (8) Chapter X reorganizations. Many important changes have developed in this field in the past decade, especially with respect to the supervisory powers of the Securities and Exchange Commission and the Interstate Commerce Commission.

Depreciated securities. A serious decline in the market value of a security may arise from causes that are either external or internal with respect to the particular issue. The rapid fall in all bond values in the latter part of 1931, led by United States Government bonds (which declined from a 3.25 per cent basis in September to a 4.25 per cent basis in December), was due to a fundamental change in the condition of the money market. The disfavor into which railroad securities, as a class, have fallen in recent years has harmed the position of all securities in this group, irrespective of the relative prosperity of individual companies. Depreciation which arises out of such external causes comprises a general problem in investment management, the most

practical solution of which is to be found in careful selection
and intelligent diversification.   Depreciation which arises out
of internal causes, however, presents a group of specific problems that must be solved separately.

The utmost care and prudence exercised in the selection
of investments does not always suffice to prevent loss through
depreciation in value.   Every investment commitment is essentially a wager on the future.   A fatalistic attitude that the
die by which the future will be fashioned has already been
cast would appear unwise in the light of investment experience.   The future is always "in the making" in that the events
of each day influence the developments of the next.   To foresee the ultimate result of innumerable factors operating with
varying effects over any given period of time would be to
transcend the recognized limits of intellectual vision.   Sound
though a security may be at the time of purchase, later developments may transpire to change completely the quality
of the commitment.   Practically every investor, howsoever
cautious as he may be, finds that some of his securities turn
out poorly because of unfavorable developments with respect
to those particular issues.

Depreciation in this sense refers to major rather than minor
declines in value.   Price fluctuations within a reasonable
range are rarely significant, since they reflect what might
be termed the normal action of the market.   Declines dis-
proportionate to those shown in comparable issues, a condition indicating clearly an "out of line" situation, are more
serious.   Delay may be dangerous, in view of the rapidity
with which a weakened financial condition may grow worse.
Moreover, the mental hazard involved in the acceptance of
a small loss is less disturbing than that concerned with a large
decline.   Under ordinary conditions, a decline of 10 per cent
or more in the value of any investment security would make
the wisdom of its retention questionable.

The problem which confronts the holder of depreciated
securities is that of determining whether to sell and thereby
accept what is often a substantial loss, or to continue to hold
in the hope that eventually a higher price may be realized.

A peculiar psychology exists with respect to the latter alternative, which somewhat fallaciously holds, first, that no loss is actual until definitely realized and, second, that further decline is unlikely.   Moreover, the belief prevails that selling in such a situation is less courageous than holding.   The dilemma in which the investor is placed is too often allowed to become more serious because of the natural inclination to postpone an unpleasant decision.

Equity proceedings.   The investor who owns securities in companies which are in default, and who prefers to hold the issues rather than dispose of them at the sacrifice prices which then prevail, will be asked to assist in the reorganization of the company either through depositing his securities with protective committees under equity proceedings or through approving a readjustment plan under statutory proceedings.   In either case, the doctrine of absolute priority under which creditors who have prior claims receive preferential treatment, is the basis of reorganization.   In order to prevent delays which frequently arise in equity proceedings when small minority dissenting groups are able to block plans acceptable to the majority of interested holders, the law now provides an alternative method of statutory proceedings under which minority interests are bound by the action of the majority. As a result, the newer method of statutory reorganization has largely superseded the older method of equity proceedings.

Under equity proceedings, default in the payment of interest by a company ordinarily results in the appointment of a receiver (usually an officer of the company or a person acceptable to the management) by the Federal court of jurisdiction. Concurrently protective committees are formed (usually self-appointed) for each class of securities.   These committees invite other holders to coöperate with them through depositing their securities at a specified depository.   Sometimes competitive committees are set up for the same group of securities, the one receiving the smaller support usually retiring.

The protective committee is created for the protection of the numerous bondholders, who generally comprise many small holders located at inconvenient distances from one another. For reasons of economy as well as of convenience, it is highly desirable that coöperative action be taken in mutual interest. The committee members are usually selected by the investment firm that originally distributed the issue, and comprise representatives of the house and of some of the larger bondholders. Because of conflicting interests, it is customary to have separate protective committees for each class of security holders.[1]

The protective committees advertise in the leading financial papers, requesting the deposit, with specified banking institutions, of securities, against which depository receipts are issued. These receipts are fully negotiable and may be bought and sold at the prevailing price,[2] as freely as the original instruments. Security holders are urged to deposit their issues in order that the committee may feel legally qualified to act and to evidence such qualification before proper judicial authority. In order that the committee may evidence such qualification, a large majority of the securities must be deposited with it. At least two thirds in amount of the outstanding securities must be deposited to insure effective action. Although the investor is not compelled to coöperate with the committee, it is clearly to his interest to do so unless he has reason to the contrary, such as lack of confidence in the particular committee appointed.

---

[1] Receivers for the Seaboard Air Line Railway Company were appointed on December 23, 1930. Within one month, no less than eight distinct protective committees had been formed to represent as many classes of security holders. The committees were as follows:

Committee Representing:	Members
First Mortgage Bonds	5
Refunding Mortgage Bonds	4
First and Consolidated Mortgage Bonds	7
Secured Notes	4
Adjustment Mortgage Bonds	3
Seaboard—All Florida First Mortgage Bonds	6
Preferred Stock	5
Common Stock	9
Total Membership	43

[2] The price of the free certificates tends to be above the price of the depository certificates since the former may usually be converted into the latter, whereas the reverse is not always permitted.

As soon as the requisite number of securities are deposited, the committee takes formal action in behalf of the security holders. Joint meetings are held with committees representing other interests, sometimes resulting in the appointment of a central committee, with one representative from each group, to expedite matters. Conferences are held with officials of the company and court representatives in an endeavor to ascertain the best plan for meeting the situation. Except in rare cases, a reorganization plan is worked out and submitted to the security holders.

Reorganization plan. Companies which default in the payment of interest are customarily declared insolvent and are placed in charge of a receiver appointed by the courts. The duty of the receiver is to continue the business for the time being and to conserve the assets for the benefit of the creditors. With permission of the court, he may issue *receivers' certificates,* having a prior lien upon the general assets, to procure cash for this purpose. He coöperates with representatives of the various interests in the determination of a reorganization plan; or, if reorganization is inadvisable, he liquidates the business and distributes the proceeds, less receivership expenses, among the creditors. Receiverships may be terminated within one year; more frequently they run for several years.

Corporate reorganizations are occasionally accomplished without receiverships. Such readjustments that save considerable time and money involved in receiverships are ordinarily possible only in cases where no funded debt is outstanding. The Goodyear Tire and Rubber reorganization in 1921 is a notable example of a voluntary readjustment.

The preparation of a reorganization plan requires proper consideration of the relative priorities of the various claimants. Some of the creditors usually have preferred claims because of legal protection, as in the case of employees, or because of the pledge of specific security, as in the cases of collateral bank loans. The order in which claims are arranged with respect to priority generally conforms to the following sequence.

I. Secured Claims:
1. Expenses of the receivership
2. Wages of employees
3. Taxes
4. Secured loans
5. Senior mortgage bonds
6. Junior mortgage bonds

II. Unsecured Claims (rate alike):
7. (a) Debenture bonds
    (b) Unsecured loans

III. Stockholders:
8. Preferred stock (if preferred as to assets)
9. Common stock

The reorganization plan must provide funds for the payment of those items, such as taxes and wages, that have the earliest claim on the assets. It should not seriously disturb the position of the senior bonds, which are entitled to full payment before any distribution may be made to subsequent claimants. The burden of sacrifice must therefore fall on those groups that are in the weaker position—namely, the junior bondholders and the unsecured creditors—as well as upon the stockholders, who usually learn that their equities have been lost.

The objectives sought in the reorganization plan are readily apparent. In the first place, current indebtedness must be paid, and a satisfactory working capital position must be restored. In the second place, fixed charges should be materially lowered. In the third place, the capital structure should be simplified in all cases where numerous issues are outstanding. In the fourth place, the plan should be sufficiently drastic to afford more than temporary relief. In the fifth place, the plan should be flexible enough to provide for future financing. The preparation of a plan that will accomplish these objects without undue hardship to existing security holders is a highly difficult task.

The purpose of the reorganization plan is to devise a new capital structure which will permit the attainment of these objectives. The new structure may allow some of the senior issues to remain undisturbed, or it may provide a clean slate of new securities. First and foremost, it should be so arranged as to reduce annual fixed charges, through the substitution of contingent charge issues, such as income bonds and stocks, for a substantial part of the old funded debt. Secondly, it should provide new securities sufficiently attractive to be sold for cash either to old security holders on a preferential basis or to newcomers. Thirdly, it should provide for the simplification of debt structure through a mechanism whereby several former issues are exchangeable into a single new issue. The new financial structure should accomplish these desired results if it is to function satisfactorily.

As an essential part of a reorganization under equity proceedings, the new plan must be approved by practically all of the old security holders. A dissenting minority representing 15 per cent of the old issues may effectually prevent the operation of the plan. The old security holder may be asked to consent to the placing of a prior lien before his existing claim, or to exchange at least part of his fixed charge bonds into income bonds or preferred stock, or to purchase additional securities in the new company through payment of an assessment.

The old security holder is not obliged to approve the new plan. He will consider the proposals and determine, so far as he can, their relative fairness. He will further come to some conclusion as to the probable success of the plan in operation and as to the time required for eventual recovery. He will give thought to nonfinancial factors, such as the character of management and the economic position of the industry, before reaching a decision. As a practical matter, he will decide either to stay through the reorganization by approving the proposed plan, or to dispose of his holdings at the best price obtainable.

In the event that the reorganization plan has been accepted by a substantial majority of each class of security holders, the court will then order a public sale of the corporate property. Representatives of the new company provided in the reorganization plan then "buy in" the property at a minimum "upset price" determined by the court. Dissenting security holders are thus "frozen out" because they have no claim upon the new company and are entitled to participate only in the meagre distributable assets of the defunct company.

The steps followed in an equity receivership would be as follows:

(1)   Formation of separate protective committees for each class of securities.

(2)   Deposit of securities with protective committees.

(3)   Formulation of reorganization plan by protective committees and receiver.

(4)   Approval of reorganization plan by holders of securities.

(5)   Court order for sale of property at minimum price.

(6)   Sale of property and distribution of proportionate proceeds to dissenting holders.

(7)   Issuance of securities by new company as provided in reorganization plan.

Statutory reorganizations.   In an endeavor to simplify and expedite the reorganization of debtor corporations, numerous amendments have been made to the Federal bankruptcy law during the past decade. Since the enactment of these amendments, which are known as "Section 77" in connection with railroad reorganizations and "Chapter X" (which has replaced "Section 77B") in connection with other corporate reorganizations, practically all important reorganizations are being effected through the statutory provisions now available. The principal advantage afforded by these amendments is the mandatory requirement that minority creditors are bound by the action of a two-thirds majority (in amount) and may not block the completion of an acceptable reorganization plan.

Railroad reorganization.   At various periods in the economic history of the nation, certain of the larger railroad systems have been in financial difficulties and have been obliged to go through receivership proceedings in order to regain solvency. In 1894, no less than 192 companies, including the Atchison, the Norfolk and Western, and the Union Pacific, operating nearly 41,000 miles of railroad, were in receivership. In 1915, some 75 companies, including the Rock Island, the Wabash, and the Missouri-Kansas-Texas, operating nearly 42,000 miles of railroad, were in receivership.   In 1940, some 109 companies, including the Chicago and North Western, the New Haven, and the St. Paul, operating more than 77,000 miles of railroad, were in the hands of receivers or trustees.

Prior to the past decade, railroad receiverships occurred during periods of economic depression and were caused by the inability of certain companies to earn enough to cover interest charges at such times.   In most cases, a moderate reduction in the fixed charges, coupled with an ensuing recovery in business conditions was sufficient to insure the success of a reorganization plan without the need for adopting drastic economies.

So long as the country was growing rapidly and the railroad companies enjoyed a practical monopoly in the field of transportation, the problem of working out a successful reorganization plan was not unusually difficult.   Under present conditions, however, with a considerably diminished rate of national growth and with powerful competitors obtaining an increasing share of available traffic, the formulation of a practicable reorganization plan has become highly difficult.   No longer may successively higher economic peaks be relied upon to bring the volume of traffic revenue necessary to support an optimistic appraisal of future earnings.   It is now believed that only that plan of reorganization which is based upon actual earnings in the poorest years affords a realistic approach to a solution of the problem.

Section 77 reorganizations.   Although this amendment to the bankruptcy law was enacted in 1933, the results thus far have been most disappointing.   The procedure which must be followed as outlined below has required far more time and resulted in much more dissension than was originally foreseen.   A complete reorganization requires seven steps:

(1)   The debtor company is given six months to prepare a tentative plan which usually favors the stockholders against the creditor bondholders.

(2)   The creditor bondholders also present plans (usually through protective committees) which are rarely acceptable to the stockholders.

(3)   After hearing arguments on both the creditor and debtor plans, the Interstate Commerce Commission appoints an examiner to prepare a compromise plan.

(4)   The Commission thus formulates an official plan after hearing arguments on the examiner's plan.

(5)   The Commission plan is submitted to the Federal Court.

(6)   After hearings, the Federal Court either approves or disapproves the I. C. C. plan.

(7)   If approved by two thirds of all classes of security holders voting, the plan is finally approved, the trusteeship is ended, and the new securities are issued.

PROPOSED RAILROAD REORGANIZATION PLANS [3]
(ALL AMOUNTS IN MILLIONS OF DOLLARS)

System	Bonds			Annual Interest		
	Before	After	Reduction	Before	After	Reduction
Missouri Pacific.........	$ 661	$ 308	$ 353	$24.8	$ 7.3	$17.5
St. Paul..............	627	224	403	14.9	4.3	10.6
Chicago & North Western	431	222	209	16.5	3.4	13.1
New Haven..........	390	230	160	13.5	6.4	7.1
St. Louis-San Francisco.	373	116	257	12.6	3.0	9.6
Erie.................	305	191	114	13.6	7.5	6.1
Total..........	$2,787	$1,291	$1,496	$95.9	$31.9	$64.0

In view of the time required to reconcile the various claimants and to adjust the plan to conform with concurrent changes in the earning power of the company, it is scarcely surprising that progress has not been more rapid.   Certain of the larger companies are in the final stages as this section is being written. The outstanding characteristic of the reorganization plans thus far approved has been a drastic reduction in the amount of annual fixed charges.   As shown in the accompanying table,

[3] From Interstate Commerce Commission summary as of July 31, 1940.

the fixed charges of the five companies listed have been reduced from $96 millions to $32 millions, or a reduction of 67 per cent.   In the great majority of cases, the corporate stocks of the companies were entirely eliminated on the basis of evident insolvency.

A readjustment rather than a reorganization of the finances of the Baltimore and Ohio Railroad was accomplished in 1939 under special Federal legislation which is no longer in effect. After being accepted by the holders of 88 per cent of the securities affected, and approved by the Federal Court, the company extended $166 millions of near-by maturities for a period of from five to ten years and interest payments in the former amount of $31.4 millions were modified so that $19.6 remained fixed and the balance became contingent on a cumulative basis for eight years.   It is obvious that this plan affords the company only temporary relief inasmuch as the payment of the fixed charges is delayed rather than reduced.

The readjustment of the finances of the Boston and Maine Railroad was achieved in 1940 in a remarkably short period, without recourse to either Section 77 or the Chandler Act, through voluntary surrender on the part of the first mortgage bondholders of their fixed charge bonds on the basis of a new $500 senior fixed charge bond and a new $500 junior contingent charge bond for each old $1,000 bond.   As a result, the annual fixed charges were reduced from $6.8 millions to $4.0 millions.

Industrial reorganizations. Industrial reorganizations have been more numerous but less spectacular and, as a group, less successful than railroad reorganizations.   Statutory proceedings are usually necessary, as shown in the cases of Westinghouse Electric in 1908 and Baldwin Locomotive in 1937, but may be avoided, as shown in the cases of Corn Products Refining in 1906 and Goodyear Tire and Rubber in 1921.   Industrial reorganizations involve problems of management to a greater extent than problems of finance.   The financial structure of an industrial company is generally simple, seldom providing more than two classes of bondholders and often none at all.   The Goodyear reorganization was greatly facilitated by the complete absence of funded debt in the old corporate

structure.   The reorganization plan in this instance included:
(1) an issue of first mortgage bonds to provide new money;[4]
(2) an issue of debenture bonds to fund the bank loans and
to provide additional money; (3) an issue of prior preference
stock to care for trade creditors; (4) an issue of second preferred stock to replace the old preferred; and (5) an issue of
new common stock of no par value to replace the old common
stock of $100 par value.

Chapter X reorganizations.   The reorganization of industrial companies under Chapter X of the bankruptcy law (which
has replaced Section 77B) has been accomplished more rapidly
than the reorganization of railroad companies under Section
77.   The greater success in this respect is due partly to the
relatively simple capital structures of industrial companies and
partly to a less elaborate method of procedure.   The following
steps must be followed:

(1)   Preparation of reorganization plan by debtor company,
or a creditor, or the trustee.

(2)   Approval by court of any plans before they are submitted to interested parties.

(3)   Review by Securities and Exchange Commission if
debt exceeds $3,000,000.

(4)   Approval by state public service commission if company is subject to supervision.

(5)   Acceptance by two thirds in amount of each class of
creditors.

(6)   Acceptance by majority of each class of stockholders if
assets exceed liabilities.

(7)   Final confirmation of court making plan effective.

The review by the Securities and Exchange Commission,
acting in an advisory capacity, has become one of the most
important protective features of these reorganizations.   In
determining the fairness of a proposed plan, the Commission

---

[4] So stringent was the condition of the investment market when these bonds
were issued in 1921 that the first mortgage bonds, due in 1941, bore a coupon
rate of 8 per cent, were payable at 120 at maturity, and were offered to investors at a discount!

approves only those plans which give full recognition of claims in the order of priority and which deny participation to equity owners unless a residual value is plainly indicated. In determining the feasibility of a plan, the Commission requires evidence indicating that adequate working capital is to be provided, that fixed charges are to be less than reasonably anticipated earnings, that capitalization is to be commensurate with asset value, and that bonds will be retired in due course. Although disapproval by the Commission does not eliminate any particular plan, the action of the Commission has had a wholesome effect in the formation of sound reorganization plans.

It is encouraging to observe that many of the reorganizations already arranged under Chapter X have been realistic in the scaling down of fixed charges. In numerous realty reorganizations, entire issues of mortgage bonds carrying fixed charges have been converted into income bonds bearing contingent charges (as in the case of the 40 Wall Street Building in New York). In certain industrial reorganizations, all outstanding bonds have been converted into stock (as in the case of National Radiator).

Reorganization plans which have permitted stockholders to retain an interest in a company despite a failure to pay creditors in full are contrary to the doctrine of absolute priority. Such plans, even though approved by more than the required two-thirds majority, have been denied court approval.[5] In such cases, stockholders would be expected to make further contribution to retain an interest in the enterprise.

---

[5] The principle of absolute priority was clearly confirmed by the United States Supreme Court in 1939 in the Los Angeles Lumber Products Co., Ltd. case.

13

TAXATION OF SECURITIES

❖ıınıınııcııınıınıııcııınıınıcııınıınıcııınıınıcııınıınıcııınıınıcııınıınıcııınıınıcııınıınıcııınıınıcııınıınıcııınıınıc❖

Scope. The purpose of this chapter is to discuss the various tax levies to which securities are subject and the extent to which certain securities are exempt from these taxes. The order of discussion is: (1) Federal income taxes, (2) corporate income taxes, (3) state income taxes, (4) Federal estate taxes, (5) Federal gift taxes, (6) state estate taxes, (7) property taxes, and (8) transfer taxes. The tax position of exempt securities may be substantially changed as the result of legislation under consideration in connection with national defense expenditures.

Taxes on securities. The investor is constantly confronted with a wide variety of tax levies that must be carefully considered in the determination of investment policy. The Federal Government imposes income, gift, and estate taxes; the state governments impose income, estate, and property taxes; and the local county and municipal bodies impose property taxes. Furthermore, foreign securities of internal issue are subject to taxes imposed by foreign governments. The incidence of these taxes does not apply uniformly to all securities, or to all investors, or in all localities. The problem of taxation varies with the position of the individual investor with regard to the nature of his income, the size of his estate, the place of his residence, the number of dependents, and the location of his commitments.

The term *tax free,* or *tax exempt,* used in connection with securities, has a meaning much more restricted than might at first appear. It usually refers only to income taxes and generally to Federal income taxes. The bonds of the municipality of Boston, Massachusetts, are known as tax-exempt issues. If these bonds are owned by an investor in Albany, New York, no Federal tax is imposed upon the interest income, but the New York State income tax applies, as well as the Federal and New York State estate taxes, in the event of the death of the holder. Tax exemption, therefore, applies primarily to income taxes and not to estate, gift, and property taxes.

The tax position of the investor is complicated by overlapping taxes. The income available for dividend payments by a corporation is substantially reduced by corporate income taxes (which in 1942 were imposed at rates as high as 65 per cent). The dividend income of the stockholder is further reduced by personal income taxes (which in 1942 were imposed at rates as high as 81 per cent). The estates of investors are subject to taxation by both the Federal and state governments (at rates as high as 77 per cent in 1942). Profits from the sale of securities are regarded as additions to income for tax purposes without an equivalent provision for losses arising from the same source. Corporate property is subject to property taxes in areas where located, and securities representing the ownership of the corporate property are frequently subject to similar taxes in the areas where the investors reside.

Personal income taxes. Income taxes levied by the Federal Government comprise the heaviest tax burden which investors carry. Apart from state income taxes which are imposed independently and run as high as 15 per cent of income, the Federal Government in 1942 imposed a personal income tax which was the aggregate of two separate taxes as here stated:

(a) a *normal* tax of 4 per cent of all income in excess of a personal exemption of $750 for single persons and $1,500 for married couples, plus $400 for each dependent;

(b) a *surtax* on all income in excess of the personal exemption, at graduated rates starting at 6 per cent on the first $2,000 of surtax income, and advancing to 77 per cent on income in the highest bracket (over $5,000,000).

An investor with a taxable income of $16,000, with wife and two dependent children, would be subject to the following taxes:

(a) a normal tax of 4 per cent on the taxable income of $16,000 less a personal exemption of $2,300, or $548.

(b) a surtax of 6 per cent on the first $2,000 of taxable income above the personal exemption of $2,300, or $120; plus 9 per cent on the next $2,000, or $180; plus 13 per cent on the next $2,000, or $260; plus 17 per cent on the next $2,000, or $340; plus 21 per cent on the next $2,000, or $420; plus 25 per cent on the next $2,000, or $500; plus 29 per cent on the last $1,700, or $493—making a total surtax of $2,313.

The total Federal income tax would thus be $2,861, or 17.8 per cent of the taxable income (without allowance for earned income credit). The tax rate on the highest income bracket in this case would be 29 per cent, which is the effective rate with respect to the investment income of the taxpayer.

A study of the prevailing rates indicates that the tax levy increases rapidly with the size of the annual income. Investors of limited means pay less than one tenth of their incomes as taxes, whereas wealthy investors are compelled to pay over one half. To the latter group, securities that are exempt from Federal income taxes naturally make a strong appeal. Such securities may be divided into three classes—namely, (1) free from both taxes, (2) exempt from the normal tax, (3) exempt from part of the normal tax under indenture covenants.

Securities that are free from both normal taxes and surtaxes include the following issues:

1. United States Government bonds:
   Short-term notes (one to five years) when so designated. (National Defense notes are not exempt.)
   Long-term Treasury bonds, up to a maximum of $5,000 principal amount (issued before 1941).
   3 per cent Panama Canal bonds, due in 1961.
2. United States Territorial bonds.
3. Federal Land and Joint Stock Land bank bonds.
4. State and municipal bonds of domestic issue.

Securities that are exempt from the normal tax but subject to the surtax comprise principally the United States Government bonds that were issued previous to 1941. Since the surtax levy is much heavier than the normal tax, exemption from the latter is much less valuable to wealthy investors.[1]

Securities that bear tax-free covenants are those upon which the issuing corporation pays part of the income tax imposed upon the holder. As the amount paid by the corporation is usually "up to 2 per cent," the advantage to the holder is almost insignificant.

It should be carefully noted that income taxes are charged against the income received and not against the principal of the investment. An investor subject to a tax rate of 10 per cent pays a $3 tax on the $30 received annually from a 3 per cent bond, which payment reduces his income to $27. Obviously, the purchase of a tax-free 2.70 per cent bond at par will produce the same net return to that individual as a taxable 3 per cent bond at par. In like manner, the purchase of a tax-free 3 per cent municipal bond at par will afford the same return as a taxable 4 per cent corporate bond at par to the investor who is required to pay a tax rate of 25 per cent.

---

[1] Repeated proposals to remove the tax-exemption features of state and municipal bonds have been unsuccessful up to the time of writing. The general belief exists that such legislation, by either statute or constitutional amendment, would affect the taxability only of those securities issued thereafter and would not be retroactive in such manner as to remove the exemption from the bonds previously issued.

Investment policy with respect to Federal income taxes under existing levies is determined by the size of the annual personal net income. As the total tax rate is small to investors of limited means, such investors will find it profitable to buy taxable securities and to pay the tax. Investors with annual incomes in excess of $25,000 will find the purchase of tax-free securities more advantageous. As shown in the ac-

EQUIVALENT YIELDS ON TAX-FREE AND TAXABLE SECURITIES
(UNDER REVENUE ACT OF 1940)

Tax-free Yields..........................			2.00%	2.50%	3.00%
Individuals (including normal tax, surtax and super-tax, but excluding state income taxes):					
Surtax Income	Average Tax Rate	Maximum Tax Rate			
$ 10,000.........	8%	13%	2.67	3.33	4.00
25,000.........	19	34	3.85	4.81	5.77
50,000.........	30	48	4.88	6.10	7.32
75,000.........	39	59	5.71	7.14	8.57
100,000.........	45	66	6.25	7.81	9.38
250,000.........	59	69	6.90	8.62	10.34
500,000.........	66	75	8.33	10.42	12.50
1,000,000.........	72	79	9.09	11.36	13.64
Corporations (excluding excess profits tax)..			2.63	3.94	5.26

companying table, an investor with a taxable income of $50,000 annually would have to receive a yield of 7.32 per cent on a taxable bond to have it equal a yield of 3.00 per cent on a tax-free bond. Although the repeated reductions in Federal income tax rates during the decade from 1920 to 1930 lessened the interest in tax-free securities, the more recent increases in these tax rates reëmphasize the attractiveness of these issues to wealthy holders.[2]

---

[2] The tendency on the part of wealthy investors to avoid income taxes through the purchase of tax-exempt bonds was well-illustrated in the estate of Senator James Couzens of Michigan, who died in 1936 leaving an estate of $34,119,537, of which $33,270,000 was invested in Government and municipal bonds.

The effective tax rate to an investor is that applicable to his highest income bracket inasmuch as income from investments is reported *in addition* to regular income from other sources. An investor with a surtax income of $50,000 pays 43 per cent of total income as Federal taxes but pays at the rate of 59 per cent in his highest bracket, which usually contains his income from investments. Hence he must receive 4.88 per cent from a taxable bond in order to have 2.00 per cent remaining after paying the 59 per cent tax.

Profits and losses which arise from the purchase and sale of securities affect the tax liability of individual investors according to the length of time the securities were owned. On securities held less than 18 months, all profits in excess of losses sustained are regarded as income and are fully taxable; losses in excess of profits on such short-term holdings may not be deducted from other income but may be carried forward for one year. On securities held from 18 to 24 months, net profit or net loss may be included in taxable income up to 66⅔ per cent of the amount involved. On securities held over 24 months, net profit or net loss may be included in taxable income up to 50 per cent of the amount involved.

Corporate income taxes. Under the Revenue Act of 1941, the Federal tax on corporate income is the sum of (1) an *excess profits tax* graduated from 35 per cent of the first $20,000 of earnings in excess of either 95 per cent of average net income from 1936 through 1939 up to 60 per cent of excess profits exceeding $500,000, or, alternatively, in excess of 8 per cent on the first $5,000,000 of invested capital plus 7 per cent on the remainder, plus (2) a *normal tax* of 24 per cent on the earnings remaining after excess profits taxes, plus (3) a surtax of 7 per cent on the net income subject to the normal tax. As a consequence of these taxes, with the prospect of even higher rates under war-time conditions, it is most probable that income available for corporate security holders will lessen rather than increase irrespective of the volume of industrial activity.

State income taxes. A recent compilation showed that more than 30 of the 48 states now levy personal income taxes in addition to those imposed by the Federal Government. Although the personal exemption limits are somewhat lower than those permitted on the Federal returns and the rates are considerably lower on higher incomes (the maximum in New York being 8 per cent and in California being 15 per cent), the levy is based upon the full taxable income without deduction for Federal income tax payments. An investor residing in New York State in 1940 with a total income of $16,000, with a wife and two dependents, would pay a state income tax of $763, or 4.8 per cent of total income, but would pay a rate of 8.0 per cent on $3,700, which is that part of his income in the highest bracket. On the $15,237 remaining, he would pay a Federal tax of $1,221, or 8.0 per cent of net income, but would pay a rate of 17.6 per cent on $437, which is that part of his income in the highest Federal bracket. Such an investor would therefore be paying a total Federal and state tax of no less than 25.6 per cent of that part of his income which fell in the highest Federal bracket.

Federal estate taxes. Estate taxes are imposed by Federal and state authorities under the principle that the right to transfer title to property is a privilege granted by the state rather than an inherent right of the citizens. The tax may be levied against the entire estate of the decedent or against the individual legacies of the beneficiaries, as inheritances. The Federal Government and most states follow the former practice.

The Federal estate tax levy follows the general pattern of the Federal income tax. All estates above a specified minimum are subject to a graduated tax, increasing in rate with the size of the estate. (Under the Revenue Act of 1926 as amended by subsequent Revenue Acts, an exemption is granted on estates up to $40,000. The first $5,000 above the exemption is taxed at 3 per cent, the next $5,000 at 7 per cent, the rate continuing to advance until a maximum of 77 per cent is imposed on that part of the estate in excess of $10,000,000.)

On that part of the Federal estate tax covered by the 1926 Act, a credit up to 80 per cent is allowed for estate taxes paid to state governments; but no similar credit is allowed on that part of the tax covered by the subsequent Acts. The tax applies to the entire net estate above the $40,000 exemption. No securities are exempt. The payment of the tax may not be avoided through outright gift, as is shown in the subsequent paragraph.[3]

Federal gift taxes. In an endeavor to prevent avoidance of the Federal estate tax through lifetime gifts, a graduated tax was placed upon all gifts having a value in excess of $40,000. The gift tax rates are uniformly three fourths of the corresponding estate tax rates. They range from 2¼ per cent on the first $5,000 to a maximum of 57¾ per cent on amounts in excess of $10,000,000.

State estate taxes. With the exception of Nevada, all states in the United States now impose estate or inheritance taxes in addition to those imposed by the Federal Government. The immediate thought that Nevada might afford favorable residence opportunity is refuted by the policy of the Federal Government in allowing the states to collect a substantial part of the estate taxes. The aggregate tax on Nevada and New York estates of equal size is the same, the technical difference being that all of the tax on the Nevada estate is paid to the Federal Government, whereas a large part of the tax on the New York estate is paid to the New York State government. An interesting and not surprising result of the liberal credit granted by the Federal Government for taxes paid to

---

[3] The drastic effect of estate taxes upon large estates is shown in case of the estate of F. W. Vanderbilt, who died in New York on June 29, 1938. Despite the fact that more than $50,000,000 out of a total fortune of $72,588,284 was invested in tax-exempt bonds, total taxes paid to the Federal and state governments amounted to $41,272,109.

state governments is the practice of states to make the state tax equivalent to the maximum credit granted by the Federal Government.

Prior to 1925, the tendency on the part of state governments to impose inheritance taxes upon the transfer of securities of local companies, left in the estates of nonresident decedents, greatly complicated the work of executors. Since that time, however, the enactment of reciprocal legislation by many states leaves less than ten states in which this problem still exists, none of which is of outstanding corporate importance.

Although the tendency on the part of the state governments is to take full advantage of the Federal credit by making the state tax 80 per cent of the 1926 Federal tax, the effect is more applicable to large estates. Generally speaking, the state governments set a smaller exemption figure and thereby tax many estates which are not subject to the Federal tax. (Under the New York law in effect in 1940, estates under $2,000 are not taxed. Exemption amounts to $20,000 for widow or husband and $5,000 for each relative as legally specified.)[4]

Property taxes. Taxes on real and personal, tangible and intangible properties are imposed by state and municipal governments. Investors are especially interested in those taxes that apply against securities which are generally regarded as personal intangible property. Some states impose taxes specifically against security holdings, as, for example, the Pennsylvania tax of four-tenths of 1 per cent annually (the four mills tax) on the value of securities held by residents of that state. The more general practice is to impose on intangible personal property such as securities the same tax rate as that

---

[4] The method by which the Federal and state governments share in the division of estate taxes may be observed from the estate of C. H. Geist of Pennsylvania, who died in 1939 leaving an estate valued at $54,130,684. Under the Revenue Act of 1926, the tax of $9,353,500 would be divided on the basis of $7,482,800 (80 per cent) to the state and $1,870,700 (20 per cent) to the nation. Under subsequent Revenue Acts, a further tax of $23,009,100 is entirely retained by the Federal Government. The total tax liability of the estate was therefore in excess of $33,000,000 of which about $25,000,000 was payable to the Federal Government and about $8,000,000 (including a normal transfer tax of 2 per cent of the estate) was payable to the State of Pennsylvania.

levied on tangible real property such as land and buildings. The levy and collection of taxes on personal property of either a tangible or an intangible nature are much more difficult than in the case of real property. In New York City, for illustration, personal property tax revenues were so small as to cause the abolition of this tax in 1933. It would appear that the significance of such taxes to the investor depends upon the seriousness with which they are regarded in the community in which he is a resident. It is interesting to observe that the location of issuer of the securities and the domicile of the security instruments are factors to be considered, in addition to the place of residence of the owner, in the assessment of these taxes.

Despite the fact that some states endeavor to impose property (as well as income and estate) taxes on securities held within those states for the account of nonresidents, the general practice is to the contrary. The Constitution of New York State guarantees that the state will not impose any property, income, or estate tax on any securities held within the state for nonresidents of the state, in safe-deposit boxes or in safe-keeping, custodian, or trust accounts.

Transfer taxes on securities. Transfer taxes are now imposed on many transactions in securities by the Federal Government as well as by certain state governments. The Federal transfer tax on the sale of stock in 1940 was six cents per share if the price was $20 per share or more, and was five cents per share if less than $20. The Federal transfer tax on the sale of bonds, other than domestic public issues, was five cents per $100 of face value, or fifty cents per $1,000 bond.

The New York State transfer tax applied only on sales of stock and was four cents per share on stock selling at or over $20 and was three cents per share on stock selling under $20 per share in 1940.

14

INSTITUTIONAL INVESTORS

Scope. The purpose of this chapter is to discuss the investment policies and practices, as well as the legal restrictions upon the more important financial institutions of the country. The order of discussion is: (1) corporate trustees, (2) savings banks, (3) commercial banks, and (4) life insurance companies. These institutions hold securities in an amount exceeding $60,000,000,000 and comprise a major segment of the investment business. Collectively, the policies of these institutions represent a consensus of conservative investment practice as employed by the most experienced and the most successful buyers of securities in the United States.

Fiduciary restrictions. A notable development over recent years in the investment field has been the growing importance of institutional investors. The group includes banks, trust companies, insurance companies, trustees, administrators, executors, fraternal organizations, educational institutions, and various others. In all cases, the individuals act in a position of trust, investing not their own money but the funds of others entrusted to their care. It naturally follows that such fiduciary relationship requires a degree of prudence and caution beyond that which the individuals might employ in the selection of their own commitments. The latitude within which fiduciaries may exercise discretion depends upon the nature of the trust, the powers granted by the maker, and the various Federal and state laws governing the investment of fiduciary institutions. The purpose of the present chapter is to indicate investment procedure in this important field, surrounded as it is by many restrictions that do not confront the private investor.

Not all institutional investors are obligated to observe the laws governing the investment of trust funds. Fraternal organizations and educational institutions may establish investment policies of their own and may purchase any securities they desire, restricting their activities only by self-imposed conditions. Trustees, banks, and insurance companies, however, are usually obliged to purchase only those securities that are legally eligible. Owing to separate legislative acts, moreover, a particular security, which may be a "legal investment" for one class of fiduciaries, may be ineligible for another. As will be shown later, the restrictions are generally conservative as applicable to savings banks and life insurance companies, and liberal as to commercial banks and fire insurance companies.

Investment trust company securities are discussed elsewhere in this book and not in the present chapter. The title of these institutions is unfortunate and misleading. The term *investment trust* should connote a fiduciary relationship vastly different from that which exists between investors and managers of the typical American investment trust company. That sense of personal responsibility which should pervade every act of the trust manager is practically nonexistent in the selection of securities by American investment trust companies.

Part 1. Trustee Investments

Trustee investments. Trust funds are administered by trustees appointed by the maker of the trust. The trust may be *voluntary*, to go into effect at any time, or *testamentary*, to become effective upon the death of the maker. The investment policy of the trustee will be governed by the instructions, if any, in the trust instrument. [1] In the absence of documentary instructions, the trustee must follow the procedure set forth in the laws of the state of jurisdiction governing the investment of trust funds. In the event that the particular state has no legislation in this respect, the trustee must observe a code of procedure which has become known as the *American rule* and which was admirably stated over a century ago in a celebrated case:

All that can be required of a trustee to invest is that he shall conduct himself faithfully and exercise a sound discretion. He is to observe how men of prudence, discretion and intelligence manage their own affairs, not in regard to speculation, but in regard to the permanent disposition of their funds, considering the probable income, as well as the probable safety of the capital to be invested.[2]

State laws governing trustee investments are far from uniform. Trustees in New York are not permitted, in the absence of expressed power, to purchase stocks of any description, not even high-grade preferred issues. Trustees in the contiguous State of Massachusetts may buy common stocks if they so elect. The New York law restricts trustee investments, with a few minor exceptions, to those securities that are eligible for savings banks.

Common stocks in trust funds. The contention that trustees should be allowed to invest trust funds in common stocks without specific instructions has been repeatedly upheld by trust company officials during recent years. Trustees have faced, on one hand, the difficulty of finding acceptable bonds at a satisfactory interest rate and, on the other hand, the problem of protecting the value of the fund in a period of inflation. When given permission to do so in trust instruments, many trust companies have placed as much as 25 to 33 per cent of a trust fund in common stocks. Stanford University

---

[1] The instructions may be conservative or liberal, as is well illustrated in two recent important testamentary cases. The H. P. Whitney will granted "absolute discretion, without regard to the restrictions placed by law," whereas the P. M. Warburg will specifically limited the types of securities which might be purchased.

[2] Harvard College v. Armory, 9 Pickering 446 (1830).

received permission from the courts in 1936 to invest endowment funds in common stocks as a means of receiving a higher rate of return and as a hedge against inflation.

Acting under laws enacted in 1937, the Chancery Courts in New Jersey recently gave permission to trustees in that state to invest in common stocks without having specific authority to do so in the trust agreement, in one case, up to 20 per cent of the fund, and, in another, up to 25 per cent. In the second instance, the Court went so far as to approve a list of 36 common stocks as eligible for trustee investment.[3]

The advisability of the purchase of common stocks by trustees is doubted by many persons of unquestioned financial standing. A New England banker of the very highest reputation has stated his opinion in these words:[4]

Experience has shown that the trustee who becomes a partner in a corporation by the purchase of stock is taking a speculative risk, and that in the long run the trustee who loans money, that is, purchases bonds, comes out best.

Of collateral value as evidence is the opinion of the president of one of the largest life insurance companies in New York regarding the suitability of common stocks for life insurance companies:[5]

Common stocks have been available for a century or longer and it is recent developments only that have made them so attractive.

---

[3] It might be of interest to list the stocks which were regarded as acceptable under this ruling in 1939. It is significant to observe that the list contains no railroad stocks and only 3 public utility stocks and 33 industrial stocks, of which two are oil stocks and four are mining stocks. The complete list is here shown: Allied Chemical, American Can, American Chicle, American Telephone, Beech-Nut, Bristol-Myers, Commercial Credit, Commercial Investment Trust, Consolidated Edison, Corn Products, du Pont, Eastman Kodak, General Electric, General Foods, General Motors, Homestake Mining, Household Finance, International Business Machines, International Harvester, International Nickel, Liggett and Myers, Monsanto, National Steel, New Jersey Zinc, Penney Stores, Phelps-Dodge, Procter and Gamble, Public Service of New Jersey, Reynolds Tobacco, Sears-Roebuck, Sherwin-Williams, Standard Oil of New Jersey, Texas Corporation, Union Carbide, Union Tank Car, and United States Tobacco.

[4] From letter written by Frederick H. Prince, quoted in *The Wall Street Journal,* January 6, 1934.

[5] From letter written by Thomas A. Buckner in 1929, quoted in *The Wall Street Journal,* March 12, 1936.

To change a fundamental law because of what has happened in the last five years, would, in my opinion, be ill-advised for it would be basing a permanent decision upon temporary grounds.

Corporate trustees. Trustees are personally responsible for their acts and may be surcharged for any losses in the trust fund arising from carelessness or fraud. They are therefore financially as well as morally obligated to fulfill their trust. In view of this responsibility and in further consideration of the growing complexity of the investment business, it is not surprising to observe the trend toward the appointment of corporate trustees. The ensuing table, which covers only national banks in the United States and therefore excludes an equally impressive showing for state banks, indicates how rapidly this development has progressed over recent years:

TRUST OPERATIONS OF NATIONAL BANKS

Year	Trust Depts.	Trusts	Trust Assets
1926	1,104	26,053	$ 922,328,677
1940	1,540	137,629	9,345,419,682
Increase	40%	429%	913%

A cogent reason for the increase in the creation of trusts has been the development of newer forms of trust instruments. In interesting contrast to the older type of testamentary trusts, greater use is now being made of voluntary trusts, or *living trusts,* under which the property is immediately placed with the trustee, and income is thereafter payable to the beneficiaries. A specialized trust gaining in popularity is the *life insurance trust,* under which the proceeds of life insurance policies are trusted for the beneficiaries under the policy. In 1940 the national banks of the United States alone had been named trustees under some 15,500 life insurance policies aggregating over $590,000,000 in face value.[6]

[6] A favorite argument advanced for the creation of a life insurance trust is the statement that the life insurance payments usually are quickly dissipated. The truth of such a statement is seriously questioned by the life insurance companies. Evidence to the contrary is afforded in the *Report of the Association of Life Insurance Presidents for 1927,* pages 207-214.

Common trusts. A *common trust* is one in which several small trust funds are combined for purposes of economy and efficiency of administration. Such consolidated funds are specifically permitted under the laws of at least seven states and are not prohibited under the laws or banking regulations of any of the other states.[7] Although state banking institutions must operate common trusts in accordance with the laws of the state in which the bank is located, national banks must follow a uniform plan as here stated. The maximum participation of any one fund is restricted to $25,000 in order to limit the trust to small funds on which administration expenses are relatively high and in which adequate diversification of risk is difficult to obtain. The trust may not invest more than 10 per cent of its assets in any single enterprise other than United States Government securities. Cash and readily marketable securities, defined as subject to frequent dealings in ready markets, should comprise about 40 per cent of the trust. Participations and withdrawals are permitted only on quarterly valuation dates. Funds may not participate in a common trust if any assets in the trust are illegal for the fund to hold. Documents which evidence participation in the trust must be nonnegotiable. In New York State, common trusts are permitted to invest only in securities which are eligible for purchase by savings banks.

Duration of trust funds. Although the statutory limitations on trust funds is generally stated as two generations, numerous funds have been created to carry through three generations, and several are now in effect which will carry through four generations. The will of William Rockefeller, who died in 1922 leaving a net estate of $50,000,000 after the payment of debts, taxes, and administrative expenses, created in effect a group of trust funds under which the estate is to be kept intact for the great-grandchildren of the decedent. The will provided that the estate should be preserved for ultimate distribution in four equal parts to the grandchil-

---

[7] The seven states which have authorized the commingling of trust funds into common trusts are Delaware, Indiana, Minnesota, New York, Ohio, Pennsylvania, and Vermont.

dren of each of the four children of Mr. Rockefeller. To assure such distribution, separate trust funds were established out of each quarter of the estate for the sons and daughters of each of the children of the testator, of whom there were fourteen living in 1937. These trust funds of the grandchildren of the testator were to be held for distribution to their children, the great-grandchildren of Mr. Rockefeller, of whom twenty-eight were living in 1937, on the death of their parents. Under this plan, a considerably longer period was established than through the device of using the life of the youngest grandchild as the duration of the trust.

Investment procedure. The investment procedure of a trustee is complicated by the fact that the wishes of not one but three parties must be respected—namely, the trustor who created the trust, the present beneficiaries who are entitled to the income from the fund, and the ultimate beneficiaries who will receive the principal of the fund at the expiration of the trust.

It is not uncommon for trustors to make restrictions that hamper the trustee. In some cases, the trustee is required to hold certain securities which might better be sold. [8] In other cases the trustee is not given the power to purchase certain securities which in his judgment would be appropriate for the purpose. [9]

The present beneficiaries in a trust fund, who desire as high a rate of income as might reasonably be expected, naturally object to any attempt on the part of the trustees to buy only the very safest securities, on which the rate of return is low. On the other hand, the trustee must be mindful of the ultimate beneficiaries, called "remaindermen," who

---

[8] A trust fund created by a donor in 1912 in favor of the Metropolitan Museum of Art comprised 1,200 shares of stock of a certain bank, having a market value of $1,000,000 at the time and producing an annual income of $48,000, and contained a restriction against the sale of the stock. Within ten years, the bank closed and the stock was worthless.

[9] The trustees of a fund in New York in 1935 applied for permission to place common stocks to the extent of 35 per cent of the total amount in a trust fund restricted to legal investments on the plea that an "emergency" existed in the "probability of inflation" which warranted the request. The court refused on the ground that "any change in the class of legal investments must be the subject of legislative and not judicial action."

are entitled to the principal of the fund as nearly intact as conservative stewardship can preserve. Between the opposing viewpoints, the trustee must steer a middle course, concentrating neither in the highest-grade issues with low yields or in the low-grade issues with high yields. As safety of principal is paramount, however, he must not go below medium-grade issues and should prefer the higher-grade issues. In a market where the yield on the best grade of long-term bonds is under 3 per cent, an average rate of return as high as 4 per cent would be an unreasonable expectation from a conscientious trustee.

It is universally held that it is outside of the duty of a trustee to increase the value of a fund. Appreciation should be eliminated on the general principle, that, in testamentary cases at least, death should end the risk of accumulation. The argument in favor of common stocks for trust accounts should be settled on the basis of income prospects rather than appreciation possibilities, unless it can be maintained that the duty of the trustee is to preserve purchasing power as well as dollars.

Investment conditions during the past decade have made the work of the trustee increasingly difficult. The situation was summarized in succinct but realistic fashion in a recent address of a trust company official: [10]

Shall those of us who have the final say in trust investments buy railroad bonds, in spite of the threat of wholesale reorganizations and the scaling-down of fixed charges? Shall we buy utility bonds when the government is free to lend money to municipalities to compete with local operating companies on a red-ink basis, with the taxpayers holding the bag?

Shall we purchase industrial bonds and take a chance on the obligor corporation being legislated out of business by hour-and-wage regulations or by drastic methods of taxation? Shall we buy stocks and face possible litigation if we don't get out at the right time? Or shall we confine ourselves to government bonds and pray for a cessation of budget deficits?

British trustee investments. A statement of the restrictions upon trustee investments in England affords interesting

---

[10] From address by Robertson Griswold, of Maryland Trust Company, at American Bankers Association Conference at New York, on February 15, 1938.

comparison with the requirements in vogue in the United States. The American investor who is surprised to note that United States Government bonds are not legal investments in England is in the same position as the British investor who finds that bonds of Great Britain are barred as legal investments in the State of New York.

Under the Trustee Act of 1925, trustee investments in England are limited to the following securities:

1. Bonds of governments included in the British Empire.
2. Bonds of the larger British municipalities.
3. Bonds and preferred stocks of British railroad companies, provided 3 per cent dividends have been paid on the common stock for the preceding ten years.
4. Bonds and preferred stocks of British water-supply companies, provided 5 per cent dividends have been paid on the common stock for the preceding ten years.
5. First mortgages on real estate located in the United Kingdom.

Part 2. Savings Bank Investments

Function of savings banks. Eighteen of the forty-eight states in the nation have enacted legislation authorizing the establishment of banks to be operated primarily for the deposit of savings by people of moderate means. Although some of these states allow accounts in savings banks as high as $25,000, the general practice is to restrict balances to amounts below $10,000. New York State has set a $7,500 maximum on single accounts, a restriction which is easily evaded, however, through the opening of similar accounts in other savings banks in the state.

As the purpose of savings banks is to help people of limited means to save rather than to provide a depository for the funds of wealthy people, *savings* accounts which are gradually accumulated over long periods of time are encouraged and *investment* accounts which are usually created by large single deposits are discouraged. Apart from the savings function of the banks, a secondary reason for the discouragement of investment accounts is the probability that such accounts are usually placed in savings banks when investing opportunities are poor and are withdrawn when conditions are favorable. Moreover, banks with large investment accounts must keep relatively large amounts of idle funds in order to meet occasional demands from a small number of their depositors. Deposits in savings accounts are much more permanent, being subject to withdrawal only in the event of personal emergency. The bank can invest savings funds. in securities of limited marketability, such as home mortgages, which are adequately safe and pay a higher rate of income than do the more marketable securities in which investment funds.would normally be placed.

In view of the purposes for which savings banks have been established, the legislatures of most of the states in which these banks operate have imposed restrictions upon their investment powers in order to safeguard the deposited funds. Many states require that savings banks be mutually owned in order to reduce the hazard of investment policies designed to bring profits to stockholders more than income to depositors. As no two states have a uniform law regarding the eligibility of securities for savings banks, a comparative exhibit of such requirements is beyond the scope of this volume. Because the New York law is representative of the most conservative legislation in this respect and because the designation of any security as a "legal investment in New York State" is a mark of the highest respect in the investment world, the following discussion is applicable only to those savings banks (and trustees) located in the State of New York.

Legal investments in New York State. The present legal list in New York has resulted from an evolutionary development over the past century. Prior to the Civil War, only the bond issues of the state itself, and of municipalities within the state and real estate mortgages therein, were eligible. During the Civil War, United States Government bonds and the bonds of specified states and cities outside of New York were made eligible. Some thirty years later, bonds of other states and outside cities were allowed to qualify under a general test rather than through specific authority. About the same time, corporate bonds were first admitted on the basis of certain issues of designated railroad companies; subsequently, railroad bonds were allowed to qualify under a general rule applicable to such issues. Public utility bonds were not admitted prior to 1928 when the law provided a general rule under which utility bonds might qualify. Despite their most impressive record of safety, railroad equipment obligations were not made legal until 1929. Industrial bonds were finally made eligible in 1937 under a decided change in the policy of the Legislature whereby the power was granted to the State Banking Board to admit to the legal list any corporate *bonds,* otherwise ineligible, which the Board may determine to be worthy of purchase.

It is at least interesting to observe that no stocks of any kind, either preferred or common, or foreign securities of any description, may qualify as legal investments for savings banks in New York.

Although the New York legal list has not provided complete protection against investment losses, as the record of eligible railroad bonds during the past decade plainly shows, the solvency record of New York savings banks is sufficient testimony to the efficiency of the law. Not only did no savings bank fail in New York during the banking crisis of 1932-1933, but no savings bank has failed in New York during the past thirty years, and no depositor in a New York State savings bank has lost money by reason of the failure of the bank during the present century.

A brief summary of the securities which are legal investments in New York is here given. An official list of the securities which are regarded as eligible is prepared by the State Banking Department and issued at the beginning of July in each year. [11]

---

[11] A convenient source of reference on other states is provided in the semi-annual *State and Municipal Compendium* of *The Commercial and Financial Chronicle.*

Savings banks in New York State may invest only in the following securities:

1. Direct obligations of the United States.
2. Bonds of New York State.
3. Bonds of other states in the United States not in default.
4. Direct obligations of New York State municipalities.
5. (a) Bonds of certain counties, cities, and school districts in adjoining states, having a minimum population of 10,000 and a maximum net debt ratio of 12 per cent of real property valuation.

(b) Bonds of certain counties, cities, and school districts in nonadjoining states, having a minimum population of 30,000 and a maximum net debt ratio of 12 per cent of real property valuation.

(c) Bonds of any city in the United States that has taxable real property in excess of $200,000,000, a minimum population of 150,000, and no tax-limit legislation in effect.

(d) Bonds of counties, cities, and school districts outside of New York State issued after December 31, 1938, must not be subject to any tax-limit legislation which does not exclude debt service.

6. Bonds and mortgages on unencumbered real property situated in New York State up to 60 per cent of appraised value on nonresidential property, and up to 66⅔ per cent on residential property (except F.H.A. mortgages).

7. (a) Mortgage bonds of certain domestic railroad companies, direct or assumed, including equipment trusts, which have at least 500 miles of line, have annual revenues of at least $10,000,000, have earned fixed charges at least one and one-half times in previous year and in five out of six previous years, have paid cash dividends equal to one fourth of fixed charges or earned fixed charges at least one and one half times in previous year and in nine out of ten previous years, and have had no default in the past six years. (This provision was nonoperative from 1931 to 1938 with respect to bonds previously legal. Subsequent to 1938, bonds had to

show fixed charges earned at least once in five out of six test years preceding investment under a moratorium which extended until 1941.)[12]

(b) Debenture bonds of companies included in the preceding paragraph which show all charges earned at least two times in previous year and in five out of six previous years, and which show a net income of $10,000,000 after all charges have been deducted.

8. Consolidated debenture bonds of the Federal Land Banks and the Federal Home Loan Banks.

9. Mortgage bonds of certain domestic electric and gas companies that have annual operating revenues of at least $1,000,000 have earned fixed charges at least two times in previous year and on an average basis for five previous years, and show a balance available for dividends of at least 4 per cent on two thirds of the funded debt. The bonds must be part of a minimum issue of $1,000,000, and must represent a first or refunding mortgage not exceeding 60 per cent of the value of the physical property pledged.

10. Mortgage bonds of certain domestic telephone companies that have annual operating revenues of at least $5,000,000, have earned fixed charges at least two times in previous years and on an average basis for five previous years, and show a balance available for dividends of at least 4 per cent on outstanding stock. The bonds must be part of a minimum issue of $5,000,000, and must represent a first or refunding mortgage not exceeding 60 per cent of the value of the physical property pledged.

11. Corporate interest-bearing obligations not otherwise eligible, which, in the opinion of the State Banking Board, are suitable investments for savings banks.

12. The maximum proportion of total assets that may be invested in certain of the preceding groups is as follows: real estate mortgages, 65 per cent (exclusive of Federal Hous-

---

[12] A striking picture of the decline in the position of railroad bonds is shown in the statement that approximately 7.6 billion dollars in par value railroad bonds were "legal" in 1931 and less than 1.0 billion dollars were eligible on the same basis in 1939.

ing Administration insured mortgages); railroad obligations, 25 per cent; electric and gas bonds, 10 per cent; telephone bonds, 10 per cent.

The total face value of all securities on the legal list in New York in 1940, excluding United States Government obligations and real estate mortgages, amounted to approximately 18 billion dollars. The list included 254 railroad bonds, 143 public utility bonds, and 566 state, county, city, and school district areas outside of New York State. Despite the eligibility of such a huge total of available securities, the savings banks in New York had invested less than 20 per cent of their deposits in this group, having placed around 30 per cent in United States Government securities and 50 per cent in real estate mortgages at the beginning of 1941.

Part 3.   Commercial Bank Investments

Investment restrictions. The investment policies of all commercial banks which are members of the Federal Reserve System, including all national banks and the state-chartered banks which have joined the system, are governed by the rules and regulations established under the Federal Statutes as amended by the Banking Act of 1935. State banks which are not members of the Federal Reserve System are governed by the banking laws of the state where located. Because the member banks in the Federal Reserve System comprise nearly one half of all commercial banks in the country and hold more than 70 per cent of all banking assets, the following discussion is devoted chiefly to the investment procedure of those banks which are governed by the Federal Statutes.

Commercial banks are not permitted to participate as principals in the marketing of corporate securities. They are permitted to buy securities for their own account if the securities are of adequate quality and marketability. They are not permitted to buy any securities in which the investment characteristics are distinctly or predominantly speculative. They may buy no securities which are in default of either principal or interest payments. They may buy no convertible bonds at a price above their nonconvertible value. They may purchase no stocks of any kind, either preferred or common. They may, however, hold any securities acquired through foreclosure on collateral, or acquired in good faith by way of a claim compromise.

The requirement that all securities bought by commercial banks have adequate marketability is especially important. Marketability is defined in the official regulations as "salable under ordinary circumstances with reasonable promptness at a fair value." Evidence of marketability must exist in either (a) public distribution of the particular issue, or (b) public distribution of other issues of the obligor. If there has been no public distribution, eligible bonds are limited to ten-year (or less) obligations of established enterprises, having sound values, under an acceptable sinking fund plan of amortization.

For purposes of bank examinations, securities are divided into four groups of quality. All eligible securities are placed in Group I and are valued on the basis of cost, less amortization if any; appreciation or depreciation is disregarded. Securities in Group II are primarily of a speculative character and are valued at the average market price for the preceding eighteen months. Securities in Group III are bonds in default. All stocks are placed in Group IV. Groups III and IV are valued at cost or market, whichever is lower. Bonds purchased at a premium must be amortized. Profits from the sale of securities must not be considered as earnings until adequate reserves for actual and estimated losses have been provided. The purchase of securities for speculative profits is officially regarded as being opposed to sound banking principles.

Investment policies. The investment policy of a commercial bank is usually determined by (a) the nature of the deposit liabilities, and (b) the relationship between deposits and capital funds. Commercial banks which normally carry large demand deposits must maintain a higher degree of liquidity of assets than those in which time deposits predominate. Banks which have capital funds in the form of capital stock, undivided profits, and surplus amounting to less than ten per cent of deposits must adjust their investment commitments accordingly to prevent depreciation on securities from impairing the integrity of the capital investment.

The assets of a commercial bank consist of cash and balances in other banks (known as primary reserves), short-term obligations in the form of call loans and commercial paper (known as secondary reserves), investment securities (known as the bond account), commercial loans and discounts, and real estate mortgages. The distinction between secondary reserves and the bond account has been well expressed in the following paragraph: [13]

Secondary reserve bond investments will be presumed to be of such unquestioned credit quality and of such short term duration that they cannot cause the bank any loss whatsoever which is not infinitesimal in its consequence. Considering the true function and nature of the secondary reserve, this should not be a difficult policy. The bond investment account, however, is of a more permanent nature, and, what is most important, it is designed to perform a distinctly different function, namely, the investment for return of a portion of the bank's funds. Hence, it does bear, in our opinion, a most definite relationship not only to the amount and nature of deposits but to the condition of the capital account.

In determining the relative proportion of total assets to be placed in each of these five groups, a commercial bank faces the difficult problem of trying to maintain adequate liquidity and still derive a reasonable income. The primary reserves are completely liquid but pay no income; the term *excess reserves* so frequently heard in banking discussions during recent years arises out of primary reserve holdings greatly in excess of legal requirements. The secondary reserves are extremely liquid but pay a very small rate of return. The bond account will also return a small yield if the securities are primarily Government issues of high marketability, often called "money bonds" because of immediate salability; higher yields are obtainable only at the sacrifice of lower quality and less marketability. Commercial loans

---

[13] From *Commercial Bank Management*, Booklet No. 19, issued by Bank Management Commission, American Bankers Association.

and discounts usually give favorable yields but are not dependable sources of funds at short notice. Real estate mortgages also give favorable yields but are the least liquid of the entire portfolio.

Bond investments have long been a popular type of bank commitment. Even in times when the demand for commercial loans was in excess of the supply of loanable funds, banks bought bonds partly for liquidity and diversification of risk as well as for the favorable rate of return afforded. It was assumed that good bonds could be readily marketed to provide cash in the event of emergency. The fallacy of this assumption was demonstrated in the banking crisis of a decade ago, which was caused chiefly by "frozen assets" in the form of unmarketable securities. Between 1930 and 1933, the average depreciation on a representative group of listed bonds was 40 per cent, with declines varying from 10 per cent on the highest-grade issues to more than 50 per cent on the low-grade bonds. Banks which held securities of the average grade to the extent of more than 250 per cent of their capital funds were therefore technically insolvent. Banks which had invested in excess of 300 per cent of their capital funds in lower-than-average bonds were hopelessly insolvent. Only those banks survived which had purchased primarily high-grade bonds and had kept their bond account within conservative proportion to their capital funds.

Investment procedure. The ability on the part of bank management to put a sound policy into effect is dependent upon the condition of the money market. A desire to keep 50 per cent of total assets in commercial loans can be carried out only if a concurrent demand exists. A resolve to keep the bond account down to 20 per cent of total assets may be frustrated by the holding of excessive reserves for which there is no commercial demand. A decision to keep Federal holdings below 30 per cent of assets may be inexpedient if no alternative securities are available at acceptable prices. Actual procedure, therefore, must be based upon conditions, not theories.

An accompanying table shows the distribution of all bank

investments in the United States. A certain allowance must be made for the fact that the figure for state banks includes savings banks as well as commercial banks. The figures for national banks, however, cover only commercial banks and are therefore more applicable to the present discussion. As of June 30, 1939, the national banks were carrying over 21 billion dollars in loans and securities in the respective ratios of 40 and 60 per cent. Approximately 10 per cent of the total loans was in real estate mortgages, and about 30 per

ANALYSIS OF BANK INVESTMENTS IN THE UNITED STATES
COMPTROLLER OF CURRENCY REPORT, AS OF JUNE 30, 1939
(AMOUNTS IN MILLIONS OF DOLLARS)

	National Banks		State Banks		All Banks	
	$	%	$	%	$	%
United States Government bonds	8,769	41.5	10,021	34.8	18,790	37.7
Other bonds..................	3,784	17.9	5,812	20.2	9,596	19.2
Total bonds..................	12,553	59.4	15,833	55.0	28,386	56.9
Real estate loans.............	1,829	8.7	7,085	24.6	8,914	17.9
Other loans..................	6,744	31.9	5,857	20.4	12,601	25.2
Total loans..................	8,573	40.6	12,942	45.0	21,515	43.1
Grand total..................	21,126	100.0	28,775	100.0	49,901	100.0

cent was in business loans. About 20 per cent of the total bonds was in municipal and corporate bonds, and no less than 40 per cent was in the direct or guaranteed obligations of the Federal Government. These percentages are irrespective of the large primary reserves carried in cash and balances in other banks.

The investment position of the fifteen largest banks in New York showed that 56 per cent of total loans and investment had been invested in United States Government obligations on December 31, 1940. The same compilation showed that primary reserves amounted to 42 per cent of all assets and were in excess of all securities which amounted to 39 per cent and of all loans which amounted to 17 per cent of total assets.

Part 4. Insurance Company Investments

Investment restrictions. Apart from the various Federal insurance corporations which insure the safety of bank deposits, of deposits in savings and loan associations, and of real estate mortgages on residential property, all of which have Federal charters and invest only in Government obligations, the insurance companies of the country operate under the laws of the states of incorporation. These laws usually distinguish between the life insurance companies and those which insure against contingency losses such as fire and accidents. The restrictions on the investment powers of life insurance companies are naturally more severe than those on the casualty companies. As has been stated in a previous chapter, the fire and casualty companies have almost unrestricted powers in the selection of securities. Because of variations in state laws regarding the investment power of insurance companies, the present discussion is necessarily limited to the restrictions in New York State. The New York restrictions on life insurance investments are probably as conservative as those in any state in the Union.

Securities which are eligible for purchase by life insurance companies in New York State under the revised statutes effective in 1940 are as follows:

(1) Federal, state, and municipal bonds of domestic issue.

(2) Secured domestic corporate bonds of predominantly investment character on which fixed charges have been earned on the average one and one-quarter times or better.

(3) Unsecured domestic corporate bonds on which fixed charges have been earned on the average one and one-half times or better.

(4) Preferred or guaranteed stock of domestic origin on which all charges including prior interest have been earned one and one-half times or better.

(5) Domestic real estate mortgage loans not in excess of

two-thirds of appraised value. Such loans must not aggregate more than 40 per cent of total assets, excluding F.H.A. insured loans.

(6) Canadian Government loans, not in excess of 10 per cent of total assets.

Fire and casualty insurance companies in New York are permitted to purchase any income-producing securities, thereby being prohibited from buying bonds in default or stocks which are not on a dividend-paying basis. Such companies, however, must comply with the requirements for life insurance companies as to eligible investments to the extent of 50 per cent of the unearned premium reserve and reserves for estimated losses.

Investment policy. The investment policies adopted by the life insurance companies of the United States have been established more on a basis of empiricism than legislation. They have set up their own principles of operation and standards of acceptability based upon experience and observation extending far back in the past century. They have gained the reputation of being perhaps the most intelligent buyers of securities in the investment market.

The nature of the life insurance business permits the establishment of a most conservative investment policy. In the first place, the liabilities of a life insurance company are essentially long-term obligations, thus permitting investment in longer-term less marketable issues which offer the more attractive rates of return. In the second place, revenue is constantly being received in the form of premium payments, income from investments, and redemption of securities in such volume as to keep a high degree of liquidity adequate for emergency needs as might arise out of a sudden demand for policy loans. In the third place, the premium rates charged to policyholders assume a moderate rate of return on investments, thereby eliminating any necessity of obtaining yields higher than those provided by high-grade securities. And last, but not least, the life insurance companies can afford investment departments qualified to make the most intelligent analysis of available securities and to maintain the most careful supervision of securities owned.

The principles which underlie the investment policy of life insurance companies were concisely stated in a recent address of the president of one of the largest companies:

1. The tradition of priority of liens, supported by reasonable earnings, strong ownership, and ample equities.

2. The tradition of invariable amortization of mortgage loans, correcting changes or overestimates in market value.

3. The tradition of diversification of investments, as to general character, location, and number.

4. The tradition of constant analysis and criticism of holdings.

5. The tradition of moderation as to income yield being an accurate yardstick of quality.

6. The tradition of honest charge-offs at frequent intervals, correcting errors of judgment. [14]

It should be observed that the policy of the American life insurance companies has always been in opposition to the suitability of common stocks for their portfolios. Although such a policy is already incorporated in the legal restrictions in New York, insurance officials in that state have repeatedly expressed an unwillingness to buy common stocks for their companies even if such procedure were to be legally permitted.

The investment policies adopted by the fire and casualty companies in the United States have been based upon principles fundamentally different from those in the life insurance field. Unlike the life insurance companies which must provide reserves for long-term obligations running as long as fifty years and further into the future, the fire and casualty companies must meet short-term obligations rarely exceeding three years in time. The question of liquidity, therefore, is much more important to these companies, requiring that they invest chiefly in securities of high marketability.

---

[14] From *Investment Trends and Traditions,* by William A. Law, an address before the Association of Life Insurance Presidents, December 10, 1931.

The question of profit from security trading seldom arises in life insurance companies because of the absence of stockholders seeking large profits from the enterprise. Fire and casualty companies, however, are to a substantial degree owned and operated as much for the interests of stockholders as for policyholders. Because common stocks do afford a high degree of marketability and an attractive opportunity for profit through appreciation, it is not surprising to observe that common stocks are usually more popular than bonds or mortgages with these companies.

Investment procedure. An examination of the investment holdings of the American life insurance companies over the period from 1906 to 1940 shows that drastic changes were made in investment procedure in order to keep fundamental policies in effect. [15]

Mortgages on farm property had increased from 9 per cent of total assets of 1906 to nearly 19 per cent in 1924, after which time the companies apparently became concerned over the agricultural situation and placed new funds in other fields. Farm loans in 1929 were almost as large as in 1924 but amounted to only 12 per cent of assets. In 1940 farm loans had been cut to less than 3 per cent of assets, a substantial part of the reduction being offset, however, by real estate acquired through foreclosure proceedings.

Mortgages on farm property had increased from about 20 per cent of total assets in 1906 to 30 per cent in 1929, but in 1940 had declined to 16 per cent, or lower than in 1906. Total mortgage ratios advanced from nearly 30 per cent in 1906 to 43 per cent in 1927, but had fallen to 19 per cent in 1940. It is interesting to observe that new investments made in farm mortgages in 1939 and 1940 were 2 per cent of all new securities acquired and new purchases of non-farm mortgages were 16 per cent of all new investments, indicating that the portfolio percentages represent satisfactory proportions under the conditions then existing.

United States Government bonds first became of importance

---

[15] From data prepared by the Association of Life Insurance Presidents and *The Wall Street Journal* as reported in the *Federal Home Loan Bank Review*.

to life insurance companies during World War years when heavy subscriptions to war loans brought the ratio in excess of 10 per cent. By 1930, this ratio had declined to 2 per cent, but in 1940 had risen to 20 per cent. New purchases

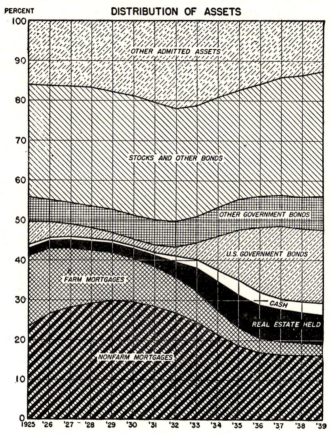

American Life Insurance Companies. (From *Federal Home Loan Bank Review,* Federal Home Loan Bank Board, Washington, D. C., April, 1940.)

of Government issues in 1939 and 1940 amounted to about 32 per cent of all new investments acquired.

Bonds of foreign governments, other than Canada, have never appealed to the life insurance companies. Holdings were under ½ of 1 per cent in 1924 and were less than ⅒ of 1 per cent in 1939. The life insurance companies were thus spared the embarrassment of facing the numerous defaults which have developed in this group.

State and municipal bonds have shown a gradual increase in popularity with the life companies, the ratio increasing from 4 per cent in 1906 to nearly 6 per cent in 1940. New purchases were about 7 per cent of total purchases in 1939 and 1940.

Railroad bonds, which comprised nearly 35 per cent of total assets in 1906, made up only 20 per cent in 1926 when the industry apparently reached its peak development, and represented only 11 per cent in 1940. New railroad securities bought in 1939 and 1940 represented less than 8 per cent of total purchases.

Public utility securities advanced from a ratio of 5 per cent in 1906 to 9 per cent in 1929 and to 14 per cent in 1940. Purchases of utility bonds in 1939 and 1940 represented 22 per cent of new investments.

Industrial and miscellaneous securities represented 3 per cent of all assets in 1929 and 6 per cent in 1940. Purchases in this group in 1939 and 1940 represented between 10 and 15 per cent of new investments.

Total corporate securities, which represented 50 per cent of all assets in 1906, had declined to a ratio of 40 per cent in 1925 and to 31 per cent in 1940. Purchases amounted to about 30 per cent of all new investments made in 1939 and 1940.

A recent study of life insurance investments covering the year 1938 disclosed interesting aspects of life insurance. Income from bond investments, including Government issues, averaged about 3½ per cent and provided about 50 per cent of total investment income. Income from mortgages averaged about 4¾ per cent and provided about 25 per cent of the total. Income from policy loans averaged about 5¾ per cent and provided about 20 per cent of the total. [16]

----

[16] *Securities and Exchange Commission, 1940.*

15

INVESTORS OF LIMITED MEANS

Scope. The purpose of this chapter is to discuss the investment opportunities available to the person of limited means who has only a few thousand or a few hundred dollars to invest. The order of discussion is: (1) financial objectives, (2) life insurance, (3) savings banks, (4) postal savings, (5) United States Savings Bonds, (6) home ownership, (7) savings and loan associations, and (8) securities. The negative conclusion is ventured that the purchase of bonds and stocks by the small investor may be less advisable than an account in a savings institution or the purchase of life insurance or a home.

Financial objectives. Investors of limited means should formulate a financial policy in which the purchase of securities is but one of several objectives. Although investors include persons with only a few hundred dollars as well as others with many thousands, it is probably true that the individual with less than $1,000 at his command would be well advised to place his funds in a savings institution rather than in securities. It might well be argued that the individual with less than $5,000 might follow the same plan because it is only at the $10,000 level that the investor approaches the point where he may intelligently spread his risks of investment. Elusive as the "average investor" may be, it would be more correct to assume that he is a man with a fund of $50,000 or more, rather than any smaller amount.

If the investor is a family man with dependents, the question of cash reserves, life insurance, and home ownership should be carefully considered before that of investing in securities. A married man with dependents should hold a reserve in a cash savings account available for emergency use equal to three months' income. He should carry enough life insurance to assure the protection of his children until they become of age, in the form of low-cost term insurance in the event that the cost of whole-life insurance should be prohibitive. He might well consider the purchase of a home for his family as an investment which will return intangible social dividends in addition to the economy which ownership often affords.

Even after adequate provision has been made for emergency reserve, life insurance, and home ownership, the investor might well consider depositing his funds in thrift institutions such as savings banks and savings and loan associations in order to be relieved of the inconvenience and risk involved in the direct purchase of bonds and stocks. He would be following the example of the largest financial institutions in the country at the present time if he loaned his funds to the Federal Government through either a postal savings account or United States Savings bonds. In other words, the purchase of a small number of shares of the common stock of as outstanding companies as General Motors or American Telephone would be advisable only after many other alternative investments were properly considered.

Life insurance as an investment. The life insurance companies have long provided the most popular form of savings in the country. The annual premium payments received by the life companies exceed 3 billion dollars and represent the larger part of the actual savings of the American public. The life insurance business has long outgrown its original function of providing protection to dependents; it is now widely used by persons who desire to provide protection for themselves as well as for others.

The reasons why life insurance appeals to investors of limited means are unusually pertinent. In the first place, the individual transfers to an experienced organization the difficult problem of selecting good securities. In the second place, the payments are pooled into a large fund which may be so widely diversified as to minimize to individual policyholders the effect of occasional losses. In the third place, the companies have established a most impressive record of safety and reliability over a period of many decades. In the fourth place, the majority of the companies are mutually owned, thus assuring against any diversion of earnings to outsiders. In the fifth place, a large variety of policies are available, thus permitting individuals to buy contracts to meet their particular needs. In the sixth place, practically all policies have loan values and surrender values which make the commitment liquid at all times. And last but not least, life insurance benefit payments are exempt from estate taxes to a substantial amount ($40,000 under legislation in effect in 1940).

Although all life insurance policies have investment features, some have more than do others. *Term* policies, valueless after the expiration of the stated term—from one year to twenty years) have the smallest investment feature, since the possibility of cancellation by expiration reduces the required reserve fund; *whole life* policies (payable at death) have a larger investment feature than term policies, since the probability of eventual redemption must be provided through the establishment of an adequate reserve fund; *limited life* policies (payable at death after a limited number of annual premiums) have a larger investment feature than ordinary life policies, since the reserve fund is built up more quickly; *endowment* policies (payable at a certain age or in the event of prior death) have a larger investment feature than limited life policies, since each endowment policy is a combination of two separate types of insurance—namely, term (payable only in the event of death before expiration) and pure endowment (payable only in the event the insured lives to expiration date); *annuity* policies (payable for life in annual installments after an agreed age), which have the largest investment feature of all, have greatly increased in popularity during recent years. Under the provisions of the Federal Social Security Act, deferred annuities to begin at age 65 are now being purchased by some 30,000,000 eligible workers on the basis of a pay-roll tax deduction. Unlike private annuities, the Federal annuity payments are not directly proportionate to contributions. [1]

Although it is not debatable that a life insurance policy offers an interesting combination of protection and investment, a careful analysis of the respective features reveals that the investment aspect is not unusually good. The rate of return on that part of the premium which represents an investment commitment is generally below that which the individual himself can procure from the direct purchase of sound securities. To the man of limited means, however, the amount involved may be too small to warrant the inconvenience of personal investment. He is inclined, moreover, to purchase securities without the degree of caution employed by the large life insurance companies. Incidentally, the compulsory feature of the premium payment under the life insurance contract may well be contrasted to the optional feature of the personal investment policy of the average person. [2]

Savings banks. The savings bank is regarded as the logical depository for the investor of limited means. This is particularly true in the case of the mutual, or trustee, type of savings banks, which are operated solely for the depositors. Such institutions exist primarily for the small investor who requires a maximum of safety and who is not in a position to select his own securities. The maximum deposit is usually limited by law to an amount that is unattractive to the wealthy investor. In most states, as previously ex-

---

[1] The cost of life insurance varies according to type of policy and age at the time the policy is written. At 35, approximate annual premiums would be $10 for term, $20 for whole-life, $30 for limited-life, and $40 for endowment policies. Costs would be less on insurance taken at a younger age and higher if taken at an older age.

[2] An excellent article on "The Investment Element in Life Insurance Contracts," by S. H. Nerlove, appeared in *The Journal of Business* of the University of Chicago, Vol. 1, No. 3, p. 273 et seq.

plained, savings banks are permitted to invest their deposits solely in securities approved by law.

Not all savings banks, however, are of the mutual type. In fact, mutual savings banks are found in less than twenty of the forty-eight states. Illinois and Michigan have none whatever. They are quite popular in Massachusetts, New York, and Pennsylvania, having found a fertile field of development in the populous industrial-immigrant sections. In view of the splendid record which these institutions have achieved, it is regrettable that the facilities are not available to everyone.

The total deposits in all mutual savings banks in the United States amounted to more than $10,400,000,000 on January 1, 1940. Mutual savings banks in New York State, however, accounted for $5,500,000,000, or more than one half of the total. Savings banks in New York State discourage what might be termed "investment" accounts through the restriction of a maximum of $7,500 (exclusive of accrued interest) on single accounts in each bank. The objection to the "investment" account is that it is subject to withdrawal in full on short notice. Such a condition compels the bank to invest too heavily in low-yielding short-term Government bonds to the detriment of "savings" accounts which are seldom disturbed and which are entitled to a higher rate of return. The rate of interest paid on deposits in New York savings banks varies with changes in economic conditions but is rarely less than 2 per cent or more than $4\frac{1}{2}$ per cent annually.

The accompanying statement of The Bowery Savings Bank (which has the reputation of being the largest in the world) shows clearly the manner in which the deposits are protected. It should be particularly noted that the surplus belongs to the depositors and is a reserve for them. The mutual savings bank provides a safe place for small savings (as little as one dollar), diversified investment, legal protection, and a reserve fund as added protection. It is significant that each depositor has an equitable share in the surplus, irrespective of the period of his deposit.

Postal savings. The savings facilities provided by the Federal Government through the post offices afford a government-guaranteed depository for small accounts. Nonnegotiable registered certificates in denominations ranging from $1 to $500 are given to depositors. The certificates are redeemable at any time and bear simple interest at the rate of 2 per

---

THE BOWERY SAVINGS BANK, NEW YORK CITY
STATEMENT, JANUARY 1, 1941

Assets

Cash in vaults and on deposit		$ 18,059,379
Bonds:		
United States Government	$166,093,703	
States of the United States	2,753,575	
Municipalities	37,335,538	
Railroads	16,963,340	
Public Utilities	5,909,380	
Miscellaneous	1,323,500	
Total bonds		230,379,036
Loans on bonds and mortgages		258,422,397
Banking houses		5,630,000
Other real estate		21,420,933
Interest accrued		3,502,688
Other assets		7,254,366
Total assets		$544,668,800

Liabilities

Deposits (404,126 depositors)	$500,358,256
Special reserves	147,409
Taxes and other liabilities	763,135
Surplus	43,400,000
Total liabilities	$544,668,800

---

cent per annum. Interest may be collected only through the exchange of an old certificate for a new one. The maximum amount of certificates which may be held by one person is $2,500, all of which must be in a single account.

Total deposits in postal savings accounts amounted to about 1.3 billion dollars in 1940, which total represented only a moderate increase over the 1.2 billion dollars in 1935 and an extremely modest amount in view of the 30 years of existence of the system.   The development of deposit insurance and the competition of savings bonds has restricted the popularity of postal savings accounts.

United States Savings bonds.   A new form of investment, known as United States Savings bonds, has gained remarkable popularity in the relatively few years which have elapsed since being placed on the market in 1935.   The Series E bonds are designed for investors of limited means and include many distinctive features.

(1) These bonds are issued in face value denominations as low as $25, $50, and $100, as well as $500 and $1,000.

(2) The bonds do not bear any stated rate of interest but are issued for a term of years and are sold at a large discount. As a consequence, the holder of the bond does not collect any interest until the bond is redeemed.   Under the present plan, the bonds are issued for 10 years and are sold at 75 per cent of face value.   The 25-per-cent profit collected when the bond is due represents interest for the period and is equivalent to an annual rate of $3\frac{1}{3}$ per cent simple interest and 2.9 per cent compound interest for the period.

(3) The bonds are redeemable at the option of the holder at any time after the first two months of purchase at a fixed price schedule under which the redemption price gradually increases from the purchase price during the first year to the face value at the end of the last year.   Under this plan, the investor is protected against any depreciation in the value of his investment during the entire period.   All other securities in the American market are subject to fluctuations in market values.   In the event that the bonds are redeemed prior to maturity, the rate of income return as indicated by the established redemption prices will be somewhat less than that obtainable if the bonds are held until the maturity date. Moreover, if the bonds are redeemed for reinvestment purposes, the rate of yield voluntarily surrendered on the unexpired period of the bonds will be higher than the maturity rate.   As shown in the accompanying table, if a bond is redeemed at the end of five years, the redemption price of 82

would afford a yield of 1.79 per cent for the five-year period but would indicate that a yield of 4.01 per cent would be required from an alternative investment to equal that which would have been obtainable through holding the savings bond to the maturity date.

UNITED STATES SAVINGS BONDS (SERIES E)
REDEMPTION VALUES AND INCOME YIELDS

Period After Issue	Redemption Value	Yield Gained (If Held)	Yield Lost (If Redeemed)
First year.............	75%	0.00%	2.90%
1 to 1½ years...........	75½	0.67	3.15
1½ to 2 years...........	76	0.88	3.26
2 to 2½ years...........	76½	0.99	3.38
2½ to 3 years...........	77	1.06	3.52
3 to 3½ years...........	78	1.31	3.58
3½ to 4 years...........	79	1.49	3.66
4 to 4½ years...........	80	1.62	3.76
4½ to 5 years...........	81	1.72	3.87
5 to 5½ years...........	82	1.79	4.01
5½ to 6 years...........	83	1.85	4.18
6 to 6½ years...........	84	1.90	4.41
6½ to 7 years...........	86	2.12	4.36
7 to 7½ years...........	88	2.30	4.31
7½ to 8 years...........	90	2.45	4.26
8 to 8½ years...........	92	2.57	4.21
8½ to 9 years...........	94	2.67	4.17
9 to 9½ years...........	96	2.76	4.13
9½ to 10 years.........	98	2.84	4.08
At maturity...........	100	2.90	0

(4) The bonds are nonnegotiable securities and are redeemable only by the registered owners, thus protecting the holders against loss arising from theft, forgery, fire, and similar causes.

(5) The bonds may now be purchased only by individual persons and will not be issued in the names of corporations, banks, trustees, or guardians. The bonds may be registered in the name of one individual or of two individuals as co-owners (either of whom may redeem the bond) or as owner and beneficiary.

(6) The maximum holding of these bonds permitted to any person is $5,000 in face value for each calendar year of

issue. Only through the purchase of $5,000 in face value in each of ten consecutive years could the ultimate maximum of $50,000 be obtained.

(7) The bonds may be purchased through banking institutions, at the post offices, or directly through the Treasury Department at Washington.

(8) The bonds are direct obligations of the United States Government which, unlike Treasury bonds which are payable only on designated dates, are redeemable at the pleasure of the owner.

Home ownership. Just as the investment aspect of life insurance is obscured by the external influence of protection, so the investment aspect of home ownership is complicated by the presence of social as well as economic considerations. From a purely financial viewpoint, home ownership has definite limitations as an investment. If proper allowance is made for maintenance, depreciation, and loss of interest on capital, it is doubtful if home ownership can be regarded as a profitable investment. On the other hand, if allowance is made for social as well as economic advantages, a strong case can be made for the home owner. The purchase of a home can be made the finest kind of an investment if income is measured in terms of units of satisfaction as well as dollars. From a financial viewpoint, it might be stated that the home should be well-built and favorably located, with a total cost not exceeding 250 per cent of the annual income of the owner, purchased with a cash equity of at least 20 per cent and a mortgage for a period of not less than 10 years. What frequently appears to be a substantial loss on the resale of a home might more properly be regarded as deferred depreciation which should have been charged off during the period of ownership.

The determination of the investment status of home ownership may be illustrated in the case of the purchase of a $10,000 home.

(1-a) If the home is bought outright for cash, the owner loses the income on $10,000 which might otherwise produce about $400 annually at 4 per cent interest.

(1-b) If the home is bought under a 60 per cent mortgage at 5 per cent interest repayable in installments over 20 years, his original investment of $4,000 gradually increases to $10,000, indicating an *average* investment of $7,000 which might otherwise produce about $280 annually. The annual interest charge would gradually decline from $300 in the first year to $15 in the last year, indicating an *average* interest cost of $157.50 annually. The total cost under this plan would thus be $437.50 annually (excluding various fees and expenses in connection with placing the mortgage).

(2) The annual property taxes might be as low as $100 (1 per cent) or as high as $400 (4 per cent) but might be estimated at $200, which is close to the national average for urban residences.

(3) The annual cost of fire insurance would probably be not less than $15 and might be as high as $50.

(4) The cost of necessary repairs to the building and maintenance of the grounds would probably be not less than $150 (1½ per cent) annually.

(5) The depreciation of the building (valued at $8,000) on a 40-year basis would amount to $200 per year.

The total cost of ownership, excluding costs of operation such as fuel and services which are usually paid by tenants, would therefore be around $1,025 annually, or $85 monthly. If comparable premises can be rented for less than this amount, the ownership of the property is justifiable more for social and psychological than for financial reasons.

Savings and loan associations. The investment position of savings and loan associations has been greatly strengthened as the result of recent legislation which permits these associations to obtain Federal charters and to offer insurance protection to shareholders. Share accounts are opened with buyers who may be home owners who have borrowed from the association or who may be investors seeking income on their savings. The funds of the association are ordinarily loaned on mortgages and installment contracts on residential property on a monthly repayment basis. Certain practices in vogue with these institutions under state supervision were found to be unwise under the conditions which developed in realty during the depression years of the past decade. As a consequence, many associations, like banks, were forced to suspend operations and undergo painful reorganizations.

Under legislation enacted in 1933 and 1934, the Federal Government is now granting charters to the associations which desire such supervision and is insuring the safety of payments made to such institutions. State-chartered associations have been allowed to transfer to Federal supervision. Due to a desire to avoid Federal supervision and to the inability of some to meet the admission requirements of the Federal group, many associations are still operating under state charters.

The Federal savings and loan associations are local in character and mutual in operation. Supervision is provided by the Federal Home Loan Bank Board over the operating and lending policies of the local institutions. Insurance is provided by the Federal Savings and Loan Insurance Corporation. Loans are limited to first mortgages on residential properties located within fifty miles of the association office. The largest loan on any property is 80 per cent of appraised value, but not exceeding $20,000. The mortgage period may not exceed twenty years and must be amortized on a monthly payment basis. *Investment share certificates* in units of $100 are sold for full cash payments. *Savings share accounts* are available to persons who desire to buy shares on the installment plan.

The owner of an investment share certificate may withdraw $100 or any part thereof upon demand. On amounts exceeding $100, a 30-day notice is required. On amounts exceeding $1,000, repayment will be made only after all other waiting applications for repurchase have been filled. From an investor's viewpoint, there may be decidedly limited liquidity to any *substantial* sum invested in these associations.

Dividend payments by Federal savings and loan associations are currently being made at rates between 2 and 4 per cent. Although the state-chartered associations maintained substantially higher rates, between 6 and 8 per cent for many years preceding the past decade, it is now generally recognized that such payments were too liberal and most state associations are now paying from 3 to 6 per cent.

Investors in shares of all Federal and many state savings and loan associations are insured up to $5,000 in each individual account by the Federal Savings and Loan Insurance Corporation. In addition to the initial capital of $100,000,000 provided by the United States Treasury, a surplus of $20,000,000 had been created in 1940 through annual premium payments by associations based on $\frac{1}{8}$ of 1 per cent of respective liabilities.

Investing in securities. The great difficulty which confronts the investor of limited means in the purchase of securities is the problem of securing adequate diversification. With the exception of United States Savings bonds, few bonds are readily obtainable in less than $1,000 units. The relatively few bonds which are available in $100 and $500 prices have such limited marketability that buying prices are usually higher and selling prices lower than the corresponding quotations on the $1,000 units. In view of the general belief that not more than 5 per cent of a fund should be placed in any one commitment, and in consideration of the difficulty in obtaining bonds in less than $1,000 units, the smallest fund which might be invested in bonds would be around $20,000. The bond investor with a few thousand dollars must concentrate to a greater extent than is believed to be prudent.

Although, as explained elsewhere in this volume, the unit of purchase of the popular stocks on the New York Stock Exchange is 100 shares, units as small as five shares may be bought at practically the same price as 100-share lots. The investor of limited means who desires to purchase stocks may therefore obtain adequate diversification with a much smaller fund than would be practicable in the purchase of bonds.

In view of the difficulty experienced by the small investor in the direct purchase of securities, it is regrettable that the investment trust companies have not been able to afford a more attractive opportunity to such persons. In the true sense of the term, however, the great thrift institutions such as the life insurance companies and the savings banks are investment trusts in that they accept small deposits which are commingled into large investment funds. Moreover, the mutual ownership of these institutions, under which all earnings are retained by the policyholders and depositors, further emphasizes their function as true investment trusts.

The accumulative incentive. Investment serves the dual purpose of providing a safe place for savings and an income for the use of the funds. The income factor is likely to exercise little appeal to the investor of limited means because the amount derived annually from a small fund seems too small to deserve consideration. The fact that savings can grow into substantial amounts over a period of years is ignored by many people who have failed to appreciate the productive power of money. Benjamin Franklin is credited with this pertinent statement:

> Remember that money is of a prolific, generating nature. Money can beget money, and its offspring can beget more, and so on. The more there is of it the more it produces every turning, so that the profits rise quicker and quicker.

The problem of buying something that will increase in value is not exclusively a matter of speculation. The opinion is offered that as many personal fortunes have been built upon the gradual appreciation from reinvestment of income as from the rapid increase resulting from a successful speculation. The accompanying tables are presented in an endeavor to show, from a purely mathematical viewpoint, the productive power of money. The first table shows the relatively small *monthly* investment required to accumulate a fund of $10,000 over periods ranging from 10 to 40 years, assuming the semiannual reinvestment of income at 3 per cent per annum interest return. Savings of $23 monthly will provide a $10,000 fund in 25 years. The second table shows the extent to which savings of $10 per month will grow in value over periods ranging from 10 to 40 years under the same assumption of semiannual reinvestment of income of 3 per cent per annum interest return.

Approximate Monthly Savings Required to Accumulate $10,000 at 3 Per Cent		Accumulation of Principal on Savings of $10 Monthly Invested at 3 Per Cent	
Amount	*Years*	*Years*	*Amount*
$11......................	40	10......................	$1,375
14......................	35	15......................	2,230
17......................	30	20......................	3,225
23......................	25	25......................	4,375
31......................	20	30......................	5,710
45......................	15	35......................	7,255
73......................	10	40......................	9,050

PART TWO

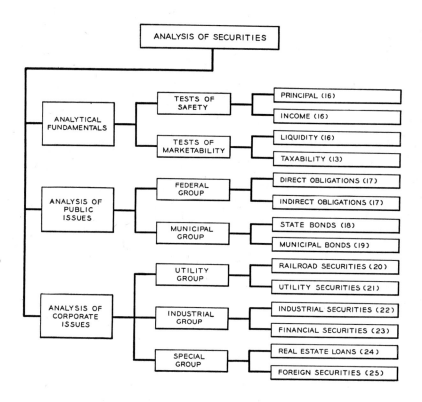

ANALYSIS OF SECURITIES

ANALYTICAL FUNDAMENTALS

- TESTS OF SAFETY
  - PRINCIPAL (16)
  - INCOME (16)
- TESTS OF MARKETABILITY
  - LIQUIDITY (16)
  - TAXABILITY (13)

ANALYSIS OF PUBLIC ISSUES

- FEDERAL GROUP
  - DIRECT OBLIGATIONS (17)
  - INDIRECT OBLIGATIONS (17)
- MUNICIPAL GROUP
  - STATE BONDS (18)
  - MUNICIPAL BONDS (19)

ANALYSIS OF CORPORATE ISSUES

- UTILITY GROUP
  - RAILROAD SECURITIES (20)
  - UTILITY SECURITIES (21)
- INDUSTRIAL GROUP
  - INDUSTRIAL SECURITIES (22)
  - FINANCIAL SECURITIES (23)
- SPECIAL GROUP
  - REAL ESTATE LOANS (24)
  - FOREIGN SECURITIES (25)

16

GENERAL TESTS OF QUALITY

Scope. The purpose of this chapter is to provide an introduction to the second half of the book, which is concerned with the problems of securities analysis. The three prime tests of investment quality—safety, income, and marketability—are discussed in general fashion. The specific applications are reserved for the subsequent chapters in their respective fields. The general observation is pertinent at this point that investment safety is almost directly proportionate inversely to the rate of income return which the investor seeks. The importance of quality in investment procedure cannot be overstated.

Investment tests. The tests of a good investment are primarily a consideration of safety and secondarily a consideration of convenience. All other factors must be subordinate to that of maintenance of the integrity of the principal sum invested. The degree of marketability, the tax position, the maturity date, and the time of income payments are interesting features worthy of attention, but are essentially less important than the degree of risk assumed in any particular commitment. The whole business of intelligent investing may be concisely stated in five words: *adequate safety with reasonable income.*

The ascertainment of quality in an investment security requires careful consideration of numerous factors, many of which cannot be resolved into a mathematical equation. An application of accounting principles is needed for the analysis of income accounts and balance sheets just as an application of engineering principles is necessary in the checking of the operating efficiency of an industrial undertaking. An application of economic principles is of basic importance in the judging of the "timeliness" of investment selections. A knowledge of new developments in the fields of pure, as well as applied, science will often influence a decision to the advantage of the investor, since new industries are constantly in the making. Geography shows the natural resources of the world and indicates a variety of things of economic significance, such as the relative wealth of nations, the accessibility of minerals, climatic influences, international frontiers, and trade routes. The often-quoted remark that "history teaches nothing" must be qualified in investment finance; one of the most intelligent criticisms that can be made of modern investment practice is that too much, not too little, reliance is placed upon historical precedent. The past is a helpful, but not an infallible, guide to the future. Psychology can never be ignored, since the attitude of the public carries security prices at one time to peaks that "discount the millennium" and at another time to valleys that appear to indicate economic chaos.

The investor who would attempt precisely to evaluate such influences would need a "philosopher's scale" to supplement the yardsticks known to mathematics. He quickly learns of the imponderable nature of many elements that he must consider. Fully one half of the factors that should be analyzed in the selection of an investment are not subject to mathematical measurement. Hence, there is always ground for wide variation of opinion. So broad is the field of investment and so varied are the factors in each group of securities, that investment knowledge is necessarily relative. In professional work, the analysts of highest reputation are those who specialize in one field, such as municipals, or steam railroads, or electric power companies.

The admission of the debatable theory that all known factors can be satisfactorily measured would not carry assurance against loss from unknown factors that can develop without warning.   Earthquakes, fires, wars, epidemics, riots, accidents, and fortuitous and adventitious events of every description occur to invalidate the most carefully prepared investment analysis.   The problem is protean and the solution can never be more than an incomplete answer.   The task of the investor is to ascertain the nature of those tests that will indicate relatively rather than absolutely the degree of risk involved in the purchase of any security.

The measurement of safety.   It is the common experience of all investors that "absolute safety" in a security commitment is an idealistic concept rather than a practical condition. Not even the safest securities afford guarantees against loss. Investors who bought British Government "Consols" at 90 in 1903 had the unhappy experience of watching them decline below 50 in 1920 and again in 1931.   Intelligent investors, therefore, seek "adequate" rather than "absolute" safety. Incidentally, adequacy in this respect does not signify a uniform degree for everyone.   Those investors who are not in a position to assume the risk of loss require more protection than others more fortunately situated.

Although the payment of income and the repayment of principal would appear to be distinctly different operations requiring separate analysis of the safety of income as distinguished from the safety of principal, the distinction is more apparent than actual.   The price of a share of common stock (which is redeemable only through liquidation) is the estimated present value of a series of dividend payments anticipated in the future.   The price of a bond is the estimated present value of the semiannual interest payments plus the present value of the principal.[1]   Safety of principal and

---

[1] In all long-term bonds, the present value of the interest payments exceeds the present value of the principal. As demonstrated elsewhere in this volume, an investor who pays $1,150 (115) for a 4 per cent bond due in 20 years is actually paying about $596 for the coupons and only $554 for the principal.

safety of income are thus woven inextricably together. It seems illogical to separate the two considerations, even though safety of principal would appear much more important. From a practical viewpoint, safety of income is more significant; if the income payment is safe, the principal is likewise secure, because the earning power that provides the income gives value to the asset securing the principal. Moreover, inability to pay income seriously impairs the value of the principal, as is invariably shown in the decline of security prices when default occurs.

All investment commitments are, in large measure, credit transactions. The investor is advancing his funds and expects to have them safely returned at some time in the future. Even when he buys a bond with a distant maturity date, he feels that he can recover his investment at any convenient time through sale in the open market. The indefinite maturity of the "loan" does not change its essential credit character. Investors might consistently follow the general rules of credit granting set up by business houses, with a certain adaptation to the security field. Credit men have long based mercantile credits upon what are popularly known as the three C's: Capital, Capacity, and Character. The investor would interpret Capital as the worth of the borrower, as disclosed in the financial statement of assets and liabilities; Capacity as the earning power, as demonstrated in the income statement of revenues and expenses; and Character as the reputation, as shown in the history of the borrower and the record of the controlling personnel.

While it may truly be said that few investment tests may be uniformly applied to all securities, some are sufficiently broad in scope to be applied to the general list. One group of tests is especially applicable to foreign public loans; a second, to domestic public loans; a third, to domestic corporate issues, with variations according to the kind of enterprise; and numerous others applicable to similar distinct classes of the field. Many of these are reserved for appropriate chapters that follow. Those that are discussed in this chapter are more generally applicable to all securities.

One of America's leading financiers, the late J. Pierpont Morgan, has been quoted as follows: [2]

> While, of course, unforeseeable disaster may overtake an enterprise, and the most sagacious and prudent find themselves involved by mistaken calculation and judgment, there are standards and measurements which ordinarily protect the thoughtful man.
>
> Impulse is dangerous, listening to intrusted persuasion is dangerous, taking things generally for granted is dangerous, depending upon Wall Street legerdemain is stupidly dangerous. Sane people do not put themselves into such dangers. Worse than a mistake, it is a risk that is a crime to invest carelessly.

Factors of safety. The amount of risk contained in any investment security is indicated by certain features of somewhat technical nature that should be carefully investigated. These features include the *type of security,* the *nature of the enterprise,* the *legality of issue,* the *degree of seasoning,* and the *personnel of management.* An extensive knowledge of finance is not required for a reasonably adequate examination of at least three of these features.

The *type of security* purchased by the investor may be a prior lien bond with wide safety margins or a common stock representing a thin equity in the corporate property. Despite interesting exceptions to the contrary, senior mortgage bonds are safer than junior mortgages, secured bonds are safer than debentures, debentures are safer than preferred stocks, and preferred stocks are safer than common stocks. Such priorities are plainly stated in the respective instruments. The terms of the investment contract are therefore closely related to the safety of the issue.

The *nature of the enterprise* is a matter of prime importance. Some undertakings are inherently more uncertain than others. The loans of government bodies, dependent upon taxes rather than profits, are more secure than the bonds of corporate borrowers. Public utility securities, by reason of greater stability of revenues, are intrinsically safer than industrial issues. Domestic securities are subject to fewer disturbances as a class than are foreign issues. In this general respect it

---

[2] Quoted by Henry Alloway in *The Wall Street Journal,* October 26, 1923.

may be observed that the service which the money renders is an excellent test of the safety of the commitment. If the borrower is able to put the funds to productive employment, the payment of income and the repayment of principal are directly facilitated.

RELATIVE EARNING POWER[a]

NET INCOME OF 1,054 AMERICAN CORPORATIONS
Table A (in millions of dollars)

Group	1929	1932	1937	1938
Steam railroad (141 cos.).......	$ 897	−$151[b]	$ 99	−$123[b]
Public utility (82 cos.).........	413	299	300	268
Industrial (831 cos.)..........	2,813	−38[b]	2,184	1,105
Total (1,054 cos.).......	$4,123	$110	$2,583	$1,250

Table B (in percentages of 1929)

Group	1929	1932	1937	1938
Steam railroad................	100%	0%	11%	0%
Public utility................	100	72	72	65
Industrial...................	100	0	78	39
Total................	100%	3%	63%	30%

[a] Data from Monthly Bulletin of Federal Reserve Bank of New York, April 1, 1939.
[b] Deficit.

The relationship of the nature of the business enterprise to the stability of corporate prosperity is clearly shown in the accompanying table, which includes four of the most and least prosperous years in the decade from 1929 through 1938. All companies in the compilation had aggregate earnings of $4,123,000,000 in 1929, after payment of taxes and interest charges. In 1932, total profits had declined to $110,000,000, or only 3 per cent of 1929. In 1937, earnings increased to $2,583,000,000, or 63 per cent of 1929, but in 1938, fell back to $1,250,000,000, or 30 per cent of 1929.

The steam railroad companies had total earnings of $897,-000,000 in 1929, which fell to a deficit, after interest charges, of $151,000,000 in 1932, recovered to $99,000,000 in 1937, or only 11 per cent of 1929, and again showed a deficit of $123,-

000,000 in 1938. The failure on the part of the railroad companies to regain their earning power of a decade ago has resulted in a substantial lowering in the quality of three securities as investments.

The public utility companies had total earnings of $413,-000,000 in 1929 in contrast to $299,000,000 in 1932, a decline of only 28 per cent. Earnings in 1937 were $300,000,000, or about the same as during the worst depression year, and in 1938 were $268,000,000, or even less than in 1932. It has been only within the past few years that utility earnings have indicated any adverse effect of economic or political developments.

The industrial companies had total earnings of $2,813,000,-000 in 1929, which was in startling contrast to the comparable loss of $38,000,000 in 1932. Profits in 1937, however, recovered to $2,184,000,000, or 78 per cent in 1929, but in 1938 declined to $1,105,000,000, which represented a drop of nearly 50 per cent in a single year. Such instability of industrial earning power has tended to make the securities of these companies more popular as speculations than as investments.

The *legality of issue* is particularly significant with respect to public securities, such as municipal bonds. A corporate bond that has been issued illegally is usually valid and collectible; a similar municipal bond is invalid and uncollectible. *Legality of issue* should not be confused with the term *legal investment,* which means eligibility for purchase by fiduciaries.

The *degree of seasoning* is applicable to the industry as well as to the issue, but ordinarily refers to the latter. New securities are issued at arbitrary prices that may or may not be accepted by the market at large. The price tends to fluctuate over a seasoning period, which may vary from a few weeks to several months. It is not uncommon for new securities to decline in market price after the primary distribution has been completed, which decline is due to the removal of artifical support. The age of the industry and the company likewise require consideration. Investors should avoid new enterprises in the experimental stage, as well as old industries in the saturation stage, and should endeavor to choose newer companies that are sufficiently seasoned to show definite earning power.

The *personnel of management* should also be carefully considered. Corporations are business enterprises generally controlled by a few leading executives. The investor should hesitate before advancing any funds to such enterprises unless he has a basis for confidence in the management. He should be relatively cautious with regard to companies in which a single individual is the dominating influence.[3]

Financial tests of safety. The financial tests that an investor should apply are explained in considerable detail in subsequent chapters, with proper emphasis upon the features pertinent to the respective fields. At this point, the nature of the tests, rather than specific applications, is discussed. The financial statements of governmental bodies, which are essentially different from those of corporations, are not included in the following discussion, which is devoted to corporate balance sheets and income statements.

The *balance sheet* is a statement of resources and liabilities, the difference between the two, the *balance,* being the net worth of the enterprise. The various items are listed with a *book* value shown for each. Since the basis of valuation is usually the cost price, which seldom indicates prevailing value, any attempt to measure asset protection from the balance sheet is subject to distinct limitation.[4]

The *test of fixed assets* is the determination of the relationship between the value of the fixed assets (land, buildings, and equipment) and the face value of securities outstanding.

---

[3] Holders of securities issued by the investment trust companies sponsored by the late Samuel Insull suffered almost total loss because of mistaken confidence in the promoter of those enterprises.

[4] "By its very nature, that report, unless well understood and interpreted, is at variance with reality. For in the accountant's report, a continuum is represented by a cross-section; a growing thing is pictured as static. Instead of a motion picture, we get a snapshot, a "still." A year's account is, in and of itself, a fiction; it depicts frozen motion, an organism as if it were inorganic, a flowing stream as if it were a pane of glass. The year, at best, is an arbitrary and artificial measure which may falsify the trend of events in a business. And to reflect even that year by a calculus of conditions at one moment of that year is indeed to indulge in artificiality."—From address by Jerome N. Frank, Chairman, S. E. C., in New York, Oct. 10, 1939.

Under the assumption that the properties have been properly maintained and have been adequately depreciated, the value of the fixed assets should be substantially in excess of the funded debt to the company.

The *test of liquid capital* is the determination of the working capital position. The current assets (cash, inventories, and receivables) should show a comfortable margin above the current liabilities (accounts payable), irrespective of the magnitude of fixed assets.

The *test of capital structure* means a comparison of the amounts of outstanding securities of a company as shown on the balance sheet. The nature of the enterprise is a governing factor in this regard, since companies with relatively stable earnings may safely issue a larger proportion in bonds. Investors should favor those companies that have the smaller percentages in bonds.

The *income statement,* more often called the *profit and loss account,* shows the earning power of the company as disclosed in the revenue and expense figures. Unlike the balance sheet, which is largely a reflection of opinion since values are stated arbitrarily, the income account is primarily a statement of fact, since very few of the items are arbitrary estimates.

The *test of earning power* is an examination of the profit-producing capacity of the enterprise. More truly than any other criterion, it measures the real worth of the enterprise. The amount of profit should be adequate with respect to the volume of business and to the value of the invested capital.

The *test of fixed charges* is a comparison of the annual interest charges with the total income available for the payment of these charges. The margin of safety should be adequate to carry assurance that interest charges are safely earned and will be promptly paid.

The *dividend payment test* is a study of the relationship between the amount paid in annual dividends and the net profit available, as well as an inquiry into the dividend record of the company over a period of years. As dividend payments are conditional charges, the investor in stocks should constantly be cognizant of the fact that current earnings are the chief determining factor. Recent experience has shown that unbroken dividend records extending for decades do not convey assurance of future payments.[5]

UNBROKEN DIVIDEND RECORDS
(At Least 30 Years)

	Company	Business	Since	Years
1.	Pennsylvania Railroad............	Railway	1848	94
2.	American Telephone & Telegraph..	Telephone	1881	61
3.	Diamond Match................	Match	1882	60
4.	Standard Oil (N. J.).............	Petroleum	1882	60
5.	Consolidated Edison (N. Y.)......	Utility	1885	57
6.	Commonwealth Edison (Chicago)..	Utility	1890	52
7.	Procter and Gamble.............	Soap	1891	50
8.	Coca-Cola.....................	Beverage	1893	49
9.	Standard Oil (Indiana)..........	Petroleum	1894	48
10.	General Mills....................	Flour	1898	44
11.	Borden........................	Dairy	1899	43
12.	General Electric................	Electric	1899	43
13.	National Biscuit................	Bakery	1899	43
14.	Standard Brands................	Food	1899	43
15.	United Fruit...................	Fruit	1899	43
16.	Union Pacific...................	Railway	1900	42
17.	Eastman Kodak................	Photographic	1902	40
18.	Texas Corporation..............	Petroleum	1903	39
19.	E. I. duPont de Nemours........	Chemical	1904	38
20.	American Tobacco..............	Tobacco	1905	37
21.	National Lead..................	Lead	1906	36
22.	Detroit Edison.................	Utility	1909	33
23	International Harvester..........	Agricultural	1910	32
24.	Socony-Vacuum................	Petroleum	1911	31
25.	F. W. Woolworth...............	Merchandise	1912	30

The factor of income. The statement has been previously made that the problem of investment analysis is the task of finding adequate safety with reasonable income. The relative size of the income, as related to the amount invested, usually indicates the degree of risk assumed. The receipt of a high rate of return upon an investment commitment is evidence of uncertainty with respect to future payments. Hence, the rate of return varies directly with the degree of risk involved. Investors who are willing to purchase securities with relatively uncertain futures naturally demand compensa-

---

[5] In the severe economic depression in 1931 and 1932, many important companies were obliged to stop dividend payments after impressive records. New York Central discontinued dividends on its common stock in 1932 for the first time since 1870.

tion in the form of a higher rate of return as a premium for the risk they undertake. Investors who demand only securities with relatively assured futures must be willing to accept lower rates of return.

Interest rates are set by the value of money, which, in turn, is determined by conditions of demand and supply. As these fundamental conditions change, the value of money changes, resulting in low rates at one time and high rates at another. Furthermore, as the money market is divided into credits of varying durations and borrowers of varying responsibilities, it follows that there is no such thing as a single interest rate prevailing at any one time. The short-term, or commercial, interest rate is subject to more rapid variations and wider swings. The long-term, or investment, interest rate changes less rapidly and within narrower limits.

The trend of long-term interest rates is between an extreme range of from 2 to 8 per cent and a more normal range of from 3 to 6 per cent. In other words, investors should not feel obliged to accept less than a 3 per cent rate of return or to seek more than 6 per cent. A further refinement of this test would indicate that from 4 to 5 per cent is the average rate that should be expected in ordinary times. To the investor who objects that such a return is too low, the answer may readily be given that the attainment of an average rate of return of 5 per cent per annum over a period of years is regarded as a commendable performance in the professional field. When securities decline in value, the depreciation is heaviest in the high-yielding group. The fallacy of risking the loss of principal to gain a few dollars more in income is too obvious to warrant elaboration.

The annual rate of return, expressed in percentage relationship between the annual income and the amount invested, is called the *yield* and is the most practical yardstick of investment quality. A low yield indicates a safe security, just as a high yield indicates a weak security. In the first case, the yield is low because it is relatively sure to be received; in the latter case, it is high because it may not be long continued. Securities are customarily divided into gradations of quality from the best to the poorest, with the respective yields indicating the allocation. The accompanying table shows approximately the yields prevailing on securities of varying qualities, first, under normal conditions, and, second, under the abnormal conditions prevailing at the time of writing.

Class	Normal	(1940)
Highest grade...........	Under 4%	Under 3%
High grade.............	4% to 4½%	3% to 3½%
Good...................	4½% to 5%	3½% to 4%
Fair...................	5% to 6%	4% to 5%
Speculative............	Over 6%	Over 5%

While the yield is the most serviceable criterion of quality in a security, it should not be regarded as infallible. It is much less reliable in the case of stocks than in the case of bonds because of the contingent nature of dividends and the greater influence of speculation as a motivating force in stock purchasing. It is not always reliable even in the case of bonds, owing to the influence of technical features that prevent the price from reaching a natural level. The more important of these qualifying factors are here listed.

1. *Marketability.* Securities issued by large enterprises are better known than those issued by smaller companies. As a consequence of the greater demand, the former issues command a higher price and afford a lower rate of return.

2. *Redemption option.* Some securities are subject to redemption at the option of the issuer at a fixed price prior to the date of final payment. As the market price will rarely exceed the redemption option price, the effect of the redemption feature is to keep the market price down to the call price at times when it might otherwise go higher. A noncallable 5 per cent bond may be selling around 120 and thereby giving a yield of less than 4 per cent at the same time as an equally good 5 per cent bond, redeemable at 105, will be selling around 105 and thereby giving a yield of nearly 5 per cent.

3. *Tax position.* The income from certain securities is not subject to income tax liability. Such exemption naturally causes these issues to command relatively high prices and to afford correspondingly low yields. Because of greater tax exemption, the bonds of New York State afforded lower yields than the bonds of the Federal Government in 1940. Despite the higher yield, the Federal bonds were definitely superior to the state bonds on a quality basis.

4. *Maturity.* Short-term securities are generally preferred to long-term issues. The earlier maturity makes them more liquid and less subject to future contingencies. It is not uncommon to find the short-term obligations of a company offering a yield of 2 per cent at a time when the long-term obligations of the same company are selling to yield over 3 per cent.

5. *Legal qualification.* Securities which are eligible for purchase by savings banks and trustees sell at somewhat artificially high prices due to the fact that such investors must confine their purchases to these issues. The higher price is reflected in the lower yield afforded to the investor.

6. *Conversion privilege.* Securities which may be converted into other securities at the option of the investor tend to rise in market price when the second security advances. At the time of writing, certain bonds of a large public utility company which were convertible into stock of the company at a favorable ratio were selling at a yield of only about 2 per cent when other bonds of the same company which were of higher ranking but which were not convertible were selling to yield nearly 3 per cent.

The factor of marketability. Marketability in a security is its relative attractiveness to a prospective purchaser. The term connotes the degree of readiness with which securities may be sold without sacrifice of value. Since prices of securities do not remain fixed in the sense that the cost of many commercial articles do, but are constantly changing, even from hour to hour, a "fair price" for a security can be only a theoretical concept. As a practical matter, a security is worth what it can be sold for at the time, irrespective of what it might have cost or what it might bring a month hence. The appraisal ideal of a willing buyer and a willing seller rarely applies to security values.   American investors are mercurial in their successive stages of hope and despair.   At one stage of the business cycle, eager buyers meet reluctant sellers, and, at another stage, eager sellers meet reluctant buyers.   As a consequence, prices move in a wide range, usually to the discomfiture of the investor who has relied upon a more stable market.   The buyer of a security should realize that, far from there being any assured price at which he may recover his investment, he might find himself possessing a security for which there may be no demand at all when he desires to sell.

Marketability in a security is not a static condition.   Like its synonym, popularity, it is subject to many changes.   Certain qualities in a security definitely affect its marketability, however, even though these qualities may later change.   Relative prosperity of an industry is a big factor in this respect, as may be illustrated in the prevailing interest in aviation and chemical securities and the lack of interest in railroad securities.   Bonds are most popular in periods of economic depression just as stocks are most popular in periods of prosperity. Foreign securities of all kinds went into startlingly quick disfavor as a result of the "Blitzkreigs" in 1940.

Apart from such developments which affect whole groups of securities, the marketability of individual security issues seems to be determined largely by the following factors:

1. *Listing.*   Securities which are listed on any of the National Securities Exchanges have a centralized market where buyers and sellers may conveniently place orders.   It is interesting to observe that many people, especially bankers, regard only those issues which are on the New York Stock Exchange as listed securities.

2. *Size.*   A large issue of securities attracts more attention and usually is held by more investors than a smaller issue. Price quotations which appear in the daily newspapers generally include only large issues.

3. *Reputation of issuer.* The securities issued by companies which are well and favorably known usually have good marketability. It is difficult to believe that securities of companies such as General Electric or General Motors would ever lack buyers.

4. *Institutional appeal.* Securities which qualify for institutional purchase, because of either legal requirement or inherent quality, generally have excellent marketability. The financial institutions, including the banks and life insurance companies, are collectively the largest buyers of securities in the country.

5. *Seasoning.* Securities which have been outstanding a year or more are regarded as "seasoned" issues with greater price stability than new issues. Such issues are preferred by many investors.

6. *Tax position.* Securities such as municipal bonds on which, at the time of writing, income is exempt from taxation are popular with wealthy investors who buy them in large volume in order to reduce tax liability.

The degree of marketability in a security may be determined at any time by seeking a price quotation. If the quotation is easily secured, either in the daily newspaper or immediately through a broker, and if the "spread" between the price asked and the price offered is close, good marketability is indicated.

Marketability is important to all investors. While it is especially significant in temporary investments, it should not be overlooked by permanent investors. Emergencies may arise that would require immediate liquidation of security holdings. Since marketability "costs money" in the sense that the more marketable security gives a lower yield, the average investor should seek a reasonable rather than a maximum degree. The plight of holders of real estate securities in recent years is due in large measure to the inherent lack of marketability in these issues.[6]

---

[6] The marketability factor in a security is generally considered to represent about 1 per cent in yield, or about 20 per cent in income. Of two equally safe bonds, the one with an active market would normally yield about 4 per cent while the other with a limited market would yield about 5 per cent.

A noteworthy feature of marketability is its close relationship to collateral value. Investors almost invariably find, when they offer securities as collateral for a bank loan, that the bank is much less interested in the quality of the security from a safety viewpoint than in the marketability of the issue.

17

UNITED STATES GOVERNMENT BONDS

Scope. The purpose of this chapter is to discuss the predominating position which the bonds of the Federal Government and its agencies have attained in the investment field. The order of discussion is: (1) types of bonds, (2) ability to pay, (3) willingness to pay, (4) savings bonds, (5) territorial bonds, (6) agency bonds, (7) instrumentalities, (8) tax position, and (9) market position. Federal bonds outstanding in 1940 amounted to $50,000,000,000 and represented about 70 per cent of the total public debt at that time. Federal loans comprised about 25 per cent of the assets in American banks and about 20 per cent of the assets in American life insurance companies in 1940.

Types of Federal bonds. The financial operations of the United States Government have become so extensive as to involve numerous types of obligations which were unknown at the beginning of the present century. At that time, all Federal bonds were uniformly the direct obligations of the Government and were issued for the general purposes of the Treasury Department. During the first decade, several issues of Panama Canal bonds, one of which is still outstanding, were made as direct obligations for the purpose of financing the construction of the interocean waterway. During the second decade, three different types of bonds were created: (1) the *Postal Savings* bonds which are no longer sold but which were used to enable depositors in the postal savings system to invest more than the maximum of $2,500 permitted in a savings account; (2) the *Liberty Loan* and *Victory Loan* bonds, all of which have now been retired, which were issued in order to finance World War expenditures; and (3) the *Federal Farm Loan* bonds, better known as the *Federal Land Bank* and the *Joint Stock Land Bank* bonds, which were issued under the provisions of the Farm Loan Act of 1916 as *instrumentalities*

Federal Financing During Civil War Period.

rather than obligations of the Federal Government.   During the third decade, *Treasury* bonds came into prominence, being issued as direct obligations primarily for the purpose of refunding higher-interest war loan bonds.

It became the lot of the fourth decade to witness a bewildering assortment of new types of Federal Government loans.

United States Government
Liberty Loan of 1917

The Secretary of the Treasury has announced the offering of these bonds. The terms are summarized as follows:

AMOUNT	**$2,000,000,000**
INTEREST RATE	3½% per annum
INTEREST PAYABLE	December 15 and June 15
CONVERSION PRIVILEGE	If, before the termination of the war, bonds are issued bearing a higher rate of interest, the holders of the bonds now to be issued may convert them into bonds bearing such higher rate, such bonds to be identical as to maturity of principal and interest and terms of redemption with these bonds, but otherwise substantially identical with the bonds of the new issue.
TAX EXEMPTIONS	Both principal and interest exempt from all Federal, State or local taxes, except estate or inheritance taxes.
PRINCIPAL PAYABLE	In 30 years — June 15, 1947. Redeemable after 15 years at par and accrued interest, at option of the United States Government.
DENOMINATIONS	Coupon Bonds: $50, $100, $500, $1,000. Registered Bonds: $100, $500, $1,000, $5,000, $10,000, $50,000, $100,000.
SUBSCRIPTIONS	At par and interest will be received until June 15, 1917, unless subscription books are closed earlier.
SUBSCRIPTIONS PAYABLE	In Full on allotment, except in amounts over $10,000, upon which two weeks' notice of intention to pay in full is required, or in Instalments as follows: 2% on application; 18% on June 28; 20% on July 30; 30% on August 15; 30% on August 30, 1917.
DELIVERY	About July 1, 1917, or on completion of payments.

For complete information regarding the Liberty Loan reference should be made to Treasury Department Circular, No. 78, copies of which may be obtained from any Bank or Trust Company or from

Liberty Loan Committee

EQUITABLE BUILDING
ROOM 518

120 BROADWAY, NEW YORK
TELEPHONE, RECTOR 7920

Federal Financing During First World War Period.

An institution known as the *Federal Home Loan* banks, patterned somewhat after the Federal Farm Loan banks, was created in 1931 with authority to issue similar types of so-called instrumentalities.   In 1932, the *Home Owners' Loan Corporation* was created under Federal auspices with authority to issue bonds guaranteed by the Federal Government in exchange for home mortgages in default at that time.   In the same year, the *Federal Farm Mortgage Corporation* was established with similar authority to issue guaranteed bonds in exchange for farm mortgages in default.   And, also in 1932, the *Reconstruction Finance Corporation* was established with power to issue obligations backed by the guarantee of the Federal Government for the purpose of making loans to business organizations in need of financial assistance.   Subsequently, the *Commodity Credit Corporation*, the *Federal Housing Administration*, and the *United States Housing Authority* were created with power to make loans bearing Federal Government guarantees.   In 1935, *United States Savings* bonds were authorized, to be sold directly to investors, primarily through the post offices, in limited amounts on a discount basis as earlier explained.   In addition to these new issues which have been sold to the public, several additional special types have been created for internal fiscal purposes, notably the unemployment insurance and old-age retirement trust funds authorized under the Social Security Act of 1935.

Federal loans for periods of one to five years are usually made in the form of *Treasury notes*, whereas loans for periods less than one year are issued as *Treasury bills*.

The general philosophy of Federal borrowing has undergone radical charge in the United States during the past decade.   In addition to borrowing in order to meet inadequacies of tax revenues during abnormal years involving wars or depressions, Federal loans are now being made in order to finance personal relief, public works, national defense, agricultural benefits, and corporation loans.   The Federal budget which was formerly a prosaic financial document has become an adventure in sociology on a magnitude never before approached.

The direct obligations of the United States Government are invariably issued as unsecured debenture bonds. The guaranteed obligations, however, such as the H. O. L. C. bonds and the F. F. M. C. bonds, are protected by a prior claim upon the mortgages for which they were issued in exchange.

The test of ability to pay. The investment quality of the bonds of the United States Government depends primarily upon the ability and willingness of the American people to carry the national debt. Desirable as early repayment of the existing debt might be, it is not essential that this be done in order to keep American credit secure. An economist might readily see disadvantages arising from a policy of rapid debt reduction. The task of carrying the present debt, even at its astronomical level, does not impose an impossible financial burden because the annual interest charge is a very small percentage of national income. The problem is more complicated because the annual interest on the debt has become a relatively small part of the annual budget. The real question is whether or not the American people can carry, not an annual interest charge of, say, 1 billion dollars, but an annual budget of 10 billion dollars. Despite the fact that tax revenues were probably the highest then recorded, the fiscal year 1940 showed a deficit of nearly 4 billion dollars.

Statistics are none too helpful in a discussion of governmental credit. Intangible qualities such as reputation and good faith outweigh monetary values or physical units of wealth. Wealth and income data, however, do provide a reliable basis for appraising ability to pay. An estimate of the total wealth in the United States, recently prepared by competent authority, showed a valuation exceeding 300 billion dollars in 1936.[1] Of this total, tax-exempt property represented less than one eighth, leaving more than 250 billion dollars on which the Federal debt has virtually a first mort-

---

[1] The Conference Board *Economic Record,* October 5, 1939.

gage.   An estimate of the total income of the American people, prepared annually at Washington by the Department of Commerce, shows variations ranging from less than 50 billion dollars in poor years to more than 70 billion dollars in good years. Although these totals are many times the annual service charge of 1 billion dollars on the Federal debt, they are not nearly so reassuring in comparison with an annual budget in excess of 10 billion dollars, in view of the many living costs, other than Federal taxes, which must be met out of the national income.

The ability on the part of the American people and, therefore, the Federal Government to carry and eventually to redeem the present national debt is not open to serious question.   The longer look ahead, however, is less favorable. Unless the continuous succession of budget deficits is checked, the point will eventually be reached when the burden will become highly inconvenient.   Any attempt to indicate at just what sum that point would be reached seems gratuitous at this writing.   It might, perhaps, be expressed better in terms of psychology than of finance.

The accompanying table, which shows the composition of the national debt in 1940, has been amplified to include the guaranteed issues as well as the direct obligations.   The guaranteed issues are not included in the published figures of Federal debt, under the assumption that they are self-liquidating and therefore do not comprise a charge against tax revenue. This assumption has debatable validity because of inadequate assets held by some of the issuing agencies.   Although this table has been compiled from official sources, mortgages insured under the F. H. A. plan and bearing the equivalent of a Federal guarantee are not included.   Such insured mortgages are outstanding to the extent of around $3,000,000,000 and would bring the grand aggregate to an amount in excess of 50 billion dollars on June 30, 1940.

The test of willingness to pay.   It is an axiom of the investment business that the "will to pay" must be present in every good loan.   Even though unwilling debtors can at times be forced to pay, no investor voluntarily buys into

THE NATIONAL DEBT OF THE UNITED STATES GOVERNMENT
(As of June 30, 1940)

	Amount Outstanding
External public issues:	
Treasury bonds.........................	$26,555,000,000
Treasury notes.........................	6,383,000,000
Savings bonds.........................	2,905,000,000
Treasury bills.........................	1,302,000,000
Miscellaneous.........................	1,047,000,000
Subtotal.........................	$38,192,000,000
Internal department issues:	
Old-age retirement.........................	$ 1,738,000,000
Unemployment insurance.........................	1,710,000,000
Federal retirement.........................	559,000,000
Federal insurance.........................	525,000,000
Miscellaneous.........................	243,000,000
Subtotal.........................	$ 4,775,000,000
Direct obligations.........................	$42,967,000,000
Guaranteed obligations:	
Home Owners' Loan Corporation.........................	$ 2,637,000,000
Federal Farm Mortgage Corporation.........................	1,271,000,000
Reconstruction Finance Corporation.........................	1,096,000,000
Commodity Credit Corporation.........................	407,000,000
Miscellaneous.........................	121,000,000
Total.........................	$ 5,532,000,000
Grand total direct and guaranteed.........................	$48,499,000,000

a law suit. Government bonds, moreover, are issued by sovereign powers which are usually immune from suits by creditors.[2] And it has been a sad commentary upon international finance during recent years that convenience has dictated debt payment more than wealth in numerous governmental loans.

It has been truly stated that the only real basis for government loans is confidence in the good faith of the borrow-

[2] "There is no constitutional or inherent right to sue the government; on the contrary, the immunity of the sovereign from suit is a principle of universal acceptance, and permission to bring such suits is an act of grace, which, with us, may be granted or withheld by the Congress."—Message of President F. D. Roosevelt, June 27, 1935.

ing nation. The best test of good faith is to be found, not in laws or treaties or oratory, but in the simple record of past transactions. It is only too easy for nations which do not desire to repay their loans to find a convenient method of evasion. The experience of American investors with foreign government loans has been most unhappy in this respect.

In a relative sense, the debt record of the Federal Government of the United States has been excellent. At no time in the entire history of the nation has there been an actual dollar default in the payment of interest or principal on a Federal bond bearing the direct obligation of the government. The record, however, is not the perfect performance that it appears to be. At three different periods, each after a great war, there have been currency difficulties which were not settled in accordance with strict justice. The repudiation of the Continental currency issued during the Revolutionary War, the long default in the redemption of the "Greenbacks" issued during the War Between the States, and the repudiation of the gold redemption feature on gold certificate currency during the past decade comprise at least minor blemishes on the credit escutcheon of the United States.

More serious was the cancellation in 1933 of the gold payment clauses in the government bonds. These gold clauses were placed in the bonds as a method of guaranteeing buyers against any loss which they might suffer from the loss of purchasing power of their money in the event that the nation should either reduce the gold content of the dollar or abandon the gold standard entirely. Irrespective of the fact that the holders of those bonds did not or, at least up to 1941, had not suffered any actual loss by reason of the cancellation of the gold clauses, candor compels the statement that the Federal Government acted arbitrarily in this instance and not in entire good faith with the investors from whom the money had been borrowed. The further statement should be made, in the interest of fairness, that at the time the gold clauses were canceled, holders of bonds which were not then due were permitted to have their bonds redeemed immediately at face value, thus permitting holders to employ their money in any alternative commitment which might seem preferable in the light of possible monetary inflation.

As indicated in the preceding section, however, the test of willingness to pay is more likely to arise in the future than it ever did in the past. With the Federal debt already at a record high level and with no indication that it will stop rising in the immediate future, the possibility of the creation of a national debt beyond the convenient paying capacity of the people should not be ignored.

United States Savings Bonds. Three different classes of Federal savings bonds are now available to investors. These bonds are nontransferable and may be redeemed only through the Treasury Department or the Federal Reserve Banks. In all cases, the redemption prices are so arranged as to provide yields at substantially lower rates than are obtainable if the bonds are held to maturity.

(1) The *Series E Savings Bonds* are a 10-year obligation, available to individual buyers only, in yearly amounts of not more than $5,000 face value. As explained in detail in Chapter 15, these bonds are sold on a discount basis at 75 per cent of maturity value (equal to a yield of 2.90 per cent). The Series E bonds are redeemable at any time (after the first 60 days of issue) at values stated on the bonds.

(2) The *Series F Savings Bonds* are a 12-year obligation, available to all buyers (except banks) in yearly amounts of not more than $50,000 face value (including Series G bonds). These bonds are sold on a discount basis at 74 per cent of maturity value (equal to a yield of 2.53 per cent). The Series F bonds are redeemable on 30 days' notice (after the first six months of issue) at values stated on the bonds.

(3) The *Series G Savings Bonds* are a 12-year obligation, available to all buyers (except banks) in yearly amounts of not more than $50,000 face value (including Series F bonds). These bonds are sold at face value and bear interest at the rate of 2.50 per cent. The Series G bonds are likewise redeemable on 30 days' notice (after the first six months of issue) at values stated on the bonds.

Territorial bonds. Territorial bonds are those issued by the insular possessions of the United States—Puerto Rico, Hawaii, and the Philippine Islands. As all territory within the Federal jurisdiction which is not included in any state is under the complete legislative authority of the Federal Congress, it follows that the Federal Government is at least indirectly responsible for the safety of loans incurred by such possessions. Although the loans are made by fully constituted governments, the issuance and repayment thereof are under the direct supervision of the Federal Government, which has ample power to compel repayment. Under regulatory acts, the debt limit of each territory has been set at 10 per cent of the assessed valuation of the taxable property.

The relationship of the Federal Government to the bonds issued by territorial governments was clearly stated in the following quotation from the opinion of the Attorney General of the United States in approving an issue of bonds of the Philippine Government in 1921: [3]

This issue and sale of bonds is authorized explicitly by the National Power, and while in the strict and legal sense the faith of the United States of America is not pledged as a guaranty for the payment of the loan or for the due use of the proceeds or the observance of the sinking fund requirements, the entire transaction is being negotiated under the auspices of the United States of America and by its recognition and aid. There can be doubt, therefore, that the National Power will take the necessary steps in all contingenies to protect the purchasers in good faith of the securities.

Although territorial bonds have always been regarded as good investments, the Philippine issues have become less popular owing to the legislation under which the islands may elect to become an independent government in 1946. Although bonds issued prior to 1934 are indirectly guaranteed by the United States Government, bonds issued subsequently are less likely to be paid since such bonds are expressly only the obligation of the Philippine Government.

Agency bonds. The investment position of the bonds issued by Federal agencies such as the Home Owners' Loan Corp-

---

[3] As quoted in *Moody's Manual of Government Securities*.

oration, the Federal Farm Mortgage Corporation, the Reconstruction Finance Corporation, the Commodity Credit Corporation, the Federal Housing Administration, and the United States Housing Authority does not require a detailed discussion of the work of these agencies or the sources of their reserves. While it is true in each instance that the bonds issued are secured by claims against revenue-producing assets, the popularity of the bonds arises chiefly out of the fact that they are fully guaranteed by the Federal Government and are therefore entitled to a status equal to that of the direct obligations.

Federal instrumentalities. The bonds issued by institutions such as the Federal Farm Loan banks and the Federal Home Loan banks have been termed *instrumentalities* of the Federal Government rather than obligations. Consequently, buyers of these obligations must look solely to the issuing institutions for the safety of their investments.

The Farm Loan banks were created under the provisions of the Farm Loan Act of 1916, which was enacted for the purpose of supplying long-term credit to farm owners. Two types of lending institutions were authorized: Federal Land banks and Joint Stock Land banks. In either case, an eligible loan must represent a first mortgage on unencumbered farm property in an amount not exceeding 50 per cent of the value of the land and 20 per cent of the value of improvements thereon, repayable in installments over a period of between 5 and 40 years. These mortgage loans become the collateral security for bonds issued by the banks to investors.

Loans handled by the Federal Land banks are made principally through local National Farm Loan Associations in which the borrower is obliged to buy stock to the extent of 5 per cent of his loan. The associations, in turn, guarantee each loan which they pass on to the Federal Land bank in which they share ownership with the Federal Government. Although bonds may be issued individually by any one of the 12 banks, in which event the other 11 banks are jointly liable, the present practice is to issue *Consolidated Federal Farm Loan bonds* representing the joint obligation of the entire group.   The interest on these bonds is exempt from all Federal, state, and local income taxes.

Loans made by the Joint Stock Land banks were made directly to farmers on the same basis as loans made through the Federal Land banks.   Bonds issued by the Joint Stock Land banks to investors had the same type of collateral security, but the bonds represented only the obligation of the issuing bank and not the joint obligations of all Joint Stock banks.   Under the provisions of the Farm Relief Act of 1933, the Joint Stock banks are now prohibited from making any new loans to farmers except in connection with old loans then outstanding.   Since that time, the banks have been gradually liquidating their loans and redeeming their bonds.   In some cases, unfortunately, the final liquidation of these banks will represent severe losses to bondholders due to individual cases of imprudent lending policies.

The Federal Home Loan banks were created under the provisions of the Home Loan Act of 1932 for the purpose of giving greater liquidity to first mortgages on residential properties.   These banks deal with lending institutions such as life insurance companies and savings and loan associations which customarily carry large holdings in home mortgages.   These institutions, which become members of the system through the purchase of stock in one of the twelve regional Federal Home Loan banks, may borrow on mortgage collateral which is eligible under the Act.   To be eligible as collateral, the loans must be first mortgages, due within 15 years, on residential property having a value of $20,000 or less.   The amount of the bank loan cannot exceed 60 per cent of the unpaid balance on the mortgage or 40 per cent of the property value.   The banks may issue bonds to investors secured by the mortgages offered as collateral by borrowing members aggregating 190 per cent (in unpaid principal) of the bank bonds.   Although these bonds may be issued by separate banks, in which event the other banks are jointly liable, the present practice of the Federal Home Loan banks, as in the case of Federal Land banks, is to issue Consolidated bonds as the joint liability of all 12 banks.   Unlike the Farm Loan Bank bonds, which are exempt from both Federal normal income tax and surtax, the Home Loan Bank bonds are exempt from the Federal normal tax but subject to the surtax.

Tax position of Federal bonds. As explained in detail in a preceding chapter, income from securities is subject to Federal, state, and local taxation according to the laws of the respective authorities. The income on all Federal bonds is exempt from state and local taxes. All Federal bonds except National defense issues are exempt from the normal tax, but certain bonds are subject to the surtax. Exemption from the normal tax, which is imposed at a relatively low uniform rate, is not regarded as particularly beneficial to investors. Exemption from the surtax, however, which is imposed at graduated rates running in excess of 50 per cent on incomes of large size, is of great advantage to persons of wealth. The following Government issues are exempt both from the Federal normal tax, the Federal surtax, and the Federal supertax on individual incomes and from income taxes on corporations:

(a)   Panama Canal bonds;

(b)   Postal Savings bonds (not United States Savings bonds);

(c)   Treasury notes (except National Defense notes);

(d)   Treasury bills;

(e)   Treasury bonds up to an aggregate par value of $5,000;

(f)   Federal Land Bank bonds;

(g)   Joint Stock Land Bank bonds;

(h)   Territorial bonds.

Included among the Government bonds which are subject to the Federal surtax are the Treasury bonds and Savings bonds (in excess of $5,000 in face value), which represent about 75 per cent of the direct obligations, and the entire group of agency bonds, including principally the H. O. L. C., the F. F. M. C., and the R. F. C. issues.

The market for Government bonds. With more than 50 billion dollars in direct and guaranteed bonds outstanding, United States Government issues have a dominant position in the American investment market. They comprise the chief earning asset of the commercial banks of the country and are rapidly growing in importance in the portfolios of the leading investment institutions such as the savings banks and the life insurance companies. In addition to having become the most popular institutional security, they are equally popular with individual investors who desire a maximum degree of safety.

Concurrently with the growing popularity of Government bonds and a contributory factor thereto, has occurred a most substantial decline in the volume of new financing by municipal and corporate borrowers, thus diverting to the Government market funds which formerly went elsewhere. As a consequence, the market for Federal bonds has become extremely active in contrast to prewar days when practically all the Government bonds outstanding (less than 1 billion dollars in 1915) were owned by the national banks and pledged as security for national banknotes. Close spreads of as little as $\frac{1}{32}$ of 1 per cent are frequently found between the asked and offered prices of large blocks of these bonds.

The average interest rate on the entire national debt on June 30, 1940, was 2.58 per cent, which represented the annual cost to the Government of the loans. In view of the substantial premiums at which many issues were selling at that time, the average yield to the investor was much less, ranging from below 1 per cent on the short-term issues to 2.35 per cent on the long-term bonds. The low yields afforded by Government issues at that time was due partly to conditions in the money market, wherein a limited demand for commerical loans contrasted with a large supply of loanable funds, and partly as a result of Administration policy to keep interest rates low in a period of deficit borrowing. Enormous imports of gold from abroad, seeking a haven of safety from war-stricken areas, created huge credit balances by member banks in the Federal Reserve Banks, far in excess of legal reserve requirements. These excess credit balances, on which no interest is paid, were invested partly in Government bonds which af-

GOVERNMENT BOND YIELDS (1900-1939)

Year	United States Treasury Bonds	British 2½% Consols	French 3% Rentes
1900................	* —	2.75%	3.50%
1901................	—	2.89	2.92
1902................	—	2.89	3.00
1903................	—	2.81	3.06
1904................	—	2.84	3.09
1905................	—	2.81	3.03
1906................	—	2.84	3.09
1907................	—	2.97	3.19
1908................	—	2.94	3.15
1909................	—	2.97	3.06
1910................	—	3.08	3.06
1911................	—	3.16	3.19
1912................	—	3.33	3.26
1913................	—	3.47	3.48
1914................	—	3.47	3.79
1915................	—	3.97	4.41
1916................	—	4.31	4.71
1917................	—	4.63	4.91
1918................	—	4.31	5.00
1919................	—	4.54	4.84
20-year Average.......	—	3.35%	3.58%
1920................	5.32%	5.21%	5.26%
1921................	5.09	5.10	5.36
1922................	4.30	4.54	5.08
1923................	4.36	4.31	5.45
1924................	4.06	4.38	5.55
1925................	3.86	4.38	6.25
1926................	3.68	4.46	6.00
1927................	3.34	4.46	5.26
1928................	3.33	4.38	4.28
1929................	3.60	4.61	3.94
1930................	3.29	4.49	3.42
1931................	3.34	4.40	3.46
1932................	3.68	3.75	3.82
1933................	3.31	3.40	4.35
1934................	3.12	3.10	4.12
1935................	2.79	2.89	3.73
1936................	2.65	2.94	3.87
1937................	2.68	3.29	3.90
1938................	2.55	3.39	4.04
1939................	2.36	3.76	4.26
20-year Average.......	3.54%	4.06%	4.57%
40-year Average.......	—	3.71%	4.08%

forded about the only favorable investment opportunity available.

In view of the fact that the yield on Government bonds has become abnormally low, apprehension is felt from time to time that higher yields must ultimately come and cause substantially lower market prices. In view of the effect upon the market of a sudden loss of confidence in the prospective prices of Government bonds, and of the consequential disturbance to Federal fiscal plans and possible embarrassment to the institutions which hold such large volumes of these issues, the general belief that market support is officially given in periods of liquidation is quite reasonable. Such direct and indirect influences as the Treasury Department is able to bring upon the market undoubtedly give color to the belief entertained in many circles that the market for Government issues is largely artificial. Although some evidence may be found to warrant that belief, it is probably true that the natural forces have outweighed the artificial influences in the establishment of market prices.

The factors which will ultimately bring about higher yields and lower prices on Government bonds are most likely to be the converse of those which brought low yields and high prices. Those factors would be: (1) an increased demand for commercial loans from business enterprises; (2) an outflow of gold exports from the United States as political stability returns to areas now disturbed; (3) a fiscal situation at Washington which will obviate the necessity of continuous deficit borrowing; (4) a change in the gold buying policy of the Treasury Department; and (5) the creation of a natural market for Government bonds at all times through the cessation of supporting operations. The fact that few of these factors may appear likely to develop at any particular time does not preclude their ultimate possibility. Moreover, the anomaly of a constantly increasing debt at a constantly lower interest rate must eventually correct itself.

18

STATE BONDS

Scope. The purpose of this chapter is to discuss the investment position of the bonds of the various states which comprise the Federal Union. The order of discussion is: (1) state sovereignty, (2) purpose of issue, (3) sources of revenues, (4) ability to pay, (5) willingness to pay, (6) legality of issue, and (7) investment position. State bonds outstanding in 1940 amounted to about $2,500,000,000 and represented about 4 per cent of the total public debt at that time.

State sovereignty. Bonds issued by the various states that comprise the United States are the obligations of sovereign powers with respect to the creation and the payment of indebtedness. Under the Federal Constitution as originally adopted, and as further asserted in the Tenth and Eleventh Amendments, each state arranges its financial affairs without interference from the Federal Government. With the single exception of New York, where the state constitution specifically grants such permission, state governments may not be sued in either the state courts or the Federal courts. Such legal disability naturally has considerable bearing upon the investment position of state bonds. Investors must rely principally upon the good faith of the states, since the law does not provide redress in the event of default. The fact that state bonds are accorded high investment rating despite the legal disability feature is a noteworthy testimonial to the reputation of the issuing states. The observation may be made, as clearly demonstrated in the case of state bonds, that investors generally place greater reliance upon the intangible factor of reputation than upon tangible property and legal protection.

Purposes of issue. States borrow principally to finance the construction of long-term improvements. Although the early history of state debt in the United States is replete with numerous borrowings arranged for undertakings such as railways, canals, and banks, most of which are now regarded primarily as private enterprises, the later history has followed more definitely accepted public projects. The great popularity of the automobile has resulted in the construction of improved roads to such an extent that highway bonds have become the most important part of the indebtedness of many states. The tremendous increase in state debt from about $500,000,000 in 1915, when the automobile owner was exceptional, to $2,500,000,000 in 1940, when nearly every family had a motor car, was due chiefly to road construction expenditures. Closely related to the increase in highway expenditure has been the increase in park development. New York had nine different park bond issues outstanding in 1940, as compared with only one in 1915. A third purpose that has become increasingly important over recent years is the building of state institutions in accordance with the growing belief that the care of the unfortunate is a state rather than a local obligation. A fourth purpose, which reached its peak about 1936, was that of providing funds for emergency relief purposes. A fifth purpose, important as yet in but a few states, is that of grade-crossing elimination. A sixth purpose is the improvement of waterways, most of which work is now undertaken by the Federal Government.

Sources of revenue. The sources of the revenues from which state governments meet their obligations comprise the various taxes levied by the respective legislatures. Although at one time a state property tax, collected by the local authorities with the municipal property taxes, provided the chief source of revenue, income from this source is less important today than revenue from special taxes largely imposed for state purposes. Practically all states now impose estate taxes, which, under an arrangement with the Federal Government, divert to the states a substantial part of the tax levied upon decedents' estates. Furthermore, states generally impose automobile and gasoline taxes, which provide large revenues. Many states impose income taxes on corporations and individuals, in addition to taxes on retail sales. Other sources are corporate organization and stock transfer taxes. The relative importance of these sources naturally differs according to the laws of the various states. The accompanying table includes the more important items in New York State revenues in 1940.

SOURCES OF STATE REVENUES IN NEW YORK

YEAR ENDED JUNE 30, 1940

Source	Amount	Per Cent
Personal income tax	$ 92,718,000	23.6%
Motor fuel tax	62,063,000	15.8
Corporation income tax	46,970,000	11.9
Motor vehicle tax	38,149,000	9.7
Alcoholic beverage taxes	32,176,000	8.2
Estate tax	27,955,000	7.1
Franchise tax	25,958,000	6.6
Cigarette tax	20,437,000	5.2
Stock transfer tax	19,182,000	4.9
Miscellaneous receipts	27,934,000	7.0
Total revenues	$393,542,000	100.0%

An inspection of the various sources of state revenues reveals some interesting aspects. The absence of any predominant source affords an advantageous diversification that tends to promote stability of income. On the other hand, the tendency to rely less upon the relatively stable property tax and more upon fluctuating special taxes is an offsetting disadvantage. It is to the direct advantage of the state and to the indirect benefit of the investor in state bonds to have state revenues as stable as possible.

Although most of the revenues are used to pay the operating expenses of the state, the amount required for debt service must be provided for adequately. Debt service includes the annual interest charge and the provision for repayment of principal, either by redemption of maturing serial issues or by provision for sinking fund. Even though the debt service usually requires less than 15 per cent of the total budget and legally ranks with the other operating expenses in equality of claim, expediency generally places the debt charge in a position subordinate to the operating expense. Budget deficits thus endanger the position of state bonds, a condition forcibly brought home to many investors in recent years.

Ability to pay. The first test of the investment position of a state bond is *ability to pay*. The ideal method of measuring this capacity would be to compare the debt of the state to the aggregate value of its resources. Unfortunately, such comprehensive compilations as the latter implies are not available in complete or authentic form. Consequently, the practice in the investment field, for general comparative purposes, is that of using only those statistics which show population and property value. Such procedure was less subject to criticism when states relied primarily upon property taxes for revenues. It is especially objectionable in New York, which no longer imposes any state property tax, relying, as previously shown, entirely upon revenues from other sources. Pending the general acceptance and publication of more comprehensive data such as income tax returns, automobile registrations, and the value of manufactured and agricultural products, population and property values will remain the chief criteria of ability to pay.

The *net debt per capita* of a state is ascertained mathematically through the division of the net debt (as later explained) by the population figure. A tabulation giving the net debt per capita for all 48 states in 1937, which appears later in this chapter, shows an average figure of $18.90 per state. Experience has shown that states which keep their debts below an average of $50 per person are usually able to maintain a good credit record. Only two states showed higher averages in 1937.

The *net debt percentage* of a state is ascertained mathematically, through the division of the net debt by the assessed value of the taxable property therein. Unfortunately, assessment methods vary greatly throughout the country, thus impairing the comparative utility of such data. A conservative maximum for this criterion is regarded as 2 per cent of true value. A net debt of 2½ per cent in a state using an average appraisal basis of 80 per cent of value would be equivalent to 2 per cent on true value just as a net debt of 4 per cent in a state using an average appraisal basis of 40 per cent of value would be equivalent to 1.6 per cent on true value.

The financial condition of New York State was recently reported as follows:

STATE OF NEW YORK
FINANCIAL STATEMENT, JULY 1, 1940

Assessed valuation of taxable real property		$25,752,029,264
Gross bonded debt	$635,544,000	
Sinking funds	145,371,852	
Net bonded debt		$490,172,148

Population (1940)	13,479,142
Debt percentage	1.9%
Debt per capita	$36.23

As shown in the statement, the net debt amounted to about 1.9 per cent of the assessed value of the real property in the state. As the assessed value averaged about 86 per cent of the full value, the true debt percentage was even less than the figure shown. It would be unfair to assume, however, that the state debt here shown comprises the entire public debt against the property, since the reported indebtedness does not include the local municipal debts. The net state and municipal debt of New York in 1939 amounted to about $3,650,000,000, or $260 per capita.

The annual debt service charge for New York in 1940 amounted to about $55,000,000, of which $19,000,000 comprised interest and $36,000,000 represented repayment of principal on serial bonds and appropriations for sinking funds (on bonds issued prior to 1920). The debt service amounted to approximately 14 per cent of the total state revenues, and

FINANCIAL STATISTICS OF STATES, 1937[1]
(EXPRESSED IN THOUSANDS)

States	Assessed Valuation of Taxable Property	Net Debt	Net Debt Per Capita
New England			
Maine................	$ 663,532	$ 29,969	$35.05
New Hampshire........	585,628	13,901	27.31
Vermont.............	48,044	7,843	20.53
Massachusetts.........	6,269,393	22,772	5.15
Rhode Island..........	(a)	26,966	39.60
Connecticut............	2,978,740	0	0
Middle Atlantic			
New York.............	25,667,926	525,900	40.62
New Jersey............	6,249,659	86,905	20.04
Pennsylvania..........	3,747,490	121,670	11.98
East North Central			
Ohio.................	(a)	10,427	1.55
Indiana...............	5,069,098	4,458	1.29
Illinois...............	(a)	200,539	25.50
Michigan.............	337,589	34,123	7.10
Wisconsin.............	4,816,474	1,184	.41
West North Central			
Minnesota.............	2,042,102	62,559	23.66
Iowa.................	3,242,806	6,458	2.53
Missouri..............	3,797,473	119,215	29.89
North Dakota..........	487,266	0	0
South Dakota..........	44,680	2,511	3.63
Nebraska.............	2,174,013	531	.39
Kansas...............	2,716,560	21,467	11.46
South Atlantic			
Delaware.............	(a)	3,118	11.99
Maryland.............	2,650,730	50,787	30.27
Virginia..............	534,437	23,892	8.88
West Virginia..........	1,737,626	76,019	41.11
North Carolina........	161,235	136,420	39.25
South Carolina........	360,000	40,771	21.83
Georgia..............	1,060,314	23,492	7.61
Florida...............	601,954	0	0
East South Central			
Kentucky.............	2,449,220	14,929	5.14
Tennessee............	1,474,958	91,007	31.60
Alabama.............	924,791	72,591	25.14
Mississippi...........	442,508	51,460	25.53
West South Central			
Arkansas..............	427,173	163,859	80.44
Louisiana.............	1,338,883	126,325	59.25
Oklahoma.............	(a)	11,936	4.70
Texas................	3,247,532	26,649	4.33

a Not reported.
[1] From *Summary Bulletin* of United States Department of Commerce.

FINANCIAL STATISTICS OF STATES, 1937 (Continued)

States	Assessed Valuation of Taxable Property	Net Debt	Net Debt Per Capita
Mountain			
Montana..............	334,015	9,850	18.41
Idaho................	381,047	2,204	4.49
Wyoming.............	285,140	3,215	13.68
Colorado.............	1,103,564	30,056	28.12
New Mexico..........	288,389	15,243	36.12
Arizona..............	359,991	1,598	3.91
Utah.................	524,417	3,901	7.53
Nevada..............	181,773	662	6.56
Pacific			
Washington..........	1,083,330	12,547	7.62
Oregon..............	892,808	26,389	25.82
California...........	612,759	106,332	17.40
Total...............	$94,397,068	$2,424,648	$18.90

to an insignificant percentage of the aggregate income of the people of the state.

A similar analysis of the financial condition of the other states in the Union would result favorably in practically all cases. Despite the great increase in state debts over recent years, in few individual instances has the charge become inconveniently burdensome. The accompanying table shows the gross, net, and per capita debt of all states in 1937.

Willingness to pay. The second test of the investment position of state bonds is *willingness to pay*. While it may be said that the sovereign position of state governments in debt matters places willingness ahead of ability to pay, experience has shown that willingness is closely related to convenience, and convenience, in turn, is largely dependent upon ability. Willingness to pay is judged in two ways: past record and present condition. As present condition refers primarily to ability to pay as shown in the financial statements previously disclosed, the discussion at this point will be confined to an examination of the debt record of the various states since the adoption of the Federal Constitution in 1789, when

State	Dates of Default
Alabama	1861–1872–1876
Arizona	No default
Arkansas	1841–1873–1878–1933
California	1854
Colorado	No default
Connecticut	No default
Delaware	No default
Florida	1840–1873
Georgia	1871–1877
Idaho	No default
Illinois	1844
Indiana	1840
Iowa	No default
Kansas	No default
Kentucky	No default
Louisiana	1866–1874–1879
Maine	No default
Maryland	1842
Massachusetts	No default
Michigan	1841
Minnesota	1860
Mississippi	1840–1842
Missouri	1861
Montana	No default
Nebraska	No default
Nevada	No default
New Hampshire	No default
New Jersey	No default
New Mexico	No default
New York	No default
North Carolina	1868–1879
North Dakota	No default
Ohio	No default
Oklahoma	No default
Oregon	No default
Pennsylvania	1842
Rhode Island	No default
South Carolina	1862–1872–1879
South Dakota	No default
Tennessee	1865–1875–1879–1883
Texas	1848
Utah	No default
Vermont	No default
Virginia	1861–1869–1872–1882
Washington	No default
West Virginia	1863
Wisconsin	No default
Wyoming	No default

the debts of the original Colonies were assumed by the National Government.   At three different periods in the financial history of the United States, numerous states defaulted in the payment of interest and principal on outstanding bonds. The accompanying table summarizes the bond default record of the entire 48 states.   In most cases, the defaults represented repudiation rather than postponement of the payment.

The first period occurred between 1840 and 1842, during the depression years following the panic of 1837.   In the prosperous years immediately preceding 1837, the states had directly—or indirectly through subsidies—issued bonds for financing the construction of railroads and canals and the establishment of banks.   As the proceeds were to be used for productive purposes, the general expectation was that the debt would be self-supporting and would not result in any burden upon the taxpayers.   In the severe economic depression subsequent to 1837, however, these projects failed to show earnings and placed the states in the embarrassing position of increasing taxes at a time when public sentiment naturally opposed such procedure.   The prolonged continuation of the depression accentuated the problem and eventually brought about a condition that caused many states to default in the payment of their obligations, as an alternative to inconvenient payment.   As the record shows, many important states defaulted at this time; as the record does not show, the more fortunate states came very close to default before the economic horizon brightened.   Eventually, some of the defaults were met in full, and some in part; but the majority were never paid.   One state, years later, amended its Constitution to make payment of bank bonds issued during this period forever illegal! [2]

The second period of default occurred between 1848 and 1860.   The states included were widely separated, and the causes varied in each case.   Texas defaulted in the payment

---

[2] The sovereignty of states in the matter of debt settlements has been repeatedly upheld in the Federal courts.   As recently as 1934, the United States Supreme Court ruled in an action brought by the principality of Monaco against the State of Mississippi that not even a foreign state, any more than a private individual, might sue a state without the consent of the state.

of debt incurred in the War of Independence with Mexico, California defaulted in the payment of debt incurred during the inflation days of the "Forty-Niners," and Minnesota defaulted as a result of an uneconomic venture into state banking.

The third period occurred in the years following the War Between the States, when all the states that comprised the Southern Confederacy repudiated state obligations incurred during the Reconstruction Period. It should be noted that such default did not apply to Confederacy bonds, which became worthless at the close of the war. Rather did the repudiation apply to the large indebtedness incurred during the "carpet-baggers" era, when the state legislatures were not truly representative. With the withdrawal of the Union Army of Occupation in 1876, repudiation was almost inevitable from an emotional, if not from an economic or a legal, viewpoint.

The severe depression that followed the economic crisis of 1929 brought about the possibility of a fourth period of default in state bonds. The State of Arkansas, in 1933, attempted to force holders of $4\frac{1}{4}$, $4\frac{1}{2}$, $4\frac{3}{4}$, and 5 per cent bonds of that state to exchange into 3 per cent bonds at par by refusing to continue interest payments on the former issues. This difficulty, however, was adjusted through a refunding program adopted in 1934 which provided for eventual payment of interest in full.

Relatively favorable as may be the present situation and immediate outlook for state bonds, however, the longer-term prospect is slightly less encouraging. The conclusion is inescapable that state debts will substantially increase with the growing demand for sociological undertakings. The demand for old-age pensions and institutional and recreational facilities will tend to increase the supply of state bonds into the indefinite future. Moreover, the tendency in some states to issue bonds with maturities extending far beyond the life of the improvement (the State of Illinois in 1925 issued $10,000,-000 in highway bonds, none of which mature before 1945 and some in 1954) is not a wholesome practice and, if not checked, may well bring future regrets.

In the purchase of state bonds, investors should prefer the obligations of those states that not only pledge their "full faith and credit," but whose constitutions provide for unlimited taxation for debt service. At least two states (Alabama and North Carolina) have constitutional limitations on the taxing power without exception for debt service.[3]

Legality of issue. The third test of the investment position of state bonds is *legality of issue*. Experience has shown that illegality of issue has usually been given as the reason for repudiation of state debt. The importance of this factor is more apparent than real, however, since the state is the sole judge of the legality of its own debts. Practically all states now limit their debt creating capacity through voluntary restrictions that have been written into the state constitution. These restrictions vary in the different states; in general, they are as follows:

1. No state credit for private benefit.
2. Bonds only for long-term improvements.
3. Referendum approval on large issues.

New York further requires (since 1920) that all bonds must be issued in serial form, that each bond issue mature within the estimated life of the improvement, and that the proceeds of each issue be segregated into a special fund to be used only for the designated purpose and not to be combined with the general funds of the state.

The investor must necessarily rely upon the opinion of qualified attorneys in this matter of legality of issue. Such opinion is customarily secured by the investment house that offers the bonds.

Investment position of state bonds. No better testimonial to the investment position of state bonds in general could

---

[3] The Constitution of New York State provides that if annual appropriations are not made for debt service charges by the State Legislature, the State Comptroller must make such provision from the first general revenues thereafter received at the suit of any holder of outstanding bonds.

be presented than the remarks of the Governor of New York in a recent message when he stated that no nation, state, or governing body enjoyed a higher credit rating than did New York State at that time.

Several reasons of a somewhat technical nature, however, help the position of state bonds. In the first place, interest is fully exempt from Federal income taxes and also, with a few exceptions, from state income taxes when owned in the state of issue. In the second place, state bonds may qualify as legal investments for trustees and savings banks. In the third place, state bonds may be used by banks in lieu of surety bonds to guarantee the safety of deposit of state funds, and by insurance companies under state laws requiring policy

NEW ISSUE

$25,000,000

STATE OF NEW YORK

1½% SERIAL BONDS

Dated December 4, 1940 *Due Serially as shown below*

Principal and semi-annual interest, June 4 and December 4, payable in lawful money of the United States of America in The City of New York. Coupon bonds in denominations of $1,000, registerable as to principal and interest in denominations of $1,000, $5,000, $10,000 and $50,000.

Interest exempt from all present Federal and New York State Income Taxes

Eligible, in our opinion, as legal investments for Savings Banks and Trust Funds in New York, Connecticut, and certain other states; and for Savings Banks in Massachusetts.

Acceptable to the State of New York as security for State deposits, to the Superintendent of Insurance to secure policyholders, and to the Superintendent of Banks in trust for banks and trust companies.

These Bonds, issued for the Elimination of Grade Crossings, constitute, in the opinion of the Attorney General of the State of New York, valid and binding obligations of the State of New York to which the full faith and credit of the State are pledged for the payment of principal and interest.

MATURITIES, YIELDS, AND PRICES
$625,000 due December 4 in each year

1941	.15%	1949	1.00%	1957	1.30%	1965	1.45%	1973	99⅜
1942	.30	1950	1.05	1958	1.30	1966	100	1974	99¼
1943	.45	1951	1.10	1959	1.35	1967	100	1975	99⅛
1944	.60	1952	1.15	1960	1.35	1968	100	1976	99
1945	.65	1953	1.20	1961	1.40	1969	99⅞	1977	98⅞
1946	.70	1954	1.20	1962	1.40	1970	99¾	1978	98¾
1947	.80	1955	1.25	1963	1.40	1971	99⅝	1979	98⅝
1948	.90	1956	1.25	1964	1.45	1972	99½	1980	98½

(Accrued Interest to be added)

The above Bonds are offered when as and if issued and received by us and subject to approval of legality by the Attorney General of the State of New York. It is expected that interim certificates will be delivered in the first instance, pending preparation of Definitive Bonds.

J. P. MORGAN & CO.
Incorporated

KUHN, LOEB & CO.

DREXEL & CO.

DICK & MERLE-SMITH

New York, December 4, 1940

New York State Financing at Historically Low Interest Rates.

guarantees. As a consequence, the market for state bonds is largely institutional, with the demand coming primarily from banks, insurance companies, and wealthy investors.

The rate of return afforded by state bonds generally reflects the yield available on investments of the highest class. Such a relationship is shown in the appropriate yields on long-term New York State bonds during the present century:

1900	2.65%
1905	2.70%
1910	3.65%
1915	4.00%
1920	4.30%
1925	3.80%
1930	3.70%
1935	2.50%
1940	2.00%

19

MUNICIPAL BONDS

Scope. The purpose of this chapter is to discuss the investment position of the bonds of the many political subdivisions of the states, such as counties, cities, towns, and local districts. The order of discussion is: (1) political background, (2) purposes of issue, (3) nature of obligation, (4) revenue bonds, (5) special assessment bonds, (6) tax district bonds, (7) ability to pay, (8) willingness to pay, (9) legality of issue, (10) municipal bond market, and (11) tax position. Municipal bonds outstanding in 1940 amounted to about $17,000,000,000 and represented about 25 per cent of the total public debt at that time.

Political background. Municipal bonds comprise the obligations of the political subdivisions of the various states. These subdivisions include not only counties and cities, but also towns, villages, and numerous varieties of districts, many of which overlap each other. Municipalities have certain powers that have been delegated by state authority in order that they may act as agencies for local administration. Generally speaking, they are incorporated under a general state law or receive special charters under separate legislative acts. The powers usually delegated are: (1) police power, in which the maintenance of law and order is but part of the comprehensive welfare of the community; (2) taxation power, from which necessary revenues are secured; and (3) eminent domain, that confers the right to take private property, at fair compensation, for public use. The four major classifications of municipalities are counties, cities (including towns and villages), local tax districts, such as school, park, and drainage districts, and authorities which are governmental agencies created to finance the construction and operation of revenue projects such as bridges and power plants.[1]

Purposes of issue. The field of municipal activity is constantly growing wider. In addition to those activities that are expressly stated in the city charter or state constitution, many others are implied with the widening scope of municipal functions. In the furtherance of their duties, municipalities constantly face extraordinary expenditures that cannot conveniently be met from current revenues. In such cases, loans are arranged in such fashion as to spread the cost over a period of years. The ordinary purposes for which bonds are issued by municipalities are here listed:

Bridges	Markets
Buildings	Parks
Fire equipment	Public utilities
Grade crossings	School
Harbor improvements	Sewage disposal
Highways	Street improvements
Libraries	Water supply

Street improvements, schools, and water works still comprise the main purposes for municipal loans, but loans for other purposes have increased in number and amount. Municipal loans for relief purposes represented nearly 40 per cent of all borrowing in 1933, but such loans declined to only 10 per cent in 1936 and have become relatively unimportant in this field. Loans for refunding purposes have greatly increased as municipalities have taken advantage of lower interest rates to redeem high coupon bonds whenever possible. Loans for revenue-producing projects such as toll-bridges have also become more prevalent.

Under modern legislation, municipalities are rarely per-

---

[1] Investment dealers usually include state bonds in the municipal group as a matter of convenience.

mitted to issue bonds with maturities beyond the estimated period of life of the improvement financed.[2]   New York State in 1939 followed the example of New Jersey and other states by enacting legislation specifically limiting the maturities for which municipalities may issue bonds.   The limits set under the New York law are shown in the accompanying table.

NEW YORK BOND MATURITY LIMITS

Airports	10 years
Apparatus, fire and police	5 years
Bridges	40 years
Buildings:	
Fireproof	30 years
Not fireproof	15 years
Additions	15 years
Alterations	10 years
Docks	50 years
Electric plants	20 years
Gas plants	20 years
Grade crossings	30 years
Parks:	
Land	30 years
Improvements	10 years
Rapid transit railroads	50 years
Roads and streets:	
Sand	5 years
Concrete	10 years
Sewers and incinerators	20 years
Water supply	50 years

From the viewpoint of the investor, school and water bonds are regarded as the most desirable types of municipal bonds, not only because they represent universally recognized municipal functions and most essential services, but also because of excellent reputation based upon thorough seasoning over a long term of years.   Although all municipal bonds are unsecured debenture obligations, many investors rate the purposes of issue as indicators of quality, just as buyers of secured

---

[2] The town of West Farms (now in New York City) issued street improvement bonds in 1873 to mature 274 years later, in 2147!   The streets improved under this loan will have been relaid at least 10 times before the loan is repaid.

corporate bonds rate one type of security ahead of another type.

Nature of obligation. In the broad sense of the term, municipal bonds include all obligations of the various municipalities of the country. In the narrow interpretation, municipal bonds include only those for which the full credit of the entire community is pledged, with no tax limitations that might prevent ultimate payment. Hence, bonds payable out of special revenues or assessments, which are often called *limited* obligations, as well as bonds issued in communities having tax limits, are not regarded as true municipal bonds in the technical sense, and are considered distinctly inferior in most cases. The difference is important in view of the fact that, in many cases, the limited obligations substantially exceed the direct debt. The City of Seattle reported a total debt of $86,100,000 on December 31, 1938, of which special revenue bonds amounted to about $55,000,000 and special assessment bonds to $18,000,000, leaving but $13,000,000 in bonds with a general lien upon the city. It is not suggested that the limited obligations are poor securities, since, in most instances, the specified sources of revenue are ample for the purpose. It is emphasized, however, that such limited obligations, called *revenue* or *assessment* bonds, rank below the direct obligations of the city except in the cases of cities with poor credit ratings. In those cities a lien on revenues is regarded as superior to a lien on taxes. This distinction naturally does not apply in the case of cities like New York, where the assessment bonds are backed by the full credit of the city.

As most states have tax-limit legislation in effect, it would appear that few municipal bonds would deserve the *no-tax-limit* title. In many states, however, the tax limit does not apply to the debt service, for which payment unlimited taxes may be levied. Property taxes in New York are limited to a legal maximum of 2 per cent, but rates actually in effect in most New York municipalities are in excess of $2.00 per $100 annually, after the inclusion of the debt service. All New York State municipal obligations are therefore regarded as no-tax-limit bonds. A similar tax limit in Alabama does not exclude the debt service, however, which condition places all Alabama municipal debt in the tax-limit class. An even smaller tax limit in Ohio, which also does not exclude the debt service, is less objectionable because of a state court ruling that the debt service charge has priority of claim over operating expenses, an interesting exception to the general rule in other states that operating expenses are payable before debt service. Under a recent constitutional amendment, municipalities in New York State must now place debt service charges ahead of operating costs.

During recent years, agitation on the part of real property owners for a reduction in real estate taxes has resulted in the enactment of tax-limit legislation in many important states restricting the total tax rate which may be imposed for all purposes, including debt service, to levies as low as 1½ per cent yearly. The advantage of such legislation is debatable, however, as the credit position of the community is seriously injured, resulting in a higher interest rate on future loans. Under the prevailing law in New York State, bonds issued by municipalities after 1938 must be no-tax-limit obligations in order to qualify as legal investments in that state.[3]

Municipal revenue bonds. As previously stated, municipal revenue bonds are those which are payable out of revenues derived from the operation of a public facility such as a water plant or a toll bridge rather than out of general tax collections or assessments against specific properties. The use of the revenue bond to finance the construction or acquisition of public works has become popular in all parts of the country for a variety of projects as varied as toll bridges, express highways, electric light and power plants, gas plants, water works, sewer systems, swimming pools, and, in at least one instance, a planetarium.

As the position of these bonds depends solely upon the earning power of the project, it is evident that they should be regarded in a class distinctly different from ordinary mu-

---

[3] Tax-limit legislation, without exception for debt service, was in effect in the following states in 1940: Alabama, Arkansas, Indiana, Michigan, Minnesota, Nevada, Ohio, Pennsylvania, Texas, Washington, and West Virginia.

nicipal bonds which are payable from tax collections. On the other hand, revenue bonds are in a stronger position than the corporate bonds of public utility companies for four important reasons. First, the basic rate charged for the use of the facility can be raised, in most states, without the necessity of securing approval of a regulatory commission. Second, the enterprise is usually tax-free, thus avoiding the burden of corporation taxes which take as much as 20 per cent of the gross revenues of private utility companies. Third, income from revenue bonds is regarded as exempt from Federal income taxes including surtaxes. Fourth, the enterprise is in little, if any, danger arising out of competition or expiration of franchise privilege.

The argument is advanced in investment circles that revenue bonds are entitled to as good rating as general lien bonds because the projects are self-supporting, self-liquidating, and independent of tax collections. It has been shown that, in certain cases, interest on revenue bonds has been maintained by cities in default on their bonds payable from taxes. During periods of depression, however, the argument loses much of its validity when declining revenues impair interest payments. Moreover, the facility may lose its popularity as competitive influences develop. The City of Seattle defaulted in the payment of charges due on street railway revenue bonds in 1937, and required the bondholders to accept a substantial loss on their holdings in the reorganization of the enterprise in 1940.

Under recent practice, revenue bonds are frequently issued under a corporate title differing from the name of the municipality wherein the project is located. In New York City, municipal projects financed by revenue bonds include the planetarium (American Museum of Natural History Planetarium Authority), the produce market (Lower Hudson Regional Market Authority), the toll bridges in New York City (Triborough Bridge Authority), and the bridges and tunnels to New Jersey (Port of New York Authority). In San Francisco, the bridge to Oakland is financed with bonds issued by the California Toll Bridge Authority. The disassociation of the name of the city from the name of the project renders less likely any effort on the part of the city to come to the assistance of the project in order to protect the credit position of the municipality, but lessens the possibility of political influence upon the administration of the project.

The revenue bond has become an important part of municipal finance. When issued in connection with soundly conceived and well-managed projects, revenue bonds are entitled to the good investment rating which they have gained during recent years. It should be recognized, however, that not all projects which have been recently financed with revenue bonds offer equally attractive investment opportunities. The list of projects regarded as suitable for revenue bond financing (in connection with R. F. C. and P. W. A. loans) included enterprises as hazardous as swimming pools, golf courses, college stadia, public markets, harbor developments, refrigeration plants, and health resorts. Projects as spectacular as the Golden Gate Bridge, the Pennsylvania Turnpike, and the George Washington Bridge are brilliant engineering achievements but not necessarily indicative of sound investment opportunity. Not all of the projects financed by the Port of New York Authority have proved so profitable as has the Holland Tunnel.

It is interesting to note that New York City has issued bonds for many revenue-producing purposes such as rapid transit, docks, and water supply but has designated such bonds as general obligations payable from general revenues including tax collections. The revenue bonds issued by the city have been through the "authorities" as previously stated, rather than by the city directly.

Special assessment bonds. When municipal loans are made for the purpose of improving facilities in certain parts of the city rather than throughout the community, such as street pavements and the extension of water and sewer lines, it is customary to place the cost upon the property-owners who are directly and indirectly benefited, through assessments (usually spread over a series of years) in addition to their regular taxes. Such loans are made in the form of assessment bonds which are payable not from the general tax levy but from these assessments. Although the payment of assessments is just as mandatory as the payment of general taxes and is usually made at the same time on the same bill, it is apparent that a claim against some of the property in a city is less secure than a claim against all the property. Accordingly, assessment bonds are regarded as being inferior to general lien bonds. As a practical matter, however, city credit is at stake in the payment of assessment bonds as well as general lien obligations. Accordingly, it is customary for cities to supply from other sources funds for the payment of charges on assessment bonds in the event that assessment collections may be temporarily inadequate. Again, it might be noted that New York City follows the unusual practice of paying all bonds, including those of an assessment nature, from general tax collections.

Tax district bonds. In the educational development of the United States, school districts were established which served communities more extensive than existing incorporated areas. These districts issued bonds for the purpose of erecting school buildings, payable out of taxes levied on all property in the areas served, irrespective of whatever towns might be included therein. The bonds became general lien obligations of the entire community and, as such, gained favorable investment ratings.

The success of school district financing encouraged the application of the plan to other purposes with less favorable results. Irrigation district bonds were issued in many parts of the country, notably in the western states, for the purpose of financing the irrigation of small agricultural areas. These bonds, as a class, had an unsatisfactory record, partly because of unforeseen water shortages and partly because of generally unfavorable conditions in agriculture. Landowners abandoned their properties, leaving the bondholders powerless to enforce payment of the taxes with which to redeem the bonds.

In somewhat similar fashion, road districts were created in many states, notably in the Southwest, to finance the construction of local highways repayable from general tax levies.

Certain of these bonds worked out unfavorably, in part because of economic causes arising out of agricultural distress and in part because of legal technicalities which were not carefully observed.

A novel application of the tax district plan developed in Ohio in 1914 when the Miami Conservancy District was established in order to finance the construction of storage reservoirs which have prevented a repetition of the disastrous flood of 1913 in the Dayton area. All real property in a wide area along the Miami River was subject to taxes for the payment of the district bonds. The same idea is carried out on a smaller scale in the case of the Hudson River Regulatory District in the Sacandaga area.

A more recent application has been in the creation of Port Districts, such as at Seattle on the West Coast and at Albany on the East Coast, for the purpose of financing harbor improvements repayable out of tax levies upon property within the areas.

In addition to what might be termed the economic reason for the creation of tax districts, which is the financing of a project serving two or more incorporated areas, there has developed a political aspect which is rather unfortunate. Just as the restriction of a low tax limit tends to encourage financing by revenue bonds which are not part of the tax load (at least directly), so does the restriction of a low debt limit tend to encourage financing by district bonds which are not part of the legal debt of an included municipality. Even in New York State where the municipal debt limit of 10 per cent of the assessed value of taxable realty is usually adequate for municipal credit, the Legislature faces continual requests for the establishment of new tax districts. In Illinois, where the municipal debt limit is set at 5 per cent and where appraisal values are much lower than in New York, the inducement to evade such restriction by the establishment of tax districts is almost irresistible. In Cook County, more than 400 units of government (not all active) have power to levy general property taxes, including 201 school districts, 39 park districts, 22 road districts, and 2 mosquito abatement districts.

California permits tax districts to be formed for any of the following purposes: airport, boulevard, cemetery, fire protection, sanitation, water, garbage disposal, highway lighting, irrigation, library, health, memorial, mosquito, parks, museum, utility, recreation, and transportation.

The investment position of tax district bonds depends upon the purpose for which the district was created and the wealth of the included district. Although such bonds are usually general lien obligations, the quality is far from uniform. The favorable experience of investors with school district and port district bonds is in sharp contrast to their relatively poor experience with road district and irrigation district issues.

The existence of overlapping tax districts greatly complicates the problem of financial analysis. In 1939, the City of Albany, New York, reported a net debt of $18,615,000. Such statement, however, did not include Albany's share (87.89 per cent) of the debt of the Albany Port District ($7,080,000), but did include the school debt. In the same year, the City of Seattle, Washington, reported net debt figures which did not include a proper share either of the Port of Seattle debt (about 80 per cent) or of the King County School District No. 1 debt (about 99 per cent). On January 1, 1939, the net bonded debt of the City of Chicago was reported at about $96,000,000, which figure did not include $90,-000,000 in park bonds, $36,000,000 in school district bonds, and $115,000,000 in sanitary district bonds. Investors in tax district bonds should be cognizant of the fact that the published financial statements do not include the debts of underlying municipalities. Buyers of regular municipal bonds, in turn, should also realize that the financial statements of cities do not include the proportionate debts of overlapping tax districts, which, as shown previously, may exceed the internal debt.[4]

---

[4]The effect of overlapping districts upon comparative tax rates was clearly illustrated in the three leading California cities in 1940. The tax rate in San Francisco was set at $4.295 per $100 of assessed valuation with no overlapping areas. The city rate in Los Angeles was set at $1.70 per $100, but the total rate was $5.9091 after including four overlapping districts. The city rate in

Ability to pay. The first test of the investment position of a municipal bond, as in the cases of Federal and state bonds, is that of *ability to pay*. Since the dominant source from which cities derive revenues is property taxes, an analysis of the capacity of a municipality to meet its obligations involves primarily an examination of the fiscal condition as shown in the financial statement. Although cities publish balance sheets that list the tangible property owned by the municipality and the balances in various funds, the all-important intangible asset of taxable resources is not included. Consequently, recourse must be made to the expedient of a so-called financial statement that sets forth the salient factors indicating capacity to pay. The financial statement shows the amount of the city indebtedness and the value of the property that may be taxed for city revenue purposes. The percentage that the debt bears to the property value is the best available criterion of investment quality in municipal bonds.

The first major item that appears in the financial statement is the assessed value of the taxable property located in the municipality. In the accompanying statement, this item is listed at $211,500,000. In this particular instance, the *total* property value was $234,350,000, which sum included $12,600,000 in *exempt* private property and $10,250,000 in *nontaxable* city property. Franchise valuations are the values of that part of the property of public utility companies located on public property; these values are calculated on the basis of tangible property employed and the intangible right to occupy the public property. It is usually subject to the same tax rate as real estate and is regarded as equally productive. Of the three classes of property listed, the value of real property, land and buildings, is of outstanding importance in all municipal statements. In most communities, tax officials find the problem of appraising personal property extremely difficult, with the result that payment is readily

---

Oakland was set at $1.97, but the total rate was $5.18 after including six overlapping areas. All three cities used the same assessment basis of approximately 50 per cent.

evaded. Real estate is therefore generally relied upon to provide the bulk of tax revenue.

MUNICIPAL FINANCIAL STATEMENT
SPECIMEN FIGURES—DECEMBER 31, 1940

Assessed valuation (90% basis) of taxable property:

Real property..		$180,000,000
Franchise values...		4,500,000
Personal property..		27,000,000
Total..		$211,500,000
Gross bonded debt...............................		$ 16,750,000
Water bonds...................................	$2,125,000	
Sinking fund..................................	375,000	2,500,000
Net bonded debt...		$ 14,250,000
Population (1930)..............................	110,300	
Population (1940)..............................	121,600	
Tax rate.................	$2.12	

Tax Collections

Year	% Uncollected at End of Year	% Uncollected on Dec. 31, 1940
1937.....................	15.8	3.1
1938.....................	11.6	3.6
1939.....................	10.2	4.6
1940.....................	6.3	6.3

The basis upon which property is assessed for tax purposes varies widely throughout the United States. Whereas some cities, as shown in the following table, use a basis of 100 per cent of true value, others use as low as 37 per cent. A comparison of all local assessment bases in New York State in 1939 showed that the average rate was 85½ per cent, with the lowest rate at 41 per cent. Three counties reported between 40 and 50 per cent; five between 50 and 60 per cent; eight, between 60 and 70 per cent; fifteen, between 70 and 80 per cent; twenty-two, between 80 and 90 per cent; and nine, from 90 to 100 per cent.

A similar study, made in 1934, covering the principal cities in the United States showed a comparable dispersion, as indicated in the following table:

City	Basis	City	Basis
New York.........	90%	Cleveland..........	85%
Chicago............	37	St. Louis...........	80
Philadelphia........	90	Baltimore..........	100
Detroit............	100	Boston.............	100
Los Angeles........	46	Pittsburgh..........	75

With such variations in practice, it is readily apparent that the property values shown in municipal financial statements rarely indicate true value. Proper interpretation of such statements requires definite knowledge of the assessment basis used in each city. Debt percentages, as well as tax rates, for different cities are comparable only after adjustment for differences in assessment methods. A debt ratio of 6 per cent and a tax rate of 2.40 per cent in a city employing a 100 per cent assessment basis are exactly equivalent to a debt ratio of 9 per cent and a tax rate of 3.60 per cent in a city using 67-per-cent assessment basis.

Although property taxes provide the main source of municipal income, an increasing share of the total city revenue comes from rents for the use of city properties, fees for various services, and shares in state revenues from special taxes, such as mortgage, bank, and corporation taxes. Such revenues, however, are regarded as being primarily available for operating expenses of the city rather than for debt service.

Municipal tax power is limited by economies as well as by law. An unlimited legal power to tax might result in excessively high rates beyond the economic capacity of the taxpayers, and might thereby become ineffective. Municipal financial difficulties in recent years in Florida and Washington, to take two widely separated regions, have been due to the unfortunate combination of high tax rates and severe local depression. Unlimited tax power does not guarantee safety to investors. In most states, however, a maximum annual tax rate, restricting the charge to a reasonable limit, is imposed by law upon municipalities. As the general rule is that operating expenses take precedence over debt service, this tax limit seriously impairs the position of municipal bonds in the growing number of states which have imposed tax limits without excluding the cost of debt service on bonds.

The gross debt, as stated, may or may not include temporary obligations to be paid out of tax revenues receivable in the near future. In the illustrative statement, the gross debt figure of $16,750,000 did not include $1,160,000 in tax anticipation certificates. In like manner, the gross debt of New York City on June 30, 1940, which amounted to $2,530,-000,000, did not include the following items, all payable within one year of issue:

Revenue Bills	$66,900,000
Revenue Notes	500,000
Tax Notes	11,800,000
Total	$79,200,000

In the majority of states, debt limits have been established that restrict the borrowing capacity of municipalities, ranging from as low as 2 per cent in Kentucky to as high as 20 per cent in Florida. These debt limits are usually based upon a maximum percentage of the assessed value of the taxable property in the district. In New York, the debt limit is 10 per cent of the value of the taxable *real estate;* in Illinois, it is 5 per cent of the value of the taxable *property.* The general practice is to exclude that part of the debt incurred for revenue-producing purposes, such as water service, and amounts set aside in the sinking fund, in the determination of debt limit. The balance remaining after such deduction is called the *net debt.* The gross debt of New York City on January 1, 1940, amounted to $2,650,000,000, and included, among others, the following issues:

Purpose	Outstanding	Self-sustaining
Docks	$188,000,000	$ 65,000,000
Rapid transit	831,000,000	50,000,000
Water supply	439,000,000	439,000,000
Total	$1,458,000,000	$554,000,000

Although the total amount of bonds issued for revenue-producing purposes aggregated $1,458,000,000, only that part ($554,000,000) which was actually self-sustaining was properly deductible in the computation of net debt.

A further deduction of $390,000,000 for sinking funds is required in the New York illustration. These funds are held in the form of cash and marketable securities, principally New York City bonds, included in the gross debt. With the growing popularity of serial issues, sinking funds for the amortization of long-term bonds are becoming less important in municipal finance. It is decidedly to the interest of investors, however, that sinking fund appropriations be used principally to retire the precise bond issues for which the funds are established.

The percentage ratio of the net debt to the assessed value of the taxable property is shown in the illustrative statement as 6.74 per cent. This percentage, as before stated, is the best available indicator of municipal credit. In view of the widely accepted belief that large cities, because of the increased stability of revenue that comes from diversified interests, are better credit risks than small cities, which lack such diversification, it is impractical to set any inflexible rule, which would generally apply, on the maximum net debt percentage. Although 7 per cent is ordinarily regarded as a fair standard for a medium-sized city, 5 per cent would not be an unreasonably low limit for a small city, and 10 per cent would not be excessive for a large city. The New York State law relative to municipal bonds as legal investments for savings banks places a population minimum of 10,000 in cities in adjoining states, and 30,000 in cities in other states, with a 12 per cent debt limit (based upon the assessed value of real property only and including the proportionate debt of overlapping districts) in both cases. The New York law, moreover, places no debt limit whatever on cities with a population of 150,000 or more, provided that the assessed valuation of real property is in excess of $200,000,000 and no tax limits apply to the debt service.

The population figure shown in the illustrative statement is

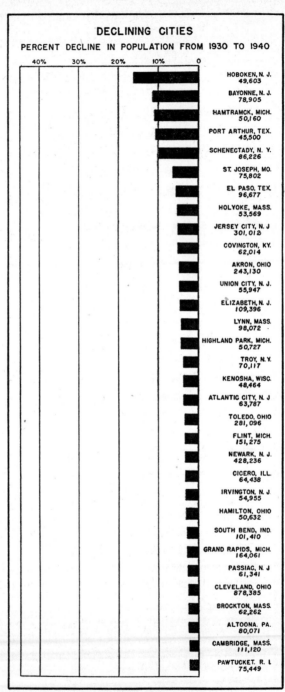

DECLINING CITIES
PERCENT DECLINE IN POPULATION FROM 1930 TO 1940

40%	30%	20%	10%	0

HOBOKEN, N. J.
49,603

BAYONNE, N. J.
78,905

HAMTRAMCK, MICH.
50,160

PORT ARTHUR, TEX.
45,500

SCHENECTADY, N. Y.
86,226

ST. JOSEPH, MO.
75,802

EL PASO, TEX.
96,677

HOLYOKE, MASS.
53,569

JERSEY CITY, N. J.
301,012

COVINGTON, KY.
62,014

AKRON, OHIO
243,130

UNION CITY, N. J.
55,947

ELIZABETH, N. J.
109,396

LYNN, MASS.
98,072

HIGHLAND PARK, MICH.
50,727

TROY, N. Y.
70,117

KENOSHA, WISC.
48,464

ATLANTIC CITY, N. J.
63,787

TOLEDO, OHIO
281,096

FLINT, MICH.
151,275

NEWARK, N. J.
428,236

CICERO, ILL.
64,438

IRVINGTON, N. J.
54,955

HAMILTON, OHIO
50,632

SOUTH BEND, IND.
101,410

GRAND RAPIDS, MICH.
164,061

PASSAIC, N. J.
61,341

CLEVELAND, OHIO
878,385

BROCKTON, MASS.
62,262

ALTOONA. PA.
80,071

CAMBRIDGE, MASS.
111,120

PAWTUCKET. R. I.
75,449

(From *Federal Home Loan Bank Review,* Federal Home Loan Bank Board, Washington, D. C., November, 1940.)

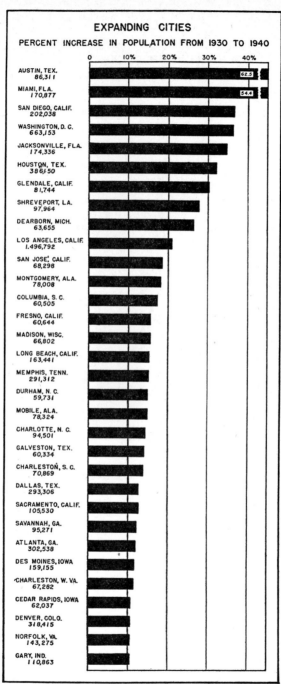

EXPANDING CITIES

PERCENT INCREASE IN POPULATION FROM 1930 TO 1940

AUSTIN, TEX. 86,311	62.5
MIAMI, FLA. 170,877	54.4
SAN DIEGO, CALIF. 202,038	
WASHINGTON, D. C. 663,153	
JACKSONVILLE, FLA. 174,336	
HOUSTON, TEX. 386,150	
GLENDALE, CALIF. 81,744	
SHREVEPORT, LA. 97,964	
DEARBORN, MICH. 63,655	
LOS ANGELES, CALIF. 1,496,792	
SAN JOSE, CALIF. 68,298	
MONTGOMERY, ALA. 78,008	
COLUMBIA, S. C. 60,505	
FRESNO, CALIF. 60,644	
MADISON, WISC. 66,802	
LONG BEACH, CALIF. 163,441	
MEMPHIS, TENN. 291,312	
DURHAM, N. C. 59,731	
MOBILE, ALA. 78,324	
CHARLOTTE, N. C. 94,501	
GALVESTON, TEX. 60,334	
CHARLESTON, S. C. 70,869	
DALLAS, TEX. 293,306	
SACRAMENTO, CALIF. 105,530	
SAVANNAH, GA. 95,271	
ATLANTA, GA. 302,538	
DES MOINES, IOWA 159,155	
CHARLESTON, W. VA. 67,282	
CEDAR RAPIDS, IOWA 62,037	
DENVER, COLO. 318,415	
NORFOLK, VA. 143,275	
GARY, IND. 110,863	

(From *Federal Home Loan Bank Review*, Federal Home Loan Bank Board, Washington, D. C., November, 1940.)

121,600, as reported in the 1940 Federal Census. Reference to the preceding 1930 census discloses an increase of nearly 11 per cent. As the average increase for the nation over the decade was but 7 per cent, it is at once evident that this city has made favorable progress. Although a rapid rate of growth is a favorable sign, it is not without its disadvantages. City expenditures must keep pace with this increase in population, with the result that bond issues are almost continuous, new issues often coming on the market before the previous ones have been absorbed. A condition of financial indigestion naturally tends to harm the position of all bonds of the city. The remarkable growth of Los Angeles and Detroit during the preceding decade was not entirely to the advantage of investors in bonds of those cities.

The per capita debt of $117 shown in the illustrative statement compares favorably with an average of about $145 in all American cities having a population of 30,000 and over. While consideration must naturally be given to the relative wealth of the community in the use of this item for comparative purposes, it is generally believed that a per capita debt of $300 is too high for convenient repayment by any municipality and that $250 is a reasonable maximum.

Age, apart from population, is also a factor to be considered under ability to pay. The splendid position of the bonds of Boston, Massachusetts, and Albany, New York, is due in large measure to the three centuries of uninterrupted existence behind both cities. Age evidences stability. It is not surprising to find municipal credit on a higher plane in the older-established North Atlantic states than elsewhere in the nation. History, not sectionalism, is the reason.

The tax rate of $2.12 shown in the statement is based upon an assessment rate of 90 per cent of full value and is therefore equal to a tax rate of $1.91 at full value. Comparisons of municipal tax rates are likely to be misleading unless proper adjustment is made for differences in assessment methods.

A recent survey showed that the average tax rate in the principal cities of the United States was around $3.70 per $100 of valuation and that the average assessment basis was

66 per cent, thus indicating an effective rate of $2.47 on true value. Although the average rate of $2.79 charged in the eastern cities seemed to be relatively low, the effective rate of $2.51, after adjusting for the average assessment basis of 90 per cent in this area, was higher than elsewhere in the country. The average rate of $4.47 charged in the western cities became an effective rate of $2.28 when adjusted for the average assessment basis of 51 per cent. The average rate of $3.27 charged in the southern cities became an effective rate of $2.19 when adjusted for the average assessment basis of 67 per cent. The average rate of $2.27 charged in the middle western cities became an effective rate of only $1.34 when adjusted for the average assessment basis of 59 per cent.[5]

Students of municipal finance believe that the cost of debt service, including both annual interest charges and provision for sinking fund or serial redemption, should not exceed 25 per cent of the annual budget. During the four-year interval between 1936 and 1940, the debt service percentage in the New York City budget was reduced from 31 to 26 per cent, at which point it was close to the standard just indicated.

Willingness to pay. The second test of a municipal bond is that of *willingness to pay*. Since municipalities may be sued, the test is less important than in the field of state debt. Communities reluctant to meet their obligations, however, can place many obstacles in the legal path of insistent creditors. Valid municipal bonds are enforcible obligations from a legal viewpoint. Creditors holding such bonds in default can sue in a court of jurisdiction and can obtain judgment. If no property is available for attachment, a writ of mandamus can be obtained, requiring the city authorities to levy and collect additional taxes to cover the claim, or to face commitment to jail for contempt of court. Although such power of collection seems complete, even the final alternative has proved ineffectual in certain instances.

Willingness is a matter of convenience and good faith. Convenience is largely a matter of capacity, whereas good faith is a matter of character. Capacity may best be judged

---

[5] Survey by Mortgage Bankers Association of America in 1938.

from the financial condition of the city and character from its financial history. A strong financial statement and an excellent debt record are therefore the best indications of willingness to pay.

Inability to pay is too frequently pleaded as a subterfuge for unwillingness to pay. The numerous municipal defaults that occurred in Florida subsequent to the collapse of the land boom in that state in 1926 were due chiefly to inconvenience in payment. While it is true that conservative debt limits were completely ignored by many Florida cities, in some cases running above 20 per cent of property values, and that a 20-per-cent debt in boom days became a 40- and even a 50-per-cent debt in depression days, too many cities prefer default to substantially higher tax rates.[6] For illustration, Miami defaulted in 1930 because annual revenues of about $4,400,000 were inadequate to cover the debt service charge of about $3,000,000 after payment of general operating expenses of about $2,500,000. A 25-per-cent increase in tax levies would not have been disastrous, especially in view of the 50-per-cent prior reduction in assessments, and would have avoided default. The investment tragedy of municipal bond defaults, aggregating in excess of $200,000,000, in 30 important Florida cities in 1930 was not wholly an economic problem.

Recent municipal bond defaults have by no means been confined to Florida, however. Reference has previously been made to defaults in tax district bonds in California, Texas, and Washington. A most unfortunate series of litigations involving assessment methods brought Chicago to the brink of receivership in 1932, because of delays in tax collections between 1928 and 1931. The prolonged depression in the textile industry, extending for almost a decade, compelled Fall River, Massachusetts, to default in the payment of three short-term issues in 1930, which, however, were paid in full with the proceeds of a funding issue in 1931.

The earlier history of the United States includes numerous examples of municipal bond defaults. Although most of

---

[6] The assessed valuation of property in Miami fell from $389,000,000 in 1926 to $97,000,000 in 1933.

these defaults were in newer communities in the development stage, the list includes several important cities. This early experience was almost as valuable as it was costly, in that it formed the basis for subsequent legislation, in state constitutions and city charters, designed to prevent a repetition of past errors. One wholesome restriction is the prohibition of public credit for private enterprise.

The observation is pertinent at this point that inability to pay because of inadequate revenues arising out of tax-limit legislations should more properly be termed unwillingness to pay. Investors should show a decided preference for the bonds of those communities that have obligated themselves to pay their bonds with no limitation as to taxes for such purpose. Tax-limit legislation once placed a large southern city in a position to force bondholders to accept a compromise that gave them only one half of the face value of their bonds in new bonds at a lower interest rate.

Another observation may further be in order, that willingness to pay is correlated with the enjoyment of the benefits to be derived from the improvement. The practice on the part of some municipalities to place maturity dates on bond issues beyond the estimated normal life of the improvement is not wholesome and may readily result in unwillingness to pay at the designated time.

In pleasant contrast to the many illustrations that might be cited of unwillingness to pay on the part of municipalities, numerous examples might be cited to the contrary. Many cities maintained the integrity of their credit ratings through a drastic reduction in operating expenses even to the point of severe inconvenience to the community welfare, and, at the same time, actually lowered the tax burden upon property owners. It is also pleasant to record the many instances where grave disasters such as fires, floods, and earthquakes did not prevent the full payment of maturing obligations. Good faith is an excellent municipal asset.

An indication of the relative willingness on the part of a community to pay off indebtedness is afforded in the tax collection record. The data which appear in the specimen state-

ment indicate that collections have been improving throughout the four-year period.   In 1937, the city collected about
84 per cent of the taxes levied during that year, about 88 per
cent in 1938, about 90 per cent in 1939, and over 93 per cent
in 1940.   By the end of 1940, the city had collected 97 per
cent of the 1937 levy, 96 per cent of 1938 taxes, and 95 per
cent of 1939 taxes.   A tax collection record of 85 per cent
during the year of levy is regarded as favorable, and a record
of 90 per cent or higher is regarded as excellent.

Legality of issue.   The third test of a municipal bond is
that of *legality of issue*.   Validity is of prime importance,
first, because creditors are allowed to sue municipalities to
compel payment, and, second, because a municipal bond that
has been illegally issued is invalid and noncollectible.
Although instances are to be found where courts, to protect
innocent investors who have acted in good faith, have held
some municipal bonds with minor technical defects as valid
obligations, the general rule is that buyers of municipal bonds
do so at their own risk and may not plead ignorance should
illegality later be established.   As all negotiations involving
the issuance of municipal bonds are open to public inspection,
and the laws regarding such issues are matters of record, a plea
of ignorance of any defect would not be an acceptable basis
in a suit for collection.

Cases involving illegality of issue of municipal bonds may
usually be divided into four groups.   The *authority of issue*
may be inadequate under the powers granted to the city.   The
purpose of issue may be outside the legitimate objectives for
which bonds may be issued.   The *process of issue* may have
violated any one of a score of minute details required by law.
The *restriction of issue* may have been ignored in the issuance
of bonds to an aggregate amount beyond the legal debt limit
of the city.   As the investor is rarely in a position to pass upon
such questions of a legal nature, he must rely upon the
advice of qualified attorneys.

The procedure followed in the issuance of municipal bonds
must be in strict accordance with legal requirements.   The
enabling ordinance must be properly drafted and introduced

at a legal meeting of the city council, approved in turn by the finance committee, the council, and, in many cases, a public referendum. The bond offering must be advertised for public sale (private sale is occasionally permitted), sealed bids submitted, and the award properly made. The bond instruments must agree in all details with the provisions of the ordinance. Failure to observe any one of the many technical requirements of the law in each of these steps endangers the validity of the obligation. As municipal law is a distinct part of the legal field, investors should be assured not alone that outside counsel has carefully checked and approved the legality of issue, but also that the particular counsel has a recognized reputation in municipal finance. So important are both of these phases that experienced investors in municipal bonds will buy only those issues that have been approved by certain attorneys. In this connection, it is significant to observe that less than 50 law firms in the entire United States have gained a national reputation in this field.

A delivery of municipal bonds from seller to buyer should be accompanied with a certified copy of the opinion of the law firm that approved the issue. The opinion states that the attorneys have verified all matters with respect to authority, purpose, process, and restriction of issue, and that adequate revenues can be made available for debt service. To save the time involved in such thorough investigation and thus to enable the bonds to be immediately offered to investors after the award has been made, many cities add a validation clause to the instrument, which constitutes a predetermination of all points that might be made the basis of litigation. Under the doctrine of estoppel, cities are thereby prohibited from advancing any claim of illegality at a later date. The effectiveness of such validation, however, is not uniform in all states.

The market for municipal bonds. Unlike important corporate issues, the majority of which are listed on the various security exchanges of the country, municipal bonds are bought and sold in the open market, which is a comprehensive term for "over the counters" of the investment houses that special-

ize in this field. Such firms often deal exclusively in municipal issues, since the purchase and sale of municipals is conducted in a manner dissimilar to that of corporate issues. The
market is largely institutional; that is, the principal buyers are
insurance companies, banks, and trustees, all of whom are
interested primarily in safety. In addition, the tax-exemption
feature appeals to wealthy investors. As a consequence,
transactions are usually carried on in large blocks and on a
narrow profit margin. Dealers in corporate bonds regard
$1,000 as the usual unit and about 2 per cent as a reasonable
profit; dealers in municipals regard $5,000 as the usual unit
and about 1 per cent as a fair profit.

The fact that municipal bonds as a class are regarded as
high-grade investments does not carry the inference that all
municipal bonds are excellent securities. As many, if not
more, gradations of quality exist in the municipal field as in
the corporate field. A high-grade municipal bond is better
than a high-grade corporate bond in most cases, but a low-
grade municipal issue is a highly speculative security. Under
normal conditions, the better grade of municipal bonds yield
about 3 to 4 per cent per annum, in contrast to yields ranging
from 5 to 8 per cent on the poorer grades. The lower grades
of municipal bonds should be bought only by individuals
familiar with the issuing community. The average investor
should confine his purchases to the general lien bonds of the
larger cities of the nation.

The tax position of municipal bonds. Income from all
classes of municipal bonds, whether general lien, assessment,
or revenue obligations, issued by municipalities, special districts, or authorities is regarded as exempt from all Federal
income taxes under prevailing regulations. This exemption
feature is of particular value to wealthy investors whose
incomes are subject to the heavy surtax rates which now prevail. In view of the natural tendency on the part of such
investors to avoid income taxes through investing large sums
in tax-exempt bonds, especially in the municipal field where
the greatest opportunity lies, repeated efforts have been made
to remove this exemption feature from such issues.

The legality of tax exemption on municipal bonds is based upon interpretation and precedent rather than upon specific legislation. Although the Sixteenth Amendment to the Federal Constitution, which gives the Government power "to lay and collect taxes on incomes, from whatever source derived," was enacted nearly thirty years ago, no attempt has been made to have it apply to income from municipal bonds because of doubt concerning its applicability to such income.

General agreement appears to exist that the most practical method of taxing the income from municipal bonds would be through the enactment of a further amendment to the Federal Constitution to that specific effect which would require the approval of at least 36 of the 48 states. Considerable doubt exists as to the probability of such approval. In the event of such legislation, bonds previously issued would probably retain their exemption, although there is no assurance on this point. Moreover, the possibility that income from municipal bonds may be made subject to Federal taxes through Congressional action without resort to a constitutional amendment and with the approval of the Supreme Court should not be overlooked.

20

RAILROAD SECURITIES

Scope. The purpose of this chapter is to discuss the investment position of the securities of the American railroad companies. The order of discussion is: (1) development, (2) regulation, (3) systems, (4) location, (5) operations, (6) income account, (7) balance sheet, (8) bonds, (9) stocks, (10) consolidations, and (11) securities analysis. Problems involved in the reorganization of railroad companies under Section 77 of the Bankruptcy Law are discussed in a previous chapter (Chapter 12—"Protection in Reorganizations"). The amount invested in American railroad securities is nearly $20,000,000,000 and represents the most important single industry in the nation with respect to capital employed and number of workers.

Development of the industry. The development of the steam railroad industry in the United States during the past century has closely followed the standard pattern of economic growth. The infancy of experimentation was followed by the adolescence of development, which, over recent years, has given place to the maturity of saturation. Some observers foresee in prevailing railway difficulties the beginning of the fourth and final stage, the senility of decline. The experimental stage began about 1830, with the construction of the short Mohawk and Hudson trackage from Albany to Schenectady, and ended in 1869, with the opening of the first transcontinental road, the Union Pacific, from Omaha to the Pacific Coast. During this period, many short lines were placed in operation and were financed chiefly by local capital. The development stage, which began at the close of the Civil War and continued until the turn of the century, brought wide expansion of new lines to all parts of the country and many consolidations of small roads into large systems. (The present New Haven System is the consolidation of 203 separate railroad companies.) The saturation stage began about 1910, attaining an apparent peak in 1926. During this third period, capital expenditure became intensive in nature rather than extensive, as shown, not in new mileage of line, but in track rehabilitation, equipment of greater capacity, increased terminal facilities, shop betterments, and power electrification. By 1926, the steam railroad industry was, to all intents and purposes, completed in the United States. No part of the country suffered by reason of inadequate railway facilities; in fact, in certain sections of the country, notably the Northwest, the facilities provided were beyond the economic warrant of the territory served. The problem of railroad management became primarily one of operating efficiency—that of procuring a satisfactory volume of traffic and of moving it at a reasonable cost.[1]

STEAM RAILROAD INDUSTRY IN THE UNITED STATES[2]
(As of 1940)

Miles of line....................	235,000	
Miles of track....................	400,000	
Locomotives in use...............	42,000	
Passenger cars..:...............	38,000	
Freight cars.....................	1,650,000	
Employees.......................	1,010,000	
Property investment....................	$26,150,000,000	
Capital stock (net)......................	6,900,000,000	
Bonds (net)...........................	10,700,000,000	
Total capital........................	17,600,000,000	
Annual revenues....................................		$4,300,000,000
Annual wages.......................................		1,900,000,000
Annual purchases...................................		800,000,000
Annual taxes......................................		400,000,000

[1] The average tractive power per locomotive increased from 36,000 pounds in 1920 to 50,000 pounds in 1939; the average freight-car capacity, from 42 tons in 1920 to 50 tons in 1939.

[2] From *A Yearbook of Railroad Information*, 1940 Edition.

With 1,000,000 employees and over $26,000,000,000 property investment, the steam railroad industry represents the largest private enterprise in the nation. Out of annual revenues around $4,000,000,000, the carriers pay over $1,900,-000,000 in wages, spend nearly $800,000,000 for material purchases, and contribute $400,000,000 in taxes. The prosperity of the railroad companies, therefore, vitally affects the economic welfare of the country at large, as well as that of investors in railroad securities.

Regulation. Through a process of evolution that began almost concurrently with the origin of the industry, railroading has become probably the most publicly regulated of all private enterprises in the United States. Legislation enacted by state and local authorities, as well as by the Federal Government, has severely restricted the powers of the company officials. As most important railroads carry both interstate and intrastate traffic, they are subject to the regulations of the Federal Interstate Commerce Commission and the Public Service Commissions of the various states. While a natural spirit of independence makes railroad management resent the constant encroachment of public regulation, investors have been helped probably more than harmed by the development. The evils of unregulated competition, as shown in the railroad history of several decades ago, were immeasurably more harmful to holders of railroad securities than the disadvantages that currently arise in rate, wage, and financial controversies.

The principal regulatory body affecting the railroads is the Interstate Commerce Commission, a Federal body appointed by the President. The powers of the Interstate Commerce Commission, which were merely observatory when the Commission was first organized in 1887, have been gradually increased, particularly in 1903, 1906, 1910, 1913, 1920, and 1933, until they now comprise a wide scope of regulatory authority over all railroad operations. Many of these powers directly affect the investment position of railroad securities.

The outstanding power of the Interstate Commerce Commission is that with respect to rate regulation. Under legislation enacted in 1933, the Commission is no longer required to give the companies any definite income such as a fair return upon a fair value, but is told to set rates sufficient to provide adequate and efficient service at the lowest reasonable cost.

The Commission has broad regulatory powers with respect to new financing by railroad companies. New securities, both bonds and stocks, may be issued only with the approval of the Commission after careful investigation of the purpose of the issue, the amount required, the nature of the security, and the cost of distribution. Although such approval does not constitute an investment recommendation, there can be no doubt that investors are protected through this function.

The additional authority that the Commission has with respect to accounting procedure and periodical earnings statements is also helpful to the investor. All railroad companies are required to keep bookkeeping accounts in strict accordance with a standard uniform system that assures reliable statements and permits ready comparison of results. Moreover, all carriers must submit monthly statements of earnings, which statements are published in the newspapers and enable investors to keep in close touch with the operations of the companies. Very few companies outside of the railroad field publish monthly earnings.

New railroad mileage may be constructed and existing mileage abandoned only with permission of the Commission. Holders of securities in existing properties, as well as prospective investors in new lines, are thus protected against the loss that would result from the uneconomic competition of facilities provided in excess of the demand. Conversely, holders of securities in unprofitable lines are not protected against continued losses incurred in the operation of such properties.

Competing railroad companies are not allowed to consolidate without the approval of the Commission. As such approval is far from perfunctory and is based chiefly upon public advantage, this veto power of the Commission has become a most potent factor over recent years. Numerous important proposed consolidations have been disapproved as being opposed to the public interest.

Railroad systems. Investors in railroad securities should recognize that the corporate title of a company rarely indicates the area served. Despite its title, the New York, Chicago and St. Louis railroad, better known as the "Nickel Plate," operates only between Buffalo and Chicago. The New York Central railroad, on the other hand, operates between Boston and St. Louis. The Chicago, Rock Island and Pacific railroad does not go beyond the Rocky Mountains, whereas the Atchison, Topeka and Santa Fe railroad operates as far east as Chicago and as far west as San Francisco. The Southern Pacific railroad handles shipments (partly in its own boats) from the North Atlantic seaboard to the Pacific Coast. The Illinois Central railroad operates as far south as New Orleans, and the Pennsylvania railroad operates as far west as Chicago and St. Louis. The so-called "transcontinental" railroads such as the Northern Pacific and the Union Pacific do not operate east of Chicago, nor do any of the "trunk" lines of the Atlantic States operate west of St. Louis. The Bangor and Portland railroad is surprisingly found to operate in Pennsylvania rather than in Maine. Only through reference to a railroad map may the territory served by any particular company be ascertained.

Railroad investors should further recognize that railroad systems and railroad companies are not identical. The New York Central railroad *company* operates only from New York to Buffalo, whereas the New York Central railroad *system* includes many leased lines, among which are the Boston and Albany (Boston to Albany), the West Shore (Hoboken to Buffalo), the Michigan Central (Buffalo to Detroit to Chicago), the Lake Shore (Buffalo to Cleveland to Chicago), and the Big Four (Cleveland to St. Louis). As the securities issued by these companies have been assumed by the New York Central, they are all grouped as New York Central issues. The Pennsylvania railroad *company* operates only from Philadelphia to Pittsburgh, whereas the Pennsylvania railroad *system* includes important leased lines, such as the United New Jersey (New York to Philadelphia), the Philadelphia, Baltimore and Washington (Philadelphia to Washington), the "Fort Wayne" (Pittsburgh to Chicago), and the "Pan Handle" (Pittsburgh to St. Louis). As in the case of the New York Central, the securities of the leased companies are assumed by the Pennsylvania and considered as Pennsylvania issues. Such a grouping of leased lines is to be found in most of the large systems but is more prevalent in the older railroads of the Northeast.

The ten most important railroad systems in the United States from the standpoint of size are shown in the accompanying table.

Rank	System	Mileage
1	New York Central......................	11,420
2	Chicago, Milwaukee, St. Paul & Pacific....	11,325
3	Pennsylvania...........................	10,890
4	Atchison, Topeka & Santa Fe............	9,625
5	Chicago, Burlington & Quincy...........	9,325
6	Southern Pacific.......................	9,130
7	Chicago and Northwestern..............	8,460
8	Great Northern........................	8,370
9	Chicago, Rock Island & Pacific...........	7,590
10	Missouri Pacific.......................	7,450

Geographical influences. Geography plays an important part in railroad prosperity. The size of the territory served, physical features, density of population, natural resources, manufacturing plants, commercial activities, and even corporate attitude directly affect the earning power of any particular company. As all of these factors do not operate with uniform advantage to any company, the conservative investor seeks a favorable combination rather than a maximum of advantage in all respects.

The size of the territory limits the distance over which traffic may be carried by the company. As freight traffic contributes the bulk of railroad earnings, as freight rates vary with the distance carried, and as the transportation cost varies more with terminal expense than with distance, it readily follows that long-haul traffic is relatively more profitable than short-haul shipments. Companies serving extended areas, such as the Pennsylvania and the Atchison, therefore have an operating advantage over those serving smaller districts, such as the New Haven and the Pere Marquette.

The topography of the territory has distinct bearing upon operating conditions. Companies serving relatively level areas, such as the Mississippi Valley region, usually operate more economically than those serving mountainous districts. Rugged terrain means additional capital expenditures for bridges, cuts, tunnels, snowsheds, and extra locomotives, as well as greater revenue expenditure for fuel and for repairing slides and washouts. In addition to these expenses is the necessity of running lighter trainloads at slower speed in a

TOPOGRAPHICAL COMPARISON OF NEW YORK-CHICAGO ROUTES

System	Mileage	Ruling Grades		Maximum Elevation (Feet)
		East Bound	West Bound	
New York Central.......	979	0.3%	0.6%	995
Erie....................	998	0.7	0.9	1,518
Pennsylvania............	908	0.8	0.9	2,160
Baltimore & Ohio........	993	0.8	0.9	2,270

district of poor traffic density. On the other hand, flood conditions are always a potential danger in low, flat areas. Proximity of terminals to ports is another factor, helpful in providing a source of traffic, but harmful in offering a low-cost competitor. An interesting illustration of the effect of topography is shown in the accompanying comparison of the routes followed by the four principal trunk lines from New York to Chicago. New York Central enjoys a tremendous natural advantage in that its maximum elevation and ruling grades are much lower than those of the other companies.

The density of the population has further bearing upon earnings. In a thickly populated region, passenger traffic is large, a negative factor in most instances, since passenger traffic is relatively nonprofitable, requiring expensive terminals and careful train operation.[3]   In such a region, property values are high, making for high tax rates; and expensive safety devices are necessary to prevent accidents.   Concentration of population, however, usually means commercial and industrial activity, both of which bring lucrative freight traffic.

Natural resources are reflected in the products of agriculture, the forest, and the mine.   Shipments of these products comprise the backbone of the freight traffic of the nation.   So important are these resources in many districts that the prosperity of the entire region, including, of course, the carriers, depends almost entirely upon a single commodity.   Cotton in the South, petroleum in the Southwest, wheat in the Northwest, corn in the Central West, coal in the Appalachian section, lumber in the South and the West, copper in the Rocky Mountain section, and iron in the Great Lakes section, all evidence the great importance of this factor.   Shipments of these commodities are usually carried profitably in bulk over long distances.   Economic distress in any commodity, however, seriously harms the earning power of the railroad companies dependent upon it.

Manufacturing and commercial activity in any area bear directly upon the prosperity of the serving carriers.   A high degree of activity and a broad diversification of enterprise make a most satisfactory background for railroad traffic. Experience has shown that such areas provide a more profitable and a more reliable source of shipments than do districts rich in natural resources.

The public attitude toward large corporations in general and railroad companies in particular varies geographically. In some states, due in part to unwise policies on the part of railroad managements, a feeling of animosity exists, which is naturally harmful to the prosperity of the companies therein located.

As railroad companies do not hold monopolies and must compete, at fixed uniform rates, with one another for traffic,

---

[3] According to the Interstate Commerce Commission computations, the passenger-operating expense ratio for all American railroads in 1938 was 121.8 per cent in contrast to 66.9 per cent for freight traffic.

the prospective investor in railroad securities in any particular
territory should carefully consider the competitive situation
in that region and endeavor to select those companies that are
offering the better service.

Operating data. The annual reports published by the
American steam railroad companies contain a vast amount of
statistical and financial data, most of which is of service only
to those intimately acquainted with railway operations. In
addition to such data, moreover, detailed elaborations are
published in the reports of the Bureau of Statistics of the
Interstate Commerce Commission. Although all of this
information directly or indirectly has a bearing upon the
investment position of railroad securities, the average investor
would find it expedient to concentrate his attention on a relatively small group of items among the operating data.

The number of *miles of line* operated indicates the size and
the importance of the road and serves as a common denominator for comparison of roads of unequal size. As before stated,
the longer roads are regarded as the better.

The *traffic density,* which is the quotient determined after
dividing the product of the aggregate revenue tonnage trans-
ported and the average distance carried by the number of
miles operated, indicates the freight productivity of the
district. In this connection, it is interesting to observe the
variations that exist in different parts of the country. The
average traffic density for the entire nation in 1938 was
1,236,000 ton-miles, but the range was from 719,000 in the
Northwest to 4,994,000 in the Pocahontas (coal) district.
Individual companies show even wider variations. A heavy
traffic density is regarded as a favorable indication.

Commodity tonnage shows the nature of the traffic handled
and is usually discussed on a percentage basis. Each company
reports commodity statistics in major groups, as well as in
separate detail. Such data throw interesting light upon the
earning power of the individual companies. As freight rates
are based upon the general principle of charging *what the
traffic will bear*—that is, proportionate to the value of the
shipment—it obviously follows that valuable commodities are

more profitably carried and that the companies which are favored by shipments of higher value are in an advantageous position. As shown in the accompanying table, the more profitable traffic comprises: (1) shipments in less than carload lots, which yield nearly $17 per average ton carried; (2) animal products, which yield over $11 per ton; (3) agricultural

ANALYSIS OF COMMODITY STATISTICS
(BASED ON 1939 TRAFFIC)

Group	Revenue per Ton	Tonnage Percentage	Revenue Percentage
Agricultural..............	$ 5.64	10.2%	15.3%
Animal.................	11.04	1.6	4.9
Mineral................	1.90	55.2	28.3
Forest..................	4.12	5.5	5.9
Manufactured...........	5.53	25.9	38.3
Total (carload)..........	$ 3.52	98.4%	92.7%
Less than carload........	16.96	1.6	7.3
All classes..............	$ 3.74	100.0%	100.0%

COMPARATIVE COMMODITY STATISTICS (1939)

Company	Agriculture	Animals	Mines	Forests	Manufactures	Less Than Carload
Atchison............	26%	6%	6%	3%	36%	7%
Atlantic Coast Line...	24	2	10	11	21	9
Burlington..........	16	9	16	5	33	7
Illinois Central.......	19	6	20	8	30	7
New Haven.........	6	3	10	2	27	11
New York Central....	6	5	23	2	33	4
Rock Island.........	24	5	12	7	33	8

products, which yield about $6 per ton; and (4) manufactured products, which yield about $5 per ton. The two least productive are: (1) mineral products, which yield less than $2 per ton; and (2) forest products, which yield slightly over $4 per ton. Profits are not directly proportionate to revenues, however, as the low-grade commodities can be moved somewhat more economically. That road is in the more favorable position which can show a fair percentage of the high-grade commodities (to gain a better average revenue per ton) and a reasonable balance of diversification over the group (to derive stability of earnings and to avoid uneconomic returning of empty cars from destination points).

An interesting comparison of the commodity statistic percentages for a selected group of companies in different sections of the country appears in the accompanying table. It will be observed that, although none of these companies shows what might be termed an ideal degree of diversification, the Western carriers carry a better distribution of traffic than the Eastern roads.

Income statement anlysis. The income statement and the balance sheet comprise the two financial statements in which the investor in corporate securities is primarily interested. Although all corporate balance sheets follow the same general form, income statements show considerable variation. The profit and loss report of a steam railroad company is prepared along lines peculiar to the conditions in that industry and differs materially from that of an industrial company. In both cases, net income is shown as the balance remaining after expenses have been deducted from revenues. The difference lies in the manner in which revenue and expense items are presented. The ensuing discussion is based upon the standard form of railroad accounts.

Total operating revenues include all receipts from railroad operations, but exclude receipts from other sources, such as income from investment securities owned by the company. For all railroads in the country, freight traffic contributes about 80 per cent of the total; passenger traffic about 10 per cent; and miscellaneous services, such as mail and express, about 10 per cent. The percentages for individual roads, in many instances, vary considerably from the group averages. New Haven shows about 57 per cent from freight and 33 per cent from passengers; New York Central, 70 per cent from freight and 18 per cent from passengers; Pennsylvania, 75 per cent from freight and 16 per cent from passengers; Burlington, 80 per cent from freight and 10 per cent from passengers;

and Missouri Pacific, 83 per cent from freight and 7 per cent from passengers. A study of railway revenues during the period from 1920 through 1940, as shown in the accompanying table, reveals these noteworthy points: (1) passenger traffic declined continuously until 1933; (2) freight revenues were relatively stable until 1930; and (3) total revenues reached a maximum as far back as 1926.

OPERATING REVENUES OF AMERICAN RAILROADS[4]

Year	Freight	Passenger	Total (All)
1920	$4,328,000,000	$1,288,000,000	$6,178,000,000
1921	3,924,000,000	1,153,000,000	5,516,000,000
1922	4,005,000,000	1,075,000,000	5,559,000,000
1923	4,622,000,000	1,147,000,000	6,289,000,000
1924	4,345,000,000	1,076,000,000	5,921,000,000
1925	4,552,000,000	1,057,000,000	6,122,000,000
1926	4,809,000,000	1,043,000,000	6,382,000,000
1927	4,643,000,000	976,000,000	6,136,000,000
1928	4,691,000,000	902,000,000	6,111,000,000
1929	4,825,000,000	873,000,000	6,279,000,000
1930	4,083,000,000	729,000,000	5,281,000,000
1931	3,254,000,000	551,000,000	4,188,000,000
1932	2,452,000,000	377,000,000	3,162,000,000
1933	2,492,000,000	329,000,000	3,095,000,000
1934	2,633,000,000	346,000,000	3,271,900,000
1935	2,790,000,000	358,000,000	3,452,000,000
1936	3,308,000,000	412,000,000	4,053,000,000
1937	3,378,000,000	443,000,000	4,166,000,000
1938	2,858,000,000	406,000,000	3,565,000,000
1939	3,251,000,000	417,000,000	3,995,000,000
1940	3,520,000,000	415,000,000	4,296,000,000

The *average revenue per ton-mile,* which is determined by dividing the annual freight revenue by the number of ton-miles reported, indicates the relative profitableness of operations. Carriers that are handicapped by a low average revenue on a ton-mile basis (caused largely by low-grade shipments) face a formidable obstacle that often prevents satisfactory profits. Although the grand average for the country was 0.983 cents per ton-mile in 1938, some districts reported as low as 0.645 cents (Pocahontas) and as high as 1.54 cents

[4] From *A Yearbook of Railroad Information.*

(New England).   It is pertinent to observe that the resources
of the territory and not the capacity of management determine
the average revenue.   Operating comparisons are always more
enlightening between companies in the same geographical
area.   Chicago Great Western suffers a fundamental disadvantage in an average ton-mile revenue of 0.90 cents in
contrast to 1.21 cents reported by Chicago and North-Western.

Total operating expenses include all the direct and indirect
expenses, such as wages of employees, cost of materials purchased, and administrative overhead, incurred in the conducting of operations, but exclude financial expenses, such as
interest on bonds.   The cost of new property, such as land,
buildings, equipment, and rolling stock, is treated as a capital
charge, and the amount is added to the assets rather than
deducted from earnings, as in the case of revenue charges.
For reasons of analytical expediency and in conformance with
long-established practice, operating expenses are not classified
in the usual corporate manner of labor, materials, and overhead, but more in harmony with the major operating divisions.
Hence, wages are included in several items rather than shown
as a single lump sum.

Maintenance of way and structures includes the cost of
materials (rails, ties, ballast, and so forth) and the wages of
labor consumed in the maintaining of the road bed and structures (bridges, tunnels, shops, and so forth) used in operations.   For the average American railroad, this item requires
an expenditure of about $2,000 per mile operated per year and
represents between 11 and 13 per cent of operating revenues.
During the period from 1935 through 1939, the actual averages
were $1,900 and 11.6 per cent, respectively, for all important
American companies (Class I).[5]

A standard somewhat more scientific than maintenance per
mile operated is offered by the Interstate Commerce Commission in its *equated track-mile,* which is based upon the relative
importance of main track as distinguished from extra tracks

---

[5] Class I companies are those whose operating revenues exceed $1,000,000
annually.   The Class I group operates about 92 per cent of the total mileage
and earns about 97 per cent of the total revenues in the United States.

and sidings. This figure, however, is not available in the annual reports of the companies.

As maintenance expenditure is controllable to a considerable degree, reports should be carefully scrutinized to ascertain the relative adequacy of the amount expended. Managements have been known to "skimp" on maintenance to show favorable earnings, obviously a short-sighted policy. On the other hand, the expenditure may be excessive, thus resulting in an understatement of earnings. During the past decade, the Western Pacific almost completely rehabilitated its line, causing the maintenance ratio over this period to run as high as 20 per cent of revenues. Companies serving mountainous districts, however, naturally must expend more for maintenance of way and structures. The adequacy of maintenance should be tested on the *per mile* basis, as well as on the *percentage of revenue* basis, with due consideration for traffic density.

Maintenance of equipment includes principally the cost of material and the wages of labor consumed in the repairing of the engines and the cars owned by the company. It also includes the amounts set aside for depreciation and retirement of equipment. For the average American railroad, this item requires an expenditure of about $3,500 per mile operated per year and represents between 19 and 22 per cent of operating revenues. During the 1935-1939 period, the actual averages were $3,200 and 19.4 per cent, respectively, for the principal carriers. Since equipment maintenance varies directly with usage, maintenance cost *per mile run* affords a further check on adequacy. Maintenance expense per mile run normally is between 25 and 30 cents for locomotives and about 2 cents for freight and passenger cars. Failure to maintain rolling stock in good condition is regarded as a serious matter, since this equipment provides the direct source of revenues.[6]

Total maintenance expense ratio, which is the sum of maintenance of way and structures plus maintenance of equipment,

---

[6] The advanced student will find many elaborate statistics indicating relative adequacy of maintenance expense in the annual reports of the companies.

is regarded as a comprehensive criterion of maintenance policy. A reasonable standard would be between 30 and 35 per cent of revenues. The interpretation is that any amount under 30 per cent for both purposes would indicate undermaintenance and that any amount over 35 per cent would show excess maintenance.

Traffic expense is a comparatively small item which indicates the expense incurred in the soliciting rather than in the conducting of traffic. The amount seldom exceeds 2 per cent of revenues.

Transportation expense is the largest item in the operating expense group, comprising chiefly the wages of stationmen and trainmen and the cost of fuel. For the average American railroad, this item requires an expenditure of about $6,000 per year per mile operated and represents between 34 and 38 per cent of operating revenues. During the 1935-1939 period, the actual averages were $5,900 and 36.1 per cent, respectively, for the principal carriers. Management has little control over this item, as wages are fixed largely by Federal authority and fuel prices depend upon economic conditions. Fortuitous though it may be, a low transportation expense ratio is an excellent commendation. Proximity to the leading coal-mining regions benefits all roads in the Pocahontas District in this regard, since they not only buy fuel cheaply but carry a commodity to other users that can be moved with maximum economy. For this reason, Chesapeake and Ohio and Norfolk and Western report transportation expense ratios of only about 25 per cent.

General expense includes chiefly administrative overhead, such as salaries of officers and clerks, legal fees, and pension benefits. The amount is relatively small, usually under 3 per cent of revenues.

All other expenses include miscellaneous items, seldom aggregating 1 per cent of revenues.

Total operating expense is the sum of the separate expense items. For the average American railroad, operating expenses aggregate about $12,500 per year per mile operated and represent between 72 and 76 per cent of revenues. During the

1935-1939 period, the actual averages were $12,100 and 74.2 per cent, respectively, for the principal carriers. It should be noted that this total does not include financial charges, such as taxes and bond interest. It is not practical to set up a maximum standard for the operating expense percentage, more popularly termed *operating ratio.* Some component items should be large, while others should be small. An operating ratio of 76 per cent, of which maintenance represents 36 per cent, is much better than a ratio of 70 per cent, of which maintenance represents 28 per cent. A standard of 72 to 75 per cent, with total maintenance of at least 32 per cent, should prove a satisfactory guide.

Net operating revenue is the balance remaining after operating expenses have been deducted from operating revenues. This amount represents the gross profit from operations and from it must be paid fixed charges in the proper sequence of claim.

Railway tax accruals represent the first charge against net revenue. These taxes are payable in part to the Federal Government, but mostly to local authorities. Taxes comprise another item that is outside the control of management. The importance of this item is less apparent in the fact that taxes require about 9 per cent of gross revenue than in the fact that they represent more than 30 per cent of total net income.

Uncollectible railway revenues represent the expense appropriation for bad debts. The amount involved is relatively insignificant.

Railway operating income is the balance remaining after deduction of the two preceding items. It is subject to adjustment in all individual cases (largely eliminated in the consolidated figures for all roads) for *hire of equipment,* under which one company pays another for the use of equipment loaned on through traffic, and for *joint facility rents,* which cover payments for the use of consolidated services, such as bridges and union passenger terminals. The amounts involved in these two items vary considerably for individual companies.

Net railway operating income is the balance remaining from operations available for the security holders. It is the return received from the capital invested in the operating property. In no year subsequent to 1930 has the average rate of return for the principal railroad systems been as large as 3 per cent upon the aggregate property investment. Although a return of 5 per cent on investment is adequate to cover all fixed charges and leave a balance for dividends to a reasonable degree, a return under 3 per cent is barely adequate to cover fixed charges alone. The failure of the combined roads to show a fair rate of return does not mean, however, that no individual companies did so.

Other income includes all revenues from sources other than direct operations. In large part, it represents interest on bonds and dividends on stocks of other railroad companies. The importance of this item, so far as individual companies are concerned, is not uniform. It means a great deal, for example, to Union Pacific, which usually derives about one third of its income from this source. It is important also to Delaware and Hudson as a large holder of investment securities. As Union Pacific learned in 1931 and 1932, however, other income is not always a reliable source of revenue when it is derived in the form of dividends on stocks of other companies.

Gross income is the sum of net railway operating income and other income.

Fixed charges represent those financial expenses that must be paid as they fall due. They include: (1) rent for leased roads, usually in the form of guaranteed interest or dividends; (2) rent for miscellaneous properties; (3) interest on funded (long-term) debt; (4) interest on unfunded (short-term) debt; and (5) amortization of discount on funded debt. Sinking fund provisions should be regarded as capital adjustments and should not be charged as expense. Total fixed charges should not exceed 12 per cent of operating revenues and should be earned at least one and one-half times. In 1932, Union Pacific reported about $115,000,000 in operating revenues, $36,000,000 in total income, and $16,000,000 in fixed charges—an impressive showing in a year of economic depression.

Net income is the balance remaining for dividends and surplus.

Dividends on preferred stock represent the priority distribution that must be made to the preferred stockholders (if any) before anything may be paid to the common stockholders.

Dividends on common stock represent payments to common stockholders. Holders of railroad common stock have learned, during the past decade, that, although dividend declarations in ordinary times seldom exceed one half of the available earnings, they are likely to be discontinued entirely in periods of depression.

Surplus is the final balance remaining after dividend payments. The amount is carried to the surplus account on the balance sheet, which includes all undistributed surpluses from prior periods.

Balance sheet analysis (assets). The outstanding item that appears on the asset side of the railroad balance sheet is the Investments account, of which Road and Equipment is the chief factor. In most instances, this item dominates the group, running as high as 90 per cent of total assets. The nature of the railroad business requires a heavy investment in physical assets. In setting up this account on the balance sheet, the companies usually include the value of equipment purchased under trust agreements and the value of improvements to leased property; the underlying value of leased property, however, is excluded. The bases upon which the property is valued are far from uniform. Prior to 1906, assets were valued largely according to the discretion of management, with grounds for at least some suspicion that book values were somewhat inflated. Since that time, however, the accounting procedure designated by the Interstate Commerce Commission has required the use of actual cost figures on additions and betterments. The book valuations, therefore, represent a mixture of valuation methods. An attempt on the part of the Interstate Commerce Commission, under the La Follette Act of 1913, to set up true values based upon physical inventories has resulted in almost utter confusion as to the relationship between stated and actual values of railroad properties. The claim that assets have been greatly over-valued in railroad balance sheets has become chiefly of academic interest in view of the adoption by the Interstate Commerce Commission of values for rate regulation that closely approximate book values.

Observation has shown that the investment in the Road and Equipment account is reasonable when the amount does not exceed four times the average annual operating revenues. With operating cost and taxes requiring approximately 80 per cent of gross revenues, the income remaining would afford a return of about 5 per cent on property valued at four times gross revenues. If the property value is five times the average revenues, the rate of return falls to 4 per cent. If the property value is more than five times the average revenues, the rate of return falls below 4 per cent.

From the investor's viewpoint, however, the condition of the property is more important than the book value. Since personal examination is usually impossible, the investor must rely upon a careful analysis of the maintenance figures for an authentic answer to this leading question.

Investments in affiliated companies represent holdings of stocks, bonds, and notes of associated subsidiary companies. Although the investment is carried in the form of securities, it would be more practical to assume that the amount represents investment almost as fixed and permanent as road and equipment. The amount involved is usually not large, but in some cases is of major importance. The Pennsylvania Railroad reported over $635,000,000 in such securities in 1939.

The values at which investments in affiliated and other companies appear in the balance sheet usually represent cost which may or may not truly reflect prevailing value. Union Pacific reported an income of about $12,330,000 in 1939 from investments carried at $197,000,000; the high rate of return, over 6 per cent, indicated conservative valuation. The investment accounts, however, are seldom as liquid as that of the Atchison, which reported, on December 31, 1939, the sum of $16,-900,000 as Other Investments, of which $13,700,000 comprised United States Government securities.

Current assets comprise principally cash on hand and in banks, accounts receivable, and inventories of materials and of supplies on hand. Important as this group is in industrial finance, much less significance obtains in the railroad field. Several reasons may be cited. In the first place, temporary investments of quick liquidity, although available for immediate requirements, are included in the Investments group. On December 31, 1938, Union Pacific reported about $56,000,000 in current assets, which figure, however, did not include over $13,000,000 in United States Government securities. In the second place, the regularity with which revenues are received on a cash basis assures a steady inflow of funds for current bills. In the third place, the roads are able, in normal times, to correct an adverse current ratio by funding short-term debt from the proceeds of the sale of long-term bonds.

Deferred assets and *unadjusted debits* are generally small, unimportant items, having only a minor technical significance of an accounting nature.

Balance sheet analysis (liabilities). The items which appear on the liabilities side of the railroad balance sheet include capital stock, funded debt (bonds), current and deferred liabilities, reserves, and surplus.

Capital stock represents the stated value of the stock outstanding. The stock, as in the case of the Atchison, may comprise both preferred and common shares, or, as in the case of New York Central, may represent only common shares.[7] The value shown is usually the par value, although some companies, as a result of comparatively recent reorganizations, have issued stock of no par value. Such companies, including the St. Paul and the Missouri-Kansas-Texas, place an arbitrary value upon the capital stock account. It is genuinely unfortunate that most railroad companies have a relatively small capitalization in stock, as compared with bonds. Although the composite net capitalization for all leading companies shows about 39 per cent in stock to 61 per cent in bonds, the position of many individual roads is obviously much

---

[7] The anomaly of Great Northern having only preferred shares outstanding signifies that such stock might more properly be termed common shares.

inferior to the average. Companies that show the stock proportion as low as one third, and even one fourth, of total capitalization are patently trading on a thin equity. It is further regrettable that the carriers did not resort to equity financing to a greater proportion than 25 per cent in the favorable stock market period from 1925 to 1929. A thin equity in stock capitalization eventually harms both bonds and stocks, as shown in a year of severe depression such as 1932, when net operating income was inadequate to meet the heavy burden of fixed charges for all roads as a group. Small wonderment should be felt that such a situation not only brought railroad bonds to a distressingly low estate, but reduced many stocks to negligible prices.[8]

Funded debt represents the outstanding bonds, or long-term debt, of the company. The amount shown is usually the total of many separate issues, each of which has distinctive features, as discussed in an earlier chapter. Conversely with stock, bond capitalization should be kept down. Any capitalization ratio that shows as much as two thirds or higher in bonds is excessively out of balance. The discrepancy is even greater than appears on the surface, since companies do not include guaranteed securities of leased lines in stating indebtedness. A usual practice is to estimate such obligations by capitalizing annual rentals at 5 per cent (multiplying by 20). The importance of rental obligations is clearly shown in the example of the Pennsylvania, where such payments are nearly twice the interest charges on the funded debt. Investors should prefer the securities of those companies, otherwise satisfactory, whose indebtedness, including capitalized rentals, does not exceed two thirds of total capitalization.

The items comprising the funded debt should be arranged according to maturities, to disclose any large issues that must be paid in the immediate future. Such maturities do not cause difficulties in years of prosperity, when refunding can be readily arranged. But in years of depression, such as 1931 and 1932, large maturing obligations brought great embar-

---

[8] New York Central common stock declined from a high of 256 in 1929 to a low of 9 in 1932.

rassment to many important companies and caused receivership in several instances.

Current liabilities include items payable within one year. The amount is of interest chiefly in relation to current assets as previously discussed.

Deferred liabilities include a group of small miscellaneous items payable at an indefinite time, usually more than one year in advance.

Unadjusted credits comprise principally reserves that have been set up for special purposes, such as *taxes, insurance,* and *depreciation.* The wide distribution of railroad property minimizes the risk of loss from fire and similar causes and enables the companies to act as self-insurers for a substantial part of the risk. Tax liability is estimated in advance of payment, subject to later revision when the tax reports are audited by the public authorities. Depreciation is accrued by all companies on equipment and, in some cases, on road as well. An annual expense charge is made against earnings, as shown previously in the discussion of maintenance provision, which is carried to the depreciation reserve, against which the value of property retired is written off. The necessity for providing for the ultimate retirement of equipment is more obvious than in the case of road. Accordingly, it is not entirely strange to find that the balance sheet of Pennsylvania on December 31, 1939, showed a depreciation reserve of $302,-000,000, or 50 per cent, against equipment in service valued at $606,000,000, in contrast to a reserve of only $38,000,000, or 6 per cent, against road in use valued at $642,000,000. It will be noted that these reserves are not funded; in other words, the amounts represented have been invested in the general assets of the companies rather than segregated into separate funds of cash and securities.

Surplus represents the excess of the aggregate value of the assets over the stated value of the liabilities, reserves, and capital stock. Most railroad companies have allotted part of the surplus account for specific purposes, under a general grouping entitled *appropriated surplus.* The most popular purpose for such segregation is "for addition and betterments," in which case the amount stated has been reinvested in property and cannot be paid out as cash dividends to stockholders. As of December 31, 1939, Union Pacific reported an appropriated surplus of nearly $35,000,000 as a "reserve for depreciation of securities."

Profit and loss represents the unappropriated part of the surplus account. It is the amount from which dividends are declared and paid. In theory, at least, it comprises the accumulated undistributed earnings of prior periods, and forms a backlog for the continued payment of dividends in years of reduced earnings. Recent experience, especially in the railroad field, has shown that a large profit and loss credit balance carries little assurance of the payment of dividends at such times. Numerous examples might readily be cited in which dividend rates have been reduced and, in important instances, have been entirely discontinued, despite large surplus accounts. The position of the cash account is more important than the size of the profit and loss account at such a time.

Railroad bonds. Railroad bonds run the entire gamut of quality from the highest-grade senior liens of the strong companies to the low-grade junior issues of weak companies on the brink of, if not already in, receivership. The prime test of quality is earnings protection.

First-grade railroad bonds include the senior mortgage issues of prosperous companies, as illustrated in the Pennsylvania Consolidated 4½'s of 1960, the Norfolk and Western First and General 4's of 1944, and the Chesapeake and Ohio General 4½'s of 1992.[9]

---

[9] The Chesapeake and Ohio General 4½'s of 1992 are secured by a first lien on 1,081 miles of line from Fort Monroe, Va., to Covington, Ky. All fixed charges were earned an average of 4.52 times during 1936-1940 as here shown:

1936	5.27
1937	4.67
1938	3.26
1939	3.87
1940	5.03
Average	4.52

The first-grade group also comprises the divisional bonds of many small properties which have been leased to large important companies under conditions whereby interest payments are guaranteed by the latter. Obviously, only those divisional bonds that are secured by valuable property fall in this group. The Oregon Short Line First Consolidated 5's of 1946 (guaranteed by Union Pacific) and the Hocking Valley First Consolidated 4½'s of 1999 (guaranteed by Chesapeake and Ohio) are good examples. Terminal bonds secured by valuable properties and guaranteed by prosperous companies, as illustrated in the Chicago Union Station First 3¾'s of 1963, are likewise in this group.

Bonds that qualify in the first-grade group are usually issued by companies which show an earnings factor of better than two times all fixed charges over the preceding five years. Under normal conditions, bonds in this group provide income yields between 3½ and 4½ per cent.

Second-grade railroad bonds include those issues that are acceptable investments in the general sense but which are relatively less secure than the highest grade. They comprise the junior issues of the prosperous companies, and, in some cases, the senior issues of the smaller companies. Examples would be the Louisville and Nashville Unified 4's of 1960, the Atchison, Topeka and Santa Fé Adjustment 4's of 1995, and the Chicago, Burlington and Quincy General 4's of 1958.[10]

Second-grade railroad bonds are usually secured by an earnings factor ranging from one and one-half to twice all interest charges over the preceding five years. In ordinary times, bonds in this class yield between 4½ and 5½ per cent.

---

[10] The Chicago, Burlington and Quincy General 4's of 1958 are secured by a first lien on 6,441 miles of main line west of the Mississippi River and by a second lien on 1,616 miles of main line east of the Mississippi. All fixed charges were earned an average of 1.45 times during 1936-1940 as here shown:

1936	1.54
1937	1.51
1938	1.37
1939	1.38
1940	1.45
Average	1.45

Third-grade railroad bonds comprise the issues of those companies which are still solvent but which show narrow margins of safety. They include issues such as the Baltimore and Ohio First 4's of 1948, the New York Central Refunding and Improvement 4½'s of 2013,[11] and the Southern First Consolidated 5's of 1994. These bonds are secured in most cases by a narrow margin of safety ranging from deficits in poor years to less than one and one-half times interest requirement in good years. Bonds in this class generally yield well in excess of 6 per cent.

Railroad stocks. Railroad stocks, long regarded as the only equities deserving investment consideration, have recently lost much of their past reputation. The decline in railroad prosperity, caused partly by general economic conditions and partly by increased competition, has compelled substantial curtailment in dividend payments. Even the Illinois Central, with an unbroken dividend record extending back some 70 years to the Civil War period, was obliged to discontinue dividends in 1931. The New York Central, with a record almost equally impressive, also stopped dividends in 1931. Union Pacific, Chesapeake and Ohio, Norfolk and Western, and the Pennsylvania were the only important railroad common stocks on a dividend basis at the close of 1933. The consequence is that the railroad stocks, as a group, have been reduced in rank from fair investments to speculative commitments. The stability of income that railroad stocks provided for many years has given place to uncertainty. Until such time as sustained prosperity returns to the industry,

---

[11] The New York Central Refunding and Improvement 4½'s of 2013 are secured by a first lien on 295 miles of road, but by sequential liens on 2,445 miles. All fixed charges were earned an average of 1.04 times during 1936-1940 as here shown:

1936	1.17
1937	1.12
1938	0.59
1939	1.09
1940	1.23
Average	1.04

INVESTMENT RATING OF PRINCIPAL AMERICAN RAILROAD SYSTEMS

(Based on Ten-Year Average, 1930-1939)

Company	Number of Times Fixed Charges Earned
Group I (over 2.0):	
Norfolk and Western	9.74
Chesapeake and Ohio	3.96
Union Pacific	2.46
Group II (1.5 to 2.0):	
Atchison, Topeka and Santa Fe	1.93
Chicago, Burlington and Quincy	1.69
Reading	1.62
Group III (1.25 to 1.50):	
Louisville and Nashville	1.41
Pennsylvania	1.34
Great Northern	1.27
Group IV (1.00 to 1.25):	
New York, Chicago and St. Louis	1.17
Southern Pacific	1.14
Northern Pacific	1.13
Atlantic Coast Line	1.00
Baltimore and Ohio	1.00
New York Central	1.00
Southern	1.00
Group V (0.90 to 1.00):	
Kansas City Southern	0.98
Illinois Central	0.97
Erie	0.92
Colorado and Southern	0.91
Missouri, Kansas and Texas	0.90

railroad equities will not be attractive from the viewpoint of the investor.

Consolidations. Joint control of competing lines, long prohibited under former legislation, is now permitted under the provisions of the Transportation Act of 1920 as amended in 1940. Such technical consolidations, whether by lease, stock purchase, or otherwise, must provide for the preservation of competition and the maintenance of existing routes and channels of trade and of commerce. Another requirement is that the arrangement must be in the public interest and the terms must be approved by the Interstate Commerce Commission. Although numerous applications were made for acquisitions under this provision in the decade that followed the enactment of the 1920 law, no important approvals have been granted. The chief reason for disapproval has been divergence from the comprehensive plan worked out with great difficulty by the Commission and submitted in final form in 1929, as representing the best complete plan in the public interest.

Future prospect. The future prospect of the railroad industry is not overbright under existing conditions. Competition in the form of the motor car, the oil and gas pipe lines, the electrical transmission line, and the aëroplane has made serious inroads into railroad earnings. Regulation of rates, routes, wages, and securities does not place the carriers in a comfortable position to offset the losses arising from decreased traffic.

For many years to come, the railroads must provide the main reliance for transportation. Self-interest alone will compel the public eventually to give the carriers fair consideration. One might be less optimistic if the competitors were in a position to take over the bulk of the railroad traffic. While railway operation may not be an essential industry, transportation is essential, and until such time as competition is able, from the standpoints of both capacity and economy, to better the railway service, the outlook is not fundamentally unfavorable. If railroad management is alert, adroit, and intelligent enough to utilize through coördination the related competitors, as provided in motors and in aviation, a comprehensive transportation industry will carry the railroad industry to new traffic peaks.

The growth of regulation, if not retarded, may eventually bring the railroad industry close to public ownership. The relative advantage or disadvantage of such a result may be left to the economists for debate. From the viewpoint of the investor in railway securities, however, it must be viewed as an unfavorable tendency. The transfer of utility ownership from private to public control is usually accomplished under terms not especially advantageous to security holders.[12]

Railroad securities analysis. The determination of the investment position of a particular railroad security involves a careful study of the priority of the issue and of the income available for the payment of interest charges. For illustrative purposes, the securities of one of the largest systems has been chosen for analysis based upon the earnings of the system during the five-year period from 1935 through 1939. Because a five-year period usually contains at least one good year as well as one poor year, an average of such a period is believed to be more representative than a three-year average which is more likely to be abnormally good or unusually poor. Moreover, a five-year average is regarded as more reliable than a ten-year average, which frequently conceals the effect of an adverse long-term trend.

Although this particular system had thirteen different securities outstanding in 1940 in the total amount of nearly $700,000,000, four of these issues were so small, aggregating less than $14,000,000, that this study is concerned primarily with the nine issues which represent 98 per cent of the capitalization of the system. In the order of priority, these issues rank as follows:

(1) Equipment trust certificates in the amount of $23,000,000, bearing interest at the rate of 2¼ per cent and 2½ per cent serially from 1940 through 1952. The interest charge on these certificates in 1940 amounted to about $540,000. The total income available for all fixed charges of the system

---

[12] Thomas F. Woodlock, eminent railroad authority, offered the following comment in an article in *The Wall Street Journal* on May 23, 1938:

"To which the present writer will add one more personal note. His experience with the *Five Per Cent* cases of 1913-14 left him with the fundamental conviction—which his subsequent experience as a Commissioner of Interstate Commerce only deepened—that the end of the road for our railroad industry is government ownership, not as a deliberately chosen public policy but as the inevitable consequence of our inability to regulate and keep in health our present system of privately owned carriers. From that conviction he has never wavered. The progressive anemia from which our carriers are now acutely suffering is the direct product of that inability, and, excluding miracles, we are now near to the end of the road."

during the five-year period 1935-1939 amounted to $22,200,-000, or more than 41 times the interest charge on the equipment certificates which, in effect, have priority of claim. The indicated safety factor is so great as to indicate clearly the maximum quality rating for the certificates. The yield of 1.60 per cent afforded by these obligations in 1940 was in line with the quality of the issue and the condition of the money market at that time.

(2) A divisional bond, having a senior lien on the most important trackage of the system, outstanding in the amount of $22,500,000, bearing interest at the rate of 4 per cent due in 1958, callable at 110. The interest charge on this issue is about $900,000 annually, which, added to the charge of $540,-000 on the equipment certificates, makes a total annual charge of $1,440,000 on both issues. The average available income in the 1935-1939 period was $22,200,000, as before stated, or nearly 16 times the total requirement on both issues, indicating a high rating for the divisional bond. The yield of 3.20 per cent afforded by this bond in 1940, which was relatively high in view of its quality, was attributable in part, at least, to the fact that the prevailing market price was very close to the price at which the bond was callable.

(3) The senior mortgage issue of the company, as distinguished from the system, outstanding in the amount of $150,-000,000, bearing interest at the rate of 4 per cent due in 1995, noncallable. The interest charge on this issue is about $6,000,000 annually, which, added to the total interest charge of $1,440,000 on the two preceding issues, makes a total charge of $7,440,000 on the three issues. As the average available income, as previously stated, was $22,200,000, the total fixed charges on the first three issues were covered about 3 times, indicating a margin of safety of 200 per cent which is considered to be adequate protection. The yield of 3.65 per cent prevailing on these bonds in 1940 was in line with comparable high-grade railroad bonds at that time.

(4) A divisional bond, having a claim on a less important part of the system, outstanding in the amount of $33,000,000, bearing interest at the rate of 4½ per cent due in 1962, callable

at 110.   The interest charge on this issue is about $1,500,000, which, added to the total interest charge of $7,440,000 on the three preceding issues, makes a total charge of $8,940,000 on the four issues.   The application of this figure to the average available income of $22,200,000 showed a coverage of 2½ times, or a margin of safety of 150 per cent.   The yield of 3.80 per cent prevailing on these bonds in 1940 was in consonance with their position as better-grade securities.

The four small issues which are not discussed individually in this survey were outstanding in the amount of $14,000,000, having various interest rates and maturity dates.   The aggregate interest charge in 1940 was about $660,000, making a total charge for these bonds and the four preceding issues of $9,600,000.   As the average income of $22,200,000 was 2.3 times this total charge, the position of these issues appears to be sound.

(5)   Two debenture bond issues, outstanding in the amount of $8,000,000 for 4 per cent bonds due in 1955, callable at 110, and $28,000,000 for 4½ per cent bonds, due in 1948, callable at 102.   The interest charge on these bonds amounts to $1,600,000 annually.   The total interest charge of $11,200,000 on all ten bonds up to this point was covered slightly less than 2.0 times by the average income available of $22,200,000, thus indicating that the debenture bonds are on the border line between bonds which are first-grade and those which are second-grade.   The yield of 3.75 per cent prevailing in 1940 on the 4½'s of 1948 contrasted with a yield of 4.35 per cent on the 4's of 1955, reflecting in part the shorter maturity and the probability that 4½'s redeemable at 102 are more likely to be called than are 4's redeemable at 110.

(6)   An adjustment income bond, outstanding in the amount of $50,000,000, bearing contingent interest at the rate of 4 per cent due in 1995, noncallable.   The interest charge of $2,000,000 on this issue is payable only if earnings (as computed under an elaborate formula) are adequate.   The addition of this contingent charge of $2,000,000 to the aggregate fixed charges of $11,200,000 makes a total of $13,200,000.   The coverage indicated by the average income of $22,200,000 was

1.7 times, indicating a second-grade security, being over 1.5 times and under 2.0 times. The yield of 4.55 per cent afforded by this issue in 1940 was in line with such classification.

(7) A preferred stock, outstanding in the amount of about $125,000,000, entitled to a dividend preference of 5 per cent, noncallable. The annual dividend requirement on this issue is $6,200,000, which, added to the $13,200,000 in prior fixed and contingent interest charges, makes a total of $19,400,000 in aggregate charges. The application of $19,400,000 to $22,-200,000, the average available income, gives an "over-all" factor of 1.1 times, an extremely narrow margin of safety, indicating a speculative position for the preferred stock. The prevailing market price of around $60 per share in 1940 reflected this investment weakness.

(8) A common stock outstanding in the amount of $240,-000,000, or 2,400,000 shares. The balance remaining for the common stock after deducting prior claims totaling $19,400,-000 from the average annual income of $22,200,000, was $2,-800,000, or about $1.10 per share annually. The position of the common stock was decidedly speculative. An indicated fair price of $11 to $13 per share (ten to twelve times average earnings) compared with a prevailing price of around $25 in 1940. It is noteworthy that earnings on this stock in 1939 of $0.95 compared with earnings of $22.70 just ten years earlier.

21

PUBLIC UTILITY SECURITIES

❖▬▬▬▬▬▬▬▬▬▬▬❖

Scope. The purpose of this chapter is to discuss the investment position of the securities issued by privately owned public utility companies such as the American Telephone and Telegraph Company. The order of discussion is: (1) franchise, (2) regulation, (3) territory, (4) management, (5) electric power, (6) gas, (7) telephone, (8) telegraph, (9) water supply, (10) street railway, (11) holding companies, (12) public ownership, and (13) securities analysis. The total amount of utility securities outstanding is around $30,000,-000,000 and represents a wider investment interest than does any comparable group of corporate enterprises.

The public utility industry. From the investment viewpoint, public utility securities comprise the bonds and stocks issued by electric light and power, gas, telephone, telegraph, water, and street railway companies. In a more technical sense, public utility companies may be described as those engaged in a business: (1) affected with a public interest; (2) usually under a franchise contract giving monopolistic privileges in the territory served; and (3) generally subject to the regulatory jurisdiction of a state utility commission. The steam railroad industry is a public utility enterprise which, because of certain inherent characteristics, such as magnitude and area, is placed in a separate investment class.

PUBLIC UTILITY INVESTED CAPITAL
(As of January 1, 1940)

Electric light and power......................	$15,000,000,000
Telephone....................................	5,500,000,000
Manufactured gas............................	3,500,000,000
Natural gas..................................	2,500,000,000
Street railways and busses....................	3,000,000,000
Water supply................................	500,000,000
Total................................	$30,000,000,000

The importance of public utility companies in the investment field is clearly indicated in a comparison with the steam railroad industry. The total amount of railroad securities held by the public aggregates around $20,000,000,000, whereas the comparable total for utility issues is nearly $30,000,000,000. The progress of the utilities during the past decade is in sharp contrast to the almost static condition of the railroads. Whereas the development of the carriers has been chiefly in intensive betterment of existing facilities, the growth of the utilities continues in extensive expansion into new fields of operation. Such comment, however, must be qualified by the statement that utility progress has not been uniform in all branches. As will be shown later, definite signs of retrogression have appeared in two important divisions of the utility industry.

The public utility industry in the United States is dominated to a great extent by holding companies that have, through stock purchase, acquired control of the majority of the important operating companies. Securities of such holding companies are inherently weaker than those of operating companies, as will be shown later. The present discussion refers entirely to securities of operating companies. Holding-company issues partake more of the nature of investment trusts.

The franchise. Public utility companies operate under franchises, which are contracts between the company and the local community served. From the standpoint of the investor, the more important agreements in the franchise relate to competition, territory, duration, and rates. Franchises may be *competitive* or *monopolistic*. The older type of competitive award has been largely replaced by the more satisfactory noncompetitive form; regulated monopoly has proved superior to unregulated competition.[1]

Franchises may be *perpetual, limited,* or *indeterminate.* Originally, franchises were granted on a perpetual competitive basis, just as corporate charters are issued; public sentiment later brought a change to the limited duration basis (10 to 50 years); more recently, the indeterminate, or indefinite, type has come into favor, under the terms of which the franchise remains in effect as long as mutually satisfactory to the community and the company. The territorial limits stated in the franchise may prevent an operating company from extending its service to rapidly growing contiguous territory.[2]

Rate restriction clauses, under which a maximum charge per unit of service is stated, appear in a majority of franchises. Such restrictions are usually binding even though losses may result, unless the community is willing to waive its contractual rights. Resort to the Federal Constitution under a claim of confiscation is generally ineffectual against a contractual agreement. Unfortunate experience with rate restriction clauses over recent years has led, in newer franchises, to the substitution of a flexible rate based on cost of service.

The franchise position is more important to the investor than past consideration would seem to imply. Vague statements to the effect that "the franchise situation is satisfactory" should not satisfy the conservative investor. The franchise situation can work definitely to the disadvantage of holders of utility securities, as recent experience in New York, Chicago, and St. Paul has shown. The most favorable type of franchise is the noncompetitive, indeterminate type with a flexible

---

[1] In many large cities, the utility companies operate under a group of franchises, granted at various times to separate companies which were eventually merged into a single group.

[2] The franchise of the Commonwealth Edison Company prevents service beyond the corporate limits of the city of Chicago. Hence, the east side of Austin Boulevard, the corporate boundary line, is served, but the west side of the same street, being in Oak Park, is not included.

rate provision; the least satisfactory is the short-term, limited type with a maximum rate restriction.[3]

Regulation. Public utility operating companies, in practically all cases, conduct an intrastate business. Hence, their operations are subject to the regulation of the various state commissions rather than to that of the Federal Interstate Commerce Commission. These commissions exist in all states, with the exceptions of Delaware and Mississippi, in which areas corporate laws are rather liberal. The state laws under which these commissions have been established are not uniform. Any discussion of regulatory powers, therefore, could not apply to all states. The summary which follows applies generally to all states, but specifically to New York State.

Rate regulation. Rate changes may be put into effect only after commission approval. In the absence of franchise restrictions, rates are set adequate to provide a reasonable rate of return on the value of the property. Hence, commissions must evaluate property in use to establish a rate base and then must determine a fair rate of return. Recent procedure, influenced largely by Federal Supreme Court decisions, has resulted in the adoption of reproduction cost as the dominant basis for valuation in the determination of the rate base, and in the acceptance of 6, 6½, and 7 per cent as fair rates of return, varying according to the type of company. A trend away from reproduction value toward the use of actual cost, prudently invested, has become noticeable, as has also a tendency to recognize lower rates of return on invested capital.

Competition. The commissions protect the interests of investors in utility securities by refusing *certificates of convenience* (which must be obtained by any new companies entering the field) to undeserving applicants. On the other hand, they may require forfeiture of franchise grants for nonuse. Certificates of convenience are issued only in the event that the operatives of the new company will not infringe

---

[3] Utility bonds maturing beyond the expiration date of the franchise are not legal investments in New York State.

upon the vested rights of any company already in the area, that the new company has adequate capital with which to carry out its plans, and that the organizers of the new company evidence successful experience as utility operators.

Securities regulation. New securities may be issued only with the approval of the commission. Only a very limited number of purposes are acceptable: (1) to construct new property, (2) to buy existing property; (3) to better existing property; (4) to refund existing debt. The amount required must be reasonable for the purpose. The form of issue, whether bonds or stock, must be in harmony with a balanced capitalization account. The terms of the underwriting (the cost of distribution) must not be excessive. While careful scrutiny on all these points does not assure complete investment protection to the public, it undoubtedly does reduce the risk of loss.

Accounts and reports. In most states, the commissions require the use of a uniform accounting procedure. Standard classifications for the more important branches of the industry have been adopted by large groups of states.[4] Such standardization of accounting procedure not only helps the accurate portrayal of financial condition but also facilitates the comparison of similar companies. Furthermore, the commissions require the compilation and submission of exhaustive reports, which provide an official source of information. In most instances, these reports are submitted annually and are open to public inspection. The information in these reports forms the basis for the summary sent to the security holders in the form of the annual report.

Territorial analysis. One of the most important considerations in the selection of public utility securities is that of the territory served. Unlike the railroads, which cover wide areas, and industrial enterprises, which are at liberty to seek markets anywhere, a public utility company may operate only in a prescribed territory. The opportunity to prosper is definitely

---

[4] A uniform classification of accounts has been adopted as the standard for electric companies in about 30 states and for gas companies in about 20 states.

limited to an extremely small area. Careful attention should therefore be given to what might be termed external features, such as geographical location, population, and resources.

Geographical location has economic as well as physical influence. The harbors of New York, Boston, Los Angeles, and San Francisco, among others, give those cities a natural advantage of inestimable value. With excellent water and rail facilities, Chicago, Cleveland, and Detroit are splendidly located. Proximity to established channels of trade is an economic advantage from a market viewpoint, just as nearness to natural waterfalls is helpful from a production standpoint. Cities in northern latitudes, which have a more rigorous climate, offer a somewhat more favorable market for the utility companies than do cities in southern latitudes. Companies located in certain sections of the country encounter public sentiment generally hostile to public utility operations.

The population of the territory served definitely indicates the size and the importance of the company. A study of the rate of growth indicated by the Federal census shows the progressiveness of the community. Investors should prefer the securities of companies located in large communities that show a favorable rate of growth.

The resources of the territory should be also carefully considered. Some communities are primarily industrial; others are commercial, agricultural, or residential. The great advantage of the large community lies in the spread, or diversity, of resources, which makes for stability of demand for utility service. Industrial and commercial territories offer better markets to utility companies than do agricultural and residential districts.

The factor of management. Management is less important than formerly. Until the recent retirement of several of the leaders of the industry, the personnel of the management of a company had perhaps greater weight with investors than the operating performance and financial results. Utility investors acted more on a basis of confidence in the management than on knowledge of the property. With the development of the industry, regulatory powers have increased and operating methods have become standardized; as a consequence, investment interest now centers around property values more than in personnel of management. To a major extent, the personal element which characterized the adolescent stage of the industry has given place to the impersonal phase of maturity.

With operating technique fairly well standardized throughout the industry, the capacity of management is chiefly reflected in its rate policies and public relations. Investors should prefer the securities of those companies whose rate schedules are liberal to the point of attracting rather than repelling service and whose public relations are not of an antagonistic nature. To adopt a simile, utility companies must live with their customers. Companies with high rate schedules and indifferent public policies do not make good neighbors. The securities of such companies are especially vulnerable in periods of economic depression.

Electric light and power. In the public utility field, the electric light and power companies comprise the largest as well as the most popular group from the investment viewpoint. In the relatively short span of 60 years, the electrical industry has grown from the small central station of 750 horse-power, serving a few near-by customers, to the modern power plant of 500,000 horse-power, serving thousands of customers over a wide area through an elaborate transmission and distribution system. At first, the electricity produced was used only for lighting, with the consequence that the plant was idle the greater part of the time. So successful have the companies been in building up a daytime load, however, that the hours of darkness now represent the *valley* rather than the *peak* of demand. The growth of the industry has been due to more extensive, as well as intensive, use of electrical energy. The accompanying table indicates the wide range of modern applications.

Electricity is now regarded as occupying a preëminent position in the field of illumination. In the power field, it has attained an outstanding position, being successfully challenged by mechanical power only under certain unusual conditions in

ELECTRICAL APPLICATIONS

Users	Light	Heat	Power
Factories	Lamps Floodlights	Furnaces	Motors
Stores	Lamps Signs	Heaters	Motors Air conditioning
Homes	Lamps Sun lamps	Ranges Cooking devices Irons Heaters	Vacuum cleaners Washing machines Refrigerators Fans—Radio
Transportation	Street lights Searchlights	Space Heaters	Locomotives

which cheap water-power is available. In the heating field, electricity has thus far proved advantageous only in special applications; coal, oil, and gas comprise a group of strong competitors for the general heating load. The construction of large, efficient generating plants by the leading utility companies has enabled them to offer power to large users at rates below the cost of production in privately owned plants.

So rapid has been the progress of the industry that the rate of growth over the past decade, annually compounded, has been about 6 per cent, which is equivalent to a 100-per-cent increase every 12 years. In view of a comparable rate of about 3 per cent per annum for the economic growth of the nation as a whole, the progress of the industry has been both impressive and significant. The spectacular growth of electrical power has resulted in wide investment interest in the industry, attracted by the favorable combination of sound development and an essential field. The significance of this rapid growth lies in the improbability of continued growth at the indicated rate. It would be illogical not to expect a decline in the rate of growth in the future. The belief prevails, however, that the industry will continue to show a satisfactory rate of progress for many years to come.

Some comments of a relatively technical nature may be of

value to investors in securities of electric power and light companies:

1. All important companies are now interconnected with neighboring plants, a condition which enables many economies to be gained from interchange of power.

2. Increased efficiency in the operation of steam plants has brought the cost of steam generation very close to that of hydrogeneration.

3. The construction of extensive hydro-electric power plants by the Federal Government in the Southeast (Tennessee Valley), in the Southwest (Boulder), and in the Northwest (Grand Coulee and Bonneville) has made available low-cost power which can affect competitively only those privately owned plants which are in the immediate areas. Electrical power cannot be economically transmitted over distances beyond 300 miles.

4. Two thirds of the total cost of electric service is involved in transmission and distribution and is therefore irrespective of the method of generation, whether steam or water-power.

5. The application of electricity to commerce and industry has progressed to such an extent that the principal opportunity for future growth is in the domestic field.

6. The sale of electricity to domestic customers, which now averages about 900 kilowatt-hours per home yearly, can be increased severalfold through the general use of electric refrigerators, kitchen ranges, and water heaters; this increase, however, can be obtained only through the wide establishment of promotional rates.

Power company analysis. The latest balance sheet and income statement of an electric power company should be carefully analyzed. Experience has shown that the better-managed companies report financial operations within recognized latitudes. Such ranges are indicated in the following comments.

With respect to the balance sheet:

1. The value of the fixed assets (land, buildings, and equip-

ment) should not exceed 5 times the operating revenue as shown on the income statement in the case of a steam plant and 10 times the operating revenue in the case of a hydro plant. The fixed assets usually represent about 90 per cent of the total assets and about 95 per cent of the "rate base" as used by regulatory commissions in establishing fair rates for service.

2. The amount of bonds outstanding should not exceed 67 per cent of the value of the fixed assets and should not exceed 60 per cent of all securities outstanding.

3. The retirement (depreciation) reserve should be at least 10 per cent of the value of the fixed assets.

4. The preferred stock outstanding should not exceed 25 per cent of all securities outstanding and should be less than the amount of common stock.

5. The common stock should represent at least 25 per cent of all securities outstanding.

6. The ideal capital structure would be 40 to 50 per cent in bonds and 50 to 60 per cent in stocks, with 10 to 20 per cent in preferred issues and 30 to 40 per cent in common stock.

7. The surplus shown in all public utility balance sheets is relatively small, owing in part to the restriction on earning power and in part to unwillingness to disclose what might be regarded as excessive earning power.

With respect to the income statement:

1. The ratio of operating expenses, including provision for maintenance, depreciation, and taxes, to operating revenues, should not exceed 70 per cent for a steam plant and 55 per cent for a hydro plant.

2. The ratio of operating profit, before the payment of interest charges, to the investment in plant and equipment as shown in the balance sheet should be between 5 and 7 per cent to show a fair rate of return earned on the rate base.

3. The ratio of interest charges to the operating revenues should not exceed 12 per cent for a steam plant and 20 per cent for a hydro plant. The total income available for the payment of these charges should be at least 2 times the requirement.

4. The ratio of the sum of the interest charges and the preferred dividend to operating revenues should not exceed 20 per cent. The total income available for the payment of these charges should be at least 1½ times the "over-all" requirement.

5. The ratio of the balance available for dividends on the common stock should be at least 15 per cent of the operating revenues.

6. A fair market value for the common stock would be around 12 times the average earnings per share, or a capitalization ratio of about 8 per cent.

SOURCES OF REVENUES OF ELECTRICAL POWER COMPANIES[5]

(BASED ON 1939 DATA)

Class of Service	Consumption		Revenue	
	Kilowatt-hours	Per Cent	Dollars	Per Cent
Residential......	19,700,000,000	18.6	$759,000,000	33.0
Commercial.....	20,200,000,000	19.0	648,000,000	28.2
Industrial.......	52,800,000,000	49.8	595,000,000	25.9
Miscellaneous....	13,300,000,000	12.6	292,000,000	12.9
Total.....	106,000,000,000	100.0	$2,294,000,000	100.0

The gas industry. The production and distribution of gas on a commercial scale has been a major public utility enterprise in the United States for considerably more than a full century. From the first manufactured-gas plant in Baltimore in 1816, with a capacity of a few hundred cubic feet daily, to the modern Hunts Point plant of the Consolidated Edison Company in New York, with a daily capacity of several hundred thousand cubic feet, the industry has shown continued progress despite almost constant competition of alternative services. Prior to the development, about 1880, of the electrical lamp, gas was used almost exclusively for illumination. As electricity gradually gained supremacy in the lighting field, the gas companies turned to the heating field with most suc-

[5] As reported by Edison Electric Institute.

cessful results.　The physical characteristics of gas make it an ideal agency for heating purposes.　As a consequence, the output of the industry has continued to grow at a rate beyond the normal development of the nation.

Until recently, the great bulk of the gas sold by the American public utility companies was manufactured through the destructive distillation of coal.　Although natural gas was used extensively in certain districts, for the main part it was available only to customers located near the producing wells.　Extensive petroleum prospecting brought in many rich natural gas wells, especially in the Southwest, which, unfortunately, were located far from any large potential users.　To find a market for this gas, companies built pipe lines, extending hundreds of miles, bringing natural gas from remote parts to metropolitan areas including Chicago, Cleveland, Detroit, St. Louis, Washington, Atlanta, New Orleans, Los Angeles, and San Francisco.　The cost of building and operating long-distance pipe lines, however, largely offsets the basic saving in production cost.　While there can be little doubt that the development of natural gas will play an increasingly important part in the entire gas industry, for many years to come the great markets of the North Atlantic seaboard, because of the enormous expense of constructing adequate pipe lines from points west of the Mississippi River, must rely primarily upon manufactured gas.

Although gas is being widely used for industrial and commercial purposes, the chief utilization is in the domestic kitchen for cooking purposes.　Even more so than in the case of electricity, from the use of which the residential revenues are less than one half of the total, the household, providing over two thirds of total revenues, is the best customer of the gas companies.　As the cooking load does not admit of wide expansion, either intensively or extensively, the gas companies are turning to other fields for future development.　While the industrial field has not yet reached the gas saturation point, coal and oil are strong competitors.　A better situation exists with respect to the house-heating field, in which the gas companies are making interesting progress and in which the convenience of gas heat tends to overcome the handicap of higher cost.

A frank appraisal of relative advantages leads to the opinion that securities of gas companies, particularly of those operating in large cities, usually make good investments, although somewhat less attractive than those of electric companies. Gas has but one primary use—heating—whereas electricity has three—lighting, heating, and power. The gas industry is relatively closer to the saturation point. The development of natural gas will necessitate the gradual abandonment of manufacturing plants and has already brought serious rate problems to the operating companies. To a degree, the large sums invested in gas transmission lines have been committed, despite uncertainties with respect to potential supply in the wells, to potential market at destination, and to actual cost of operation. Yet gas is not without its advantages. Unlike electricity, which cannot be economically stored and which must be produced at the moment of consumption, thereby causing expansive peaks, gas can be produced and stored in advance, thus permitting substantial economy from regular hourly production. Since the chief user of gas is the domestic kitchen, the stability of demand is superior to that of electricity, the use of which depends on less stable utilizations. The gas industry is more thoroughly seasoned. Operating methods have been improved to such an extent that investors have less to fear from technical changes which render expensive equipment obsolete. The development of natural gas places many companies in a position to offer a better product at a cost less than heretofore.

Gas company analysis. An analysis of the financial condition of a manufactured-gas company involves the application of recognized standards of acceptability to the actual figures shown in the published financial statements.

With respect to the balance sheet:

1. The value of the fixed assets should not exceed 5 times the operating revenue.

2. The amount of bonds outstanding should not exceed 67

per cent of the value of the fixed assets and should not exceed 60 per cent of all securities outstanding.

3. The retirement reserve should be at least 15 per cent of the value of the fixed assets.

4. The comments with respect to preferred stock, common stock, capital structure, and surplus previously made in connection with power company balance sheets are equally applicable to gas company statements.

With respect to the income statement:

1. The ratio of operating expenses, including maintenance, depreciation, and taxes, should not exceed 80 per cent of operating revenues.

2. The operating profit, before interest charges, should be at least 5 per cent of the fixed assets.

3. The ratio of interest charges to operating revenues should not exceed 12 per cent. The total income should be at least 2 times the interest charges.

4. The comments with respect to preferred dividends and balance of earnings available to the common stock previously made in connection with power company income reports are equally applicable to gas company statements.

5. A fair market value for the common stock of a gas company would be around 12 times the average earnings per share, or a capitalization ratio of about 8 per cent.

The telephone industry. A discussion of the securities of the telephone companies in the United States concerns chiefly the associated companies in the American Telephone and Telegraph (Bell System) group. The industry has become, in the short period of 60 years, an integral factor in the everyday life of the nation. In any age such as the present, which puts a premium upon speed, instantaneous communication, as afforded by the telephone, becomes of inestimable value. Progressive policies on the part of operating management in the form of quicker service (automatic dials), promotional rates (at off-peak hours), and universal connections (long-distance lines) have caused an extraordinary growth in this field.

About 90 per cent of the telephone business of the country is handled by the associated operating companies in the Bell

group. These companies are controlled through stock ownership by the parent American Telephone and Telegraph
Company; as they have separate territories, they do not compete with each other. In addition to stock control of the
operating subsidiaries, the parent company owns and operates
the connecting long-distance lines; owns outright the Western
Electric Company, which manufactures practically all of the
telephone equipment purchased by the operating companies;
and gives a supervisory service to the associated group, for
which management fees are received.

The Bell System, comprising the American Telephone and
Telegraph Company and 24 associated operating companies,
controls about 80 per cent of the telephones and 90 per cent
of the business. The remaining independent companies, num-
bering over 7,000, control about 20 per cent of the telephones
and only 10 per cent of the business. Obviously, a great
majority of the independent companies are extremely small
and do not afford good investment opportunity. Companies
with operating revenues under one million dollars yearly
fall in this class.

GROWTH OF BELL TELEPHONE SYSTEM, 1920-1940

Items	Average (1920-1929)	Average (1930-1939)	Rate of Increase
Telephones connected......	11,700,000	14,700,000	26%
Operating revenues........	$726,000,000	$992,000,000	37
Operating income..........	$150,000,000	$198,000,000	32
Total income..............	$177,000,000	$218,000,000	23
Net income...............	$132,000,000	$167,000,000	27

Telephone company analysis. An analysis of the financial
condition of a telephone company requires the application of
standards of acceptability differing somewhat from those used
in connection with electric power and gas companies.

With respect to the balance sheet:

1. The value of the fixed assets should not exceed 4 times
the operating revenue.

2. The amount of bonds outstanding should not exceed 60

per cent of the value of the fixed assets or 60 per cent of the oustanding securities.

3. The retirement (depreciation) reserve should be not less than 15 per cent of the fixed assets. A reserve in excess of 25 per cent is regarded as excessive by regulatory commissions.

4. The comments with respect to preferred stock, common stock, capital structure, and surplus previously made in connection with power company balance sheets are equally applicable to telephone company statements.

With respect to the income statement:

1. The ratio of operating expense, as previously defined, to operating revenues should not exceed 75 per cent.

2. The ratio of operating profit to fixed capital should be at least 7 per cent.

3. The ratio of interest charges to operating revenue should be not more than 12 per cent, and total income should be at least 2 times the interest charges.

4. The comments with respect to preferred dividends, balance of earnings remaining for the common stock, and fair market value of common stock previously made in connection with power company income reports are equally applicable to telephone company statements.

The telegraph industry. The telegraph industry of the United States is controlled by two companies, Western Union (80 per cent) and Postal (20 per cent). Western Union was at one time controlled by American Telephone just as Postal is now a subsidiary of International Telephone, but, since 1914, the Bell company has had no financial interest in Western Union. Although telegraphy is one of the oldest of the utility group, dating back a full century to the Morse experiments, and although it enjoyed remarkable prosperity until very recently, the outlook for the industry is now clouded in doubt. The radio, the teletypewriter, and the long-distance telephone line have diverted a substantial part of the business which formerly went by telegraph and cable. A comment which may prove premature is that telegraphy has passed its peak as a separate enterprise and that its future lies in coördination with other forms of electrical communication.   It would be unwise to believe, however, that the telegraph industry, having passed its peak, is to fade quickly from the economic picture. Handling the communication business means more than the transmission of messages; the collection and delivery service of the two telegraph companies, developed over a long period of years, is in itself a competitive asset of great value.[6]

Telegraph company analysis.   The analytical comments made in connection with telephone companies apply generally to telegraph companies.   Unfortunately, the telegraph companies have been confronted during the past decade with a declining volume of business and an increasing operating cost. As a consequence, neither Western Union nor Postal has been able to approach a satisfactory earning power.   Even after reducing the provision for depreciation far below the former standard, the operating ratio of Western Union has been running closer to 90 per cent than to the 70 per cent suggested standard.   In 1939 the operating revenues of Western Union were far below the volume of 1929, whereas the revenues of American Telephone were substantially higher.

The water industry.   Investment interest in the securities of water companies is quite limited, owing to the prevalence of municipal ownership in this branch of the public utility field.   Largely because of the close relationship between water supply and public health, the belief is generally held that water service should be a municipal function.   Relatively few large communities, notably Indianapolis, Indiana, and Birmingham, Alabama, are served by private companies.   A number of smaller cities, such as New Haven, Conn., New Rochelle, N. Y., and Wichita, Kan., have private service.   The industry is the oldest of the utilities and for centuries has retained its essential simplicity of a "pump and a pipe."

Because water has almost always been obtainable in unlimited quantity at little or no cost, its use has quite invariably

---

[6] The creation of a Federal Communications Commission under the terms of the Communications Act of 1934 is especially interesting in its significance with respect to the economic coördination of telephone, telegraph, and radio services.

been proportionate to population. As population growth in the United States is now less than 1 per cent yearly, it is apparent that the growth of water companies is equally slow. If, however, the water companies are handicapped by slow growth, they enjoy a compensating advantage in stability of revenue. As use of water is seldom contingent upon cost, the output of water companies is remarkably steady. This stability of earnings is the outstanding advantage of water securities as investments. The great disadvantage is the extremely limited supply of securities of the better companies.

Water company analysis. The following comments are offered in regard to the securities of privately owned water supply companies:

With respect to the balance sheet:

1. The value of the fixed assets should not exceed 10 times the operating revenue.

2. The amount of bonds outstanding should not exceed 75 per cent of the value of the fixed assets or 67 per cent of the outstanding securities.

3. The retirement (depreciation) reserve should be at least 10 per cent of the value of the fixed assets for the newer properties and at least 20 per cent for the older. The great hazard in this industry is not physical depreciation but public ownership.

4. The preferred stock outstanding, when added to the bonds outstanding, should not exceed 75 per cent of the securities outstanding.

5. The common stock should be at least 25 per cent of the securities outstanding.

With respect to the income statement:

1. The ratio of operating expenses, as previously defined, to operating revenues should be between 40 and 50 per cent.

2. The operating profit should be between 5 and 7 per cent of the fixed assets.

3. The ratio of interest charges to operating revenues should be between 20 and 30 per cent. The total income should be at least $1\frac{1}{2}$ times the interest charges.

4. The preferred dividend requirement, plus the interest

charges, should be earned at least 1¼ times on an "over-all" basis.

5. The balance available for the common stock should be at least 10 per cent of the operating revenues.

6. The fair market value of the common stock would be between 10 and 15 times average earnings per share.

The street railway industry. The history of the electric street railway industry during the past 50 years clearly illustrates the successive stages in an economic cycle. The experimental stage ended about 1890, with the practical application of electric motors to street cars. The development stage continued until about 1910, when a veritable network of urban, suburban, and interurban electric railways was to be found throughout the country. In congested metropolitan areas, elevated and underground railways gave rapid transit service in addition to the slower surface lines. The saturation stage continued from 1910 to 1920, passing a peak around 1912. Shortly after 1920, a fourth stage of distinct retrogression developed, which has continued to date.

The fundamental cause of the long-continued decline in traction earnings has been loss of traffic due to the great popularity of the passenger automobile. Other difficulties have faced the tractions in the form of rate restrictions and street-paving assessments in franchises; higher operating costs, especially those for taxes and wages of labor; slower service due to streets congested with motor traffic; and bus competition. These difficulties have been overcome in the majority of cases through grants of rate increases, waiving of paving obligations, lower material costs, one-man car operation, trackless trolley cars, one-way street regulations, limited parking privileges, and coördinated bus service. But earnings remain unsatisfactory because revenues have not improved. The statement is probably true that no electric railway company in the country is now showing favorable earnings and that most of them are in serious financial difficulty.

While it might be unwise to predict either an early or a complete extinction of the industry, the number of companies in receivership and the increasing mileage abandoned yearly indicate a most unfavorable investment position. The only securities worthy of any consideration are the issues of companies in large metropolitan areas where traffic congestion makes the private automobile a nuisance more than a convenience and where limited garage facilities, as well as economic disability, reduce the number of car owners.

Street railway company analysis. With practically no securities in the entire group worthy of investment ranking under existing conditions, a recital of investment tests becomes almost purely academic. The financial statements of very few companies would afford favorable comparison with the following criteria.

With respect to the balance sheet:

1. The value of the fixed assets should not exceed five times the operating revenues.

2. The amount of bonds outstanding should not exceed 60 per cent of the securities outstanding.

3. The retirement (depreciation) reserve should be at least 25 per cent of the fixed assets.

4. The preferred stock should not exceed 20 per cent of the securities outstanding.

5. The common stock should be at least 30 per cent of the securities outstanding.

With respect to the income statement:

1. The ratio of operating expense, as previously defined, to operating revenues should not exceed 80 per cent.

2. The ratio of operating income to fixed assets should be at least 5 per cent.

3. The ratio of interest charges to operating revenue should not exceed 15 per cent. The total income should be at least $1\frac{1}{2}$ times the interest charges.

4. Comment with respect to preferred dividend requirement and common stock position is omitted because of the speculative nature of such issues under conditions existing at the time of writing.

The holding company. Reference has previously been made to the predominance of the holding company in the public utility field. This condition is especially true in the electric, telephone, and water services.   These companies, for the most part, are financial organizations whose chief asset is the common stock of subsidiary operating companies.   As the operating companies customarily issue senior and junior bonds and preferred stock, which are sold to the public, it follows that the holding company has an equity seldom exceeding one third of the capitalization of the operating company and subordinate to all other claims.   In turn, the holding company issues bonds and preferred and common stocks.   The bonds may be collateral or debenture, or both.   The common stock of the holding company, therefore, has a thin equity in the earning power of the basic operating company, a condition infinitely more attenuated when several intermediate holding companies intervene, each of which issues bonds and preferred stocks. In prosperous times, increased earnings of the operating companies magnify the earning power of the holding company and create an unreliable indication of income productivity; hence the great demand for common stocks of holding companies during the decade from 1920 to 1930.   In times of depression, the reverse is true, and small decreases in earnings of the operating companies result in drastic declines in the income of the holding company; hence the great collapse in holding-company equities during the decade from 1930 to 1940.

Purchases of holding-company securities should be made with full cognizance of the added risk involved.   The advantage that diversification gives is more than offset by the risk involved in the purchase of what is at best a junior security.   A fairly representative capitalization for a holding company is as follows: total consolidated capitalization, 100 per cent; subsidiary company bonds, 50 per cent, subsidiary preferred stock, 25 per cent, total subsidiary securities held by public, 75 per cent; holding-company bonds, 5 per cent, holding-company preferred stock, 10 per cent, holding-company common stock, 10 per cent, total holding-company securities, 25 per cent.   It is obvious that the securities of such a holding company are not in a very safe investment position.[7]

[7] In favorable comparison to the capital structures of many holding companies as above stated is that of the American Telephone System which com-

It would be unfair to infer that all holding-company securities are equally poor. Some companies are more conservatively capitalized than others. Some control more valuable subsidiaries. Some enjoy advantages from control of contiguous properties. By and large, however, investors should realize that, as a class, holding-company securities are fundamentally weaker than operating-company obligations.

Holding company analysis. It should be recognized that holding companies issue two different types of financial statements. The *corporate* statements refer to the holding company only and do not include assets and revenues of subsidiaries. *Consolidated* statements include the combined finances of parent company and subsidiaries, eliminating intercompany transactions. For analytical purposes, the consolidated statements are used because they afford a more comprehensive picture of the entire group of properties. The following comments therefore relate to consolidated statements.

With respect to the consolidated balance sheet:

1. Fixed capital should not exceed 5 times the consolidated operating revenues.

2. All bonds should not exceed 60 per cent of all securities publicly held.

3. Retirement (depreciation) reserves should be at least 10 per cent of fixed assets.

4. Subsidiary bonds and subsidiary preferred stocks should not exceed 75 per cent of all securities held by the public.

5. Parent company common stocks should be at least 20 per cent of all securities outstanding with the public.

With respect to the consolidated income statement:

1. Operating expenses (of subsidiaries) should not exceed 70 per cent of operating revenues.

2. Total subsidiary charges on bonds and preferred stocks held publicly should not exceed 15 per cent of operating revenues and should be earned at least 2 times.

prises only 26 per cent in publicly held securities of subsidiary companies and 74 per cent in securities of the parent company. Moreover, 64 per cent of all securities held by the public is represented in the common stock of the American Telephone and Telegraph Company.

3. Parent company bond interest, plus subsidiary charges as just stated, should be earned at least 1¾ times.

4. Parent company preferred dividend requirement, plus bond interest, plus subsidiary charges, should be earned at least 1½ times.

5. Balance available for dividends on the common stock of the holding company should be at least 10 per cent of subsidiary company operating revenues.

6. A fair value for the common stock of a holding company would be around 10 times average earnings per share.

Public Utility Act of 1935. The position of the securities of all holding companies in the field of electric power has been profoundly affected by the provisions of the Federal Public Utility Act. Although this legislation was enacted in 1935, the main provisions calling for the integration of properties and the simplification of capital structures have yet to be put into effect as this chapter is written. A provision in the law, popularly known as the "death sentence clause" requires that only those holding companies which can justify their economic existence will be permitted to function. One test of economic fitness is geographical proximity of properties. Those holding companies whose properties are widely scattered and which are subject to "remote control" management from a metropolitan area are especially vulnerable under the law. A second group of companies which are directly affected are those with complicated financial structures involving a bewildering group of intermediate holding companies.

It has become apparent that a prolonged period of negotiation and, possibly, litigation must ensue before the Act is fully effective. The constitutionality of the "death-sentence" clause has yet to be determined by the courts. The methods by which the objectives may be obtained do not admit of speedy achievement. Properties which may not be legally retained by one holding company must be either sold to the public through investment underwriters (as has already been done in the case of Connecticut Light and Power) or sold to another holding company eligible to buy them by reason of contiguous properties, or given in exchange to another holding company where a similar problem exists.

Surveys which have been made of the effect of the Act upon the securities of a group of leading holding companies indicate the probability that the senior issues of these companies, the collateral and debenture bonds, are relatively safe. The position of the preferred stocks is less secure, especially in those companies with large bond issues. The position of the common stocks, however, is obscure in most cases to the point of negligible value in the overpyramided group.

REPRESENTATIVE PUBLIC UTILITY HOLDING COMPANIES

Company	Organized
American Gas & Electric	1906
American Power & Light	1909
American Water Works & Electric	1914
Columbia Gas & Electric	1906
Commonwealth & Southern	1929
Electric Power & Light	1925
National Power & Light	1925
Niagara Hudson Power	1929
North American	1890
Standard Gas & Electric	1910
United Light & Power	1910
United Gas Improvement	1882

Public ownership. A discussion of public utility securities as investments would be incomplete without some reference to the question of public ownership. For years, many investors refused to buy public utility issues because of the constant possibility that the properties might be taken over by the public on terms disadvantageous to the security holders. In the decade subsequent to the First World War, public opinion in this country turned distinctly against public ownership, encouraged to no small degree by the influence of customer stockholders who were encouraged to invest their savings in the local utility companies. This change in sentiment greatly broadened the market for utility securities.

More recent experience is somewhat less assuring. Utility ownership has become a political question in several important states, especially in the field of electrical power. The additional regulatory powers granted to the state utility commissions enhance the possibility of public ownership of utilities. In some states a growing belief that commission regulation is not adequately protecting the public renews interest in the alternative of public ownership.[8]

During the past decade, the Federal Government has taken considerable interest in public utility operations, especially in the electric power field. The passage of the Public Utility Act of 1935 was designed to bring Federal regulatory power over the holding companies which control the larger operating systems. The construction of mammoth hydro plants in the Tennessee Valley area with 1,500,000 horsepower, at Boulder with 1,000,000 horsepower, at Bonneville with 400,000 horsepower, and at Grand Coulee with 2,000,000 horsepower, and numerous smaller projects have brought the Federal Government decidedly into the power business. Subsidies to municipalities in the form of grants and loans at low interest rates for the construction of local municipal plants have further affected the position of privately owned electric utility companies.

It is unfortunate, therefore, that the public utility industry which has successfully surmounted all of the economic problems encountered in the development of a major industry should have to face political problems of even more serious nature. And it is even more regrettable that the investors who financed this enterprise should be the chief sufferers in the conflict between the advocates of private control and public ownership. Without arguing the merits and demerits of public ownership, simple justice requires that the owners of private enterprise be fairly compensated if their field of operation is henceforth to be regarded as a public function.

---

[8] A most substantial addition to the list of publicly owned utilities occurred in 1940 when New York City "recaptured" the rapid transit facilities leased to the Interborough and Brooklyn-Manhattan companies. For many years previous, the street railway service in Cleveland, Detroit, and Seattle has been publicly owned.

Securities analysis. The practical application of the analytical ratios suggested as standards of acceptability throughout this chapter requires the determination of five-year average records as a basis for comparisons. In the present case, the company selected is one of the largest operating electric power companies in the United States. All figures used are averages of the reported figures for the five-year period from 1935 through 1939. This analysis is simplified by reason of the fact that this company has outstanding only two classes of securities, general mortgage bonds and common stock.

(a)   During the five-year period 1935-1939, the average of the peak loads for each year was 666,000 kilowatts, an increase of 43 per cent over the comparable figure of 466,000 kilowatts for the five-year period 1925-1929, or an indicated annual gain of about 4 per cent.

(b)   During the same period (1935-1939) the average annual output was 2,900,000,000 kilowatt-hours, an increase of 32 per cent over the comparable period 1925-1929, or an annual gain of about 3 per cent.

(c)   The average amount invested in fixed capital in the period 1935-1939 was $310,000,000, an increase of 50 per cent over the period 1925-1929, or an annual increase about 5 per cent.

(d)   Operating revenues during the 1935-1939 period averaged $55,600,000, an increase of 16 per cent over the 1925-1929 period, or an annual gain of about 1½ per cent.

(e)   Operating expenses during the 1935-1939 period averaged $39,800,000, an increase of 24 per cent over the 1925-1929 period, or an annual increase of nearly 2½ per cent.

(f)   Operating income during the 1935-1939 period averaged $15,800,000, which was almost exactly the same as the income derived in the 1925-1929 period.

(g)   Fixed charges during the 1935-1939 period averaged $6,200,000, an increase of 24 per cent over the 1925-1929 period, or an annual increase of about 2½ per cent.

(h)   Net income during the 1935-1939 period averaged $9,-600,000, a *decrease* of 11 per cent from the 1925-1929 period, or an annual loss of about 1 per cent.

REPRESENTATIVE ELECTRIC POWER COMPANY

(FIVE-YEAR AVERAGE: 1935-1939)

Item	Amount	Ratio
Operating revenues.................	$ 55,600,000	100.0
Operating cost.....................	$ 21,800,000	39.3
Maintenance.......................	3,600,000	6.4
Depreciation.......................	7,000,000	12.5
Taxes.............................	7,400,000	13.3
Operating expenses.................	$ 39,800,000	71.5
Operating income..................	$ 15,800,000	28.5
Interest charges...................	6,200,000	11.5
Net income........................	$ 9,600,000	17.0
Fixed capital......................	$310,000,000	560
Depreciation reserve...............	43,000,000	13
Bonds.............................	$138,000,000	53
Common stock.....................	127,000,000	47

A summary of the preceding data disclosed the significant
fact that substantial increases in the gross volume of business
have resulted in an actual decrease in income available to
security holders. Especially significant is the fact that a 50-
per-cent increase in invested capital has not resulted in any
increase in the operating profit of the company. The favorable influence of large increases in sales has been completely
offset by even larger increases in the cost of rendering the
service.

(i) The value of the fixed assets ($310,000,000) was 5.6
times the average operating revenues ($55,600,000). This
factor is higher than the accepted standard of 4 to 5 for a steam
company and indicates a plant larger than that required to
carry the load during the period.

(j) The amount of bonds outstanding ($138,000,000) was
44 per cent of the fixed assets and 53 per cent of all securities
outstanding. In both instances, the ratios are well below the
respective maximum standards of 67 per cent and 60 per cent.

(k) The amount shown in the depreciation reserve at the

end of the period ($43,000,000) was 13 per cent of the value of the fixed assets and was therefore above the minimum standard of 10 per cent.

(l)   The amount of common stock outstanding throughout the period ($127,000,000) was 47 per cent of the total securities outstanding and was therefore well above the minimum standard of 25 per cent.

(m)   The ratio of average operating expenses ($39,800,000) to average operating revenues ($55,600,000) was 71½ per cent, which was slightly higher than the maximum standard of 70 per cent.   The high operating ratio was largely due to the fact that maintenance and depreciation expenses averaged 19 per cent of revenues in comparison with an acceptable standard of 15 per cent.

(n)   The ratio of the average operating profit ($15,800,-000) to the average invested capital ($310,000,000) was 5 per cent, thus indicating the minimum fair rate of return such companies should earn.

(o)   The ratio of the average annual interest charges ($6,-200,000) to the average operating revenues was 11½ per cent, which was within the standard range of 10 to 12 per cent. The average income available for the payment of interest charges ($15,800,000) was 2½ times the amount of the charges which exceeded the minimum standard of 2 times for bonds of good quality but which was less than the minimum standard of 3.0 times for bonds of the best quality.

(p)   The ratio of the average net income after the payment of interest charges ($9,600,000) to operating revenues was 17 per cent, which was well within the standard range of 15 to 20 per cent.

(q)   A fair market value for the common stock of this company would be around 12 times $7.50, the average earnings per share, or $90.

INDUSTRIAL SECURITIES

❖❖||||||||||❏||||||||||❏||||||||||❏||||||||||❏||||||||||❏||||||||||❏||||||||||❏||||||||||❏||||||||||❏||||||||||❏||||||||||❏||||||||||❏❖❖

Scope. The purpose of this chapter is to discuss the investment position of the securities issued by the industrial enterprises of the nation. The order of discussion is: (1) types of companies, (2) accounting problems, (3) industrial characteristics, (4) nature of enterprise, (5) consolidation, (6) income statements, (7) balance sheets, (8) bonds, (9) preferred stocks, (10) common stocks, and (11) securities analysis. Problems involved in the reorganization of industrial companies under the Federal Bankruptcy law are discussed in a preceding chapter (Chapter 12—"Protection in Reorganizations"). Investment interest in industrial securities is largely confined to a few hundred large companies out of the many thousands which operate in this field.

The field of industry. Industrial companies are those that are engaged in the production and distribution of commodities under competitive conditions with limited governmental regulation. They comprise the great extractive, productive, and distributive agencies of the nation. The extractive industries include mines, oil wells, timber, and fisheries. The productive industries include manufacturing in all phases, from automobiles and aëroplanes to textiles and typewriters. The distributive industries include merchandising operations of all kinds, wholesale, retail, and direct selling by mail. As a group, these industries provide the economic life of the country. Large as the railroad and utility enterprises are, they serve subordinately as facilitating agencies for the industrial companies. The magnitude of the industrial field is indicated by a recent official compilation which showed that more than 8,500,000 people were employed by the manufacturing plants of the United States in 1937 and that the annual value of the manufactured products was in excess of $60,000,000,000.

Accounting problems.   The problem of investment analysis is greatly complicated by the almost complete absence of uniformity in industrial operations.   Each branch of the field and each company in the respective branches have peculiar dissimilarities which make comparisons difficult and misleading. From the standpoint of the analyst, the most important factor of variation is in accounting procedure.   Although leading companies in a few important fields, such as electrical equipment, have agreed upon a uniform accounting system for that particular field, in a great majority of cases each company adopts a system of its own.   Such lack of uniformity results in noncomparable reports.   Under one system, certain expenditures are capitalized as assets, whereas, under another system, the same items are charged as operating expenses.   Furthermore, one system may require the deduction of much heavier depreciation charges than another.   Again, one system considers certain expenses as operating charges, while another would consider the same items as surplus adjustments.   Moreover, one system may permit a method of valuing securities and inventories on hand more liberal than that of another.[1]

An added difficulty from the accounting standpoint is found in the manner in which financial statements are prepared.   A few industrial companies, such as the United States Steel Corporation, publish comprehensive statements of assets and earnings.   In almost every instance, however, the published

---

[1] Numerous examples of differences in accounting procedure might be cited from recent industrial experience. One management, succeeding a previous group of officers, made a downward adjustment of $4,000,000 in the reported earnings of United Cigar Stores in 1928. The Gillette Safety Razor Co. published in 1930 a revised statement of earnings for the period from 1925 through 1929, showing a reduction aggregating no less than $11,856,000 from the figures originally reported.

reports are incomplete. Many important companies, including such outstanding examples as National Biscuit, Allied Chemical and Dye, and American Can, publish annual reports that give a minimum amount of financial information. Many companies do not give any information on sales or expenses, but report a net income figure after various adjustments of an undisclosed nature are made. This unwillingness to publish financial statements in more than partial form makes the task of intelligent investment analysis virtually impossible. Investors are compelled to base their decisions almost entirely upon the reputation of the company, or, stated otherwise, upon confidence in the product and the management.

Another factor of importance which might readily be overlooked in the industrial field is the growing tendency on the part of companies to increase the scope of their activities through the manufacture of a more diversified list of products and through the purchase of securities of other companies. It is not generally recognized that agricultural implements no longer comprise the major part of the sales of International Harvester nor is it common knowledge that this company has become the largest maker of motor trucks in the country. It may surprise many persons to realize that nearly 40 per cent of the profits of General Motors do not come from the sale of motor cars. Eastman Kodak has already entered the field of textile manufacturing. Du Pont has at least six important operating divisions in addition to a substantial stock interest in General Motors. General Electric has built up an enormous merchandise business in addition to the manufacture of industrial apparatus. New applications of glass to industry have materially affected the operations of Owens-Illinois Glass. Products recently introduced by Procter and Gamble have brought that company into new fields of activity. And it is well known that the traditional title of five-and-ten-cent store no longer applies to Woolworth or Kresge.

Industrial characteristics. Industrial enterprise has certain characteristics which constitute what might be called a group hazard confronting investors who are interested in this field. These characteristics may be stated somewhat concisely as

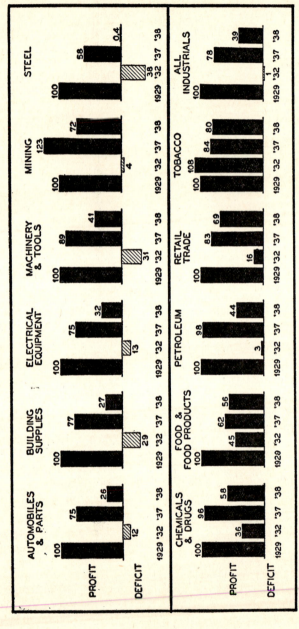

Variations in Earnings of Industrial Enterprises. (From *Monthly Review of Credit and Business Conditions*, issued by Federal Reserve Bank of New York, April 1, 1939.)

ANNUAL NET PROFITS OR DEFICITS OF 831 INDUSTRIAL COMPANIES[2]

(NET PROFITS IN MILLIONS OF DOLLARS)

Corporation Group	No. of Cos.	1929	1932	1934	1937	1938
Advertising, printing and publishing....	16	18.8	0.7	5.2	10.4	7.4
Agricultural equipment................	9	81.9	−31.3	−5.9	74.3	38.0
Automobiles........................	13	327.2	−28.7	89.9	254.8	104.1
Automobile parts and accessories (excl. tires)...........................	48	93.0	−22.0	17.5	58.3	5.6
Aviation............................	10	4.1	−1.3	0.3	5.8	12.2
Building materials and supplies:						
Brick and clay products.............	9	13.9	−4.7	1.0	5.1	0.9
Cement........................	9	11.8	−6.1	1.2	7.0	4.2
Heating and plumbing..............	17	42.6	−19.4	4.9	27.0	2.2
Paints and varnishes................	6	16.2	2.9	6.7	9.2	4.7
Other building materials............	25	55.8	−12.9	13.3	58.9	25.8
Chemicals and drugs.................	43	197.2	71.7	115.5	188.7	114.2
Containers (metal and glass)..........	6	41.6	21.6	41.5	41.1	28.3
Electrical equipment.................	35	171.3	−22.3	20.8	129.1	53.9
Food and food products:						
Bakery products....................	10	48.4	25.9	18.3	20.9	22.9
Beverages.......................	8	19.7	12.8	27.6	36.2	37.0
Confectionery....................	12	28.0	14.4	17.2	19.0	17.2
Meat packing.....................	13	38.7	−3.1	29.0	23.4	2.8
Other food products...............	29	152.1	77.8	84.9	79.1	80.5
Household equipment:						
Electrical goods...................	13	14.1	−5.4	3.5	9.3	2.9
Furniture and floor covering........	9	16.4	−9.7	3.0	13.9	1.2
Other household supplies............	15	39.9	8.3	22.3	32.0	26.7
Leather and shoes....................	13	21.0	3.2	11.2	11.4	5.6
Machinery and tools.................	76	75.5	−31.0	9.0	68.2	22.9
Mining:						
Coal............................	15	12.5	−2.7	8.9	4.1	−3.8
Copper.........................	7	41.2	−9.7	13.5	35.7	21.1
Gold............................	14	21.5	14.3	30.8	37.0	29.8
Other mining.....................	14	52.3	−7.4	27.0	79.6	44.3
Motion pictures and amusements.......	12	55.8	−15.5	21.3	47.4	30.8
Office equipment....................	12	45.8	−0.6	17.2	38.3	21.3
Paper and paper products............	26	20.1	−4.5	11.8	⌐21.8	11.2
Petroleum..........................	40	166.0	4.3	28.4	162.1	73.1
Railroad equipment..................	18	63.4	−14.9	1.1	46.9	1.2
Retail trade:						
Chain stores.....................	10	65.6	34.3	51.5	62.1	50.9
Department and apparel stores.......	21	37.1	−9.0	23.5	26.2	23.4
Food stores.....................	13	31.3	20.1	17.7	10.4	11.9
Mail order houses..................	3	45.2	−8.6	26.9	52.6	44.6
Restaurants......................	5	4.8	0.2	−0.3	0.8	−0.8
Other retail stores.................	10	8.2	−5.5	3.1	6.3	2.5
Rubber and tires....................	10	34.1	−12.5	11.3	26.8	22.6
Shipping and shipbuilding............	11	11.8	−5.3	−3.1	−1.8	−0.6
Steel..............................	33	369.2	−139.4	−14.6	212.7	1.6
Textiles:						
Clothing and apparel...............	27	22.5	−10.0	3.5	7.5	4.8
Silk and rayon....................	9	6.0	0	6.0	8.3	3.7
Other textiles....................	14	3.2	−16.6	−7.0	−0.4	−9.8
Tobacco............................	16	105.0	113.8	80.2	88.0	83.9
Miscellaneous......................	47	61.0	−3.8	13.5	28.8	15.8
Total, 46 groups...............	831	2,812.8	−37.6	910.1	2,184.3	1,104.7

[2] From *Monthly Review of Credit and Business Conditions,* issued by Federal Reserve Bank of New York, April 1, 1939.

follows: (1) wide variation in sales and profits in good and poor years; (2) excess productive capacity in many leading lines; (3) free competition among all companies for the business available; (4) overproduction problems arising out of excess capacity and free competition; (5) saturation limits for important products; and (6) prime importance of the management factor.   An appraisal of the influence of each of these factors upon the investment position of the securities of any company necessarily requires a searching investigation of the economics of the industry quite apart from an analysis of the financial condition of the particular company.   As the investor is seldom in a position to undertake this investigation, he should be cognizant of the inherent difficulties in industrial operations and should fully realize that the selection of a good industrial security is one of the most difficult problems in the investment field.

Industrial operations are notoriously unstable.   Sales are large in good years and small in poor years.   A variation of 10 to 20 per cent in annual revenues is regarded as extreme in railroad and utility operations; in contrast, annual sales by industrial companies vary as much as 60 to 80 per cent.[3]   Such variation in the volume of business has magnified influence upon earnings.   As a considerable part of operating expenses is fixed and does not vary with sales, it follows that the profit margin increases when sales are large and declines when sales are low.   If the profit margin is 10 per cent in an average year, it may run as high as 15 per cent in a good year and as low as 5 per cent in a poor year.   Bondholders should realize that an impressive margin of safety in prosperous times may entirely disappear in times of depression.   Stockholders, especially, should be as equally prepared for deficits in poor years as for surpluses in good years.   Industrial earnings in prosperous years can be extremely misleading.[4]

---

[3] Baldwin Locomotive received domestic orders for but 85 locomotives in one year (1921) and for 889 in the very next year (1922).   In 1923, Baldwin domestic sales were in excess of $80,000,000; in 1928, they amounted to only $14,000,000.

[4] The Goodyear Tire and Rubber Company reported profits of $47,300,000 for the five-year period 1915-1919, reported losses of $44,300,000 in 1920 and

As a result of ambitious expansion policies undertaken by many important companies during the decade from 1920 to 1930, output capacity was increased to a point that, in many instances, would appear to have been substantially beyond normal requirements. An urge to reduce unit costs through large-scale operation was primarily responsible for this uneconomic development. Other attributable factors were overoptimistic estimates of markets at home and abroad and the relative facility with which new funds were obtainable through the issuance of additional securities. Regardless of the cause, however, the result is a condition of high economic significance. Excess capacity reflects not only idle capital but even more harmful effects in creating intense competition and expensive overproduction. Divergent illustrations are to be found in the coal and motor industries, with present capacities equivalent to about twice the normal demand.

Competition, within reasonable limits, is more beneficial than harmful. Unfortunately, narrowing markets limiting the demand for industrial products (especially in foreign markets which are largely closed to American exports), coupled with increased productive facilities, forecast extremely keen competition for all industrial companies. Under such conditions, only the strongest companies can survive. The investor will do well to avoid those industries in which competitive conditions have gone beyond economic warrant.[5]

Overproduction is a constant menace to industrial companies. Temporary surpluses caused by changing economic conditions are much less dangerous than chronic excess outputs arising out of unregulated production. This condition is especially true of commodities, as vividly illustrated over recent years by petroleum, copper, sugar, and rubber. It is also true of certain manufactured products, such as textiles and furni-

---

1921, and again reported profits of $45,300,000 for the five-year period 1922-1926.

[5] Although more than 4,000 establishments manufacture chemical products in the United States, the three largest companies control about 66 per cent of the industry (du Pont, 25 per cent; Allied Chemical, 23 per cent; and Union Carbide, 18 per cent). The four next largest companies control only 10 per cent (American Cyanamid, 3 per cent; Texas Gulf Sulphur, 3 per cent; Hercules Powder, 2 per cent; and Air Reduction, 2 per cent).

ture. Various restrictive plans to regulate production to demand have generally failed, partly because of the illegality of
combinations in restraint of trade and partly because of the
difficulty of securing international coöperation. Prior to the
development of the oil fields in the Southwest, the petroleum
industry was exceptionally prosperous; flush production in
that area, however, has more than offset the tremendous increase in consumption, with the result that the industry has
earned less than a reasonable rate of return upon capital investment over the past decade despite the growing popularity
of the product.

Saturation points create difficult problems for industrial
companies. Every industry, following the normal curve of
economic evolution from the stage of experimentation through
the stage of development, eventually reaches the saturation
zone, at which point sales growth practically stops. The automobile industry apparently reached this point around 1930,
just as its predecessor, the bicycle, did in 1900. While the
attainment of the saturation stage does not signify an early
decline in earning power, it does indicate a cessation of substantial increases in earnings. Consequently, the position of
the industry in its growth cycle is an important consideration
to the investor. He should give preference to the securities
of those industries which have established themselves on a
sound basis but which have not entered the saturation
stage.

In view of the absence of public regulation and of the lack
of uniformity in operating conditions, the management factor
is of unusual importance in industrial analysis. Unlike the
public utility field, where management is largely a question of
personnel, management in the industrial field is more a matter
of policy. These policies are evolved out of the experience of
the company and usually reflect the principles of the founders,
applied with sufficient flexibility to meet changing conditions.
Efficiency of management is shown in a variety of ways, such
as quality of the product, production methods, marketing
policies, and credit reputation, but the outstanding test is

stability of earning power. Good management finds its best reflection in satisfactory financial statements.[6]

Nature of the industry. The selection of industrial securities should involve a careful consideration of the nature of the industry represented in each company in question. Among the more important factors to be considered are: (1) nature of the product or service; (2) monopoly position; (3) degree of integration; (4) character of inventories; and (5) tariff protection. The situation should be relatively favorable in these respects as a group.

The product or service should preferably represent a necessity rather than a luxury. Industrial companies which supply materials that are not essential to the average person do not usually offer favorable investment opportunity. Luxury trades suffer severely in years of depression. The success of certain chain stores, notably Woolworth and Kresge, which appeal to the general public on a price-economy basis, is in very favorable contrast in periods of depression to the concurrent records of the larger department stores.

Monopolistic position should not be overvalued. Control of sources of material, as currently illustrated in Aluminum Company and International Nickel, is always subject to new discoveries elsewhere. Patent protection eventually expires with adverse results to the protected company, as shown in the recent history of Gillette Safety Razor. Even the safest type of monopoly, that based on efficient production and distribution, can be disturbed by resourceful competitors, as evidenced in recent inroads by Chevrolet and Plymouth into the low-price motor field long dominated by Ford.

---

[6] "Management includes personal character, ability to organize, ability to produce, market and finance to advantage. It includes knowledge of methods and knowledge of men and markets, and skill in using this knowledge. It may include ability to take chances wisely, or to pursue a cautious course and still make profits. It must include foresight and ability to develop successors to carry on the business in years to come. This is a very brief summary of points to be considered in connection with management, but in industrial finance more than in any other, it is the men rather than the property that form the chief security for the banker's advances."—*Investment Bankers Association of America Bulletin,* May 31, 1923.

Integrated companies that control the product from raw material to the finished article enjoy considerable economic advantage over other companies that have little or no integration. The company that must buy its principal raw material from another producer and must sell its product in semifinished form, as illustrated in the case of American Woolen, suffers in comparison with an integrated company, such as United States Steel, which is in entire control of all operations from the ore mines to the finished steel product.

Companies that are compelled to carry large inventories face unusual problems. Especially is this true when the merchandise is perishable, as in the meatpacking industry, where the product cannot be held to await more favorable prices. Those companies which are not required to maintain heavy inventories of either raw materials or finished goods, or which are in a position to maintain a rapid turnover of merchandise, are not seriously affected by commodity price movements.[7]

International trade barriers, established to an increasing extent in recent years, operate to the advantage of those companies that depend upon domestic customers and to the distinct disadvantage of firms that find their best markets in foreign fields. The establishment of trade barriers in the form of exchange restrictions and barter agreements in addition to high import duties in foreign countries unfortunately comes at a time when many American manufacturers find the domestic market approaching the saturation point. General Motors, International Harvester, and General Electric are three outstanding companies that have expended large sums in the development of export trade. On the other hand, many other important firms would face severe competition at home if import duties should be substantially lowered.

Industrial consolidations. From an investment viewpoint,

---

[7] The severe decline in commodity prices during the second half of 1937 drastically affected the earnings of many large companies as reported for that year. American Woolen had an operating profit of $2,167,996 which was converted into a deficit of $1,854,902 by reason of an inventory decline of $4,022,-898. Goodyear Tire and Rubber had an operating profit of $17,600,030 which was reduced to a net profit of $7,257,287 as the result of an inventory loss of $10,342,743.

industrial consolidations in the United States have not been impressively successful. The experience of the great consolidation era from 1895 to 1905 was comparable to that of more recent years from 1925 to 1930. Even though the earlier period witnessed such gigantic combinations as United States Steel, International Harvester, American Locomotive, and International Mercantile Marine, investors in the majority of cases found actual earning power substantially less than the optimistic estimates of the promoters. And even though the recent period saw Dodge merge with Chrysler, Victor Talking Machine merge with Radio, Fleischmann and Royal Baking combine into Standard Brands, a number of theatrical firms consolidate into Fox Film, and a group of office appliance firms become Remington-Rand, the ensuing results have been disappointing.

The obvious advantages that consolidation seems to offer are more than offset by the less obvious disadvantages. This condition is particularly true when large units combine, since each component company has already gained the benefits of large-scale operation. The burden of overhead expense seems to vary with the size of the company, and seldom is economy gained in that respect. A decline in competitive effort adversely affects sales volume. The proper coördination of the departments of a large organization is a task requiring years rather than weeks or months of planning. Personal incentive on the part of the officers to a large extent varies indirectly with the size of the organization. In short, the merits are exaggerated, and the disadvantages are overlooked, when industrial consolidations are promoted.

Investors in industrial securities are therefore advised to regard consolidations as somewhat less beneficial than early proposals might indicate. Holders of securities of merging companies who elect to exchange their securities for those of the new company, as well as new investors in the latter issues, should not expect substantial benefits immediately to accrue to the new company.[8]

---

[8] A critical study of the industrial consolidations of the 1900 era appeared in the *Quarterly Journal of Economics*, Vol. 36, No. 1, p. 84. A brief study

Income statements. The income statements of almost all industrial companies fail to provide the information essential for investment analysis. While some companies issue detailed analyses of earnings and properties, as well illustrated in the informative booklets prepared by United States Steel, Bethlehem Steel, and Diamond Match, other companies publish extremely meager reports. An income statement that omits all details of operations prior to the item of net profits scarcely deserves its title. The subsequent items that appear disclose the less important factor of how the earnings are distributed; the more significant factor of how the earnings are derived is seldom available to the security holder. The following discussion is based upon the assumption that the stated information is available; as a practical matter, few industrial reports are adequately informative.

The accompanying statement of an industrial company shows in concise manner the minimum information which the income account should provide. The more important items are discussed in the following summary.

Sales billed represents the gross revenue receivable from the aggregate invoices of the company. The universal practice is to show only one total figure and not to disclose departmental results. The amount shown should be compared with sales in previous years for a study of the growth of the company. Variations from year to year are less important than the trend over a series of years.

Operating expense includes the cost of materials consumed, the wages and salaries of all employees, the rent of leased property, and many miscellaneous items such as provision for doubtful accounts.

Depreciation represents the amount set aside from earnings to provide for the ultimate retirement of physical property. Because depreciation arises out of functional obsolescence to a larger degree than out of deterioration and use, the determination of adequacy in the annual provision is most difficult. Equipment which has a physical life of 50 years may become

---

of the more recent mergers appeared in *The New York Times* on August 24, 1930.

obsolete in 20 years. Because physical service-life is more readily predictable than functional utility, practically all depreciation charges are based upon the less important of the

INDUSTRIAL INCOME STATEMENT

Sales billed..........................	$20,000,000	100.0%
Cost of sales:		
Operating cost..................	$16,000,000	80.0%
Depreciation.,..................	1,000,000	5.0
Depletion.....................	—	—
Taxes.........................	800,000	4.0
Total cost of sales............	$17,800,000	89.0%
Income from sales.................	$ 2,200,000	11.0%
Other income.....................	300,000	1.5
Total income......................	$ 2,500,000	12.5%
Fixed charges:		
Bond interest....................	$ 500,000	2.5%
Amortization....................	20,000	0.1
Total charges................	$ 520,000	2.6%
Net income........................	$ 1,980,000	9.9%
Preferred dividends................	300,000	1.5
Balance..........................	$ 1,680,000	8.4%
Common dividends................	1,200,000	6.0
Surplus..........................	$ 480,000	2.4%

SECURITIES ANALYSIS FACTORS

Factor of safety on bonds $= \dfrac{\$2,500,000}{\$\ 520,000} = 4.8$ times earned.

Factor of safety on preferred stock $= \dfrac{\$2,500,000}{\$520,000 + \$300,000} = \dfrac{\$2,500,000}{\$\ 820,000} = 3.0.$

Common stock earnings $= \dfrac{\$1,680,000}{300,000} = \$5.60$ per share.

factors. As a consequence, the statement is probably true that most industrial companies do not provide adequately for depreciation losses in their reports. The result is an overstatement of earnings. Eventually the point is reached when the value of the property as shown on the books is far above realistic appraisal. A write-down to true value at the expense of the surplus account becomes a belated acknowledgment of inadequate depreciation and overstated earnings.

Investors should appreciate that the amount provided for depreciation is an arbitrary figure as determined by the corporate management. Some companies deliberately adjust the provision to conform with earnings, increasing the charge in good years and reducing the amount in poor years. Even those companies which set aside a regular sum base their provision upon the estimated physical life of the property. The natural policy of corporations in preparing income tax reports is to claim as large an allowance for depreciation as the regulations permit. The provision for depreciation which appears in the stockholders' report is usually less than that claimed for tax purposes, although a few companies such as General Electric and Sears-Roebuck take the more conservative viewpoint that the maximum Federal allowance should be the minimum provision in the annual statements sent to stockholders.

The adequacy of a corporate provision for depreciation can be best tested by ascertaining the percentage of the annual provision to the value of the depreciable property. As 25 years is the probable service-life of ordinary corporate property, a minimum provision of 4 per cent would seem to be necessary. Because corporations rarely report the value of land, which is regarded as nondepreciable, separately from buildings and equipment, a minimum provision of 3 per cent of total property value, including land, would give about the same result as a 4-per-cent provision against the depreciable property.

Depletion represents the amount set aside from earnings to offset the actual loss of assets in the extractive industries, such as mining and petroleum. The purpose of both depreciation and depletion charges is to preserve the integrity of the investment, and therefore both indicate the return of capital rather than the distribution of earnings. This interesting distinction exists: the amount set aside for depreciation will normally be reinvested in new equipment to replace the old; the amount provided for depletion cannot be used to "replete" the extracted ore although, in some instances, the funds may be used to acquire new properties. Hence, extractive companies pay dividends partly from surplus, as a distribution of earnings, and partly from the depletion reserve, as a return of capital. The problem of properly estimating depletion is complicated by the discovery of new sources, with the consequence that many important mining companies report earnings "before depletion," thus tending to overstate profits.

Taxes is self-explanatory, including all Federal, state, and local levies. Income taxes have become the most important item in this group.

OPERATING RATIOS AND INCOME RATIOS
SELECTED MAJOR INDUSTRIES[9]

Industry	Operating Ratio*			Income Ratio†		
	1937	1938	1939	1937	1938	1939
Agricultural machinery	84.7	90.3	92.5	10.7	6.7	5.9
Automobiles...........	89.6	93.6	88.3	9.0	5.8	9.6
Chemicals............	81.7	86.4	81.8	20.3	14.1	19.2
Cigarettes............	88.8	89.2	88.5	8.9	8.7	9.0
Meat packing.........	98.6	99.8	98.2	0.9	−0.4	0.9
Oil refining...........	85.9	91.8	90.4	11.9	6.7	7.7
Rubber..............	92.8	94.2	92.0	3.4	3.6	5.2
Steel................	90.3	98.6	92.2	7.0	−0.5	5.4

* Excluding income taxes.
† After taxes and interest charges.

Total cost of sales is the sum of the preceding expense items. The percentage which this total bears to sales is the *operating ratio,* an important financial criterion which varies widely with different industries. A high rate of inventory turnover, as illustrated in the meat-packing, chain-store, and mail-order industries, permits some companies to show satisfactory profits despite cost ratios as high as 95 per cent. Few industrial companies show operating ratios under 80 per cent of sales.

[9] Source—*Survey of American Listed Corporations,* Securities and Exchange Commission.

Income from sales is the difference between sales value and cost. The operating profit should show a reasonable margin on sales value and an acceptable rate of return on property value. The adequacy of the profit margin on sales must be judged with respect to the nature of the business; 5 per cent in one line may be better than 10 per cent in another. The rate of return on property value should be at least 10 per cent in the stabilized industries and even higher in the more volatile fields. The inability of many large companies to show such earning power over the past decade would seem to require a general scaling down of fixed property valuation.

Other income represents earnings derived outside of the regular operations of the business. For the most part, the income consists of interest and dividends received on securities owned. In a great majority of cases, the amount is relatively small and is included with sales revenues and not shown separately. General Electric is a notable exception in this respect, inasmuch as one third of total income is derived from outside sources. It is further interesting to note that if "accrued" as well as "received" income from outside sources were included, this item would represent nearly 40 per cent of General Electric's total income.[10]

Total income is the aggregate earnings from operating and outside sources. It is the amount available for the security holders, over whom the bondholders have priority of claim.

Bond interest is the annual fixed charge payable to the bondholders and is determined by the coupon rate on the outstanding issues. The amount should seldom, if ever, exceed 5 per cent of average annual sales and should not exceed one third of total income.

Amortization represents the annual charge by which the discount on bonds issued by the company below par value is gradually written off during the life of the bonds. The charge,

---

[10] Perhaps a more spectacular illustration of other income in industrial companies is shown in the case of the du Pont investment in General Motors amounting to nearly a 25-per-cent interest. Over the decade from 1929 through 1938, du Pont reported average earnings of $4.80 per share of common stock, of which $2.43 was derived from the General Motors investment and only $2.37 from direct operations.

in effect, is additional interest and is clearly an expense of the business.

Sinking fund provision covers the amount which many industrial companies set aside yearly to provide a fund with which to retire bonds at maturity. Although the item is plainly a capital charge, some bond indentures require that the fund be created out of earnings, thus compelling the inclusion of the amount among the current expenses.[11]

Preferred dividends comprise the preferential payments made to the preferred stockholders. The total income should be at least 1½ times the sum of interest charges, amortization expense, and preferred dividend requirement.

Common dividends comprise the payments made to the common stockholders. The amount of the payment is contingent chiefly upon the balance of earnings available, and the prospective needs of the business. The ideal dividend policy is the retention of a part of the earnings for expansion purposes and the maintenance of as high a dividend rate as conditions permit.[12]

Surplus is the balance remaining after all dividend payments. The amount is added to the undistributed earnings of prior periods and is so reported on the balance sheet of the company.

The fact that some companies do not employ the sequence of charges here shown is more significant than may first appear. For instance, the statement of depreciation expense *after* bond interest tends to overstate the margin of safety to the bondholder. The inclusion of other income with sales tends to understate the operating ratio. For analytical purposes, statements differently arranged should be recast into the sequence here shown.

In addition to the more complete income statements issued

---

[11] Some companies evade the adverse effect of such requirement by considering the sinking fund provision as part of the depreciation charge and reducing the latter in accordince.

[12] During the ten-year period from 1925 through 1934, General Motors paid 77 per cent of earnings to stockholders and retained 23 per cent for expansion. During the first five years (1925-1929), however, dividends represented only 63 per cent of earnings whereas during the second five years (1930-1934) dividends represented 113 per cent of earnings.

annually by industrial companies, the practice of publishing quarterly summaries is growing in popularity. A majority of the more important companies now provide their security holders with such interim reports, which enable investors to keep in closer touch with current conditions.

Balance sheets. An industrial balance sheet should be construed as a statement of opinion as to the value of the various assets and liabilities prepared by the management of the company. The valuations shown are those that appear on the corporate ledger, which fact accounts for the term *book value*. The basis for value is usually original cost, but may often be an arbitrary estimate that overstates or understates intrinsic worth. The accompanying illustrative statement shows the manner in which industrial companies usually publish balance sheets. It is noteworthy that industrial balance sheets are generally reported in greater detail than income statements.

Cash represents balances carried in commercial banks.

Receivables comprise primarily short-term credits extended to the customers of the company. The amount usually shown is that after a reserve for doubtful collections has been deducted. The account should bear a reasonable relationship to annual sales, with allowance for seasonal influences and terms of credit.

Inventories represent the value of merchandise on hand. The accepted standard of inventory valuation is *cost or market, whichever is lower,* but such method should not be assumed if not so stated. The amount is sometimes shown on a *net* basis after the deduction of an unstated reserve for inventory depreciation. The amount should bear a reasonable relationship to annual sales, with due allowance for the nature of the business.

Investments in associated companies represent advances to subsidiaries. This money should be regarded primarily as a permanent commitment. The true value is indicated in many instances from the amount reported as other income in the income statement.

Marketable securities represent temporary investment of surplus funds. If shown separately, the amount should be

INDUSTRIAL BALANCE SHEET

Assets		Liabilities	
Current assets:		**Current liabilities:**	
Cash.................	$ 1,500,000	Accounts payable.....	$ 4,500,000
Receivables..........	7,500,000	Interest accrued.......	150,000
Inventories..........	5,000,000	Taxes accrued........	400,000
		Dividends payable....	950,000
Total...........	$14,000,000		
		Total...........	$ 6,000,000
Investments:			
Associated companies..	$ 4,000,000	**Reserves:**	
Marketable securities..	2,000,000	Depreciation..........	$ 5,000,000
		Contingent...........	400,000
Total...........	$ 6,000,000		
		Total...........	$ 5,400,000
Fixed assets:			
Land................	$ 5,000,000	**Funded debt:**	
Buildings............	15,000,000	Mortgage bonds.......	$10,000,000
Equipment...........	10,000,000		
		Preferred stock*........	$ 5,000,000
Total...........	$30,000,000		
		Common stock†........	$15,000,000
Deferred charges:			
Bond discount........	$ 350,000	Appropriated surplus....	$ 5,000,000
		Profit and loss surplus...	$ 3,950,000
Total...........	$50,350,000	Total...........	$50,350,000

Securities Analysis Ratios

Working capital ratio:

$$\frac{\$14,000,000}{\$ 6,000,000} = 233\%.$$

Depreciation reserve ratio:

$$\frac{\$ 5,000,000}{\$30,000,000} = 16.7\%.$$

Capitalization ratios:
Bonds ($10,000,000)   = 33%.
Preferred stock ($5,000,000)   = 17%.
Common stock ($15,000,000) = 50%.

* Represented by 50,000 shares of no par value.
† Represented by 300,000 shares of no par value.

considered as part of current assets. Unfortunately, many companies include this item with the previous one under the general term of investments.

Fixed assets comprise Land, Buildings, and Equipment, which accounts are usually grouped and reported at a composite valuation. Moreover, intangible items, such as Goodwill and Patents, are often included in this amount. The value stated may represent original cost, but, in numerous instances, is based upon periodical reappraisals. The true value is shown, however, not in the balance sheet but in the earning power evidenced by the income statement.

Bond discount is the unamortized balance of the difference between the face value of bonds and the price received for bonds issued below par.

Current liabilities include obligations payable within 12 months. The total should not exceed one half of current assets. Inability to meet current debts creates a position of insolvency, a condition which may necessitate the appointment of a receiver to take charge of the company.

Depreciation reserve is an amount set aside from earnings, as before illustrated, to offset the obsolescence and deterioration of the physical property. The account is credited annually with the amounts appropriated from earnings and charged with the book value of property abandoned. The amount stated is not segregated into a special fund, but is reinvested in the general assets of the company. The size of the reserve may vary from as low as 10 per cent of the plant account, as reported by Woolworth, to as high as 75 per cent of the plant account, as reported by General Electric. A practical standard would appear to be around 30 per cent.[13]

Contingent reserve is usually a small amount provided to meet contingencies not otherwise covered.

Secret reserve is a term loosely applied to undisclosed surplus. The understatement of any asset or the overstatement

---

[13] A practice long popular in Europe and recently advocated in the United States is to set up a depreciation reserve equal to the entire plant investment. Ultraconservative as such procedure would appear to be, the ultimate effect is diametrically opposite when it results in the elimination of depreciation charges and permits the return of capital to take the guise of earned dividends.

of any liability automatically creates a secret reserve. The usual manner in which such reserves are created is that of stating an asset on a *net* basis after the deduction of an undisclosed reserve. Another popular method employed is that of setting up valuable outside investments at a nominal figure. Such practices result in an understatement of the true worth of the company.[14]

Funded debt may take the form of mortgage or debenture bonds. In either event, the amount should seldom exceed the net working capital (which is the difference between current assets and current liabilities), should never exceed 40 per cent of tangible assets, and should not exceed one fourth of the total capitalization in bonds, stock, and surplus.

Preferred stock represents the value at which this class of stock is carried on the balance sheet. The value shown is the nominal, or face, value of the stock, except in the case of no par stock, in which event an arbitrary value is used.

Common stock represents the value at which this class of stock is carried on the balance sheet. As in the case of preferred stock, an arbitrary value is employed for no par issues. Some companies that have no par stock have adopted the expedient of combining the stock and surplus accounts on the balance sheet. The *book value* of the common stock is the proportionate equity of each share of common stock in the net assets of the company. In the illustrative balance sheet previously shown, the aggregate value of the tangible assets is $50,000,000, against which $21,400,000 is deductible to cover current liabilities, reserves, and funded debt, leaving a remainder of $28,600,000; a further deduction of $5,000,000 must be made under a provision whereby the preferred stock has a preference as to assets at the rate of $100 per share in the event of dissolution, leaving $23,600,000 as the net equity of the common stock; this amount is divided by 300,000, the number of shares outstanding, producing a quotient of $78.67, which is termed the book value of the common stock. In

---

[14] The annual report of International Harvester for 1931 showed the application of $11,000,000 to earnings from an inventory reserve which did not appear in previous reports.

theory, book value should indicate intrinsic worth and should have direct influence upon market price. In practice, earnings have much greater weight in the determination of market price than has book value.

Appropriated surplus is that part of the surplus account which has been reinvested in the business and which is not available for cash dividends to stockholders.

Profit and loss surplus represents the undistributed earnings from which dividends may be declared. In theory, it provides a reserve for the continuance of dividend payments in poor years. In practice, however, corporations at such times usually regard the conservation of cash as more essential than the payment of dividends. The existence of a surplus of nearly $500,000,000 did not assure dividends to United States Steel stockholders in 1932.

Industrial bonds. The investment position of industrial bonds has measurably improved during recent years. This improvement has been due partly to impairment of the general quality of railroad bonds because of reduced earning power and the effect of hostile legislation upon public utility securities, which has tended to reduce the wide margin of superiority which railroad and utility bonds traditionally enjoyed over industrial bonds. In larger part, however, the improved status is due to betterment in the industrial field. Many industrial companies—General Electric, General Motors, Eastman Kodak, International Harvester, and the Standard Oil group, just to name a few—have established impressive records of earning power and financial stability which compare favorably with the records of railroad and utility companies. It is not surprising, therefore, to observe that certain industrial bonds were added to the "legal list" of securities eligible for investment by trustees and savings banks in New York State in 1939 for the first time in the hundred years since the law was originally enacted.

It is regrettable from the investor's viewpoint that many of the more prosperous industrial companies have no bonds outstanding. An increasing number of corporations have taken advantage of the favorable conditions which have existed in the money market during recent years to redeem outstanding bonds either through surplus cash reserves or through "term-loans" at commercial banks at low interest rates. The supply of good industrial bonds has diminished to the point of acute scarcity.

A good industrial bond should meet the following tests of acceptability:

1. The total bonds of the company should not exceed 25 per cent of all securities outstanding.

2. The total bonds of the company should not exceed the net working capital of the company.

3. The maturity of the issue should not exceed 30 years.

4. A sinking fund provision should be provided adequate to retire a substantial portion of the bonds before maturity.

5. The annual interest charge should not exceed 3 per cent of the average annual sales revenue.

6. The average total income for the five preceding years available for the payment of interest charges should be at least four times the charges.

7. The issue should be at least $10,000,000 and should preferably be listed on a National Securities Exchange.

8. The company should be in a growing industry, supplying an essential product or service, fairly well integrated, and not primarily interested in export sales.

It may be the "counsel of perfection" to advise such selectivity in a limited field. It may be said in justification that industrial bonds seem to be either very good or very bad. The prudent investor must act accordingly. A wide range of quality exists between the Standard Oil of New Jersey 2¾'s of 1953 quoted at the time of writing on a yield basis of 2.40 per cent and the United Drug 5's of 1953 quoted to yield 6.50 per cent.

Preferred stocks. Preferred stocks of industrial companies are entitled to investment recognition only upon the basis of demonstrated earning power on the part of the issuing companies. Especially is this true, as earlier stated, when the company has no bonds outstanding, thus giving the preferred stock, in effect, a prior lien on earnings and assets. The existence of many excellent issues, such as International Harvester Preferred, General Motors Preferred, and National Biscuit Preferred, might readily create the false impression that industrial preferred stocks, as a group, are good investments. An acceptable industrial preferred stock should meet the following tests:

1. The preferred stock of the company should not exceed 33 per cent of all securities outstanding.

2. The average total income for the five preceding years available for the payment of interest and dividends should be at least 2½ times the average preferred dividend requirement plus the average bond interest, if any bonds are outstanding.

3. The issue should preferably be noncallable and listed on a National Securities Exchange.

4. The issue should preferably be one of a company which has no funded debt.

5. (See No. 8 for industrial bonds.)

The investor in industrial preferred stocks should realize that preferred dividend payments are always optional with the company and that neither a large corporate surplus nor a long unbroken dividend record assures the continuation of dividends in years of adversity.

Common stocks. Few common stocks of industrial companies deserve investment consideration. The fluctuating nature of industrial earnings, coupled with the dividend discretionary power of corporate management, makes the position of the common stockholder uncertain at all times and precarious in periods of business depression. Probably few conservative investors would rank any industrial common stocks as good investments. Investors with a more liberal attitude might list a limited group such as General Electric, E. I. du Pont, Eastman Kodak, and Woolworth as deserving investment ranking. In any event, common stocks of industrial companies should be bought only by persons able and willing to assume a relatively large degree of risk.

The selection of industrial common stocks as acceptable

investments involves the application of tests which eliminate the great majority of such issues from consideration.

1.   The common stock should have an unbroken dividend record for the preceding 10 years.

2.   The market price should not be more than 20 times the average earnings per share for the preceding five years.

3.   The prevailing dividend rate should afford a return on the cost price of not less than 3 per cent per annum.

4.   The issue should be listed on a National Securities Exchange.

5.   (See No. 4 for industrial preferred stocks.)

6.   (See No. 8 for industrial bonds.)

The purchase of industrial common stocks as long-term investments would obviously require the consideration of additional factors.   Such commitments can, and often do, work out advantageously, just as do many other forms of speculation.   Economic forecasting, however, is always hazardous. The long-pull investor faces the double hazard of selecting not only the industries which will be prosperous 10 years hence but also the particular companies which will benefit from that condition.   The chance of finding the right combination seems too remote to warrant terming such a commitment an investment.

Securities analysis.   The procedure followed in the analysis of the financial statements of an industrial company may be illustrated through application to the reports rendered by a large manufacturing company over the five-year period from 1935 through 1939.   (The figures here shown have been rounded out in order to facilitate the presentation.)

Sales billed averaged 350 million dollars, which is taken as a basis of 100 per cent for analytical comment.

Operating cost averaged 245 million dollars, or 70 per cent of the sales revenue.   All production costs, including labor, materials, and administrative overheads, are included in this item.

Maintenance expense averaged 35 million dollars, or 10 per cent of the sales revenue.   The relatively high cost of maintenance is due to nature of the business, as this item rarely exceeds 5 per cent in industrial plants.

Depreciation expense averaged 28 million dollars, or 8 per cent of the sales revenue. As this provision was about 4 per cent of the value of the plant and equipment, it was probably adequate for the purpose.

Tax expense averaged 14 million dollars, or 4 per cent of the sales revenue. Even more significant is the statement that taxes consumed 33 per cent of the balance remaining after the preceding items.

Operating expense, the sum of the four preceding items, averaged 322 million dollars, or 92 per cent of the sales revenue. This percentage is popularly known as the operating ratio. The percentage here shown is regarded as standard in this industry. During the five-year period, it varied from a low of 90 per cent to a high of 96 per cent.

Operating income averaged 28 million dollars, or 8 per cent of sales revenue which is complementary to the operating ratio.

Other income averaged less than 1 million dollars and is not a factor in this instance.

Total income therefore averaged 28 million dollars, or 8 per cent of sales revenue.

Bond interest averaged 7 million dollars, or 2 per cent of sales revenue. This percentage is within the 3-per-cent maximum suggested for industrial bond interest. The total income averaged 4 times the bond interest, equalling the factor of 4 times as previously suggested for a safe position. The bonds may therefore be considered as reasonably safe. A bond interest ratio of 1 per cent of sales or less and a times-earned factor of 5 or better would be required for a high-grade rating.

Preferred dividend requirement averaged 7 million dollars, which, added to the bond interest charge of 7 million dollars, made a total of 14 million dollars in priority payments. As the total income was 2 times the total priority payments, in comparison to a minimum of 2.5 times as previously suggested, the investment position of the preferred stock was not sufficiently secure to warrant more than a moderately good rating.

A times-earned factor of 4 or better would be required for a high-grade rating. The market price of 120 quoted on this 7-per-cent preferred stock in 1940, affording a yield of nearly 6 per cent, was in contrast to prices as high as 160 on comparable preferred stocks of higher ratings.

Common stock earnings averaged $4.67 per share for the five-year period ended in 1939. The market price of 80 quoted on this stock in 1940 was about 17 times average earnings for the preceding five years, which is below the maximum of 20 times previous suggested but above the factor of 15 times earnings which is more frequently regarded as a fair price. As the dividend record of this stock was most irregular during the decade from 1930 to 1940, it did not merit investment consideration under the test previously suggested.

Bonds outstanding on December 31, 1939, amounted to 190 million dollars, or nearly 33 per cent of total capitalization. This position is relatively unfavorable, as the bond ratio should not exceed 25 per cent. The moderate rating accorded to these bonds is due primarily to the effect of a heavy debt structure.

Preferred stock outstanding on December 31, 1939, amounted to 110 million dollars, or 20 per cent of total capitalization. Although this percentage is within the maximum previously suggested, the preferred stock in this case is subordinate to 33 per cent in bonds, making a total of 53 per cent, or more than one half of the total, in priority securities. It is obvious that the preferred stock is in a relatively weak position.

Common stock outstanding on December 31, 1939, amounted to 280 million dollars, or 47 per cent of total capitalization. As the common stock represents less than one half of the total capitalization, it is apparent that the available earnings are subject to wide fluctuations as sales volumes change, thereby harming the investment position. Although earnings over the 1935-1939 period averaged $4.67 per share of common stock, income in 1938 was not sufficient to cover preferred dividends, leaving a deficit of 2 million dollars instead of any surplus for the common stock.

23

SECURITIES OF FINANCIAL COMPANIES

Scope. The purpose of this chapter is to discuss the investment position of the securities of financial companies such as banking institutions which are owned by stockholders in contrast to those which are "mutually" owned by depositors or policyholders as the case might be. The order of discussion is: (1) bank stocks, (2) insurance stocks, and (3) investment company securities. To a substantial degree, the assets of financial companies are reinvested in securities of other companies; investors in these companies are therefore delegating to others the investment of their funds.

Part 1. Bank Stocks

Classification of banks. The banks in the United States may be classified: (1) either as *national* or *state,* depending upon the source of charter; (2) either as *commercial* or *savings,* depending upon the nature of operations; (3) either as *member* or *nonmember,* depending upon membership in the Federal Reserve System; (4) either as *insured* or *noninsured,* depending upon participation in the Federal deposit insurance plan; and (5) either as *stock* or *mutual,* depending upon the nature of ownership. The investor should be cognizant of the significance of each of these distinctions.

National banks are chartered by the Federal Government and are subject to uniform supervision by national bank examiners. (The title "National" must appear in the name of all national banks and may not be used by state banks.) State banks are chartered by state governments and are subject to varying methods of supervision by state banking boards in accordance with the laws of the incorporating states. National banks as a group were formerly regarded as stronger institutions than state banks, a tradition which has been largely invalidated under the supervisory powers of the Federal Reserve System and the Federal Deposit Insurance Corporation.[1]

Commercial banks deal primarily with businessmen in doing a general commercial banking business, in accepting both demand and time deposits, in handling checking accounts, in making loans and investments, in performing trust functions, and in executing orders from customers. Savings banks which operate in the more restricted field of handling savings deposits and making long-term investments are found in less than 20 of the 48 states. Commercial banks, as a rule, operate savings departments in addition to commercial departments.

Member banks, which comprise all of the national banks and the large state banks which have elected to participate, are believed to be somewhat stronger than the nonmember banks due to potential assistance from the Federal Reserve banks in periods of emergency and through the supervision of the Federal Reserve authorities.

Insured banks, which comprise practically all of the commercial banks of the country, are regarded as sound institutions because of ability to meet the eligibility requirements of the Federal Deposit Insurance Corporation. Investors should observe that the insurance applies to depositors and not to stockholders.

Mutual banks are those which have no stock outstanding, being owned and operated by the depositors.[2] Investment

---

[1] The total number of banks in the United States in 1930 was around 30,000, of which 10,000 were national banks and 20,000 were state banks. In 1940, the total number had declined to around 15,000, of which 5,000 were national banks and about 10,000 were state banks.

[2] All savings banks in New York State are required to be mutually owned. Some states, however, permit stock-ownership of savings banks.

interest is necessarily confined to the commercial banks which are owned by stockholders.

Sources of earnings. The operating revenues of commercial banks are derived from five sources: (1) interest on loans, (2) income from investments, (3) fees for trust services, (4) charges for checking accounts, and (5) miscellaneous items such as rents and commissions. Their relative importance is in the order stated.

Interest on loans provides from 40 to 80 per cent of revenues, depending upon the relative volume of loans outstanding. In past years, interest on loans provided the chief source of bank earnings, amounting to as much as 80 per cent of revenues. During recent years, the demand for business loans has fallen to such an extent that loans now represent less than one half of the earning assets of the commercial banks (actually only 41 per cent in the national banks in 1939). The decline in the volume of loans has been accompanied by a decline in interest rates. As a consequence, interest on loans has fallen to less than 50 per cent of bank revenues. The declining revenue from loans has compelled bank officials to seek increased earnings from other sources.

Income from investments provides from 20 to 40 per cent of revenues, depending upon the relative volume of securities owned. The revenue from this source has materially increased during recent years as surplus funds not used in loans are invested in securities. As Federal bonds and notes now represent about 40 per cent of all earning assets in the banks of the country, and nearly 70 per cent of all securities owned by the banks, the rate of return from investments is much lower than was previously earned from securities.

Fees for trust services provide from 5 to 10 per cent of revenues. The importance of this item lies less in the relatively small percentage than in the fact that it is gradually increasing as banks become more active in this field.

Charges for checking accounts, better known as *service charges,* provide from 3 to 5 per cent of revenues. In past years, banks were more than willing to handle checking accounts without charge—in fact, paid relatively high interest rates on average balances for the use of the money. With changing conditions, banks are now compelled to impose charges to cover the actual expense of handling the account. The revenue from this source is negative in that it barely offsets the cost of the service.

Miscellaneous items make up the balance of revenues, aggregating from 10 to 15 per cent of the total. This percent-

LOANS AND INVESTMENTS OF FEDERAL RESERVE SYSTEM BANKS
(As of June 29, 1940)

United States Government bonds......	$14,700,000,000	43%
Other bonds........................	5,700,000,000	16
Total bonds..................	$20,400,000,000	59%
Real estate loans....................	$ 3,000,000,000	9%
Other loans.........................	11,000,000,000	32
Total loans...................	$14,000,000,000	41%
Grand total.............	$34,400,000,000	100%

age varies according to the activity of the bank in real estate holdings, in orders for securities to be bought or sold, and in fees for numerous minor services.

The operating expenses of commercial banks may be divided into four groups: (1) salaries and wages, (2) interest on time deposits, (3) taxes, and (4) miscellaneous items. These items normally require about 70 per cent of the operating revenues.

Salaries and wages amount to about 40 per cent of total expenses and require between 25 and 30 per cent of revenues.

Interest on time deposits amounts to about 25 per cent of total expenses and requires from 15 to 20 per cent of revenues. Under the provisions of the Federal banking law, interest may not be paid on demand deposits, better known as checking accounts.

Taxes amount to about 10 per cent of total expenses and require from 5 to 7 per cent of revenues.

Miscellaneous items, including the more recently levied assessments for deposit insurance, amount to about 25 per cent of expenses and require from 15 to 20 per cent of revenues.

The operating income, which is the operating revenue less operating expenses, is normally about 30 per cent of the revenues. This item is frequently referred to as the "gross income" of the bank in published reports.

The gross income is subject to further increases arising out of profits gained on securities transactions and recoveries made on losses previously charged off. It is subject to further decreases because of losses sustained on securities transactions and other losses sustained from banking operations.

It is the general custom of banks to report only gross income and dividend payments. The investor can only surmise the extent to which the actual figures would approximate the standards here set forth. He can, however, estimate the extent to which the reported earnings were increased or decreased by subsequent adjustments of profits and losses by comparing the surplus accounts in the balance sheets at the beginning and end of the period.

The unwillingness on the part of bank managements to issue a detailed income statement is an obvious handicap to the investor who would like such information as a guide to his judgment. Even more objectionable, perhaps, is the practice on the part of certain banks to make variations from year to year in the method of reporting earnings, thereby making comparisons unreliable.[3]

Bank statements. The financial statement of a bank is a balance sheet showing assets, liabilities, and capital as of a certain date. The assets comprise the cash on hand and on deposit in other institutions, items in the course of collection, securities owned, loans outstanding, real estate owned, and

---

[3] "Among bankers themselves there is a common tendency to speak slightingly of the bank earnings reports as presented. Bankers have behind them a long and even respected tradition in favor of falsifying earnings reports. The tradition, in its respected form, merely requires that the falsification be in the direction of disclosing less than the actual earnings by storing away "hidden" reserves. It is a common thing for bankers to boast of not showing all their earnings."—From article by E. V. Bell in *The New York Times,* January 22, 1939.

miscellaneous items. The liabilities include amounts due depositors, accounts payable, capital stock, undivided profits, surplus, reserves, and minor items. The interest of the investor is chiefly in the capital stock, undivided profits, and surplus accounts, as the sum of the three represents the equity of the stock.

Capital stock is the stated value of the outstanding stock as carried on the books of the bank.

Undivided profits is the amount of surplus earnings from which dividend payments are made.

Surplus is the remainder of the surplus earnings which have been allowed to remain in the bank on a relatively permanent basis as an additional factor of safety to depositors. It is increased from time to time through transfers from the undivided profits account and reduced upon occasions to offset unusual losses.

From the standpoint of the bank depositor, it is believed that the total equity of the stockholders, including capital, surplus, and undivided profits, should be at least 10 per cent of the deposit liabilities. From the standpoint of the bank stockholder, it is believed that the market value of any bank stock should not exceed $1\frac{1}{4}$ times its proportionate equity.

The financial statement that a large metropolitan bank recently published gave the following information:

Deposits....................	$950,000,000
Capital stock ($10 par).......	25,000,000
Surplus....................	50,000,000
Undivided profits............	24,000,000

The total equity of $99,000,000 was slightly more than 10 per cent of total deposits, which meets the first test previously stated. The total equity of $99,000,000 divided by the number of shares, 2,500,000, gives a book value of nearly $40 per share. The prevailing market price of $52 per share was 1.3 times the book value, or slightly higher than indicated fair value under the second test.

Bank stock analysis. The statistical analysis of a bank stock requires the determination of three mathematical relationships. All of these ratios have been computed for five selected banks in the accompanying table.

(a) The market value should not exceed 1¼ times the book value per share. All five stocks in the table come within this restriction, the factors ranging from a low of 0.87 to a high of 1.22. Under this test, stock *D* is most favorably priced and stock *A* is least favorable.

(b) The market value should not exceed 15 times average earnings per share. It is interesting that stock *D*, which was

BANK STOCK ANALYSIS
(ALL FIGURES ON A PER-SHARE BASIS)

Bank	Book Value (12/31/39)	Market Value (12/31/39)	Dividend (1939)	Earnings (1935–39)	MV / BV	MV / E	D / MV
A.........	$ 42.50	$ 52.00	$ 2.00	$ 2.80	1.22	18.6	3.9%
B.........	31.50	33.50	1.40	1.80	1.06	18.6	4.2
C.........	43.50	54.00	3.00	2.60	1.19	15.0	5.5
D.........	305.00	265.00	12.00	13.10	0.87	20.2	4.5
E.........	27.40	26.00	1.00	1.80	0.95	14.4	3.9

most favorably priced under the first test, is least attractive under this test, in which stock *E* is the most attractive.

(c) The annual dividend should afford a yield of not less than 4 per cent of the cost price. As the dividends ratios on four of the five stocks are close to this figure, they all meet the required test. The one stock which is affording a yield over 5 per cent is "out of line" either because of a possible reduction in the dividend rate or for reasons not apparent in the data.

Investment position of bank stocks. Bank stocks, which were regarded as the most conservative of all stock investments at the time of the First World War, rose to the peak of security popularity during the decade from 1920 to 1930 and fell to complete disfavor during the decade from 1930 to 1940. The collapse of bank stock prices between 1929 and 1933 when quotations on eight of the leading bank stocks in New York declined from 85 to 96 per cent of their former prices—when one out of every two banks in the country was forced to close —profoundly affected the investment market. Despite the drastic price readjustment, the market for bank stocks from 1933 to 1940 remained in the doldrums except for brief unsustained periods of activity.

The prospect for improvement in the investment position of bank stocks depends primarily upon business expansion, which is expressed in a larger volume of bank loans and higher interest rates both on loans and on investments. If past experience is to be a guide, it is only a question of time until these factors develop. Admittedly, in the interval, new conditions may arise. The various lending agencies of the Federal Government mentioned in an earlier chapter are only some of the credit institutions now operating under Government supervision. All of these agencies are more or less in competition with the commercial banks of the country. The answer may take the form of nationalization of the banking system on one extreme or may take the opposite extreme of a return to the practices of a decade ago. It is by no means impossible that bank stocks may again regain a large part of their former investment popularity.

Part 2. Insurance Stocks

Insurance company stocks. The insurance companies in the United States in which there is a major investment interest are the stock-owned fire and casualty companies. Most of the life insurance companies, including nine out of the ten largest, are mutually owned by the policyholders. A substantial number of the fire and casualty group is likewise of the mutual type in which there is no stock-ownership.

From the viewpoint of the investor, fire and casualty companies represent the combination of an operating enterprise and an investment holding company. The principal business of such companies is obviously that of writing contracts, called *policies*, under which fire and other risks are insured. The secondary business is that of investing the large reserve funds which such companies must carry for the protection of their policyholders. An insurance company therefore faces the double hazard of unprofitable underwriting and unfortunate investing. Profits made in one department may be offset by losses in the other.

The profitable operation of the underwriting end of the insurance business is dependent upon the receipt of income from premiums in sufficient amount to exceed payments of commissions to agents, administrative expenses, and losses to policyholders. As the business is extremely competitive, premium rates cannot be changed according to the loss experience of separate companies, but must be determined more in line with the experience of the more efficient companies. The annual fire losses in the United States vary over wide ranges as shown in the experience of a selected group of 30 leading companies whose total losses dropped from $400,000,000 in 1926 to $300,000,000 in 1928, rose to more than $450,000,000 in 1930, dropped to nearly $250,000,000 in 1935, and rose to $320,000,000 in 1939. As premiums are based upon average years, it necessarily follows that individual years can show results extremely favorable or unfavorable.

The successful operation of the investment division of the insurance business is dependent upon the receipt of an income as large as is consistent with the safety of the funds. Because insurance premiums are payable in advance on contracts which run from one to three years into the future, insurance companies have the use of funds which are repayable in the form of loss claims, over prolonged periods. Even if the entire premium revenue is eventually returned in payments on losses, the contract may still prove profitable in that funds were provided which produced income retained by the company. Unlike life insurance companies which are largely restricted in the choice of investments under the laws of many states (not being permitted to invest in common stocks under New York State law), fire and casualty companies have wide freedom of choice and are permitted to purchase speculative issues if they so desire.

It is generally recognized that the investment policies of fire and casualty companies are less conservative than those of life insurance companies. Certain fire insurance companies do concentrate in bond investments, but more companies purchase common stocks freely, partly because they are proponents of the theory that common stocks make good long-term investments and partly because of the appreciation in values which is gained on a rising stock market.

The investor in fire insurance stocks shares with the company the dangers involved in a business which comprises two distinct hazards, either of which may bring about substantial losses. The favorable record of certain of the old established New England companies such as Hartford and Aetna should not mislead investors into the belief that insurance stocks generally make excellent investments.

Insurance company statements. The financial statements issued by insurance companies to the public are usually balance sheets prepared according to the regulations of the state of incorporation. Income statements showing profits and losses from operations are filed with the insurance departments in the various state capitols, however, and are available for public inspection.

The income account is customarily divided into two sections, the underwriting exhibit and the investment exhibit. The underwriting exhibit shows premiums received, underwriting expenses, losses incurred, and the net profit or loss from insurance operations. The investment exhibit shows income received, profit or loss on sales, appreciation or depreciation on holdings, and the net gain or loss from investment operations. The practice of showing unrealized "paper" appreciation or depreciation on securities in the earnings statement of a company is most unusual in corporate procedure. The result of such reporting is to cause the indicated earnings to rise and fall with the trend of the securities market more than with the results of insurance operations. The sum of the net profits or losses represents the combined gain or loss for the year. This amount, divided by the number of shares outstanding, gives the indicated earnings per share.

As an investment criterion, earnings per share, calculated in this fashion, are of little practical value. They do afford an "over-all" picture which serves as an interesting summary of the results of the year but which is misleading as a basis for determination of fair value. As stated earlier, American fire insurance companies suffered unusually high losses on insurance claims in 1930. Despite this handicap, a certain Rhode Island company showed a net gain from insurance operations. Furthermore, the company received nearly $1,000,000 in income from investments during the year. Both gains, however, were completely offset by a depreciation of more than $5,000,000 on securities held, which compelled the company to show a combined loss of more than $4,000,000 for the year. A substantial part of this depreciation was later recovered, a development which resulted in an overstatement of earnings in subsequent years just as the original depreciation caused the understatement of earnings in 1930.

The balance sheet shows the assets, the liabilities, the reserves, the capital stock, and the surplus. Unlike banks which usually carry investments at cost, insurance companies carry securities at "convention values" as set by the state insurance commissioners. These values are arbitrary in many cases, theoretically representing "fair value" in contrast to "market value" in the cases of securities which are selling at relatively low prices. As premiums are collected in advance, a substantial reserve must be maintained to cover future losses which are to be paid out of premium revenues. The experience record of insurance companies indicates that loss ratios average about 50 per cent of premium collections. It is therefore customary to assume that at least 40 per cent of the unearned premium reserve will eventually become earned surplus. (It should be observed that the 40-per-cent margin is a gross profit, subject to reduction for expenses already incurred and to be incurred on the policies.) The capital stock and surplus accounts represent the equity of the stockholders based upon the book value of the assets at arbitrary rather than liquidating values. The sum of the capital stock, the surplus, and 40 per cent of the unearned premium reserve, divided by the number of shares outstanding, gives the book value per share.

It is obvious that neither the reported earnings per share, as affected by "paper" profits or losses, nor the reported book value per share, as affected by "convention values," affords a reliable criterion of investment value. The suggestion is made that earnings per share for the preceding five years be recalculated without including investment profits or losses, actual or potential, and that result be multiplied by the factor of 15 (which capitalizes earnings on the basis of a 6⅔ per cent rate of return), in order to determine a fair value for the stock. The further suggestion is made that a fair basis for appraisal would be not more than the book value as calculated according to the formula previously stated. It is interesting to observe that the average ratio of market value to book value for a representative group of companies was around 1.1 in 1925, was as high as 1.6 in 1928, was as low as 0.7 in 1932, and had returned to about 1.0 in 1940.

Part 3. Investment Company Securities

Nature of investment companies. The title of investment company has been applied to those institutions which engage in the business of investing funds of individual persons who prefer not to make their own commitments for reasons of safety and convenience. The individual investor may not have enough time at his disposal to make the necessary investigation which should precede the purchase of securities, or may not have adequate knowledge of investment values required to make an intelligent selection, or may not possess the capital essential to a proper distribution of the risks incurred, or may not be in a position to watch his investments carefully after purchase. It is apparent that the investor of means can obtain these services either through the establishment of trust fund or custodian accounts, or through the employment of professional advisers. The investment company therefore appeals primarily to investors of limited means who do not have access to these conveniences.

If the business of investing were an exact science, if analysts could foresee the effect of economic forces as engineers forecast the influence of physical forces, the investment company would be the ideal institution for investors. The investment company has all the advantages of capital, skill, training, and experience which the average investor lacks. Consequently, the investment company should operate much more efficiently and more profitably than the average investor.

Some 50 years ago, investment trust organizations were formed abroad, notably in Scotland and Holland, for the purpose of providing an investment service to individuals who felt either unable or unwilling to select their own securities. In view of the general success of these earlier trusts, it seems pertinent to point out certain conditions and principles under which they operated:

(1) Domestic investment opportunities were greatly limited due to small geographical areas and highly developed enterprises.

(2) New domestic securities issues were not available to small investors because of the preferred position of large subscriptions.

(3) The more attractive fields of investment were in foreign securities, the selection of which required greater skill than did the choice of domestic issues.

(4) The capital of the investment trusts was secured practically without cost on the basis of voluntary, unsolicited subscriptions.

(5) The capital structure of the investment trusts comprised debenture bonds for investors desiring the largest degree of safety, preference stock for investors desiring a higher rate of return and a priority position, and ordinary stock for investors able and willing to accept the largest degree of risk in order to be entitled to the highest rate of return.

(6) The practice of the investment trusts was to buy a diversified group of securities primarily on the basis of income revenue rather than on the basis of appreciation possibilities. Accordingly, bonds and preferred stocks, having relative stability of value, were purchased to a greater extent than were common stocks.

(7) Profits derived from the sale of securities were not included in reported earnings but were placed in reserve accounts. Losses sustained were charged against these reserves rather than deducted from operating earnings or surplus. The omission of trading profits and losses from reported earnings stabilized the reported earnings to a notable degree.[4]

(8) The operating expenses were kept down to a moderate percentage of income because of small operating staffs which, in some instances, served a group of investment trust organizations.

American experience. The success of the British and Scottish investment trusts during the early years of the present century encouraged the formation of investment organizations in the United States. This development began shortly after 1920 and reached its peak in 1929 when stock market prices reached extremely high levels. The concurrence of the two peaks was more than a coincidence.

American investment companies were organized along lines distinctly different from those adopted by the European companies. Despite the theoretical advantages of this method of investing, it cannot be said that a natural demand for the establishment of such companies has ever existed in this country. Certain of the basic conditions which brought about the creation of investment trusts in foreign nations were not present in the United States. The country was large, developing rapidly, welcomed small investments, and provided a more attractive field than did foreign areas. The earlier American companies were formed as corporate promotions which involved heavy expenditures for advertising and solicitation of subscriptions. High-salaried operating staffs were

---

[4] The cumulative effect of a balanced capital structure and substantial reserves upon the earning power of an investment trust common stock may be illustrated from the report of a Scottish investment company in a recent year. The company earned about 7 per cent on total capital but, because of lower fixed interest rates on the bonds and preferred stock, this was equal to over 11 per cent when the balance remaining after the prior charges was applied to the common stock and reserves combined, and to nearly 37 per cent when applied to the common stock alone.

employed, as much to impress prospective subscribers as to produce profitable operations. Investment policies were adopted which attracted capital from speculators more than savings from investors. The claim that the American companies had adapted the investment trust to meet the requirements of the American market was merely another way of saying that the movement was much more artificial than natural from an economic viewpoint.

The American companies operated far less conservatively than did the European companies. They sought trading profits as a prime source of income and selected common stocks to a much greater extent than bonds or preferred stocks. They reported profit on securities sold as part of operating earnings, relying upon their skill as market analysts to avoid losses in years of declining prices. They gave wide publicity to unrealized appreciation on securities owned, thereby influencing high market prices on their own issues and attracting speculative buyers. Several of the larger companies were formed as affiliated organizations of established investment banking firms and brokerage houses and thereby became, in some cases, "dumping grounds" for inferior securities owned by the sponsoring firms, or the source of substantial brokerage commissions from the purchase and sale of securities.

The experience of the American investment companies during the 1927-1932 period of declining security prices was most unfortunate. Practically all of the companies had invested chiefly in common stocks when the market reached its ultimate peak in 1929 and failed to liquidate on the declining markets of the next two years. The losses sustained were enormous since many of the large companies were formed in 1928 and 1929 just prior to the collapse of the market.

During the period from 1933 to 1937, the investment companies which survived the 1929-1932 debacle continued in large part to pursue the same policy of investing principally in common stocks. It is all the more regrettable therefore that they were no more able to foresee the disastrous drop in stock prices in 1937 than they had been in 1929. Despite a professed ability to take advantage of the swings of the business cycle through careful "timing" of purchases and sales, the investment companies have fared little better, if as well, than did the ordinary investor.

Types of investment companies. The original type of investment organization as developed abroad is known as the *management* company. As the name implies, control of the fund is left entirely to the discretion of the management. A newer type, developed in the United States but now rather popular abroad, is the *fixed* type, also known as *unit investment trusts,* under which a definite group of securities is permanently retained. A variation of the management company is found in those which concentrate in the securities of certain industries, such as chemicals or aviation. A variation of the fixed type is found in those trusts which permit substitutions to be made under unusual conditions. *Installment trusts,* also known as *face-amount certificate companies,* are separate trust funds, bought under monthly payments, invested entirely in the shares of a sponsoring investment company.

The capital structure of a management company may comprise only common stock but more frequently represents bonds and preferred stocks as well. As in the case of a business corporation, the bonds have a fixed interest charge and, except in the unusual case of collateral bonds, have an unsecured priority of claim on the assets. The preferred stock usually has a preference with respect to both assets and earnings over the common stock. The capital structure of a fixed company comprises only common stock which is in the form of certificates of beneficial interest in blocks of the specified securities deposited with a trustee. A *mutual* investment company is one which has only common stock outstanding, which follows a policy of investing primarily for income, and in which the shareholders have the option of redemption at approximately liquidating value at all times.

Investment companies may be of the *income* type in which the procurement of regular income is the main objective, or of the *accumulative* type in which the receipt of immediate income is subordinated to the long-term appreciation possibilities of the securities purchased.

Fixed trust analysis. In the creation of fixed trusts, definitive blocks of certain dividend-paying stocks are purchased which are deposited with a trustee and against which certificates of ownership are issued in small denominations. Ten shares each of 30 different common stocks of well-known companies might be purchased at a total cost of $12,000, and deposited with a trustee against the issue of 10,000 shares of stock. These shares might be sold at $1.32 each, thereby giving the sponsors a gross profit of $1,200, known as the "markup," out of which distribution expenses would be paid. As dividends are received by the trustee, a small fee is retained, and the remainder is distributed proportionately to the shareholders. After the first block of 10,000 shares is sold, the process is repeated indefinitely, the sales price being adjusted each day to prevailing quotations on the deposited securities. The deposited stock remains in the custody of the trustee for a fixed term, usually 20 years, and is exchangeable for trust shares only when offered in full block units of 10,000 shares.

In the earlier issues of fixed trust shares, provision was made for the elimination of deposited issues only in what was then regarded as the unlikely complete discontinuation of dividend payments on such issues. In that event, the provisions required the immediate sale of the stock and the proportionate return of the proceeds to shareholders. The disadvantage of this provision which forced a sale at an inopportune time and forbid the reinvestment of the proceeds in another issue at any time became apparent during the years subsequent to 1929 and led to the development of the semifixed type under which stocks may be held even if dividends are passed and other specified stocks may be substituted if any of the original issues are sold.

The provisions under which fixed trust shares are issued usually require that the trustee make a complete distribution of all income received, whether in the form of cash, stock, or rights. In that event, shareholders should realize that all distributions in excess of cash dividends are not income but are return of capital investment.[5]

The determination of fair value in a fixed trust share is arrived at through the ascertainment of liquidating value of the deposited shares. Such calculations are being made constantly by the sponsoring firms and the trustees. If the trust is of the mutual type which makes redemption mandatory at the option of the shareholder, the liquidating value largely fixes the market value. If the trust is not mutual, however, and especially if the sponsors are no longer active, the holder of such "orphan" shares may have difficulty obtaining a fair price.

Management company analysis. As has been previously stated, management companies are operated under the complete discretion of the officers and directors. Confidence in the capacity of the management, therefore, should be an important factor in an investment analysis. Good management should, and once did, command a premium in terms of market appraisal over poor management. Actual performance, however, has not warranted such a distinction—indeed, performance has been so uniformly poor that most management company shares sell at a discount from their indicated values.

The investment policies of the representative management companies in the United States seem to have two things in common: first, most of the companies still believe that common stocks offer the most attractive opportunities despite the large losses already sustained from such purchases; and second, few of the companies have been able to recognize a favorable time for the sale of their stocks despite repeated experiences in missing the market. Perhaps not even the investment companies should be criticized for failing to recognize the peak of a market; the censure is for failing to take advantage of prolonged periods of favorable prices prior to the attainment of the ultimate peak. One might hazard the suspicion that few

---

[5] A recent dividend of $1.16 paid by a fixed trust represented only 17 cents in dividend income, as 18 cents came from the sale of stock dividends, 3 cents from the sale of rights, and 78 cents from the sale of stock received as the result of recapitalization plans.

investment companies have the courage to sell in favorable markets because of the fear that higher prices later might embarrass them in comparison with competing companies.

Most management companies diversify their securities so widely as to have no voice in the control of the companies or no influence in managerial problems. The concentration which they practice more generally takes the form of favored industries than particular companies. Perhaps the best-known of the large management companies, however, is definitely committed to the opposite policy of large investments in individual companies for the purpose of control, particularly in "special situations" where an unusual profit opportunity may seem to be afforded. This company takes the frank position that dividend income should not influence the market value of its shares, because the policy of the company is to invest in long-term commitments which may not be productive for years.

The determination of fair value of management company securities is based primarily upon the value of the securities in the portfolio. The common practice of valuation is to apply the prevailing market value to the securities owned under the theory that such prices could be realized in liquidation. Although such a method is open to the objection that any attempt to sell sizable blocks of securities on short notice would adversely affect the prevailing price, yet it does afford a reasonably sound basis for appraisal. Undoubtedly it provides a more acceptable approach than would the use of actual cost prices.

It has become the practice of investment analysts to calculate the asset position of investment companies as the prime determinant of value. An investment company reported securities held at the beginning of 1940 with an approximate market value of $50,000,000. Unsecured loans from banks amounted to $10,000,000, debenture bonds amounted to $10,-000,000, preferred stock amounted to $20,000,000, and common stock was outstanding in the amount of 2,500,000 shares. The debenture bonds shared first claim with the bank loans and showed an asset coverage of $2,500 per $1,000 bond. The preferred stock had priority on the remainder of $30,000,000 after allowance for bonds and bank loans, and showed an asset coverage of $150 per $100 share. The liquidating value of the common stock was therefore $10,000,000, or about $4 per share.

The common stock in the preceding illustration has what is popularly termed "leverage," inasmuch as a moderate change in the market value of the entire portfolio exerts a much greater change in the liquidating value of the common stock. An increase of 10 per cent in the value of the portfolio would increase the equity of the common stock from $10,000,-000 to $15,000,000, or a gain of 50 per cent. On the other hand, a decline of only 5 per cent in the value of the portfolio would decrease the equity of the common stock from $10,000,-000 to $7,500,000, or a loss of 25 per cent.

Investment Company Act of 1940. Under Federal legislation enacted in 1940, all investment companies are now required to register with the Securities and Exchange Commission and to operate in accordance with the detailed provisions of that Act. Under this law, investment companies are divided into three groups, known respectively as "face-amount certificate companies," "unit investment trusts," and "management companies." The face-amount certificate companies are those which issue certificates of stated maturity value, such as $1,000 or $1,500, which are payable on the installment plan under an arrangement whereby the annual dividends are credited toward the unpaid balance. The unit investment trusts are those which are organized under a trust indenture under which units of specified securities are deposited for the benefit of holders of redeemable certificates of ownership. The management companies are those which may issue bonds, preferred stocks, and common stocks to investors and reinvest the proceeds into a diversified group of securities as selected by the company.

Investment companies are allowed to act as underwriters of securities but are not allowed to buy on margin, to sell short, or to participate in a joint trading account. Management companies may not issue bonds unless asset coverage is at least $3,000 per $1,000 bond, and may not issue preferred stock unless the asset coverage is at least $200 per $100 share. On installment plan certificates, the sales profit (markup) may not exceed 9 per cent of the total payments thereon, and not more than one half of the first 12 monthly payments may be deducted on account of sales profit. All registered investment companies must make semiannual reports to stockholders showing income statement, balance sheet, and securities held.

Management investment companies are subdivided into two groups known as "open-end" and "closed-end." The open-end companies issue one class of redeemable shares which may be redeemed at any time at the option of the holder at approximately their net asset value as computed daily upon the basis of the prevailing market value of the securities held in the portfolio of the company; the open-end companies are continuously selling new shares to investors partly to offset redemptions of old shares and partly to increase the size of their funds. Closed-end companies are those which usually issue several classes of securities to investors and which do not issue redeemable shares or make continuous offerings of new issues.

24

REAL ESTATE SECURITIES

Scope. The purpose of this chapter is to discuss real estate mortgages and real estate mortgage bonds. The order of discussion is: (1) real estate as an investment, (2) nature of instruments, (3) guaranteed mortgages, (4) insured mortgages, (5) farm mortgages, (6) home mortgages, (7) commercial mortgages, (8) vacant land mortgages, and (9) mortgages as investments. The amount invested in real estate mortgages in the United States in farm, home, and commercial mortgages is now in excess of $30,000,000,000 and is second in importance in the investment field only to the United States Government bonds.

Real estate investments. Real property in the form of land and buildings has long provided a popular basis for investment. No other form of property which might be used as an investment medium seems to afford so favorable a combination of the factors which make for stability of value and dependability of income. Unlike public and corporate securities which must, to a great extent, be bought on faith more than upon personal investigation, real estate securities are bought by persons who may easily inspect the property which underlies their investment. Moreover, a limited degree of professional skill is needed in a general appraisal of the value of the property from the aspects of location, condition, use, and productivity. It is estimated that more than one half of the wealth of the nation (about 55 per cent) is represented by land, leaving less than one half as the value of all other forms of property.

Money invested in real estate is usually represented by deeds or mortgages. *Deeds* evidence the ownership of real property and are instruments by which title is transferred from the seller to the buyer. As deeds are nonnegotiable, they are not securities in the strict meaning of the word. However, the sale of real property may be readily consummated through the preparation of a new deed. *Mortgages* are fixed claims against real property and are instruments which establish the respective interests of borrower and lender in the property.

A detailed discussion of the relative advantages and disadvantages of real estate ownership as an investment is beyond the province of this book just as would be a detailed discussion of the relative desirability of the direct ownership of a business enterprise. Some persons have a natural aptitude for real estate just as other persons have an inherent ability to operate a retail store. Yet certain comments may be in order at this point. It is true that numerous American fortunes have resulted from the purchase of well-located real property. It is also true that no other form of investment has conserved wealth over long periods of time more safely than has real estate; and it cannot be denied that the ownership of good real property is one of the best means of protecting capital against the loss of purchasing power which occurs during periods of monetary and credit inflation. Some investors claim, however, that the rising burden of property taxes, which cannot be recovered from increased rentals, tends to make real property constantly less productive. Moreover, Federal assistance on new buildings in the form of F. H. A. and U. S. H. A. loans has created a competitive influence which on one hand adversely affects income through influencing lower rentals and on the other hand affects capital investment through causing faster depreciation arising out of the obsolescence of the older buildings. The sharp decrease in the rate of population growth shown in the 1940 census, with many large cities and some states showing actual declines, necessarily is an adverse factor in the real estate market.[1]

It is interesting to observe that relatively few attempts have been made to finance publicly the ownership of real estate through the issuance of preferred or common stocks, and that the results in those few cases have been generally unfavorable. Most of the realty stocks on the market have been issued in connection with the reorganization of properties in involuntary exchange for defaulted loans.[2]

Mortgage investments. The magnitude of the real estate mortgage business in the United States is indicated in the accompanying table which shows that the volume of outstanding farm and home mortgages, excluding apartments, hotels, clubs, educational, religious, and commercial buildings, exceeded 25 billion dollars in 1939. Comparatively speaking, real estate mortgages thus comprise the largest individual group in the investment field. Because each mortgage is a distinct investment in itself, these loans are not negotiated through investment banking houses nor are they bought and sold through regular investment dealers. In a great majority of cases, the loan is arranged directly between the borrower (the mortgagor) and the lender (the mortgagee). As mortgages are negotiable instruments, they may be transferred from one owner to another. Such transactions are usually handled by mortgage brokers and realty companies instead of through investment dealers and brokers. Consequently, mortgages are less marketable than other securities.

---

[1] Although real estate ownership is usually evidenced by the possession of a deed, it is occasionally found in the form of *land trust certificates* representing the equitable ownership of a parcel of real estate divided into a designated number of equal parts. The ownership of real property worth $3,000,000 may be vested in 3,000 land trust certificates, each representing a 1/3,000 part and having a face value of $1,000. Income is received by the certificate holders in the form of rental distributions derived from the use of the land. As land trust certificates are virtually deeds, they are non-negotiable. They may not be issued under the laws of some states.

[2] Many buyers of real estate protect themselves against outside claims on property purchased by obtaining a title guaranty insurance policy issued by an insurance company which has made a careful search of the public records to determine if any unsatisfied claims have been filed against the property and if the seller is the true owner of the property. Mortgage lenders usually insist upon such protection in their own interest.

Nature of instruments. Loans on real estate are mortgage, mortgage bond, mortgage leasehold, debenture, or income instruments.

A *real estate mortgage* is an instrument under which real property is pledged as security for a loan. The owner of the property, the mortgagor, is borrowing money from a lender, the mortgagee, under a contract whereby the property is pledged as security for payment of interest and principal. Title and

FARM AND HOME MORTGAGES IN THE UNITED STATES
(1925-1939)

Year	Farm Mortgages*	Home Mortgages†	Total
1925........	$9,913,000,000	$13,589,000,000	$23,502,000,000
1926........	9,726,000,000	15,730,000,000	25,456,000,000
1927........	9,671,000,000	17,930,000,000	27,601,000,000
1928........	9,765,000,000	20,085,000,000	29,850,000,000
1929........	9,761,000,000	21,559,000,000	31,320,000,000
1930........	9,631,000,000	21,841,000,000	31,472,000,000
1931........	9,462,000,000	21,280,000,000	30,742,000,000
1932........	9,213,000,000	19,850,000,000	29,063,000,000
1933........	8,638,000,000	18,318,000,000	26,956,000,000
1934........	7,887,000,000	17,989,000,000	25,876,000,000
1935........	7,786,000,000	17,684,000,000	25,470,000,000
1936........	7,639,000,000	17,349,000,000	24,988,000,000
1937........	7,390,000,000	17,404,000,000	24,794,000,000
1938........	7,214,000,000	17,721,000,000	24,935,000,000
1939........	7,071,000,000	18,415,000,000	25,486,000,000

* From *Agricultural Finance Review*, May, 1940.
† From *Federal Home Loan Bank Review*, Sept., 1940.

possession remain with the mortgagor until such time as default may occur, in which event the mortgagee usually claims the property through foreclosure proceedings.

The mortgage instrument recites the terms of the loan and a description of the property pledged. Covenants are customarily inserted to prevent misunderstandings, under which the mortgagor promises to pay taxes and assessments and to keep the property fully insured and in good condition. An acceleration of maturity clause is usually inserted, which makes the principal of the loan due immediately in the event of default in payment of interest or any failure with respect to the covenants. Mortgages are customarily recorded in the public records of the community to protect mortgagees against any claims of third parties against the property.

A *first mortgage* is one that has a prior claim upon the pledged property, subject to operating expenses and taxes. Any subsequent mortgages have subordinate claims, payable only after the first mortgage claim has been entirely satisfied. First mortgages in properties in the course of construction are also subject to liens for unpaid materials and services.

A *second mortgage* is one that has a claim upon the pledged property after that of the first mortgage. As first mortgages are usually placed for the largest amount which conservative investors are willing to lend on the property, the position of the second mortgage is generally too hazardous for safe investment.

An *amortized mortgage* is one that is repayable in regular installments for the duration of the loan.

A *first mortgage leasehold* is a mortgage upon a long-term lease of real property and, therefore, is subordinate to the rental contract between the lessor and the owner. Such a mortgage is often placed upon property erected on leased land and, consequently, is in effect a first mortgage on the building and on the lease of the land. Even under this interpretation, the instrument has a junior claim upon the earnings of the property and seldom provides a sound investment.

A *real estate mortgage bond* is a participation certificate, usually $1,000, in (a) a large real estate mortgage, or (b) a group of several mortgages, which are deposited with a trustee for the bondholders. The construction of the General Motors Building in Detroit, which cost over $20,000,000, was financed in part from the sale of $12,000,000 in first mortgage bonds in units as low as $100 each.

A *real estat⌣ debenture bond* is a unit, usually $1,000, of a large unsecured loan issued by the owners of an important parcel of real estate, generally a hotel or an office building. The lack of pledged security makes such issues unattractive investments.

A *real estate income bond* is one on which the payment of interest is not a fixed charge but is contingent upon the earning power of the real estate on which it has a claim. Such bonds are issued almost solely in connection with the financial reorganization of a property which has been in receivership.

Guaranteed mortgages. Real estate mortgages may be guaranteed as to the payment of interest and principal by a third party other than the mortgagor. In practice, this outside guarantor is usually a real estate finance company which acts as a dealer in securities as well as a title guaranty and mortgage guarantee company. These firms, in connection with the buying and selling of mortgages, offer mortgages for sale, adding their own guarantee to that of the original mortgagor. Large mortgages are divided into units of participation certificates, and payment of these units is guaranteed to purchasers by the finance company. Due in part to a concentration in short-term mortgages and in larger part to the adverse effect of the prolonged depression of the past decade upon real estate values, most of these companies were unable to meet their obligations arising out of defaulted mortgages which they had guaranteed. Holders of guaranteed mortgages were not seriously harmed because they occupied the same position as holders of unguaranteed mortgages and could deal directly with the mortgagor in the protection of their claims. Holders of guaranteed bonds and certificates, not being in possession of the actual mortgages, could only act in concert with each other through the trustees of the issues. A special Mortgage Commission appointed in New York in 1933 to look after the interests of thousands of small investors scattered throughout the country required over five years to reorganize the status of $600,000,000 of the $700,000,000 in certificated mortgages issued in that state.

As a result of the unsatisfactory experience with this type of securities, no companies in New York State have been permitted to engage in the business of guaranteeing mortgages since 1933. It is interesting to observe that this prohibition is in the form of a temporary suspension rather than a permanent injunction.

Insured mortgages. Certain mortgages which have been issued in accordance with the provisions of the National Housing Act have been insured for the protection of investors under the supervision of the Federal Housing Administration. Mortgages eligible for F. H. A. insurance are first mortgages on residential property conforming to construction standards as set by F. H. A. They have been issued in three different groups, as follows:

(a) Twenty-five year amortized loans on a 90 per cent original basis on homes valued at $6,000 or less (maximum of $5,400);

(b) Twenty-year amortized loans on an original basis of 80 per cent of value on homes valued between $6,000 and $20,000.

(c) Twenty-year amortized loans on apartment buildings and residential subdivisions on an original basis of 80 per cent value (maximum $4,000,000).

The maximum mortgage interest rate was 4½ per cent at the beginning of 1941, with the mortgagor paying an additional ½ of 1 per cent as an insurance premium to the F. H. A. Approximately 3 billion dollars in F. H. A. insured mortgages were outstanding on January 1, 1940.

In view of the fact that the Federal Government, in effect, has guaranteed the payment of principal and interest on all F. H. A. insured mortgages issued prior to July 1, 1941, such mortgages are virtually direct obligations of the Government and are so regarded in the investment world. In view of the fact that all F. H. A. mortgages are amortized on a monthly basis requiring the collection of interest, principal, taxes, assessments, and insurance twelve times yearly, the servicing of these mortgages involves constant attention and considerable detail. As institutions are far better equipped than individuals to handle such loans, insured mortgages may be purchased only by institutions which have met the eligibility requirements of the F. H. A. and are not available to individual investors.

The investment position of insured mortgages issued after

the termination of the Government guarantee will depend largely upon the financial responsibility of the mutual insurance fund.   In view of the traditional belief that the conservative maximum for a good real estate mortgage is two thirds of fair value, mortgage loans on an 80- to 90-per-cent basis cannot be regarded as good investments even though the principal is subject to constant reduction through amortization.   The insurance feature improves the quality of such loans, but the omission of the Federal guarantee on future issues must adversely affect their investment position.   F.H.A. insurance has yet to gain public confidence.

Farm mortgages.   The farm mortgage situation in the United States has presented an acute problem for the past decade.   Despite Federal assistance to agriculture on a scale never before attempted, the investment position of farm loans remains a perplexing problem of first magnitude.   Although the following figures were compiled as of 1935, subsequent changes have not substantially altered this picture.[3]

The 6,800,000 farms in the United States had a total value of about 33 billion dollars in 1935, or an average value of about $5,000.   Approximately 2,350,000, or 35 per cent, of these farms, having a value around 15 billion dollars, were mortgaged in the amount of 7.6 billion dollars, or an average debt of $3,250.   As the average value of the mortgaged farm is considerably higher than that of the unmortgaged farm, the average percentage of loan to property value is close to 50 per cent.

Of the 3,200,000 farms operated by full owners, having a total value of nearly 15 billion dollars, mortgaged farms number 1,270,000, having a value of 7.3 billion dollars, and loans of 3.7 billion dollars.   The average mortgage of $2,900 on such farms was 50 per cent of the average value per mortgaged farm of $5,800.   In individual states, however, the averages varied considerably.   Iowa reported an average mortgage loan of $7,500 and an average farm value of $11,500, or a ratio of about 65 per cent.   Wisconsin reported a ratio of $6,500 to $12,000, or 55 per cent.   Texas reported a ratio of $3,200 to

---

[3] Data from Farm Mortgage Indebtedness in the United States, Department of Agriculture, Aug. 26, 1937.

$7,400, or 45 per cent. California reported an average loan of $5,100 against an average farm value of $13,000, or a ratio of 39 per cent.

During the critical five-year period from 1930 to 1935, farm mortgage indebtedness declined from 9.2 to 7.6 billions of dollars, mainly as a result of foreclosures and distress transfers which cancelled mortgage loans. Such enforced liquidation took place despite the fact that unprecedented liberality on the part of creditors and financial assistance on the part of the Federal Government were made available to farm borrowers. Such aid took the form of reductions in interest rates, deferments of principal payments, and extensions running as long as 10 years. Properties were taken in foreclosure actions only under extreme cases where mortgagors were unwilling to coöperate in the re-establishment of their credit.

DISTRIBUTION OF FARM MORTGAGES[4]

JANUARY 1, 1940

Investor	Amount	Percentage
Federal Land Banks..................	$1,905,000,000	27%
Land Bank Commissioner.............	691,000,000	10
Farm Security Administration.........	38,000,000	1
Total Federal..................	$2,634,000,000	38%
Insurance Companies.................	883,000,000	13
Commercial Banks...................	534,000,000	8
Individual and Miscellaneous.........	2,858,000,000	41
Total.......................	$6,909,000,000	100%

The general experience of investors with farm loans during the past decade has been relatively unfavorable. As a consequence, the demand for farm mortgages has declined considerably. The American life insurance companies which in the past were large investors in this field have substantially reduced their holdings. In 1921, the life insurance companies had invested 1.3 billion dollars in farm mortgages, or about 18 per cent of total assets of 7.5 billion dollars; in 1940, the companies had invested only 0.9 billion dollars in farm loans, or less than 3 per cent of total assets.

[4] From *Agricultural Finance Review*, Vol. 3, No. 2, November, 1940.

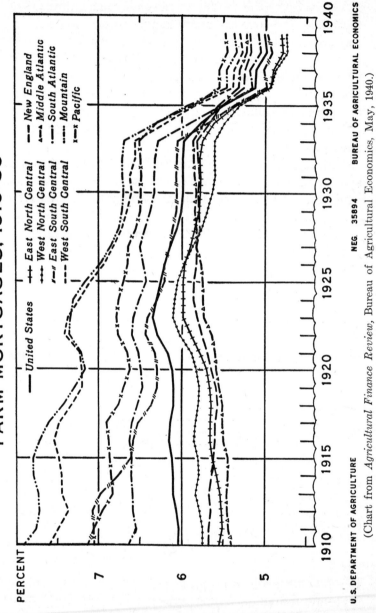

AVERAGE INTEREST RATES ON OUTSTANDING FARM MORTGAGES, 1910-39

PERCENT

United States —— New England
East North Central —— Middle Atlantic
West North Central —— South Atlantic
East South Central —— Mountain
West South Central —— Pacific

7

6

5

1910   1915   1920   1925   1930   1935   1940

U.S. DEPARTMENT OF AGRICULTURE   NEG. 35894   BUREAU OF AGRICULTURAL ECONOMICS

(Chart from *Agricultural Finance Review*, Bureau of Agricultural Economics, May, 1940.)

The cause of the decline in the investment position of farm mortgages is due to the many factors which have harmed agricultural profits during recent years. Surplus accumulations of farm products, arising out of increased production and decreased demand, have brought low prices and poor earnings. Long-term mortgage loans, made on the basis of 50 per cent of appraised values during years of prosperity, became hazardous speculations when interest payments went into default and land values fell as much as 30 to 40 per cent.

Perhaps the best lesson learned from the unfortunate experience with farm loans during the past decade has been the development of appraisal methods based upon earning power rather than upon cost price or upon prevailing values. It is now widely recognized that the earning power of the mortgaged land should be a most important factor in an appraisal. To avoid the adverse effect of abnormal prices prevailing at any time, earning power of farm property is best estimated by applying normal price averages to the yields of the past several years. Such is the method now used in connection with loans through the Federal Land Banks. Other important factors in farm values are neighborhoods, roads, schools, churches, markets, and suitability to multiple line farming.

An analysis of the present distribution of farm mortgages discloses the interesting fact that the Federal Government, through its agencies such as the Federal Land banks and the Federal Farm Mortgage Corporation, now holds 38 per cent of the farm mortgage debt of the country, a substantial part of which represents distress loans which were taken over from private investors and institutions. Insurance companies hold about 13 per cent, banks about 8 per cent, and individual lenders hold the remaining 41 per cent of farm mortgages outstanding in 1940. Of the new farm mortgages recorded in 1940, however, the Federal agencies closed only 12 per cent, the insurance companies closed 21 per cent, the banks 30 per cent, and individual lenders closed 37 per cent, thus indicating a return of institutional confidence in these loans.

Home mortgages. The home mortgage situation, as distinguished from farm mortgages and mortgages on business properties, in the United States has shown a slow but steady improvement since the depression years of 1930-1935. The magnitude of this field of investment is indicated in the accompanying table, which shows that nonfarm mortgages outstanding on January 1, 1940, amounted to over 18 billion dollars. In contrast to the situation in farm mortgages, Federal agencies held only 11 per cent of the total home indebtedness at that time.

First mortgages on residential property have long been regarded as an almost ideal investment. Relatively small losses have ever been suffered from the purchase of first mortgages on well-constructed and well-located homes under loans not exceeding two thirds of fair value. Investors have learned that a margin of safety of one third of the value of the property —in other words, one half of the amount of the loan—is necessary to cover losses arising out of depreciation, obsolescence, neighborhood changes, economic conditions, and foreclosure expenses in the event of default on the part of the mortgagor.

A home which is well-constructed depreciates in value more slowly than one which has been poorly built. From the standpoint of physical deterioration, a well-built home should last from 40 to 50 years, whereas a cheaply constructed home may not survive 25 years. In the former case, the annual rate of depreciation is about 2 per cent and in the latter instance is about 4 per cent. Even in well-built homes, the factor of obsolescence is important and tends to increase the rate of depreciation. Old-fashioned houses quickly become unpopular.

A home which is well-located is less subject to depreciation arising out of neighborhood changes. Although such changes cannot be accurately foreseen, the movement is constantly in progress in most localities. All neighborhoods are in the process of change, some improving and others declining in value. Homes located in improving areas naturally offer the better investment opportunities.

Periods of prosperity and depression cause real estate values to rise and fall. Unfortunately, defaults are most likely to occur during depression periods when resale values are low. A small margin of safety is quickly lost when properties are offered for sale in bad times. The basis of real estate loans is the value under normal conditions, a figure which is usually in excess of liquidation value when times are poor.

FORECLOSURES: AVERAGE TIME REQUIRED TO COMPLETE COMPARED WITH AVERAGE COST, BASED ON H.O.L.C. EXPERIENCE

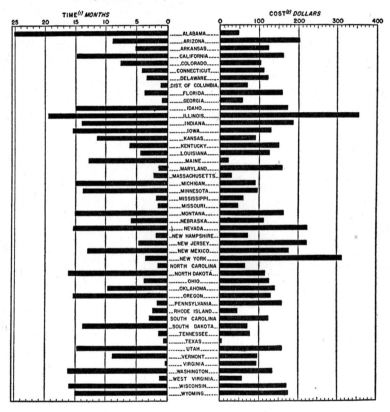

¹ In case of foreclosure in court, the time has been computed from the date of the filing of the petition to foreclose to the date of acquisition of title, free of all rights of redemption.
In case of foreclosure under power of sale contained in the mortgage or deed of trust, the time has been computed from the date of the first publication of notice of sale or of intention to foreclose, where such is required, to th e date of acquisition of title, free of all rights of redemption.
² Costs do not include salaried personnel; in both Texas and Massachusetts salaried attorneys handle foreclosure.

(From *Federal Home Loan Bank Review,* Federal Home Loan Bank Board, Washington, D. C., November, 1937.)

Foreclosure proceedings are necessary when mortgage loans fall in default unless the mortgagor is willing to surrender the premises without litigation. As shown in the accompanying chart, foreclosure action requires considerable time and involves expenses which may not be recoverable. In most states, the minimum time required is six months, and the minimum cost is $100. In nineteen states, the minimum time is twelve months, and, in five states, the minimum cost is $200. In the two important states of New York and Illinois, the minimum cost is over $300.

The argument is advanced with considerable validity that the margin of safety should vary with the value of the property. On homes having a value of $20,000 and upwards, the market is so restricted that loans should not exceed 50 per cent of value. On homes valued between $5,000 and $10,000, loans should not exceed 70 per cent; and on homes valued at $5,000 and less, where the potential resale market is almost unlimited, loans may safely be made up to 80 per cent of value. An interesting confirmation of this contention is found in the experience of a large mortgage company in New York State which reported that less than 5 per cent of loans under $7,000 were in default over a period of 28 years from 1906 to 1934, whereas $12\frac{1}{2}$ per cent of loans between $7,000 and $50,000, and 20 per cent of loans between $50,000 and $200,000, and 43 per cent of loans of $200,000 and higher were either foreclosed or in difficulty.[5] The same study revealed that only 5 per cent of loans made on single-family homes were in trouble over this 28-year period in contrast to 31 per cent of loans on apartment houses.

Investment interest in residential mortgages is primarily institutional, as shown in the accompanying table which gives the distribution of residential mortgages on January 1, 1940. Out of more than 18 billion dollars in outstanding home mortgages on that date, about two thirds were held by banks, insurance companies, and loan associations. The savings and loan associations not only held the largest volume (21 per cent) but further increased their lead through purchasing over one third (34 per cent) of the new mortgages recorded in 1939. Savings banks, which held about one sixth of the total (15 per cent), purchased only one twenty-fifth (4 per cent) of the new

[5] From *A Mortgage Analysis,* by E. A. Lodge, Comptroller, Home Title Guaranty Company, New York.

issues in 1939.   Commercial banks and trust companies, which held about one tenth (10 per cent) of the volume at the close of 1939, increased their proportion by buying over one fifth (22 per cent) of the new issues during that year.   Insurance companies, which held one twelfth (8 per cent) of the home mortgages at the close of 1939, increased their position slightly through buying nearly one tenth (9 per cent) of the 1939 issues.   Individual investors, who held about one sixth (18 per cent) of the outstanding mortgages at the close of 1939, purchased about the same part of the new issues during that year.

DISTRIBUTION OF NONFARM HOME MORTGAGES[6]

(JANUARY 1, 1940)

Investor	Amount	Percentage
Savings and loan ass'ns..............	$ 3,957,000,000	21%
Savings banks......................	2,680,000,000	15
Home Owner's Loan Corp............	2,038,000,000	11
Commercial banks..................	1,810,000,000	10
Insurance companies................	1,490,000,000	8
Individuals.......................	3,240,000,000	18
Other mortgagees..................	3,200,000,000	17
Total.......................	$18,415,000,000	100%

The improvement in the investment position of home mortgages as evidenced by increased investments on the part of important institutions does not mean that these instruments are about to regain their former popularity as investments. Estimates by competent experts to the effect that there was an "overhang" of repossessed home properties to the value of 4 billion dollars in the United States in 1940 may be greatly exaggerated and still reflect a serious threat to price stability in the realty market.

The investment position of all real estate mortgages, and of home mortgages in particular, has been weakened through legislation designed in most cases to help the mortgagor. An illustration is afforded in the moratorium law in New York

[6] From *Federal Home Loan Bank Review*, Sept., 1940.

State, which has been renewed each year since 1933, denying the mortgagee the right to foreclose a mortgage for default in the payment of principal if taxes and interest payments are not in arrears.

Commercial mortgages. Mortgages issued on business property, such as hotels, clubs, garages, and office buildings, are not regarded as favorably as loans on strictly residential property. Revenues from such special utilizations are relatively unstable, being especially subject to the influence of the business cycle. The resale value of this type of property is discouragingly low, with the result that bond creditors are virtually forced to accept whatever settlement is offered in a reorganization plan.

When the amount of the mortgage is relatively large, it is customary to divide the loan into $1,000 units which are sold as real estate mortgage bonds as previously described. Investment experience with such bonds has been distinctly unfavorable due to a combination of adverse factors. In numerous cases, mortgages were issued in amounts as high as 80 and 90 per cent of appraisal values which were optimistic, to put it mildly. Estimates of earning power in the case of new buildings were misleading due to failure to allow adequately for vacancies and to provide sufficiently for carrying costs. Rent reductions necessitated by poor business conditions further reduced income available for bondholders.

In the reorganization of many of these business properties, so serious has been the decline in earning power that bondholders have been obliged in many cases to surrender their fixed-charge obligations and accept contingent-charge debentures on which interest is payable only if earnings permit.[7]

Vacant land mortgages. Mortgages secured by the pledge of vacant land are rarely regarded as investments. As the earning power of the property is nil, save perhaps for automobile parking in city areas, the mortgagor must rely on out-

---

[7] Despite the fact that they have a first charge after operating expenses, taxes, and ground rent, on what is probably the finest hotel property in the world, holders of the income debenture bonds of the Hotel Waldorf-Astoria in New York received only 1 per cent interest in 1936, only ½ of one per cent in 1937, and no interest in 1938, 1939, and 1940.

side sources for the repayment of the loan. In most areas, the demand for vacant land is so limited that its resale value is highly problematical. It is noteworthy that New York State recently removed loans on unimproved property from the legal list for trustees and savings banks.

Mortgages as investments. Despite the relatively unfavorable experience of the past decade, real estate mortgages remain the most important group of private investments in this country. The readjustments necessitated by the numerous foreclosures of the past 10 years have eliminated many of the harmful practices which brought about the realty crisis of 1930 to 1935. As a consequence, confidence is returning, as evidenced in the larger institutional commitments made in this field during recent years.

The short-term stationary mortgage which had to be renewed every few years has been replaced by the long-term amortized mortgage which is gradually reduced through monthly payments.

The high interest rates which compelled many borrowers to pay as much as 7 to 9 per cent on mortgage loans have been reduced to the more reasonable rates of 4 to 6 per cent which now prevail generally throughout the country.

The lack of liquidity which traditionally has been a great disadvantage in mortgages has been largely eliminated through the functions of the Land Bank Commissioner and the Federal Home Loan banks which afford mortgagees an opportunity to realize upon their mortgages without forced liquidation at sacrifice prices.

The heavy expenses formerly incurred in connection with placing and renewing mortgage loans, such as legal fees, brokers' commissions, premiums, and discounts, have been substantially reduced as a result of standard practices adopted by agencies such as the Federal Housing Administration.

The expense and time involved in foreclosure proceedings have been lessened to a considerable degree as a result of the practices of the Home Owners' Loan Corporation.

On the other hand, a substantial amount of distress loans is still overhanging the market in the form either of repossessed property awaiting sale or of loans far in arrears. A general improvement in the realty field must await the elimination of such loans.

The continuation of moratorium laws in many states, including (in 1940) California, Michigan, New York, and Ohio, remains a disadvantage to investors who are thus prevented from enforcing the payment of past-due loans. The number of such state laws in force is being gradually reduced with general recognition of the passing of the emergency which was the original cause of the legislation.

Although new mortgage loans are now averaging only about one half of the volume of a decade ago, new capital is again entering the mortgage field in substantial amounts. In the home-loan field, new mortgages placed with private investors increased from an average of about $800,000,000 in 1933-1934 to an average of $2,400,000,000 in 1937-1938. In the farm-loan field, new mortgages placed with private investors increased from an average of about $450,000,000 in 1933-1934 to an average of $650,000,000 in 1937-1938. Unlike the securities of specialized industries such as the railroads and the public utilities which are adversely affected by competitive conditions, real estate mortgages on residential property have an inherent stability which is not subject to the influence of industrial life cycles.

25

FOREIGN SECURITIES

Scope. The purpose of this concluding chapter is to discuss the investment position of foreign securities in the United States. Unfavorable developments in international affairs caused American purchases of foreign securities to drop from an aggregate of more than $5,000,000,000 in the 1920-1930 decade to approximately $1,000,000,000 (mostly Canadian issues) in the 1930-1940 decade. The order of discussion is: (1) exportation of capital, (2) nature of foreign loans, (3) foreign public loans, (4) foreign corporate investments, (5) American investments abroad, (6) tariff barriers, (7) blocked currencies, (8) defaults on foreign issues, (9) foreign expropriations, (10) government protection, and (11) protective agencies.

International obligations. The purchase of securities of one country by residents of another nation may be accurately regarded as the export of capital by the latter country. The natural desire on the part of investors to keep their money at home and their reluctance to subject their funds to the relatively unknown risks of foreign commitment are offset by considerations involving income, trade, and sentiment. A fourth consideration of an artificial nature may unfortunately be added: that of the profit inducement to the distributing agencies.

The *income factor* is of prime importance. Capital flows

naturally toward the places where it is most highly valued. At times when domestic income rates are low, as witnessed in England in the latter half of the nineteenth century and in the United States during the first decade of the twentieth century, investors look abroad for more favorable opportunities. A rate of return of 6 per cent on a foreign security seems attractive when domestic issues of apparently comparable quality are yielding less than 5 per cent. Obviously, an increase of 25 per cent in annual income without sacrifice of safety is a strong inducement. The natural question immediately arises, however, as to the sacrifice of safety, since the higher yield afforded by the foreign issue may be due almost entirely to a greater degree of risk.

The *trade factor* is also important, but more from the standpoint of national welfare than from the viewpoint of the individual investor. The relationship has been admirably stated by a leading authority as follows:[1]

> While it is a fact that trade follows the flag, it is equally true that preference in trade is naturally given to those who will also finance the transactions. The supremacy of European countries in foreign trade and the intense development by them of this field of enterprise, have been primarily due to the facilities extended to foreign merchants for financing their purchases in the country with which they were dealing.

American interest in foreign trade has been greatly stimulated by a natural desire to expand commercial activity. Many industrial companies in this country ship a substantial part of their output abroad. The belief prevails that manufacturing plants in the United States have been built up to a point beyond domestic consumptive capacity and that exports are therefore essential to national prosperity. While the necessity for providing adequate arrangements for financing foreign trade is freely admitted, the investor is privileged to place his personal protection ahead of all other considerations and to refuse to assist in financing any export trade on

---

[1] "Foreign Securities and the American Investor," an address by M. L. Schiff, of Kuhn, Loeb & Co., on December 7, 1915.

other than a sound investment basis.　In this respect it should be noted that the purchase of the securities of numerous domestic companies involves indirectly a substantial foreign commitment.　Some of the important American companies that have made extensive investments abroad are International Telephone, General Electric, International Harvester, Electric Bond and Share, and General Motors.

The *sentiment factor* is of secondary importance.　A large share of the immigrant population in any country retains an inherent loyalty to the fatherland and is often willing to invest savings in the securities of the latter country.　The factor of sentiment assumes a political cast when loans are made to "friendly" nations.　A favorable sentiment toward Japan in its war with Russia brought a cordial reception to Japanese bonds in the American market in 1904 and 1905. More recent aggressive Japanese policies in China have decidedly changed this sentiment.

The *profit factor* has played an inconspicuous but influential part in the distribution of foreign securities.　The underwriting margin of profit on the sale of foreign securities is usually substantially above the margin on domestic issues. As a consequence, investment firms have been induced to distribute more foreign issues than the quality of the securities or the position of their investor-clients would warrant.　Competition among these houses for foreign issues has prevented the careful scrutiny which all new financing, especially in the international field, should require, and, incidentally, has led many foreign countries to borrow extravagantly.[2]

Nature of foreign securities.　The chief difference between domestic and foreign securities lies in the circumstances under which they are issued rather than in the form in which they appear.　The same types of securities exist: public and corporate; mortage, collateral, and debenture bonds; preferred and common stocks.　Securities distributed within the coun-

---

[2] Testimony before the Senate Finance Committee in 1932, investigating foreign loans, disclosed gross profit margins as high as 13 per cent on some foreign issues sold in the United States.

try are *internal* and naturally are issued in denominations of the domestic currency; securities distributed outside of the country of issue are *external* and are issued in denominations of foreign currencies.   United Kingdom bonds issued in England are an internal issue in pounds; United Kingdom bonds issued in the United States are an external issue in dollars. Practically all of the foreign securities in the American market are external issues in dollar denomination.   In theory, external issues are not affected by foreign exchange fluctuations; in practice, such issues are indirectly sensitive.   United Kingdom external dollar bonds declined sharply when London suspended gold payments in 1931, despite the fact that interest and principal on these bonds were payable in American dollars.   The practice of issuing international securities in multiple currency form, giving the investor the choice of accepting payment at a fixed ratio in any of several currencies, has been followed in several large recent issues, including the German International Loan of 1930, the Roumanian Monopolies Institute Loan of 1929, and the Greek Stabilization and Refugee Loan of 1928.[3]

The difficulty confronted in the investment analysis of a foreign security is the necessity of using extra dimensions beyond the measurements employed in domestic analysis.   A given set of conditions is accepted as applicable to all domestic securities.   Uniformity of fundamental factors such as law, currency, governmental stabilty, and commercial procedure permits the domestic analyst to devote his entire time to an intensive study of the security itself.   The almost complete lack of such uniformity in the world at large compels the foreign analyst to make an extensive study of numerous factors which are quickly passed over in the domestic field.

The world has no international code of laws, ethically or morally speaking.   The American investor in domestic securities has the uniform protection of the Federal Constitution behind all of his commitments.   He is reasonably sure

---

[3] The term *tranche* is used to designate the separate sections of an international loan; for example, one issue of Brazil external bonds is divided into a French tranche, a British tranche, and a United States tranche.

to receive fair treatment in any court action under laws with which he is conversant and which he is obliged to respect. The investor in foreign securities does not have an equal measure of assurance. Not only are foreign laws different, but courts of jurisdiction naturally have a friendly bias to domestic debtors. It is perhaps as unreasonable as it is unwise to assume that foreign laws conform with American practice.

The currency problem is troublesome because of instability of the values of the respective units. The inability of the leading nations of the world to keep their currency units on a parity with established gold value has caused great monetary confusion. The depreciation in the value of the national currency directly harms the position of the securities of the country through the increase of the burden of debt service. Currency fluctuation adds another variable to the problem of foreign analysis.

Governmental stability is a third additional factor of high importance in foreign investment. So unsettled have national governments become that a veritable epidemic of revolutions has occurred in recent years. The list of countries that have changed their governments by force since the First World War is both impressive and significant. In some cases, the new administrations have fully honored the debts of the old regimes; in other cases, less fortunate developments ensued; but in all cases, investment values have been impaired.

Commercial procedure is far from uniform in the nations of the world. The payment of debt is regarded more seriously in some parts of the world than in others. The attitude taken by the American nation with respect to the retirement of indebtedness is in direct contrast to that taken by other nations that attach less importance to the necessity of reducing the principal of their debts. Perpetuity of public debt is the rule rather than the exception in many parts of the world. This attitude was clearly expressed more than a generation ago by Henry C. Adams in the following quotation, which is almost as true now as it was then.[4]

---

[4] Adams, Henry C., *Public Debts*, 1887, p. 240.

The policy adopted by the United States with regard to the expungement of its obligations is not of wide acceptance. From the time that Gallatin assumed control of the Federal Treasury to the present, the American people have manifested a strong dislike to the perpetuation of a funded debt, but in other countries this sentiment fails to find response. It is true that England and Holland appear to appreciate the arguments for the extinction of public obligations; but the Latin peoples, whether in Europe or in South America, as well as those peoples of Eastern and Asiatic civilization who have come in contact with and imitate European manners, do not attach much importance to the necessity of reducing the principal of their debts.

Public issues. American participation in foreign securities has been confined to a major extent to the bonds of government bodies, including nations, states, and municipalities. The tests of quality are the same as those in the domestic field: ability to pay, willingness to pay, and legality of issue. Ability to pay is reflected in the sources of revenue, willingness to pay in the default record, and legality of issue in the pertinent legislation. Information with respect to these tests, however, is not easily available in times of peace and is practically unavailable in times of war.

The sources of revenue of foreign states are similar to those previously discussed in connection with domestic public loans, with some noteworthy additions. Direct taxes of various kinds, including property and income taxes, are levied to a greater extent in countries that are *capital rich*. Indirect taxes, such as import duties, are used to a greater degree in countries that are *capital poor*. In some countries, export taxes are levied upon the shipment of raw commodities, such as coffee in Brazil, tin in Bolivia, and nitrates in Chile. In other countries, monopolies have been established on important articles of popular use, such as salt, tobacco, and matches, whereby the government directly, or indirectly through franchise grant, controls the market and profits through the maintenance of artificially high prices. In numerous instances, countries of inferior credit standing have issued bonds secured by a prior claim upon revenues from such special sources. Experience has taught, unfortunately, that this priority is not always observed when other sources of revenues fail.[5]

From an idealistic viewpoint, the improvement financed from the proceeds of the bond issue should provide the revenue for the service charge. This desirable result is naturally possible only when the loan has been arranged for a definitely productive purpose. An interesting comment in this respect appears in a further quotation from an authority previously cited:[6]

To take up, first, the matter of government finance, it is very important that the investor should be assured that the borrowing country is economically administered; that in its annual budget income and expenditures balance; and that the proceeds of any loan are to be used for productive purposes. From the point of view of the investor dreadnoughts and rifles are not good security. A country should provide, preferably out of its own budget, through taxation of its own people, or by internal loans provided by them, for all that might be called non-productive expenditures, and it should restrict, if possible, its foreign borrowing to such purposes—public works, railroad, irrigation, etc.—as may be self-supporting.

The possession of natural resources is not a trustworthy indicator of abilty to pay. Some nations possessing vast natural resources—Mexico, for example—are poor credit risks. Other nations, without natural assets—Finland, for illustration—have excellent financial reputations. Moreover, statistics that are prepared to show the magnitude of national resources are not especially reliable, inasmuch as they are usually based upon liberal approximations of value.

The financial statements that disclose debt position, revenues, and expenditures are worthy of careful study. While it is never possible to estimate accurately the debt capacity of a nation, such a limit does exist, as tax levies eventually show. While numerous defaults in public issues in various parts of the world have usually been the direct result of extravagant

---

[5] Peruvian National Loan bonds are secured by a prior claim on 60 per cent of revenues received by a local depository. Despite such contractual promise, the Peruvian Government in 1931 ordered that all of such revenues be paid directly to the national treasury. Subsequent default on the bonds became inevitable.

[6] *Foreign Securities and the American Investor,* by M. L. Schiff.

borrowing policies, in other cases inability to pay has arisen out of economic misfortune. Rather drastic scaling down of the public debt in some important countries appears necessary, if those nations are to meet their future obligations regularly.

The dominating importance of good faith in international finance has been admirably stated by the late Dwight W. Morrow in an analysis which is a classic of its kind:[7]

You may ask me what then is the security for a foreign government loan. The answer is clear. Loans are made to foreign governments in reliance primarily upon the good faith of those governments. The intelligent investor recognizes that in the long run a government that defaults upon its obligations hurts itself even more than it hurts its creditors. Even where specific taxes or customs are allocated for the service of a loan the main reliance of the creditor must be upon the desire of the debtor government to see the particular revenues maintained and made available. Even where a foreign expert is placed in charge of revenues the arrangement is helpful only when made with hearty concurrence of the debtor government, and with the belief and expectation on the part of the debtor government that the fiscal arrangement will redound to its own advantage.

Yes, it is upon good faith that lenders to foreign governments rely. And I need not say to a group of business men that it is upon good faith also that you rely in almost all of your domestic dealings. It is true that there is a sanction ultimately applicable to domestic contracts. The proper legal steps may be taken, the breach of contract may be proved, and execution may be issued through the sheriff against property of the domestic debtor who fails to pay. But you do not in practice put much reliance upon the help of a sheriff in enforcing your contracts. You do not willingly deal with one upon whose property you expect to have to levy execution. In the overwhelming majority of your business transactions you must rely upon the ability and the willingness of your debtor to pay. On no other principle could modern business be conducted.

In international loans there is no ultimate effective sanction analogous to the domestic sheriff. But there still remains our reliance upon good faith, our reliance upon that law which is older than statute law—the acknowledged customs of mankind. The

[7] From "The Investor in Foreign Bonds," an address made by Mr. Morrow on April 23, 1926.

credit of governments is not easily built up. It may easily be shattered. And it must never be forgotten that there are rules of conduct accepted by the silent approval of civilized men, the breach of which hurts the one committing the breach much more than the one against whom it is committed. We rely in short upon good faith. If good faith cannot be relied upon it is better that the loan be not made.

Foreign corporate issues. American investment interest in foreign securities has been confined chiefly to public issues. A few foreign corporate bonds and stocks, however, have found a ready market in the United States. Some companies of purely domestic origin, such as International Telephone and Telegraph and American and Foreign Power, conduct the larger part of their operations abroad. American investors have long been large holders of Canadian corporate issues, notably Canadian Pacific and International Nickel; of South American issues, notably Chile Copper and Cerro de Pasco; and of Cuban issues, such as Cuba Cane Sugar and Consolidated Railways of Cuba. More recently, European corporate issues have gained prominence in America, as shown in Ford and Associated Electrical Industries of England; Royal Dutch and Shell Union of Holland; and United Steel Works and General Electric of Germany.

An interesting aspect of foreign stock participation is shown in the creation of so-called "American shares," which are in effect the external equivalent of the internal issue. One "American share" may represent one full original share, or a fraction, say one-tenth, of a full original share, deposited against it. The stock of Ford of England, listed at present on the New York Curb Exchange, is *depository receipts*, issued share for share for the original stock held in London by a trustee.[8]

The analysis of foreign corporate issues presents added difficulties to the investor. Financial information is not disclosed by foreign companies so frequently as by American

---

[8] The depository receipts are bought and sold in New York on a *dollar* basis even though the deposited stock bears a stated value in *pounds*. The original stock would not be acceptable delivery for a sale on the Curb Exchange whereas the depository receipts would be unacceptable on the London market.

companies. The data published are much less complete, as a rule. Accounting procedure follows radically different lines. For illustration, European companies usually show earnings barely adequate to cover dividends, carrying surplus profits into reserve accounts; fixed assets are often carried at nominal values in the balance sheets; substantial fees, proportionate to current earnings, are customarily paid to directors. The computation of investment ratios, as followed in domestic

IMPERIAL CHEMICAL INDUSTRIES, LTD.
INCOME ACCOUNT

(British Method)	£	(American Method)	£
Net earnings..............	5,780,000	Net earnings..............	5,780,000
General reserve...........	529,000	General reserve...........	529,000
Balance..................	5,251,000	Balance..................	5,251,000
Brought forward..........	109,000	Preference dividends.......	1,407,000
Total....................	5,360,000	Balance..................	3,844,000
Carry over..............	351,000	Ordinary dividends........	3,385,000
Balance..................	5,009,000	Balance..................	459,000
Preference dividends.......	1,407,000	Deferred dividends........	217,000
Balance..................	3,602,000	Surplus..................	242,000
Ordinary dividends........	3,039,000	Previous surplus..........	109,000
Balance..................	563,000	Total surplus.............	351,000
Ordinary dividends........	346,000		
Deferred dividends........	217,000		

security analysis, generally requires a realignment of the sequence of items in the income account, as illustrated in the accompanying comparison of the European and American methods of preparing income statements.

American foreign investments. The American people were holding foreign investments, either in the form of securities of foreign borrowers or in the form of foreign properties owned by American corporations, in the total amount of some $11,-750,000,000 in 1940. In addition, the Federal Government held the so-called War Debt bonds of some $13,000,000,000 (including interest arrearages) of the allied nations, practically all of which have been in default for many years.

As shown in an accompanying table, the direct investments of American corporations in foreign properties amounted to nearly $7,000,000,000 in 1937, distributed primarily in the Western Hemisphere. Of this total, some 1.6 billion dollars were invested in public utility enterprises, about 1.4 billion dollars in manufacturing plants, about 1.1 billion dollars in petroleum production, and about 1.0 billion dollars in mining and smelting enterprises.[9]

Foreign securities held by American investors in 1940, as shown in a second table, amounted to approximately $3,300,-000,000. During the decade from 1930 to 1940, the amount of such issues declined more than one half, due partly to an almost complete cessation of foreign borrowing in this country and partly to redemption through maturity retirements or through repatriation in the form of open-market purchasing for the account of foreign buyers. The substantial discounts at which many of these securities could be purchased during recent years afforded many borrowing nations an opportunity to retire their bonds at costs far below face values.

Foreign investments in the United States in 1940 amounted to about $6,700,000,000, of which 1.9 billion dollars represented direct investments in American enterprises, 2.9 billion dollars represented securities of American corporations, and 1.9 billion dollars represented bank balances which had been transferred to this country during the "flight of capital" from European nations before and after the opening of hostilities on the Continent in 1939.

Tariff barriers. Nations which have made extensive foreign investments are creditor nations, just as nations which have borrowed extensively are debtor nations. Foreign loans are usually made in the form of merchandise exports rather

---

[9] Increased American investments have aroused a large measure of hostility in some countries where fear is felt that "peaceful penetration" of capital may be followed by "spheres of influence" and "foreign management" to the detriment of local interests. In recent years, large purchases of British electric and African copper stocks by American investors caused considerable resentment.

than in the form of cash, inasmuch as the exporter receives the money which the investor pays for a foreign security. Creditor nations which impose high tariff barriers are impairing the safety of their foreign loans because they thereby prevent the debtor nation from sending merchandise in payment of interest charges. One important reason why certain countries have blocked currencies is that they have been unable

AMERICAN DIRECT INVESTMENTS IN FOREIGN COUNTRIES [10]
(As of January 1, 1937)

Grand Divisions

1.	Canada	$1,952,000,000
2.	South America	1,466,000,000
3.	Europe	1,245,000,000
4.	West Indies	753,000,000
5.	Central America	628,000,000
6.	Asia	417,000,000
7.	Oceania	111,000,000
8.	Africa	93,000,000
9.	International	26,000,000
	Total	$6,691,000,000

Leading Countries

1.	Canada	$1,952,000,000
2.	Cuba	666,000,000
3.	Chile	484,000,000
4.	Mexico	479,000,000
5.	United Kingdom	474,000,000
6.	Argentina	348,000,000
7.	Germany	227,000,000
8.	Brazil	194,000,000

to send their goods abroad and thereby obtain foreign currencies for exchange purposes.

The high protective tariff which has been in effect in the United States for many decades may be entirely warranted from the broad standpoint of social and economic welfare but it is incompatible with the position of the country as a creditor nation. It has been truly said that a nation should not attempt to sell abroad unless it is willing to buy abroad. It

[10] From U. S. Dept. of Commerce, Economic Series No. 1 (1938).

may be just as truly added that a nation should not lend abroad unless it is willing to buy abroad.

American experience with foreign loans would have been much more favorable if proper consideration had been given to the method of repayment. The classic statement of the late Dwight W. Morrow to the effect that foreign loans are made primarily upon the good faith of the borrowers might

---

FOREIGN SECURITIES HELD IN THE UNITED STATES [11]
(As of January 1, 1940)

Grand Divisions

1.	Canada	$1,414,000,000
2.	South America	934,000,000
3.	Europe	619,000,000
4.	Asia	165,000,000
5.	Oceania	96,000,000
6.	West Indies	79,000,000
7.	Central America	26,000,000
8.	Africa	2,000,000
	Total	$3,335,000,000

Leading Countries

1.	Canada	$1,414,000,000
2.	Brazil	273,000,000
3.	Argentina	198,000,000
4.	Chile	192,000,000
5.	Germany (and Austria)	173,000,000
6.	Colombia	128,000,000
7.	Japan	112,000,000
8.	Australia	96,000,000

---

well be qualified to include good faith on the part of the lenders. The borrower at least has the right to assume that the lender, of all people, will not do anything to make repayment either inconvenient or impossible.

Blocked currencies. The investment position of all foreign securities has been seriously impaired by currency embargoes which have been placed in many countries upon the transfer of money to foreign creditors. Irrespective of the justification of this practice, the effect is to make almost im-

---

[11] From U. S. Dept. of Commerce news release, May 26, 1940.

possible the payment of interest or principal on foreign loans. Such funds as are licensed for transfer are generally used to settle necessary trade commitments and are not available for service payments on securities. So serious had this matter of blocked currencies become in 1940 that American investors and corporations were able to obtain only a fraction of the income that would ordinarily be received from their foreign investments. The concept of blocked currencies is in complete opposition to the principle of foreign investment.

A secondary problem which arises out of blocked currencies is that of accounting for earnings from foreign operations. It has long been customary for American companies to include profits from foreign operations whether received in this country or retained abroad, on the basis of the prevailing exchange rates. So long as balances were freely transferable, this practice was sound. But with such transfers now forbidden, the warrant for this procedure is debatable. It is not improbable that the amounts which American companies will realize ultimately from these balances will be substantially less than the amounts originally computed.

The action of the Federal Government in "freezing" the credits in the form of bank balances and securities held in this country by foreign nationals whose countries have been invaded during wars comprises a new form of blocked currencies which tends to interfere with the underlying principle of foreign investment. This practice, which has been called "the abolition of asylum rights for foreign funds," tends to prevent the payment of interest and principal to American creditors even when the amounts due are already in this country in the form of American currency and likewise tends to prevent the use of such balances to pay creditors in other countries.

Defaults on foreign issues. In contrast to conditions in the domestic field, where default means failure to pay interest or principal when due, default in the foreign field occurs in a variety of ways, many of which arise out of unwillingness and are tantamount to repudiation. Foreign defaults may occur in any of the following ways:

I. Interest:
   A. Postponement in full or part
   B. Suspension
   C. Reduction in coupon rate

II. Principal:
   A. Postponement
   B. Reduction in face value
   C. Forced conversion

III. Sinking Fund:
   A. Postponement
   B. Suspension
   C. Reduction in annual provision

IV. General:
   A. Divergence of pledged funds
   B. Repudiation of debt

The adoption of any of these expedients by a nation is considered a default and should be seriously regarded. A minor infraction, such as postponement of the annual sinking fund provision, is significant in that it is often a precursor to a more serious default.

A study of the financial history of the world reveals numerous instances of defaults on public debts. At one time, some 50 years ago, one half of the foreign government loans listed in London were in default in whole or in part. At the beginning of 1941, a substantial part of the foreign government loans listed in New York, notably of South American issue, was similarly in arrears. The investor in foreign issues is thus compelled to look closely into the debt record of each nation in which he is interested.[12]

Foreign expropriations. The action of certain foreign nations, notably Mexico and Bolivia, in seizing the properties

---

[12] A significant aspect of the purchase of foreign securities in the United States is the fact that they were largely bought by people of limited means who were attracted by the large yield promised and apparently were not cognizant of the degree of risk involved. A survey made in 1926 at a time when these issues were extremely popular indicated that 85 per cent of the people who bought foreign bonds purchased them in small amounts ranging from $100 to $5,000 and that approximately 50 per cent of the total amount was purchased by these small investors. An article written in 1940 by an official of the Foreign Bondholders Protective Council referred to the great number of aged people "in hospitals, infirmaries, county poor houses and bare homes" who claimed these bonds represented all they had in the world.

of foreign companies operating within the borders of those countries has injured the holders of securities in those companies. In 1938, Mexico seized the properties of 17 foreign oil companies on the claim that the subsoil petroleum belongs, not to the owner or lessor of land, but to the government. As no compensation of an adequate nature has as yet been received or proposed, the act is tantamount to confiscation of property valued in the neighborhood of $500,000,000. Despite protests by foreign owners including several of the largest American companies, the constitutionality of the seizure was later approved by the Supreme Court of Mexico. In 1937, Bolivia seized the oil properties of a subsidiary company of an American company on the claim that the concession under which the company operated was illegally obtained. This act of apparent confiscation was subsequently approved by the Supreme Court of Bolivia.

The desire on the part of the Federal Government to maintain a "good neighbor" policy with the other nations in the Americas has caused the adoption of a nonintervention attitude in disputes between private interests and such foreign governments. A somewhat antagonistic attitude on the part of those governments to what they term "Yankee imperialism" further impairs the maintenance of a spirit of fair play and justice in these controversies. The net result is bound to be harmful to the American investor and perhaps even more so to the foreign nation whose credit reputation is almost irreparably harmed.

Government protection. The American investor in foreign securities should be cognizant of the attitude taken by the United States Government with respect to the enforcement of payment of foreign loans. In view of the extent to which American investors must rely upon the good faith of foreign borrowers for the repayment of their commitments, the position of the Federal Government at Washington is of high significance. The statement of Elihu Root, Secretary of State in 1906, that "It has long been the established policy of the United States not to use its armed forces for the collection of ordinary contract debts due to its citizens by other governments," was amplified by Justice Charles E. Hughes, when he was Secretary of State in 1923, in the following quotation:

It must be remembered that the Government of the United States has no power to compel its citizens to lend money or to fix the terms of their investment. Nor is it in a position to control the action of other governments who desire to borrow. In this situation our Government endeavors, by friendly advice, to throw its influence against unfairness and imposition, and it has at times, with the consent of the parties—indeed, at their instance—agreed to a measure of supervision in the maintenance of security for loans which otherwise would have been denied or would have been made only at oppressive rates.

Protective agencies. An organization known as the Foreign Bondholders Protective Council was formed in the United States in 1934 under the semiofficial auspices of the Department of State to act as a protecting agency for American investors in foreign securities. In view of the substantial volume of foreign loans currently in default, some comment on the possible remedies which are available would appear to be pertinent.

In the opinion of a leading authority, "a bond claim is the lowest possible order of international claim." The bondholder is therefore in a weak position to enforce payment from a reluctant foreign debtor. The following courses of action are available:[13]

1. Suit in the domestic courts of the debtor country; a generally ineffective procedure even if a judgment is obtained.

2. Diplomatic pressure, unofficial or official; a method rarely effective.

3. Appeal to a court of arbitration; a proceeding not very helpful in the light of past international experience.

4. Reprisal; official or semiofficial sanction of retaliatory measures, such as the modern exchange clearing systems invoked against Germany.

5. Force, which may include a peaceful blockade or war; few nations have ever gone to war for the collection of debts.

[13] From address by J. Reuben Clark, Jr., to The Bond Club of New York, January 16, 1935.

In view of the limited assistance afforded in any of the suggested remedies, it might well serve the purpose again to quote from the authority previously mentioned:

Promises to pay . . . depend upon the good-will of the promissor, and that, in the last analysis, is all there is to this international bond situation. You must find in the foreign government in default a willingness to meet its obligations. Until you do find that willingness you are relatively helpless unless you are prepared to undertake the doctrine of reprisals, and later war.[14]

With due allowance for those debtor nations which are in default and with which this country has favorable trade balances which increase the difficulty of repayment, there are numerous examples of other nations which are in default despite favorable trade balances with the United States. Such nations can scarcely plead inability to pay, especially when they use funds that otherwise would be available for debt service to buy up bonds selling at low prices because of default in interest payments. It has been estimated that as much as 50 per cent of the dollar bonds of some countries have been thus retired.[15]

Investment position. The investment position of foreign securities in the United States could scarcely be more discouraging than that which existed at the beginning of 1941. Sound investment is primarily a matter of good faith which, in turn, is based upon confidence. Until such time as a durable peace can be effected, it is futile to believe that international investments can be regarded as attractive securities. And until such time as foreign investments are intelligently used to facilitate both exports and imports between borrowing and lending nations, without the impeding handicaps of high tariff barriers and blocked currencies, defaults will be almost inevitable. The possession of nearly three quarters of

---

[14] *Ibid.*

[15] Under the Federal legislation enacted in 1934, known as the Johnson Act, nations in default on war-debt obligations to the Federal Government are prohibited from negotiating any new loans in this country while the war loans are in default. The failure of this legislation to result in any resumption of payments by the nations involved up to 1940 has led many persons to believe that it is unduly restrictive and should be revoked.

the monetary gold supply of the world places the United States in a preëminent position to finance the reconstruction of a sounder economic structure than the world has yet witnessed. It is small consolation to observe that the investment experience of the leading European nations in the field of foreign loans has been little better than that of American investors. International loans must continue to be made unless all foreign trade is to revert to a barter economy. A reorientation of the position of international securities in foreign trade should result in much sounder foreign securities.

INDEX

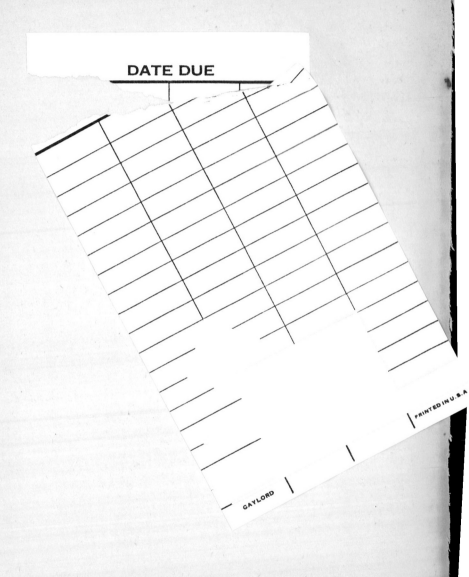

DATE DUE

GAYLORD

PRINTED IN U.S.A